BEING
CHRISTIAN
TODAY

RICHARD JOHN NEUHAUS is the president of the Institute on Religion and Public Life, in New York City, and editor-in-chief of the monthly journal *First Things*. His most recent books are *America Against Itself* (Notre Dame Press) and *Doing Well & Doing Good: The Moral Challenge of the Free Economy* (Doubleday), both scheduled for publication in 1992.

GEORGE WEIGEL is the president of the Ethics and Public Policy Center, in Washington, D.C. His book on the role of the Catholic Church in the collapse of European Communism, *The Final Revolution*, will be published in 1992 by Oxford University Press.

BEING CHRISTIAN TODAY

An American Conversation

*Edited by Richard John Neuhaus
and George Weigel*

ETHICS AND PUBLIC POLICY CENTER

The **ETHICS AND PUBLIC POLICY CENTER,** established in 1976, conducts a program of research, writing, publications, and conferences to encourage debate on domestic and foreign policy issues among religious, educational, academic, business, political, and other leaders. A nonpartisan effort, the Center is supported by contributions (which are tax deductible) from foundations, corporations, and individuals. The authors alone are responsible for the views expressed in Center publications.

Library of Congress Cataloging-in-Publication Data

Being Christian today : an American conversation / edited by
    Richard John Neuhaus and George Weigel

    p.   cm.
    Papers originally presented at a conference held in
Washington, D.C., April 1991.
    Includes bibliographical references and index.
    1. United States—Religion—1960–   —Congresses.
2. Christianity—United States—20th century—Congresses.
I. Neuhaus, Richard John.   II. Weigel, George.   III. Braaten,
Carl E., 1929–
BR526.B435   1992
261'.0973—dc20   92–13335 CIP

ISBN 0–89633–164–4 (cloth : alk. paper)

Distributed by arrangement with:

National Book Network
4720 Boston Way
Lanham, MD 20706

3 Henrietta Street
London WC2E 8LU England

Ethics and Public Policy Center
1015 Fifteenth Street N.W.
Washington, D.C. 20005
(202) 682–1200

Contents

Preface

THIS book has grown out of three remarkable days of conversation in the nation's capital. It is, in some sense, about politics. But it is far more about culture as the basis of politics, and religion as the root of culture. G. K. Chesterton's description of the United States as a "nation with the soul of a church" is as true today, it turns out, as it was at the beginning of the twentieth century. Thus the ways in which Christians live out their faith, and conceive their civic responsibilities, are matters of consequence for the whole country: not least in times like our own, when the pace of historical change at home and in the world can be both exhilarating and disorienting.

In April 1991, some ninety Christian theologians, philosophers, and political theorists gathered in Washington to think about the state of ecumenical Christian social ethics in America. The immediate occasion was the centenary of *Rerum Novarum*, the 1891 encyclical of Pope Leo XIII that launched modern Catholic social teaching. But our goal, in gathering an assembly of thinkers that included liberal and evangelical Protestants as well as Catholics of a variety of theological dispositions, was not to re-examine the past; it was to scout the future. Does the tradition of modern Catholic social teaching offer fruitful terms of reference for the ongoing ecumenical conversation about Christian responsibilities in public life? Can liberals and conservatives (in both the theological and political senses of those terms) talk seriously with each other about Christian social responsibility in modern (or post-modern) America, across the fault lines that so often divide the Church as well as the worlds of politics?

Readers will, of course, make their own judgments on those questions. Our conviction is that the essays and responses in this book contain some powerful evidence for answering yes. It is possible to break through the barriers that impede moral conversation about the American experiment in ordered liberty. And when we do so, some welcome light is shed upon what so often seem to be intractable dilemmas: abortion; individual liberty and the character of the community; poverty and the crisis of the urban underclass; America's world role after the Cold War.

The conversation that took place in Washington in April 1991 was co-sponsored by the Ethics and Public Policy Center, the Institute on Religion and Public Life, and the Jacques Maritain Center at the University of Notre Dame. Dr. Ralph McInerny served with us as co-convener and co-chairman of the conference, and to him we extend our warm thanks. The participants are listed in the appendix of this book. The conference and the book were made possible in part by generous funding assistance from the W. H. Brady Foundation, the Earhart Foundation, the Homeland Foundation, and the many other supporters of the co-sponsoring institutions. Carol Griffith and Jacqueline Stark of the Ethics and Public Policy Center staff did heroic work in shepherding a complex conversation into print. Karen Henry, Gretchen Baudhuin, Christopher Ditzenberger, and Daniel Maclellan, also of the Center staff, were of great help in mounting the conference in which these conversations took place. We are also grateful to the Most Rev. Agostino Cacciavillan, D.D., apostolic pro-nuncio in the United States, who welcomed the conference participants, expressed the interest of the Holy See in their conversations, and shared his own reflections on the importance of Catholic social thought in contemporary America.

When Abraham Lincoln asked, in 1863, whether a nation "so conceived and so dedicated" could long endure, he posed an enduring challenge to his fellow countrymen of all generations. Americans of many religious and political persuasions now seem convinced that the virtue of the American people—the character of our country as a political community—is indispensable to the survival of this ongoing experiment in self-government that we call the United States of America. May this book help to advance the public, ecumenical, and inter-religious conversation about the relation between virtue and democracy, between character and citizenship, and between a love of individual liberty and a concern for the common good.

RICHARD JOHN NEUHAUS
GEORGE WEIGEL

The Epiphany, 1992

1

Taking America Seriously: Catholicism and the American Future

GEORGE WEIGEL

THE year 1991 marked the centenary of modern Catholic social teaching and the bicentenary of the Bill of Rights to the U.S. Constitution. It might have come as something of a shock to the (very Protestant) Framers of the Constitution to be told that their work at the Philadelphia Convention might someday be assessed against criteria established by a succession of nineteenth- and twentieth-century Catholic popes—as it might have come as a surprise to several of those popes to hear that their work would be taken more seriously by some of the heirs of the Puritans than by some of the children of Rome. Yet that is precisely what happened at this juxtaposition of anniversaries. Catholic social teaching was very much "in play" in the ecumenical conversation about the future of the United States at the end of the twentieth century. And a papal encyclical celebrating the centenary of that tradition seemed to look to the United States as a kind of laboratory for testing the future prospects of human freedom and solidarity. As the metaphy-

George Weigel is the president of the Ethics and Public Policy Center. Among the books he has written are *Freedom and Its Discontents: Catholicism Faces Modernity* and *Tranquillitas Ordinis: The Present Failure and Future Promise of American Catholic Thought on War and Peace.*

1

sician Yogi Berra said when he heard that a Jew had been elected mayor of Dublin, "Only in America."

What is this Catholic social teaching by which the American experiment is being measured, ecumenically, today? By "modern Catholic social teaching" we usually mean the eleven key texts of the tradition, dating back to 1891: the encyclicals *Rerum Novarum* (1891), *Quadragesimo Anno* (1931), *Mater et Magistra* (1961), *Pacem in Terris* (1963), *Populorum Progressio* (1967), *Laborem Exercens* (1981), *Sollicitudo Rei Socialis* (1987), and *Centesimus Annus* (1991); the papal letter *Octogesima Adveniens* (1965); and the Second Vatican Council documents *Gaudium et Spes* (1965) and *Dignitatis Humanae* (1965).[1]

How can we apply the wisdom of that tradition to the many urgent questions crowding the intersection of religion and public life in contemporary America? One worthwhile approach is to analyze those key texts, historically, theologically, and politically.[2] But something more is needed today. At a time when a culture war has created a deep rift in our national life, our situation as American Christians requires that an *ecumenical* group of scholars and religious leaders consider the central issues shaping the future of the public church in America.[3] Why? Because the debate over the future of the American experiment is no longer defined in sectarian terms. And because the debate over the "public church"—its ecclesiological nature, and the themes it should most vigorously press in regard to the right-ordering of American society—is not solely, or even primarily, denominational in character today.

To put it another way, the question "How shall we be Christian in America today?" is being explored by Christians from many ecclesial communities and theological traditions who share a commitment to Christian orthodoxy and to the fruitful witness of the Church *as Church* in the American public square. The centenary of *Rerum Novarum* offers an opportunity to put the leaders of that ongoing ecumenical discussion in explicit conversation with the wisdom of modern Catholic social teaching.

So the nature of the American debate requires this kind of future-oriented and ecumenical exploration. But so does the nature of modern Catholic social teaching. For this tradition has been, from the outset, emphatically *public* in its style and in presenting itself as an instrument of culture-formation. No doubt there have been times, over the past hundred years, when modern Catholic social teaching seemed to have involved a lot of Catholic "inside baseball." Yet the tradition itself has also insisted that it is not for Catholics only. This volume is a test of that claim. It is a test for which the tradition itself calls. And in the testing, our sense of what it means to be Christian in America today ought to be advanced a step or two.

THE AMERICAN EXPERIMENT

The argument of this essay is based on two presuppositions. The first is that the United States—in historical fact, in present reality, and in future prospect—is an *experiment*, a never-to-be-completed exercise in determining whether a nation "so conceived and so dedicated" can long endure: can endure in liberty and remain dedicated to the proposition that all men are created equal. That is the "American proposition," as John Courtney Murray liked to put it, and the testing of that proposition is the story line of the United States of America. So the unfinished nature of the American experiment is part of the essence of this "proposition country," this "nation with the soul of a church," as Chesterton described us.

The continuity of America is not the continuity of blood—of race, tribe, or ethnic group. It is the continuity of *conviction*: the conviction that we can, through this *novus ordo seclorum* called American constitutional democracy, "form a more perfect Union, establish Justice, insure domestic Tranquility, provide for the common Defense, promote the general Welfare, and secure the Blessings of Liberty to ourselves and our Posterity."

The concept of America-as-experiment has a long, distinguished, and ecumenical pedigree. In contemporary usage it is most frequently drawn from the works of Father Murray; but Murray himself happily acknowledged that he had taken it from Lincoln, who in turn drew on a stream of national self-understanding that reached an early rhetorical apogee in John Winthrop's sermon aboard the *Arbella* in 1630.[4] Murray argued that the roots of the self-understanding of the American founding went even deeper than that, of course, and could be traced to medieval Christian political philosophy.[5] But that is a discussion for another day. The point here is that this is a nation *intrinsically* locked into an ongoing, public moral argument about the right-ordering of our lives, loves, and loyalties. The question is not whether that argument will take place but what sort of moral wisdom will inform it.

A CATHOLIC CONTRIBUTION?

The second presupposition of this essay is that modern Catholic social teaching—the texts identified above and the complex theological reflection that has both produced those texts and stretched them exegetically—has important contributions to make to the ongoing American debate about America.

It is worth noting that this is, at best, the second generation in which one could make that assertion without causing a (decidedly unecumenical) donnybrook. Arthur Schlesinger, Sr., was not exaggerating by much when he told the doyen of American Catholic historical studies, John Tracy Ellis, that "the prejudice against your Church [is] the deepest bias in the history of the American people."[6] And if American anti-Catholicism—or, to be more precise, American anti–*public*-Catholicism—now wears a predominantly secular, rather than Protestant, mask, it is nonetheless real, and nonetheless a factor in the continuing argument about the right-ordering of our society.

That bad news is tempered by good news: that Christian social ethics in these United States has become a thoroughly ecumenical affair into which many streams of reflection—Calvinist, Lutheran, Wesleyan, Anabaptist, and Roman Catholic—now flow. That happy fact vindicates at least one dimension of the modern ecumenical movement, as it vindicates also the claims of the Founders and Framers, James Madison prominent among them, who believed that religious liberty would be good for religion and good for the American polity. And it vindicates the hopes of such giants of American Catholic history as Archbishop John Carroll and Cardinal James Gibbons: proto-ecumenists, social reformers, and American patriots who looked forward with calm confidence to the day when American Christians would deliberate in common, and as a matter of course, on their responsibilities as believers and as citizens.

Ecumenical good manners are important. The claim here, however, is that modern Catholic social teaching has important things to offer the American debate about the right-ordering of our society. That claim may be defended on two grounds, one involving the nature of the American argument about America, and the other involving the nature of Catholic social teaching.

An Incorrigibly Religious People

In his commencement address at Yale in 1962 (a speech best remembered today for his quip that he now had "the best of both worlds, a Harvard education and a Yale [honorary] degree"), President John F. Kennedy honed the ethos of the "best and the brightest" to a particularly sharp edge by arguing that the real problems of the age were not philosophical or ideological—and thus laden with questions of meaning and value—but technical and managerial.[7]

It seems, in retrospect, an extraordinary claim. For since that spring day in New Haven, civil rights, the Vietnam war, Watergate, the place of human-rights concerns in U.S. foreign policy, nuclear deterrence, the roles of men and women in society, biomedical technology, the nature of the market economy, abortion, and the war in the Persian Gulf have all been debated throughout our society, passionately if not always wisely, in explicitly moral categories.[8]

Is this a hangover from the past, a reflection of what a New York Times reporter dismissed in early 1991 as the country's "streak of piousness"?[9] Perhaps. But the empirical evidence suggests otherwise. The far more plausible explanation is that the phrase in the Pledge of Allegiance "one nation, under God" (which means, first of all, "under judgment") continues to have impressive, even determinative, culture-shaping force. Theoretically, it is possible to construct a moral worldview capable of sustaining a democratic experiment without reference to the biblical God. But that abstract possibility (which has yet to prove itself in any concrete historical circumstance) is irrelevant to American culture and society, where 85–95 per cent of the people profess to believe that morality is derived from religion. Which means, for the overwhelming majority of the overwhelming majority, biblical religion.

Americans' instinctive reach for biblically grounded moral categories as one means of ordering the public debate about our society
and its relation to the world cannot reasonably be reduced, then, to
a matter of a "pious streak"—unless one confuses "America" with
the worldviews dominant at CBS, the *New York Times*, and the
Academy of Motion Picture Arts and Sciences. Americans will, for
the foreseeable future, continue to deploy religiously derived moral
warrants in the debate over America. That is who we are. And that
openness to religiously grounded moral argument is one reason
why modern Catholic social teaching, which is arguably the "thick-
est" body of Christian social-ethical reflection available today, will
continue to be "in play" in the American argument over America.

A "Public" Tradition

In addition, three characteristics of modern Catholic social teaching make it a particularly apt participant in this ongoing debate.

First, modern Catholic social teaching is a self-consciously *public*
tradition in terms of both its *audience* and the *warrants* it sets forth
in defense of its moral arguments.

As a matter of chronological fact, not until *Pacem in Terris* (1963)
did the tradition explicitly make the moral reflection of "all men of
good will" its concern. But the very range of the social, political,
and economic questions analyzed by modern Catholic social teaching, and the fact that those issues are addressed in the context of a
modernity (and post-modernity) that is self-evidently pluralistic in
its philosophical and theological convictions, makes it clear that the
tradition has always been interested in engaging interlocutors beyond the formal boundaries of the Roman Catholic Church. "Not
for Catholics only" is an implicit self-understanding of the tradition
from *Rerum Novarum* on; that self-understanding has become quite
explicit (if occasionally grating for some of the *fratres seiuncti*) over
the past twenty-five years or so.

The public character of its audience is complemented by the
public character of the warrants the tradition has tended to use in
support of its moral vision and its proposals for social, economic,
and political reform, within and among nations.

Modern Catholic social teaching has become more richly biblical in its language and imagery under Pope John Paul II. But it would be a considerable stretch to suggest that the tradition as a whole is an exercise in biblical theology. Rather, it has been, in the main, an exercise in a natural-law style of moral discourse, one in which appeals to the *reason* of "all men of good will" are more frequently deployed than scriptural texts.

That may seem, on the surface, a problem in the American context, given the claims made just above about the biblically derived moral warrants that the majority of Americans use in thinking about the right-ordering of our society. Yet what appears to be a problem may in fact be an opportunity. For there is no agreement among Christians on an appropriate exegesis of scriptural texts relative to questions of public policy. Nor is there agreement between Christians and Jews (or within the Jewish community) on the appropriate contemporary application of the Noahide laws. And then, as if this were not enough, there is the matter of American secularists, who have a constitutionally protected place in the public square.

In this cultural-linguistic babel, the natural-law approach exemplified in modern Catholic social teaching could provide a useful grammar for the debate, a way of bringing some order into the pluralism of American public life so that real argument could replace cacophony. Specific policy implications aside, therefore, the *style* of modern Catholic social teaching has much to commend it to a society in which public moral argument is at once both dominantly religious and determinedly pluralistic.

A Transcultural and Transhistorical Tradition

Modern Catholic social teaching is also important in the American context because it is self-consciously transcultural and transhistorical.

America may well be, as Ben Wattenberg suggests, the "first universal nation." But there are also tendencies toward provincialism and antinomianism in American culture that hinder the public moral debate. By "provincialism" and "antinomianism" I do not intend a put-down of the "average American." On the contrary: I mean to describe characteristics of the nation's intellectual and cultural elite, which often identifies its (libertine) lifestyle frettings and causes with the concerns of the entire world, and which has worked assiduously for some two generations now to deconstruct (or, at the very least, to marginalize) the notion that public moral argument ought to be conducted within a set of moral norms that are taken to be authoritative. Indeed, the very notion of "authoritative norms" is regarded as impossibly *déclassé* and hopelessly "premodern" by many of the nation's intellectual and cultural tastemakers.[10]

Confronting this elite orthodoxy, modern Catholic social thought is resolutely countercultural. It deliberately attempts to address a multiplicity of contemporary concerns, across the full range of social, economic, and political life, out of the same classic font of moral wisdom. And it continues to insist that the basic truths about the human person, human society, and human destiny that shape its social analysis are not historically contingent but are rather radically transhistorical. Indeed, insofar as modern Catholic social teaching operates against, and toward, an eschatological horizon of human transformation and redemption—a horizon that it nonetheless insists has a transformative power in the here-and-now—modern Catholic social teaching is as radical a relativizer of the elite relativizers as one is likely to find in the American debate.[11]

In sum, then, one of the considerable strengths of modern Catholic social thought is that, amidst the cacophony of democratic social and political life, it offers *points of reference* for the *authoritative guidance* of a *continuing conversation*: about America, about America's role in the world, and about the world's claims on America.

Freedom and Solidarity

Finally, modern Catholic social thought is an important partner in the American debate about America because of the two thematic poles between which its intellectual current flows: the themes frequently identified by John Paul II as "freedom" and "solidarity."

These themes have an abiding importance for a democratic experiment in which schoolchildren pledge themselves, daily, to the pursuit of "liberty and justice for all." But they also have a particular edge today. Think, for example, of the great issues that now occupy such a considerable place on the domestic policy agenda: abortion; the urban underclass; the drug crisis; the availability and cost of medical care; the failures of our educational institutions; the politicizing of the academy. In each of these cases, what is being debated is the means by which we link the liberty that is the birthright of each individual to the "justice for all" that is the promise of the American experiment. Modern Catholic social thought, in its reflection on the intrinsic (i.e., not merely accidental) relation between human freedom and human solidarity, might just have a role to play in shaping our democratic deliberation on these urgent issues.

The same is true in international affairs. In the aftermath of the Gulf War and with the collapse of the Yalta imperial system, we have become engaged in the most serious debate between internationalists and isolationists (or, as they would prefer, "new nationalists") that the country has experienced since the late 1930s. It is by no means a settled question that the American republic will accept the burdens of international leadership in a unipolar world. (Nor is there agreement, even among the committed internationalists, on what the nature, extent, costs, and means of exercising that leadership might be.) Might not modern Catholic social teaching, in its reflection on freedom and solidarity, help us find a balance between America's domestic responsibilities and America's duties beyond its borders? Given the propensity of the American people (most recently demonstrated in the debate over U.S. policy in the Persian Gulf) to conduct the argument over America's role in world affairs in explicitly moral terms, there would seem to be an important opening here.

An Available Tradition

In sum, then, modern Catholic social thought brings a number of impressive strengths to the American debate over America. First, in both audience and style it is a "public" tradition. It asks only (only!) that its interlocutors be reasonable men and women of good will. To put it another way, one can enter the debate over America according to the "grammar" provided by modern Catholic social thought without being a Catholic or, for the most part, even a believer. And yet, using that Catholic "grammar" inevitably drives one's view of policy questions, and of the underlying questions about the human person, toward transcendent reference points. This is a great advantage in the American context, given both the abiding religiosity of our people and the constitutional doctrine of ecclesiastical non-establishment.

Second, modern Catholic social teaching is the product of a magisterium that has tried to marshall its arguments in a transcultural and transhistorical fashion. This universal character of the Catholic magisterium is a great advantage, for it is a barrier against various forms of provincialism (cultural, ideological, ethnic, and the like). Moreover, because modern Catholic social teaching understands itself to be both *coherent* and *authoritative*, it is able to offer stable points of reference amidst the tremendous pace of modern technological, social, and political change. One need not accept the authoritative nature of those points of reference to be grateful for the kind of terrain-mapping that the tradition provides for the public moral debate.

Finally, the two key themes of modern Catholic social teaching— freedom and solidarity—are well suited to the contemporary American debate about the right-ordering of our domestic society and the nature of America's responsibilities in the world.

TAKING AMERICA SERIOUSLY: TWO OPTIONS

These, then, are the strengths that modern Catholic social teaching brings to the conversation. What are its weaknesses? To be specific, what about the often-heard charge that modern Catholic social teaching "doesn't take America seriously enough"? Here we open a can of worms, for those who charge that the Church, in its social teaching and elsewhere, doesn't take America seriously enough are often saying very different things. There are, in fact, two broad ways of "taking America seriously" in the Catholic context. One will be of little help in shaping the second century of modern Catholic social teaching; the other could be of considerable help.

Catholic Congregationalism

First, a temptation to be avoided: "taking America seriously" does not mean that American democracy is, in virtually all respects, a model for the internal life of the Church.

This proposal comes from what might be termed the "party of dissent" in American Catholicism. It is a party uncomfortable, in what it imagines a distinctively American way, with the hierarchical character of the Church. It is a party that tends to identify "authority" with authoritarianism: behind Joseph Ratzinger it espies the specter of Alfredo Ottaviani, and behind John Paul II the ghost of Pius IX (or Pius X). Although the party itself is dominated by elites, it lays claim to the tradition of American populism and identifies that populism with the *sensus fidelium* as defended by, say, John Henry Newman. It is a party that has taken modern Catholic social teaching seriously, although it tends to give that tradition a decidedly *gauchiste* interpretation (for instance, it highlights those dimensions of modern Catholic social teaching that it believes to be most critical of American capitalism).

It is, in short, the party of what I have elsewhere called "Catholic Congregationalism."[12] It has a distinctive interpretation of the history of Catholicism in America.[13] But its most salient claim for our purposes is that the teaching of *Sollicitudo Rei Socialis* on the right-ordering of nations should be applied to the life of the Church: "dictatorial and authoritarian" forms of governance should be replaced by "democratic and participatory" ones.[14]

This position presents a number of difficulties. At the very least, it has a certain rhetorical implausibility, even inconsistency, in that those who urge the "Americanization" of Catholicism are often the ones who have the least good to say about America as a society, a culture, and a polity.

At a more substantive level, the "Americanization" of Catholicism, were it to follow (as the party of dissent seems to wish) the path of liberal Protestantism, would be quite likely to result in a further dissipation of Christian social witness in the United States. For it seems to be an iron law of church bureaucracy in American Christianity that the quest for public-policy "relevance" radically diminishes the Church's role as a moral mentor to the wider society. No thoughtful observer of the bizarre performance of the National Council of Churches on the matter of the quincentenary of the European discovery of the Americas and on the issue of the Gulf War could reject the suggestion that the "Americanization" of Roman Catholicism on the NCC social-action model might someday drive the Catholic Church down the sorry path described by a former NCC general secretary as the road from the mainline to the oldline to the sideline.

There is also a kind of provincialism, bordering at times on hubris, in the party of dissent and its understanding of those elements of the American experience that ought to be normative for both the Church and the world. Take American feminism, a key plank in the platform of Catholic Congregationalism. To be sure, there are many feminisms. And on this question of women and men, there is certainly an ongoing debate to be engaged: one might even speculate that it is likely to be far more complex, in its argumentation and its outcomes, than is assumed by either Elizabeth Schüssler-Fiorenza or Phyllis Schlafly. It is cultural imperialism of the worst sort, however, to suggest that the relations between women and men in the United States, or between some women and some men, are somehow a normative model for everybody else in the world (or, less grandly, for the Church throughout the world). And yet that seems to be precisely the kind of claim being pressed by many feminists in the Catholic Congregationalist camp.

At bottom, though, the chief difficulty posed by Catholic Congregationalism and its concept of "taking America seriously" is not to be construed in standard left/right political terms. Rather, it is theological, and specifically ecclesiological.

Calls for "taking America seriously" that confuse the deliberative processes and structures of governance appropriate to a political community with the deliberative processes and structures of governance appropriate to the community of faith involve a category mistake of considerable proportions. The Church is the Church. It is a community of disciples gathered together by Word and sacrament.[15] It is a community whose service to the human family is, in the words of the Hartford Appeal, "against the world for the world."[16] It is a community whose *raison d'être* is the proclamation of the Truth that makes men free (John 8:32)—a truth whose contemporary meaning is determined, not by the votes of a "majority plus one," but through a complex process of discernment, reflection, debate, and prayer within boundaries established by ancient and authoritative texts and monitored by an authoritative magisterium. It is a community whose membership transcends the boundaries of human mortality, a community in which Chesterton's *mot* about tradition as the "democracy of the dead" is a crucial determinant of self-understanding.

Viewed through the lens of American voluntarism, or through the preoccupations of Catholic Congregationalism, this "thick" ecclesiology can seem to be little more than a matter of institutional prickliness. And no doubt there have been times when the boundary-setting function of the magisterium has foreclosed needed discussion. No doubt there are, in some Catholic quarters, problems of "creeping infallibilism." But, at bottom, the ecclesiological "thickness" of Roman Catholicism is not a matter of institutional self-interest; it is a matter of communal self-understanding, as authoritatively determined for the contemporary discussion by the Second Vatican Council's "Dogmatic Constitution on the Church."[17]

Moreover, the "thick" ecclesiology of Roman Catholicism should be of interest beyond the formal boundaries of the Catholic Church. For it is precisely by being the Church—by being the bearer of an authoritative set of reference points for the public argument about the right-ordering of society—that the Church makes its most distinctive contribution to this ongoing democratic deliberation. Absent that sense of obligation to the authoritative self-understanding of the community—absent that sense of Church *as Church*—"Catholic social teaching" would quickly dissolve, as other forms of Christian social teaching have dissolved, into an ecclesiastically tinged manifestation of the changing enthusiasms of what the British, with malicious wit, refer to as the "chattering classes." Catholic Congregationalism, in short, is very unlikely to provide persuasive answers to the question of how to be Christian in America today—precisely because of its ecclesiological thinness.

Seriously Taking America Seriously

On the other hand, ecclesiological orthodoxy does not require us to reject the idea that Catholic social teaching could be significantly enhanced by "taking America more seriously," and precisely as a morally grounded social, cultural, and political experiment in democratic pluralism.

On this centenary of *Rerum Novarum*, and in a spirit of respectful gratitude toward the tradition of modern Catholic social teaching, we should admit that the tradition has not, until very recently, been attentive to the American experience. When the seminal 1986 Vatican "Instruction on Christian Freedom and Liberation" teaches that "the call to freedom rang out with full force" only in 1789 with the coming of the French Revolution, and laments the further oppression that often accompanied man's subsequent efforts at worldly liberation,[18] the American Catholic wants to ask, What about the Revolution of 1776? What about American constitutionalism, which for all its failings has yet managed to channel the revolutionary energies of our people into non-violent forms of social change? What about a revolutionary tradition whose inheritors continue to declare, publicly, and at the end of the twentieth century, "In God we trust"?

The gap that some have perceived between the American experience and modern Catholic social teaching is explained in part by the European or Continental character of the theological debate that undergirded that teaching from the days of von Ketteler and Leo XIII until recent years.[19] That Continental debate continues to shape the magisterium's social teaching, as do themes drawn from the contemporary Latin American experience of Catholicism. But it is surely long past time for the responsible authorities in the Church to see in the American Catholic debate over modern Catholic social thought—particularly as that debate reflects on the distinctive experience of modernity in the United States—as formidable a body of thought on these matters as may be found in any other part of world Catholicism.

Indeed, I will make bold to suggest that the cutting edge of contemporary Catholic social theory—on matters of political structures, economics, and international affairs—is here in the United

States. Much of this work is being done by theologians, philosophers, political theorists, and economists who wish to hold themselves accountable to the boundary-setting function of the magisterium—which should only make the possibility of a greater American contribution to the future of Catholic social teaching more attractive.[20]

The United States is, for better or for worse, and usually for both, the world's great laboratory for the future, as it has been since the mid-nineteenth century. America's radical ethnic, religious, and racial pluralism (itself a microcosm of the human family as it struggles to make the transition from anarchy to political community), and America's indisputable position as the communications center of the world, should suggest the importance, for modern Catholic social thought, of "taking America more seriously."

TOWARD LIBERTY AND JUSTICE

Three aspects of the American struggle to define and secure "liberty and justice for all" should be of particular interest to Catholicism as a world church at the turn of the third Christian millennium.

1. Religious Freedom and the Catholic Human-Rights Revolution

That religious freedom is the first of human rights, and an essential guarantor of right order within nations, is a persistent theme in the social teaching of John Paul II that resonates deeply with the Catholic experience of America.[21] Indeed, it is on this question of religious freedom, in both its personal and its public aspect, that modern Catholic social thought has been most directly influenced by the American experiment. The Second Vatican Council's "Declaration on Religious Freedom" (*Dignitatis Humanae*) was decisively shaped by John Courtney Murray's creative extension of Catholic church/state theory—a development of social doctrine that was generated at least in part by the *novus ordo* of the First Amendment to the U.S. Constitution.[22]

Less well recognized perhaps is the extraordinary impact that the

Council's teaching on religious freedom—structurally extended by John Paul II into an analysis of the right-ordering of states—has had on the affairs of men and nations. Permit me, here, to make a simple, flat assertion: the transformation of the Catholic Church from a traditional defender of the *ancien régime* into perhaps the world's foremost institutional defender of basic human rights—a transformation whose real-world impact has been felt throughout Central and Eastern Europe, and from Seoul to Tierra del Fuego—would be inconceivable without the "Declaration on Religious Freedom," the American-influenced *magna carta* of the Catholic human-rights revolution.[23]

The future direction of that revolution is not altogether clear. The uncertainty is due, at least in part, to confusions that entered the Catholic human-rights debate with *Pacem in Terris*, which listed a vast range of human and societal goods under the rubric of "human rights," with little or no effort to rank or order those rights. With John Paul II, the Church has begun to ask whether some rights, when constitutionally guaranteed in law and respected in public practice, create conditions that make possible the pursuit of other social goods (whether those goods be construed as "rights" or not). That investigation is by no means complete, and may not be given priority in the development of the tradition. But it has begun.

And none too soon. The economic, social, and political failures of those societies that proclaimed their fidelity to the priority of "economic and social rights" have become evident to all but the most hardened ideologues, as has the superior performance of societies that have stressed the priority of civil liberties and political freedoms. But now, in the wake of the Revolution of 1989 in Central and Eastern Europe, and under the pressure of yet-unresolved questions being persistently pushed by some influential sectors of Western opinion, the topic has shifted to the *location* of human rights, and specifically to whether there are such things as "minority rights" or "group rights" within pluralistic societies. This may seem a bit esoteric in the United States;[24] but it is a burning question in Central and Eastern Europe, and indeed in Canada. It was, in fact, the most hotly debated topic at the 1990 human-rights review session of the Conference on Security and Cooperation in

Europe, held in Copenhagen.[25] Since then it has become painfully clear also—in, for example, the debate over religious instruction in Polish schools—that there is much work to be done in the new democracies to implement the full promise of religious freedom and to define the relationship between governmental and ecclesiastical institutions.

No claims should be made about American omniscience on either of these two points, the locus of "rights" in persons or groups, or the constitutional jurisprudence of religious freedom. Still, in no other modern setting has religious freedom been so supportive of a vibrant religious practice, which has in turn secured the cultural foundations of democracy, as in these United States. Moreover, the vigorous debate on the dimensions of a Catholic theory of human rights conducted by American Catholic theologians of various philosophical and political persuasions has often been of a very high caliber, and surely ought to have a role in shaping the future reflection by the Church's formal teaching authority on these matters.[26] Here, then, on this matter of religious freedom and the Catholic human-rights revolution, is a natural candidate for inclusion under the rubric of "taking America more seriously."

2. The Economy

From the mid-1960s through the late 1980s, a gap between the American experience and the trajectory of modern Catholic social teaching seemed to open ever wider on questions of political economy. Earlier, such a gap had not been perceived: *Rerum Novarum*, for example, was generally seen in America as a vindication of Cardinal Gibbons's defense of the rights of labor; and while there was understandable nervousness in some American circles about the corporatism that seemed implicit in *Quadragesimo Anno*, the encyclical's emphasis on the principle of subsidiarity was congruent with the American experiences of localism and federalism.

Yet even in these two early documents there were tensions in approach that would lead, over time, to the gap. The tradition focused on the ethics of wealth-distribution; Americans were certainly concerned about that (as was evident in the trade-union movement), but the characteristic national focus was on wealth-creation. There were also differences in style: Continental Catholic social thought favored an abstract style of reasoning about matters of political economy, as exemplified by the quest for a "Catholic third way" between socialism and "liberal capitalism," while Americans preferred a more inductive or empirical approach.

Then, from the late 1960s on, the Holy See's persistent criticism of a "liberal capitalism" that many American Catholics could not see in their own experience of capitalism was amplified by a brace of themes drawn from softer forms of the theologies of liberation, having to do with the "exploitation" of the Third World "periphery" by the capitalist "center." Modern Catholic social thought seemed to have learned little about the ethics of wealth-creation and wealth-distribution from the manifest failures of socialism (much less Communism) throughout the world.

Not only were these tensions resolved, but the discussion was raised to a wholly new level by the 1991 encyclical *Centesimus Annus*, which made a decisive break with the curious materialism that had characterized some aspects of Catholic social teaching since the days of Leo XIII. In *Centesimus Annus*, John Paul II endorses the "free economy," properly regulated by law and culture; and he takes the Catholic discussion in a new and welcome direction by teaching that wealth-creation under contemporary conditions has more to do with human creativity and imagination, and with political and economic systems capable of unleashing that creativity and imagination, than with "resources." And that, the pope suggests, is one of the "signs of the times" to which future Catholic social thought must be attentive.

Indeed, one of the distinctive characteristics of *Centesimus Annus* is its empirical sensitivity. Besides delivering a devastating critique of Real Existing Socialism (in a sharp analysis of "The Year 1989"), John Paul II shows that he has thought very carefully indeed about what does and doesn't work in exercising a "preferential option for the poor" in the new democracies, in the Third World, and in impoverished parts of the developed world. According to *Centesimus Annus*, the "preferential option" is a kind of formal principle: its content should be determined, not on the basis of ideological orthodoxy, but by empirical facts. And it seems that for John Paul, the evidence is in: what works best for the poor is democratic polities and properly regulated market economies. Why? Because democracy and the market are the systems that best cohere with human nature, with the "truth about man."

Undoubtedly, many streams of thought influenced *Centesimus Annus*. One of them, certainly, was the American Catholic, indeed American ecumenical, debate on questions of Christian morality and political economy. The virtually simultaneous publication, in the early 1980s, of the seminal studies by Robert Benne (*The Ethic of Democratic Capitalism: A Moral Reassessment*[27]) and Michael Novak (*The Spirit of Democratic Capitalism*[28]); the great debate over the drafting and exegesis of the 1986 U.S. Catholic bishops' pastoral letter, "Economic Justice for All"[29]; and the recent "Postcommunist Manifesto" issued, in ecumenical fashion, by Max Stackhouse and Dennis McCann[30]—all of this intellectual energy seems to have made its way, over time and by many paths, across the Atlantic. And that happy fact creates the happy prospect of an even more vigorous conversation between the Holy See and the ecumenical church in the United States on the central moral/cultural issues that will shape the free economy and the free society in the future.

3. The New World Order

Modern Catholic social teaching has also emphasized the quest for a new international political order. This reflection—which began with Pope Pius XII, reached an important benchmark with Pope John XXIII's encyclical *Pacem in Terris*, and has been deepened and extended by the social teaching of John Paul II—has important affinities with a line of American thinking about world politics that began with Woodrow Wilson, continued through Franklin Roosevelt, and has been given new currency (in a somewhat confused, or perhaps just confusing, way) by George Bush, building on the accomplishments of Ronald Reagan.

Modern Catholic social teaching and this stream of American political thought agree that "order" is, as John Courtney Murray put it in 1963, "the contemporary issue." "The process of ordering and organizing the world is at the moment going forward," said Murray. "The issue is not whether we shall have order in the world; the contemporary condition of chaos has become intolerable on a worldwide scale, and the insistent demand of the peoples of the world is for order. The question is, then, on what principles is the world going to be ordered."[31]

There also seems to be agreement between the Holy See and the American world-order advocates that those principles ought to be the principles that have guided the evolution of liberal democracies: the purpose of any "new world order," as John XXIII taught in *Pacem in Terris*, is the more effective protection of basic human rights, and the development of international legal and political instruments for the non-violent resolution of international conflict.

But the conversational (and perhaps confrontational) rubber hits the road today at two other basic points, and here there is much need of further conversation between the Holy See and American scholars and analysts. The first is unipolarity. To say that the post–Cold War world is unipolar is not an act of American self-congratulation; it is a statement of empirical fact, as the Gulf crisis proved beyond cavil. Moreover, that crisis and the tragedy of Yugoslavia have made it clear that the alternative to unipolarity, to some form of Pax Americana (or, at least, vigorous American leadership in a more wide-ranging Pax Occidentalis), is not multipolarity but chaos. Modern Catholic social teaching, on the other hand, has persistently stressed the central importance of international institutions, and particularly the United Nations, in building a "new world order"—and it has done so in ways far beyond the most Wilsonian imaginings of anyone seriously involved in policy development in the Bush administration (or any likely Democratic successor to that administration).

How can a Pax Americana (or Pax Occidentalis) give birth, over time, to effective international legal and political institutions? How can modern Catholic social teaching sketch a real-world approach to the evolution of effective international legal and political institutions without alienating two key constituencies: the Third World (where the majority of the world's Catholics reside), and those American and Western European nations that will have to bear the burden of leadership in building a minimum of order in world affairs for the foreseeable future? These are questions that urgently need exploration in the conversation between Rome and the United States.

The second area requiring far more intense conversation between the Holy See and American Christian social ethicists is the just-war tradition: what do the classic norms of that tradition mean today, and how do they (and the concept of statecraft that derives from them) relate to the pursuit of peace with freedom, justice, security, and order? The Gulf War brought to the surface a number of crucial issues that require clarification, such as the breadth of the category of "just cause," and the impact of modern weaponry on the categories of proportionality and discrimination.[32]

CONCLUDING UNSCIENTIFIC POSTSCRIPT

Seriously "taking America seriously," then, means that modern Catholic social teaching might reflect more deliberately on at least three things. (1) It should think critically and in conversation with the full range of the human sciences on the nature of American democracy as the "lead society" in the transition to the future, particularly in terms of the relation between individual liberties and the pursuit of the common good. (2) It should deepen its reflection on "democratic capitalism" as the empirically available and morally preferable alternative to "liberal capitalism" (socialism, one assumes, being moribund). And (3) it should reflect on the relation between the pursuit of a new world order and the leadership responsibilities of the Western world in general and the United States in particular, with the goal of establishing the ground rules for acceptable behavior in post–Cold War international public life.

American Catholics have taken modern Catholic social teaching seriously indeed. The development of that teaching will be strengthened if, in addition to its many other conversational partners on this vastly diverse planet, the magisterium of the Church continues to take the American experiment seriously as one paradigm for discerning the problem and possibilities of human freedom. Conversely, the future of the American experiment will be more secure if John Paul II's teaching on the inherently moral nature of human freedom is more regularly reflected in our public discourse.

In 1884, the Catholic bishops of the United States were bold enough to claim that "our country's heroes were the instruments of the God of nations in establishing this home of freedom."[33] We may prefer a more modest reading of the workings of Providence in history. But not too modest, I hope. In the renewal of the American experiment, and in the further development of modern Catholic social teaching, it is not to be regarded as merely an accident of chronology that the Feast of the Chair of St. Peter and Washington's (real) Birthday both fall on February 22.

Responses

1. GEORGE LINDBECK

To ask a Lutheran to comment on George Weigel's essay is ecumenically appropriate but risky. I am naturally inclined to compare him to Martin Luther, and however flattering that may be from my point of view, it may not be from his.

Weigel's style, like that of Brother Martin, is assertive: one would never complain of him, as Luther did of Erasmus, that he masks his opinions by "ifs," "maybes," and "under some circumstances." His tone is more like that of a Protestant testimony meeting. And he thinks, furthermore, that Rome needs to heed local (in his case, American) experience in order properly to perform its universal magisterial task. The reformatory side of me rejoices.

But Lutherans, as other Protestants have been known to complain, also have a medieval side. They like not only to testify but also to indulge in scholastic *quaestiones disputatae*. Luther in his academic role of university professor periodically engaged in these with visible enjoyment until the end of his life. I wish that in this respect Weigel's essay were a bit more medieval, a little less testimonial.

A good case can be made for beginning a discussion with assertions. Yet there is also a place for the interrogative mood, and that is the note I shall strive to strike. There is much more in Weigel's paper than I can deal with in the space allotted. Somewhat arbitrarily, therefore, I shall limit myself to comments on four of his premises regarding the character of the United States, and on three of his conclusions regarding this nation as a model society, a laboratory for the future, and the center for a unipolar world. The purpose is not to contradict but simply to note in medieval fashion objections that need to be answered.

George Lindbeck is a professor of theology at the Divinity School, Yale University.

In regard, first, to the assertion that the Church as Church (and not simply Christians as individuals) has the responsibility to participate in the public debate over the right-ordering of American society, the hidden question is Paul Ramsey's classic, "Who speaks for the churches?" Clerics by themselves cannot be trusted, Weigel would be the first to maintain; nor does he have much confidence in the laity of the new knowledge class (as shown by his remarks about "Congregationalist" Catholics). Perhaps he would agree to frame the problem in terms of Newman's "On Consulting the Faithful"; but however formulated, the question is crucial to what "being Christian today" means, communally and publicly.

A similar question arises, in the second place, regarding Weigel's assertion that "our situation as American Christians requires that an *ecumenical* group of scholars and religious leaders consider the central issues shaping the future of the public church." Who speaks for the *oikumene*? The National Council of Churches would not be Weigel's choice, as his other writings show; nor do its Roman Catholic counterparts fare much better. What, then, are the alternatives? The "American conversation" captured in this book is not, given its lack of ecclesiastical sponsorship, an instance of the public church acting ecumenically. Or is it, in some tentative, proleptic sense? The problem is worth a *quaestio disputata*.

In the third place, the claim that appeals to natural law make traditions of social teaching, such as the Catholic one, especially capable of publicly engaging in the American debate is likely to evoke the counter-question, which natural law? The epistemologically foundational varieties that have dominated both neo-scholasticism and Enlightenment liberalism in the last several centuries have lost or are losing credibility, and reformulations of premodern, non-foundational versions, such as Alasdair McIntyre is attempting, are as yet marginal. Thus it is not surprising that conservatives such as Judge Robert Bork who want to influence the national debate eschew appeals to natural law.

Perhaps also the greater emphasis on Scripture in recent Catholic social teaching is not to be interpreted, as Weigel seems to do, as a retreat from publicness. Perhaps it rather reflects a recovery of the pre-modern and anti-foundational theological conviction that sinful human beings need revelation to remind them of what is naturally good. Will people continue to believe, for example, in the inalienable dignity of the person if our culture forgets its biblical roots? Whatever the answer, it needs to be discussed, not assumed.

A fourth point in need of further exploration is Weigel's assumption that America is exceptional as an experiment in nation-building on the basis of "incorrigibly" religious convictions. One may grant that its founding convictions had a religious aspect and yet doubt the persistence, the incorrigibility, of this dimension. Gallup polls cannot supply the answer. They report that 84 per cent of the populace professes "commitment to Christ," but they do not tell us of the non-Christians (I have met some) who are not averse to using such a phrase because they believe that Jesus was a good person. In the babel of tongues that pervades the religious marketplace, Christian vocables and fragmented concepts predominate because of the history of this society, but their relation to cohesive traditions of belief and practice is often debatable, to put it mildly.

If the premises can be treated as questions, so also can the conclusions. Even those who agree that America in the past has served as a model society because of the priority it has given to "civil liberties and political freedoms" over "economic and social rights" may wonder whether this remains true. Our violence, inner-city ghettos, and disintegrating families suggest otherwise. Nor can the United States, given its deficits, faltering economy, deregulatory excesses, and S & L scandals, serve as an exemplary instance of the ethics of wealth-creation. Perhaps Catholic social teaching should look elsewhere for examples of how best to attain a humane democratic capitalism.

Much the same kind of objection applies to the claim that this country, with its pluralism and its centrality as the hub of world communications, is the laboratory in which the future is being invented. Perhaps so, but perhaps also this is the place where modernity, having survived the Marxist challenge, will undergo its final spasms.

Similar doubts arise regarding a third conclusion, that we are now entering an epoch when America will be the hub of a unipolar world. How can it possibly maintain this role for more than a very short time if it is losing its economic predominance to the European Community and the Pacific rim?

Perhaps Weigel's theses can be maintained on all or most of these issues. I would like to think so; but they need to be argued in the critical mode of the medieval disputation. To the extent that this is done, we can hope that Rome and other parts of the world will learn from the American experience; if it is not done, they will continue to ignore that experience much as before. In the meantime, we can be thankful to George Weigel for providing us with an agenda for fascinating and worthwhile work, not only in the present conversation but for a long time to come.

2. WILLIAM MURPHY

George Weigel has presented the *status quaestionis* with remarkable skill and clarity and has correctly assessed the strengths that the American "experiment" and the Catholic tradition have to offer to each other. As my modest contribution, I would like to comment on two areas with the hope that others will find them interesting enough to pursue and perhaps deepen. The first is the assessment of just what is this America today; the second, some aspects of Catholic social teaching and their relation to American goals and conduct domestically and abroad.

Weigel's assessment of these United States is of a deeply religious nation "locked into an ongoing, public moral argument about the right-ordering of our lives, loves, and loyalties." The possibility of a democratic experiment without reference to God he finds "irrelevant to American culture and society." While he does admit that there is a "cacophony" in our democratic social and political life, I sense he is rather sanguine not only about the inherent goodness of the American people but also about the power of religiously motivated democratic ideals as the major definer of America.

Here is where I have difficulty. I agree that the vast majority of Americans see themselves as religious, believe in God and in heaven

Monsignor **William Murphy** is director of the Office of Social Justice for the Archdiocese of Boston. He served on the Pontifical Commission on Justice and Peace 1980–87.

and hell (secularists seem somewhat more inclined to believe in hell than theists), and base their lives on principles of right and wrong that derive explicitly or implicitly from religious belief. That is all to the good. However, I believe it is only part of the picture of America. The other part, to my mind, leads to a more sober assessment of this noble "experiment."

While I share Weigel's judgment on the "elite relativizers," I see more and more evidence that they are winning the day precisely because they can appeal to a portion of the "American experiment" that is increasingly seen in America as being "American." This is not the place to revisit the abortion debate. That is, however, the most obvious example of what I mean.

A Society Without Norms?

To be American means increasingly that one creates oneself. Not only are there no norms that can lay claim on me: the very idea of norms is antithetical to my free pursuit of self-realization. This line of reasoning leads to a crisis of nature, a crisis of truth, and a crisis of conscience. If we can manipulate nature scientifically, then why do I have to accept any "constraints of nature" upon my choices? If truth is relative, then why can I not create the world about me and live according to what is true *for me*? If this or that choice gives me pleasure, then why am I bound to any norm of right or wrong so long as what pleases me does not "harm my neighbor"?

In an interesting article entitled "Liberalism and the American Natural Law Tradition" in the *Wake Forest Law Review* (vol. 25 [1990], 429–99), Russell Hittinger argues that the proponents of *any* kind of natural-law legal tradition in this country are exponents of a kind of self-creating individualism that renders any sense of communitarian values impossible to formulate and thus impossible to enforce. Hittinger cites legal theorists such as Laurence Tribe and Ronald Dworkin, David A. Richards and Alan Gewirth. However, the legal decisions of Blackmun and Brennan *et al.* are even more to the point. They have built on "the right to be left alone" in such a way that, from *Eisenstadt* v. *Baird* (1972) on, the concern for the "privacy of a social institution" has given way to the almost exclusive defense of the "liberty of individuals to enact their own consensual preferences through social arrangements of their choice." Such an approach undergirds Tribe's recent book *Abortion: The Clash of Absolutes*, as well as Richards's *The Moral Criticism of Law*.

I am not a lawyer, and I offer apologies if I have wandered into unknown pastures. But I do believe Hittinger is correct, and his argument gives substance to my conviction that, while America remains "religious," more and more people are increasingly shaped by a tradition of individualism that rejects any claims on the person or society that would spring from a natural-law tradition. To me there is irony in the fact that those citing any kind of natural-law inspiration are the most prominent defenders of this new self-creating individualism, which runs counter to any notion of suasive natural moral theory informed by Catholic social thought.

Let me give you a sobering example. Recently I was discussing with some students, most of whom are men preparing for the Catholic priesthood, the Church's concern for the family as the basic cell of society. I reviewed among other things the "Charter of the Rights of the Family" published in 1983 by the Holy See. Several of my students balked at the notion that the state should provide benefits to married couples that it need not extend to unmarried couples. My argument that society has a stake in the family, that stable families are needed for the good of society, caused discomfort (comfort being the latest measure of truth and right, by the way) because it seemed to the seminarians to be discriminatory against unmarried couples who live together. This category, in their view, includes gay couples, who ought to have the same rights as "straight couples," married or not.

With Weigel, I am buoyed by the religious motivation and practice of the American character. However, I believe the religious tradition will have to engage this other strand of American thought and experience in a much deeper way than it has to date. This other strand has had an enormous impact through the entertainment industry and other bearers of popular culture. But the social consequences of the legal arguments are even more disturbing; they appear to be authentic expressions of the American "experiment," and they contribute to a *weltanschauung* that regards nature, truth, and conscience as purely subjective elements in the individual's "right" to attain self-defined self-fulfillment.

My second observation builds on Weigel's characterization of the strengths of Catholic social thought. I am, if anything, more optimistic than he about what Catholic teaching can offer the American experiment. Catholic social teaching does not set out to be countercultural. On the contrary, it aims to influence and help shape culture. It is, however, countercultural to the very persons I have mentioned above. It is also countercultural to those whom Weigel defines as "Catholic Congregationalists" as well as to a whole raft of people whose normal discourse is a kind of psycho-babble, and to those whose pain at seeing dysfunctional situations leads them to redefine aberration as norm.

During the Persian Gulf conflict, I spoke in a variety of Catholic settings about just-war theory. Time and again I was challenged with great emotion by Catholics who simply refused to use categories of moral reasoning, either appealing to some phrase from the Bible in a fundamentalist way or substituting their emotions for moral discourse. This should be a cause of concern in the Church.

Being Open to Criticism

In such an atmosphere, the tranquil equilibrium of Catholic social teaching is an invaluable contribution. However, we must be ready to have that teaching not only buttress the best in our "experiment" but also scrutinize us and at times criticize us for not living up to what we proclaim so boldly as ours. I agree totally with Weigel that Catholic social thought will provide "points of reference" for our conversations. What I am suggesting is that, at times, those points of reference might make us feel uncomfortable, and that, in those cases, we should be ready to re-examine our presuppositions rather than rejecting the insight of Catholic social doctrine.

For example, freedom and solidarity are essential elements in Catholic social thought that can illuminate the responsibilities of the United States in the world. However, if this is a "unipolar world," then the United States will have to be ready for criticism from church sources if it misuses its leadership role. Underlying the concept of solidarity is the notion of the equality of nations, of relations between them as partnerships between equals. The unipolar power has to uphold certain very real and concrete obligations, lest solidarity become a code word for American hegemony.

From that point of view, modesty regarding the American experiment can be enhanced by the willingness to make use of all the elements of Catholic social thought in order to be self-critical about our own triumphs. To the extent that Weigel makes America the norm or even the most successful reference point for the principles of Catholic social thought, he runs a real risk. Chesterton's remark that history saves us from being slaves to our own era applies as well to our own country. No one can accuse me of being down on America. But everyone, I hope, would agree with me that Catholic social teaching can never canonize any nation or fail to point out defects in even the most noble of experiments.

Before closing, let me register a few other reactions to this fine essay. Weigel speaks of the considerable influence John Courtney Murray and other American churchmen had on the Vatican Council's "Declaration on Religious Freedom" (*Dignitatis Humanae*). The American contribution to this important document was indeed significant, and we should be proud of it. Yet it was not the only contribution. I suspect we speak of it and Murray so often partly because we don't have much else to point to as American contributions to conciliar teaching.

Similarly, the complaint of many "democratic capitalists" in our country that the papal critiques of liberal capitalism really don't apply here has a real foundation. They also make a valid point when they note that papal teaching has not attended as much as it should have to wealth-creation. Yet the results of the practice of international capitalism in many developing countries that John Paul II speaks of in *Sollicitudo Rei Socialis* cannot be dismissed as simply the fault of societies that don't yet know how to use capitalist market mechanisms. Developed and industrialized countries have a responsibility to examine how their practice and their control have contributed to a less-than-equal crack at wealth-creation by the poorer and developing countries.

While improvement is always possible, it is not true that the Holy

See has been blind to American contributions in this field. Regarding wealth-creation, I can say that the observations of one American Catholic were taken very seriously by at least one Roman dicastery in the early 1980s, and that this had an influence on subsequent reflection within the Holy See on this subject. I do agree, however, with Weigel's important point that an ethic of wealth-creation is urgently needed and that the ecumenical community in this country is in a privileged position to help provide that reflection. In that process, attention will have to be given to building into wealth-creation some self-correcting factors so as to avoid excesses and injustices that in the past went hand in hand with capitalist expansion.

A final word about the New World Order: I am frightened by it. It is true that the Holy See from Pius XII on has spoken in general terms about developing international instruments to further peace and good order among nations. This was seen to be one of the ends of the United Nations. The U.N. is not, however, the U.S.A. I believe the Holy See would be very reluctant to endorse a scheme of world order that was unilaterally proclaimed and guaranteed by any single nation. And I believe such reluctance would be correct from both a theoretical and a strategic point of view. I do not doubt that America is the "lead society" today. However, it is not so by any right or by any guarantee except its performance in comparison with other countries and groups of countries in the world. I may be very proud of what this country has accomplished domestically and internationally. That does not mean that it, or any other nation, should become the necessary measure for the future. Hubris is a Greek word with an unending list of practitioners far beyond the geographical and historical limits of classical Greece.

This country has much to offer, much for which we are thankful to God, and we are justly proud of our accomplishments. We must, however, be equally candid about the aspects of this society that are antithetical to some of the ideals we would like to see prevail, that in fact run counter to the tradition of Catholic social teaching. We must engage in a better and more pointed discussion with all the strands of American society. We will want to maintain openness to the principles of social teaching that can help us fulfill our role as we would want to, noting that, as John Paul II said in *Sollicitudo*, this teaching can be of "great help in promoting both the correct definitions of the problems being faced and the best solution to them."

2

Liberalism Revisited: From Social Gospel to Public Theology

MAX L. STACKHOUSE

To speak for ecumenical Protestantism today is not easy. For one thing, we are quite diverse; I cannot speak for the whole range of the "we" with whom I identify. For another, there are not many of us left who publicly admit we are religious "liberals." In some circles it is obligatory to be "radical"; in others it is fashionable to be "conservative." Only those who do not worry greatly about their image will admit to being a liberal and belonging to a liberal church. Some who formerly were in liberal churches have become evangelicals; a few have become Catholic; more have dropped out. And many of the faithful simply ignore what church leaders and national bodies say—a much easier possibility among liberal Protestants than in other communions.

Nevertheless, some of us persist in believing that key dimensions of Christianity demand liberalism, and that liberalism has not been so much refuted as shouted down. Further, we believe that the ecumenical spirit has not been mummified but is already departing the empty tomb of the politically correct, and is appearing where many do not expect it—in the convictions of the laity, in the

Max L. Stackhouse is the Herbert Gezork Professor of Christian Social Ethics and Stewardship Studies at Andover-Newton Theological School. His books include *Creeds, Society and Human Rights* and *Public Theology and Political Economy*.

33

reading habits of the clergy, in the prayers and practices of the congregations, and even in the public ethos of modernity. The future, we believe, is likely to be liberal in this sense: as Christianity in the past drew on Greek and Roman philosophy and later on the humanism of the Renaissance, so now it ought properly to acknowledge some insights from Enlightenment and post-Enlightenment thought, engage in a dialogue with both the modern sciences and other world religions, and attend to the concerns of those previously excluded from leadership. Such a liberalism can contribute to the renewal of church and society.

THE LIBERAL RECEPTION OF 'RERUM NOVARUM'

The legacy of *Rerum Novarum* both converges with and diverges from this Protestantism. Its appearance concurred with the rise of the Social Gospel, the dominant form of liberal Protestantism in twentieth-century America. Still, some of *Rerum Novarum* seemed not only quaint but suspect. For example, the appeals to natural law simply do not sing in a Protestant key.[1] We agree that it is not necessary to appeal to the "special revelation" or "saving grace" that we know in Jesus Christ at every moment of debate about public issues, and we do not believe that only Christians have a decent sense of justice. Yet we prefer to speak of "general revelation" or "common grace" when referring to the *iustitia originalis*, although this accent has been obscured by "kerygmatic theology" during this century.[2]

For most of us, however, viewing the primal—if frail—human capacity to recognize truth or justice as revelation or grace guards against the perils of self-sufficiency and pride. We want all to acknowledge that everything we know that could make a difference in life, and every means by which we know whatever we do know, is a gift of God. Thus the analysis of every area of life—politics, law, science, sexuality, technology, medicine, art, business—has to recognize sooner or later that theological issues are at stake at its deeper levels. The idea of some autonomous sphere of action that is separate from theology, or of some arena of moral independence from God grounded in "unaided reason," as natural-law arguments presume, does not ring true to us. To rely on such an idea seems not only intellectually mistaken but also confessionally Pelagian and morally arrogant.

On the other hand, the document addresses familiar issues. Protestantism had already been deeply influenced by the Emancipation movement when *Rerum Novarum* was promulgated.[3] The Social Gospel had already developed out of the pastoral encounter with industrialization. It evoked a passion for social justice. It called upon the Church to address the new realities of modernity—the city, the appearance of "classes" after the decline of feudal estates, the disputes about property, the new wave of concern for rights, the rise of the "Robber Barons." It recognized that not only the character of persons but the very structure of the common life could become destructive and wreak havoc on all in it, as Leo XIII was to recognize.[4]

Reasons for Suspicion

Despite this familiarity, we need to remind ourselves of the context of suspicion in which this and subsequent Roman teachings have been received in much of the twentieth century. *Rerum Novarum* was written within a church that, before Vatican I, had had only one council in three centuries—Trent, where Protestant ideas did not fare well. Liberal Protestantism is distinctively stamped by its love for meetings—synodical, presbyterial, and congregational. A seldom discussed but pervasive presumption of liberal and ecumenical Protestantism (and a theme that ties us to the Eastern Orthodox tradition) is the view that papal tendencies have tended to subvert the dialogical, even proto-democratic conciliarism of the faith implicit in the New Testament—as manifest in the Council in Jerusalem, for example, where the party of the belated apostle, Paul, was right and Peter was wrong.

Democratic debate and lay influence are treasured as matters of principle within liberal and ecumenical Protestantism. The Holy Spirit, we believe, is almost as likely to be present when we follow the biblical advice "come, let us reason together," as when the "Word is rightly preached and the Sacraments rightly performed." But a generation before this encyclical was issued, the preceding pope had asserted the immaculate conception of Mary as a matter of dogma, issued the Syllabus of Errors, and presided over the council that defined his infallibility. Few Protestants could read *Rerum Novarum* with a hermeneutic of trust.

To be sure, Protestants were aware that change was afoot in the Catholic world. In the nineteenth century, the old estates through which Catholic power had controlled both religion and society in Europe had been destroyed. The guilds that found their unity both in hereditary privilege and in the "worship" of patron saints had collapsed, democracy had overturned old hierarchies, the Papal States had been conquered in southern Europe, Bismarck had instigated new limits on Catholic influence in central Europe, and Protestant inventors and economists in northern Europe were developing ways of interacting with nature that both Catholics and romantics hated as mere "instrumental rationality." These new economic and technological methods were liberating the landed peasantry from drudgery and shopworkers from the tyranny of their masters, while at the same time they displaced farmers and generated that ambiguous new institution, the factory.[5]

On the whole, Protestants applauded these developments, even as they attempted to minister to those caught in unanticipated side effects. The residues of the *ancien régime*, propped up by Catholicism, were fading in society and economy as they had in religion, and Catholic populations were fleeing societies formed on Catholic principles to find their future in Protestant lands. Such changes were viewed by Protestants as the vindication of their break with, to use a Leonine phrase, those "separated brethren" who had become so Roman that they had lost their catholicity.

Besides, the conflicts that led to the Spanish-American War were already on the horizon. Few Protestants then disputed the moral and spiritual legitimacy of American involvement in Latin America and the Philippines to save our brothers and sisters in these lands from a Catholicism that kept them in a state of dependency on—as Walter Rauschenbusch put it—authoritarianism, ritualism, and superstition. Rauschenbusch, like most Protestants of that time, thought that religion was the most decisive factor in shaping the social, intellectual, political, and economic prospects of peoples everywhere. That has been, in fact, the predominant Protestant view until very recently, as we shall presently note. In any case, when this Baptist Social Gospeler turned to Catholic thinkers, he drew only on Bishop Dupanloup for his doctrine of subsidiarity and on historian Ignaz von Döllinger for his protest against the use of fraudulent relics in Catholic worship.[6]

I mention these matters not to open old wounds but to remind us of how hostile relationships have been in the past. *Rerum Novarum* pried open closed doors, although it was received in a context of suspicion, and although memories die hard (and are not all dead yet). Journals that had never had Catholic contributors published essays by priests, some of whom would write only anonymously.[7] The Episcopalian (and Fabian) W. D. P. Bliss, who edited the *Encyclopedia of Social Reform*, invited Fr. William J. Kerby to contribute to the third edition of that work. Kerby covered the thought of Bishop von Ketteler in Germany, Baron von Vogelsang in Austria, the sociologist Pierre Le Play in France, and Cardinal Manning in England, all of whom influenced Leo.[8] A sympathetic treatment in such a source was itself news.

At about the same time, the great Congregationalist leader Washington Gladden argued that Leo XIII was likely to have more influence on Christianity than any other pope since the Reformation, not only because he spoke to the needs of working people, but also because the loss of the Papal States demanded a new kind of argument from church leaders. Leo seemed to him to recognize a basic Christian principle that Gregory VII's caeseropapist empire had earlier obscured: the Church has to make its case by its capacity to persuade rather than its capacity to coerce.[9]

The Source of Rights

But perhaps the early response of William Jewett Tucker, Andover professor of ethics, soon to become the president of Dartmouth, is most characteristic of liberal Protestant responses to *Rerum Novarum*. He argued that "it is easier for a modern to accept the conclusions of the argument than the reasoning on which it rests." Tucker did not think that the industrial conflicts were due to the fact that "workmen's guilds have failed" or that "public institutions and the laws have repudiated the ancient religion," as the encyclical claims. He argued instead that the guilds "went to pieces before modern industrialism showed their utter insufficiency to meet the new situation." He wrote also that we could not conceive of modern political or material progress "under the regime of the [old] church."[10]

Tucker further noted that, despite the recognition that people have the right to organize certain kinds of groups (e.g., families, unions) without approval from the state, the papal language sometimes implies that the right of association can be withdrawn if the groups are seen as dangerous to the state or to true religion. Tucker saw the residues of a "concession theory" in which the state *allows* the people this or that right, as if rights were an artifact that states construct or dismantle. This view is in tension with other formulations where it is suggested that rights are given by God and cannot be granted or withdrawn by any state. "Rights," for liberal Protestants, is the modern way of stating what is manifestly clear in the Bible—that God has ordered human life by a justice that no political or church authority can alter. Tucker thought that if a state or a church tried to allow or disallow rights, rather than recognize and observe those that are already present in God's moral law and bestowed upon human beings at creation, that state or that church would have to be changed.

Liberal Protestants have been extremely sensitive about this point, especially as it bears on the rights of groups to organize. In fact, a major claim of liberal Protestantism for nearly four hundred years was that the right of churches to organize independently of the Caesars, the Herods, and the high priests of the world is the central organizational issue of the New Testament, and that only in societies where this right is recognized do the basic principles operate that allow the conciliar impetus, with its tendency toward democracy, to emerge. Moreover, this tradition draws from the legacy from Athanasius against the Constantinian celebrations of Eusebius.

Early in this century Ernst Troeltsch summarized this view with his massive argument about the "churches" and "sects" to show that ecclesiology is the clue to Western social history, and to ask if the confluence of Calvinist, sectarian, and humanist principles might engender a modern "Christian social philosophy." His friend Max Weber extended the sociological, analytical part of his argument cross-culturally.[11] The polity of a civilization is created in the implicit polity of its deepest religious core—and is worked out first in the communities of faith and secondarily on the anvils of social, economic, legal, and political struggle. Many Protestants hold that the struggles for the freedom of the Church brought to some degree of actualization the rights of speech, press, and association, and clarified the bases for all profound views of human rights.

The Pertinence of Locke

Tucker did not quite say about *Rerum Novarum* what was said about it later at a Boston University gathering on the topic—that throughout "John Locke is the dog that does not bark." But he might have, for Locke's arguments about rights and toleration state in secular, philosophical form the export version of what many liberal Protestants believed about these matters—celebrating the fact that the Cromwellian revolution in which Locke's family was deeply involved made English-speaking lands relatively open to Jews, Muslims, and other non-Christians. Further, Locke's view of the relationship of knowledge and will was central to the debates about the nature of freedom as developed by Jonathan Edwards (whom liberal Protestants tended to reject in favor of Locke).[12]

Locke is pertinent to this encyclical in another way as well: it contains a very high doctrine of the right of property, a view that many Protestants held at the time and many hold still. But most contemporary Protestant leaders have become more reserved about the absoluteness of this right than Leo.[13] For one thing, they know that the Founding Fathers wrote in the Declaration of Independence that certain unalienable *human* rights are endowed by the Creator—"life, liberty, and the pursuit of happiness." Those words altered the then-famous Lockean phrase "life, liberty, and property." The reasons for this change are obscure, and the protection of property as a *civil* right is in the Constitution. Nevertheless, they know that states have to tax people, and that taxation is not theft. Between the 1890s and 1910, when Henry George's proposal for a scheme for a "single tax" and the idea of different rates for "progressive taxation" were in the press daily, these matters were widely debated, and Locke's views were part of the argument.

Another reason why most liberal Protestants treat the right of property less absolutely than Leo did is that it was a matter of *status confessionis* that human dignity took priority over property rights in regard to slavery. Nearly all the Protestant churches split on this matter, and those branches that most vigorously opposed slavery became the founders of the ecumenical movements of this century—a fact that has stamped our character.

Nevertheless, Tucker spoke for many when he concluded that in Leo's concern for common humanity, in his nods toward democracy, in his embrace of human rights, in his recognition that rights apply to families, associations, and "lesser societies" and thus are not merely individualistic, and in his resistance to the doctrine that economics and society are best understood in terms of class conflict, "His Holiness . . . has ranged himself unmistakably on the side of the new (post–*laissez faire*) Political Economy."[14] No praise from him could be higher.

Such ideas were shared by those who prompted Protestantism to form councils of churches in the next generations. They have dominated most of the century's Protestant social witness. These ideas were manifest in the policies of the New Deal during the Depression; they were modulated away from a temptation toward rollicking optimism by Reinhold Niebuhr's Christian Realism as the world faced the Fascists and the Stalinists in the middle decades of the century; and after World War II, they supplied (with Jacques Maritain and others) much of the language for the United Nations Charter and Declaration on Human Rights.

THE ETHICAL TRINITY

These ideas remain as a deep substratum of liberal Protestant thought. They must, therefore, be viewed, not only historically, but also within the larger structure of modern Protestant thought as it shapes society, and particularly as it has become articulated in social ethics. One way to do this in summary fashion is to recall Richard Niebuhr's insightful work on *The Kingdom of God in America*.[15] Niebuhr argues that three motifs of Protestant thought have molded the way Americans think about the relation of religion to the common life. Each interprets a distinctive dimension of the biblical image of God's reign.

The first motif, especially characteristic of the Puritans, was the "Sovereignty of God." Here was the notion of God as lawgiver, the orderer of creation and society. Intrinsic to God's will is a universal design, a pattern for the human organization of life that was implanted in the human mind and woven deep into the fabric of human interaction. However distorted human life becomes through sin, that universal design remains vestigial in all that is, and it is unmistakably illuminated by Scripture. Some things are eternally right, some things are eternally wrong; and both church and government must structure the common life to make possible the right and to constrain the wrong in the midst of a fallen world. All persons and societies are under a universal moral law.

The second motif, especially present during the Great Awakenings, was the "Reign of Christ" in the heart of the believer. God's rule is not only without; it is also potentially within. Individuals were invited to seek a personal awareness of the redeeming presence of Christ in the soul. This would bring a new vividness to thought and action and lead persons to new levels of personal discipline, love, and responsibility for their neighbors.

And the third motif, especially powerful in the twentieth century, is the sense of the "Coming Kingdom," the recognition that the full realization of the purposes of God may become manifest in history, and that we are called to live toward a future that has already begun to break into the present. The ultimate future, even now proleptically present by the power of the Holy Spirit, involves living in expectation, participating in a "prophethood of all believers" in the formation, reformation, and transformation of communities of commitment and cooperation.

These three motifs are more than distinct expressions of particular periods of our history. They represent three decisive dimensions of an ecumenical ethic for society. They portray a kind of "ethical trinity" without which we cannot grasp the role of Protestantism in modernity or reclaim the mandate to address the world effectively today.

Society Needs Theology

What holds the three motifs together is, ultimately, God. But what makes them present in the common life is religion. This, however, creates a problem for liberals, for in the end we do not quite trust religion. Religion has no built-in rudder. It can take all kinds of forms, and not a few of them are theologically corrupt and socially pathological. The Salem witch hunts, the Elmer Gantry revivals, the temptations to "God and Country Americanism," and the spirituality of Che Guevara are equally "religious." Many varieties of "civil religions" or "social spiritualities" are not guided by an "ethical trinity."

Religion needs theology to avoid obscurantism, fanaticism, and privileged claims. Indeed, it needs "public theology."[16] If religion is to be heeded in any public discussion, it must make its case on the basis of its truth and justice as knowledge of these is accessible by "common grace" and "general revelation." If religion speaks to the society on confessional grounds alone, it runs the risk of being simply another interest group; and if it demands legal enforcement of its convictions, it coerces the conscience and leads to a lie in the soul. Theology in this sense is what tells us which religion is worth having. It is dependent upon a graceful intellectual amplitude that allows us to debate the ultimate issues, in public discourse, with those who do not already agree with us.

In this regard, theology is indispensable to society. Theology is to be seen, not as the private vocabulary of those who pray a lot, not as the distinct beliefs of this or that particular faith group, not as the rationalized religiosity of a people, and not even as the systematic reflections of professional theologians, but as the comprehending frame of ultimate reference by which human beings assess the relative truth and justice of any religion or ideology or philosophy. Only a perspective rooted in God can do that. After all, theology has been, and is in principle, the first, the most complete, and the widest-ranging systems theory ever developed; and the public to which it is pertinent is, finally, global.

Toward a Democratic Future

In some ways, we can be grateful for all that "public theology," rooted in the three motifs outlined by Niebuhr, has brought. As the century draws to a close and we begin to think of our responsibilities in the next century, we cannot fail to note that the social causes into which many liberal Protestants have thrown their lives during the last century have come to fruition. Around the world, freedom of religion is more widely established, while governments by royal lineage, colonial power, and both Fascist and Communist ideologies have been defeated. In many ways, the road is open to a democratic future with increased attention to human rights and with economies that produce effectively and create middle classes. The absence of ecclesiological foundations in many societies means that many gains are fragile. Nevertheless, Eastern Europe, Latin America, Africa (including South Africa), and large parts of Asia inch toward democratic national polities. Indeed, some democratic whispers, still faint, are heard amidst the turmoil of the Middle East.

In the United States, for all the difficulties that remain, the law, relations between men and women, the media, and economic institutions—both corporations and unions—have become more democratic internally. The modification of American social, legal, and political life in the direction of human rights under the leadership of Martin Luther King, Jr., stands as one of the most significant recent achievements of liberal Protestantism.

Indeed, within the larger household of faith, Protestants rejoice whenever the Catholic tradition more nearly approximates these themes. When the National Conference of Catholic Bishops issued pastoral letters on nuclear weaponry and economic justice that included some of these accents, some twenty-seven ecumenical communions officially recommended that local congregations study these letters along with their own denominational statements. Nothing else like this had happened since Luther nailed up his theses.

THE NEW REVISED STANDARD PROTESTANTISM

But all this does not bring rejoicing to a large number of ecumenical leaders of our day, for many have developed a quite different analysis of the nature of modern Western political, economic, and religious life. Many have adopted, in fact, the perspectives developed during the period of decolonialization, when Marxist and Leninist slogans were the preferred weapons of protest. These terms have been applied to ideas of democracy, human rights, non-socialist economics, and missions, all of which have been seen as tools of cultural imperialism. Sometimes this view has been reinforced by the pagan claim that religion is essentially a dimension of culture, and that all cultures are equally valid; or by the romantic claim that pre-modern cultures had an unrepressed, egalitarian, communitarian relationship to nature that was destroyed by Western religious "supernaturalism."

A certain modesty becomes a tradition that is tempted to triumphalism, and the public confession of sin is part of the Protestant heritage; but there are tendencies among those who hold these views to plunge the ecumenical church into ways of thinking and acting that echo more of Thomas Münzer, Menno Simons, Anne Hutchinson, or Karl Kautsky than of Luther, Calvin, Wesley, Locke, Edwards, the Social Gospel, or the Niebuhrs. They tend not only to cut ecumenical Protestantism off further from Roman Catholicism, resurgent evangelicalism, and Eastern Orthodoxy, but also to sever the important accent on social justice in the "Coming Kingdom" from its inner connection to normative views of the "Sovereignty of God" and the personal experience of the "Reign of Christ."

Perhaps the condition of the theologically and numerically depleted cluster of communions for which (and to which) I attempt to speak is no more desperate than the condition of the Roman church in the period between Trent and Vatican I. Still it must be acknowledged that the vision of the depth, breadth, width, and height of God's dealings with humanity has grown dim in ecumenical Protestantism in the last generation. And if one believes, with Paul Tillich, that religion is always the substance of culture, and that the failure of religion is due to inadequate theology, then it is reasonable to hold that the failure of religion and theology leads to failure of the civilization they have formed. And so we can expect our own society to begin to come apart at the seams. Therefore, many liberal Christians feel anguish about the condition of ecumenical Christianity at this moment.

How Things Went Wrong

Why has this happened? Many leaders of the ecumenical churches have come to believe that it is only a "conservative" concern to accent the rule of God in terms that speak of God's law, God's design—or indeed any eternal, cross-cultural principles of right and wrong to which all human beings ought to be subject. A suspicion of normative generalizations, coupled with a fascination with the contextuality and historicity of every human effort to speak about important matters, has come to dominate those segments of intellectual life to which liberal Protestants are especially attuned.[17] Normative modes of theological and ethical thinking are thus held by many to be mere abstractions, at most a residue of legalism and probably a projection of dominant elites, and usually found among those with an unresolved authority problem.

It is not the case that all concern with universalism or absoluteness is rejected. In the name of "inclusiveness," a *descriptive, sociological* universalism is sought, often in an effort to avoid or subvert *prescriptive, normative* claims about theology and ethics that were in fact less than universal but treated as absolute. Insofar as this effort does reach out to neglected and rejected peoples in new ways, it is surely to be celebrated; but it has sometimes produced an unintended rejection of all efforts to invoke any prescriptive and normative claims in faith and morals.

Similarly, the motif of a personal experience of Christ in the heart, by which the whole self becomes a vessel of piety, purity, and service, is left to the neo-evangelicals or the Pentecostals, or treated as simply another form of conservatism. In the perspective of many liberal Protestants, the believers who talk about this all the time appear to be pompous, unloving, indifferent to issues of social justice, and so fixated on questions about the authority of Scripture that they neglect the message of the gospel.

Although the concern for the personal has not disappeared, it has become a form of therapeutic or managerial individualism, as Robert Bellah has suggested.[18] "Spirituality" has a vast audience in liberal Protestant circles these days; but it is barely distinguishable from self-help pop psychology or schemes for self-realization. Any idea of conversion to something that we are not already is viewed with suspicion. Reinhold Niebuhr's suspicion of the "easy con-science" of modern secularity has come to fruition even among church members.[19]

The Victory of "Liberation"

Cut off from normative thinking and profound piety, currently influential segments of Protestant thinking have reconceived the notion of the Coming Kingdom in a specific way—liberation. Liberation theology, to be sure, has many possible forms and is currently being modified in Latin America, where it found its most forceful expression.[20] But in the forms most often adopted by ecumenical Protestantism, we find the practical victory of one theory of social analysis over every other theory. This theory, as everyone knows, was adopted by Marx from Hegel's theory of the "Master/Slave Relationship." Marx applied this to a view of bour-geois/proletariat domination.

As modified by Marx, the theory entails the notion that the oppressed proletariat is purified from its illusions by its sufferings. It thus gains a privileged epistemic position and is free to become a messianic, redemptive force in history. In modified form, this view has been adapted as the reigning metaphor for white/black, male/female, and first-world/third-world relationships.[21] Recently the terms have also been applied to heterosexism and homophilia, although the empirical and moral logic of this supposed parallelism is particularly debated and may split a number of churches. In any case, this view has given the quests for inclusiveness and personal meaning a particular bent: every non-dominant group must be heeded by virtue of its epistemic privilege, and each must express its spirituality by self-affirmation.

In many circles today, if a topic of social justice is raised, nearly everyone calls to mind some version of this model. Marx may have lost the modern world, but he conquered the modern ecumenical mind. Although few ecumenical Protestants are consciously Marx-ist, a new covert orthodoxy, under slogans of "pluralistic inclusive-ness," has been installed. Anyone who doubts this model or asso-ciates with those who do lives under suspicion. The basic meaning of "liberal" is altered. Sociologists Robert Wuthnow and James

Davison Hunter report in recent studies that "liberal"/"conservative" divisions along these lines are now decisive in Protestant churches, surpassing any denominational differences.[22]

The appeal of liberation theology is evident. Many Christians around the world have not gone through a Reformation, a Lockean Enlightenment, an Emancipation Movement, the Social Gospel, Christian Realism, or the Civil Rights Movement as theologically inspired engagements in social change. Nor have they been tutored to take the themes of the social encyclicals as central to faithful living. Multitudes of people remain trapped in pre-democratic, feudal, male-dominated societies where human rights are but a distant rumor; and Christian leaders have only sometimes been highly visible in opposing oppression. In such contexts, slogans baptized in the name of liberation condense several theories of social change into a handy scheme that seems to render a ready description of why things are the way they are, as well as a prescription for how they can become what they ought to be.

This way of thinking has been reinforced by many factors, not the least being the hiring patterns of the denominational and ecumenical agencies during the 1960s and 1970s. Protestantism's curia, insofar as we have one, became populated by a generation that accepted this analysis as gospel. Thus the leadership of this cluster of communions transmuted a legitimate and important passion for social justice into a dogmatic liberationism in which claims about the necessity of universal, transcontextual principles, or about the indispensability of personal piety and purity as an integral aspect of the struggle to know and do God's will, are viewed as "conservative" illusions. At the same time, an unofficial, revised model of how the Church is to carry out its prophetic witness for social justice has been installed.

The New and Pernicious Errors

A serious problem, however, is this: The new revised standard model contains elements that are false, and the error is consequential. At the level of social analysis, it offers a now discredited view. What it says is the case, is not the case. What it says helps, hurts. What it says oppresses, liberates; what it says liberates, oppresses.

What it says brings equality, brings only the sharing of poverty. What it touts as the "prophetic alternative" to modern patterns of technology, economics, and politics, brings social obsolescence, collapse, and tyranny. What is says enhances the actualization of justice in history, instead traps its adherents in unjust enclaves on the sidelines of history.

Christians can live with a degree of divergence in the interpretation of social reality; but these particular views tend to require theological distortion. For one thing, they deny common grace. They are held, thus, on grounds that are finally anti-ecumenical. They do not speak to or for humanity in an inclusive, cosmopolitan voice, but only to and for particular constituencies. No one can deny that we need to hear the voices of the oppressed; but it is wrong to deny that we need theological principles to help us discern what to believe. And on this point, no sociological group has an epistemic privilege.

The denial of this point often leads modern Protestant liberationists to a functional anti-intellectualism. All ideas are viewed as a function of social location. Thus the established view becomes anti-theological precisely because it asserts the priority of material praxis over metaphysical or moral insight.[23] Liberationists echo the reductionisms of Feuerbach, Nietzsche, and especially Marx as if they were theology. One is reminded of the shift made by Goethe's Faust, who rewrote the Scriptures just before making his wager with the devil:

> It is written: "In the beginning was the Word!"
> Even now I balk. Can no one help?
> I truly cannot rate the word so high.
> I must translate it otherwise.
> I believe the Spirit has inspired me
> and I must write: "In the beginning there was Mind."
> Think thoroughly on this first line,
> hold back your pen from undue haste!
> Is it mind that stirs and makes all things?
> The text should state:
> "In the beginning was Power."
> Yet while I am about to write this down,
> something warns me I will not adhere to this.

> The Spirit's on my side! The answer is at hand:
> I write, assured, "In the beginning was the Deed."[24]

Whenever and wherever there are hard times, people blame some "them." This is called the Adam syndrome: "*she* gave me the apple and I did eat." Sometimes the "other" is indeed guilty and must be called to account. But some crises, the deeper and more important and more pervasive ones, are not fundamentally due to exterior temptations or pressures. They are due to the presumed, accepted values that are woven into the fabric of a society, a culture, or a subculture—and celebrated in religion. These shape the rulers and the ruled, the rich and the poor, the whites and the blacks, the men and the women. An overthrow of the power elite, or a redistribution of property, or the development of openness to inclusiveness, cures very little at this level. Although these political actions are sometime necessary, they cannot cure the deeper ills.

The Centrality of Theology

Religion, as the chief bearer of values in every ethos, and theology, as the chief discipline to determine which values and religions are ultimately worth having, must be at the very center of every social analysis and every process of serious social change. The critique and transformation of social, political, and economic reality depend on theology, not the other way around. That is why liberation thought is so dangerous: it appears to be theological, but it has these matters backwards. The loyal opposition to it within ecumenical Protestantism struggles not against flesh and blood but against distorted principles that have become principalities, and against potentialities that have become destructive powers.

This critique must not be construed as an apology for everything that liberation thought opposes. I do not argue that theology or the Church should have nothing to do with social questions, or that some pure gospel distinct from these can and should be followed. I agree that righteousness has not been established with democracy, that human rights are not observed everywhere they are talked about, that corporate economies have not met the material needs of all segments of the population equitably, that the United States has only rarely acted with benevolence in domestic or foreign policy. I do not think that Christianity has been spread without any taint of cultural imperialism, or that liberal Protestantism has developed entirely beyond patriarchy and racism. Protestants, even liberal ones, know that a basic characteristic of everything human is sin.

Nevertheless, it seems clear that both theology and the structures of modern life need to be reconceived through post-Marxist categories of analysis, and that modern Western social life will not be found to be altogether evil. In fact, modern Western forms of social and institutional life, with all their ambiguities, may well bear within them, not only marks of the order of preservation, but hints of the order of redemption, because Christianity has generated a liberalism that has become partially incarnate in society. For the continuing sins of and within modern Western life, we must both follow the classic Protestant tradition of public confession and reclaim the Reformed strategy of *semper reformans, semper reformanda*. But neither faithfulness, nor honesty, nor justice requires a negation of modern Western civilization. Rather, we must sympathetically engage it and transform it lovingly from within.

WHITHER ECUMENICAL CHRISTIANITY?

What is to be done as we approach the twenty-first century? What might John Paul II say in a new letter on social issues that could broaden and deepen a pertinent ecumenical witness?

Any such letter would face a form of Protestantism differing from the one that received *Rerum Novarum*. It is a less confident Protestantism, but one that may now be beginning to get its own house in order once more. The cloud of evidence of this is no bigger than a man's hand, but some of the most vocal Sandinista Christians are quietly moving (or being moved) to other positions. It has not been entirely lost on key ecumenical leaders that the Catholics are winning the arguments, the evangelicals are winning the people, and the Republicans are winning the elections. Something has to change.

Furthermore, close dialogues are taking place among liberal Protestants, Roman Catholics, evangelicals, and Eastern Orthodox on matters directly relevant to social issues—especially around, of all things, the ancient trinitarian creeds. It is quite possible that these dialogues have the potential, not only to bring our communions closer together, but also to help each of the great branches of Christianity reclaim from the past and recast for tomorrow the three necessary motifs of ethical thought, as well to renew the basis for genuine ecumenical engagement.[25] Such developments could be exceedingly important as we face a series of great responsibilities in the century just ahead:

—To develop a sacramental sensibility able to guide modern technology as it extends the human mastery of nature.

—To learn to understand other world religions, especially Islam, the largest and most vigorous one and the closest cousin to Christianity.

—To seek cross-cultural principles that can frame the new levels of international law now demanded by global developments.

—To develop a deeper appreciation of the role of arts and media in shaping modern cosmopolitan consciousness.

—To reconstruct family life in the midst of rapid social change and new interpretations of human sexuality.

Two Major Challenges

No ecumenically alert community of faith can fail to address these issues. But liberal Protestantism in America is likely to have the greatest difficulty with two other challenges. The first is this: Socialism has failed, and we do not have a clear view of how to address the theological and ethical issues embedded in capitalism, corporations, market economies, modern finance, international trade, middle-class values, and profit-oriented activity, even though the argument can be made that Protestantism played a major (if not fully intended) role in bringing these into existence. The affair with liberationism has prevented us from preparing theological ethics for the pastoral and socio-political tasks at hand.

The second great challenge for contemporary ecumenical Protestantism is that we face a new Constantinian moment. We have to decide whether or not it is Providence that has capitulated the United States into a form of world leadership that, with allies in Europe and East Asia, is likely to set the economic, cultural, political, military, and legal pace for the next century or so. We know that this position will not go unchallenged. Latin American movements will remain critical, and regional powers, in which we must now include the former Soviet Union with China and India, will clearly have their own sense of how the future ought to be shaped. Furthermore, the Arabic world will surely remain turbulent for some time.

Nevertheless, we have to decide whether the fact that American leadership is at the forefront of the "New World Order" is theologically significant. Clearly, if it is, the leadership thrust upon us ought not to be seen as an opportunity for the triumph of "American interests," or of "our way of life," or of a new "manifest destiny." Instead, we ought to think of a revokable, temporary trusteeship from God that must be exercised with fear, trembling, and a commitment to stewardship that calls more to duty than to privilege.

Such a notion is a major challenge for the ecumenical churches today. The temptations to sectarianism that have always plagued our history have been reinforced by recent liberationist leadership as well as by certain trends in scholarly treatments of religion and theology. Also, much of ecumenical Christianity at home and abroad has developed a deep aversion to any hint of Western and specifically American influence. Many ecumenical Christians have been deeply involved in protesting U.S. policies in Vietnam and Central America, reenacting in their own minds Bonhoeffer's resistance to state power in Nazi Germany and Barth's role in the Barmen Declaration. Thus any claim that the Church should address the people of the one remaining superpower in terms of theological, ethical, and social principles that can make the *Pax Americana* a blessing to humanity is repugnant. To many, this smacks of Constantinianism, the "second fall" from which Protestantism rescued Christianity. Yet here we are, on the brink of a new Constantinian situation.

As we move toward and into the twenty-first century, it is likely that the chief social issues for public discourse will turn out to be doctrinal ones. What ought we to believe? Is there an orthodoxy? How does God want us to live? How do we know? What difference does it make if we hold that God's law, grace, and purpose are manifest in history, specifically in aspects of our own history? These are decisive questions that center, especially, on the nature of God, on epistemology, and on the role of divine authority in human social history. These are the prior questions—previous to the necessary attempts to address the concrete social questions.

If and when a new encyclical is issued to cap the century of social encyclicals initiated by Leo XIII, I pray that it not only will address the practical issues we face, but also will help the whole ecumenical Church with the formation of a compelling, coherent, and genuinely catholic public theology. We liberal Protestants need all the help we can get. So do the whole ecumenical Church and the emerging cosmopolitan civilization.

Responses

1. JAMES NUECHTERLEIN

Max Stackhouse's essay is perceptive, wise, and courageous. It tells necessary hard truths about the liberal or ecumenical Protestantism with which he identifies himself. I cannot imagine a more tough-minded analysis of the liberal Protestant condition issuing from within the ranks of liberal Protestantism. And I say these complimentary things not as a *pro forma* preliminary to a subsequent move for the jugular but in genuine appreciation.

I do, of course, have a few reservations (what, after all, is a respondent for?). I wonder, first, about Stackhouse's defense of liberalism's claim to the future and his implied appropriation for liberalism of the mantle of ecumenism. The liberalism of the future that he describes at the beginning of his essay is unexceptionable; it also has little to do with the actual preoccupations and practices of liberal Protestantism today. And ecumenism can be seen to depend on or follow from liberalism only if one's conception of ecumenism is promiscuously latitudinarian.

Stackhouse's analysis carries an implicit criticism of liberalism that I think needs to be made explicit: liberalism today suffers, most of all, from a crisis of faith. And that crisis suggests a weakness in the Social Gospel legacy of liberal Protestantism that Stackhouse does not here address. I think, for example, of George McGovern's remembrances in his autobiography, *Grassroots*. McGovern was the son of a Wesleyan Methodist minister, and he deeply admired his orthodox Christian father. When McGovern lost his religious faith while a teenager, he was in agony about the implied repudiation of his father's life and work until left-wing teachers suggested to him how the rhetoric of the Social Gospel could keep alive the *spirit* of his religious tradition without any close connection to its *essence*.

James Nuechterlein is the editor of *First Things* and associate director of the Institute on Religion and Public Life in New York City.

McGovern, an unbeliever, clung to the residual benefits of belief; many after him did the same thing. Walter Rauschenbusch was a man of faith and of theological sophistication, but more than a few who appropriated his message were neither.

My second point is related at least in part to the first. If a major problem of liberal Protestantism is the lapse, in much of it, from Christian orthodoxy, that problem is closely related to its weak ecclesiology. Ecclesiology is not a central concern of Stackhouse's paper, but where he does speak of Protestant ecclesiology he appears to celebrate it. This is a highly complex issue, of course, but I would argue that, at least at present, much of liberal Protestantism's disarray stems from its lack of a functional equivalent of Rome's magisterium, and that lack stems from Protestant ecclesiology. The "Protestant curia"—of which Stackhouse speaks with an appropriate minimum of enthusiasm—has been able to do the damage it has done in part because of the weakness of structures of accountability and theological ordering in liberal Protestantism. The Protestant world is one in which it is increasingly difficult to discern or even to speak coherently of any *sensus fidelium*.

My third and major point has to do with Stackhouse's proposal for a reconstructed "public theology." I have no quarrel with the proposal in theory, but my Lutheran two-kingdoms sensibilities go on nervous alert when he speaks of the need for a "sacramental sensibility" to guide modern technology or of the prospect that "the chief social issues for public discourse will turn out to be doctrinal ones." The first requirement for any reconstituted public theology, in my view, is that it be considerably more humble than the public theologies that have arisen in recent years on both the left and the right of the theological/political spectrum. I am not accusing Stackhouse of hubris or immodesty—and he makes some admirably cautionary remarks on the excesses and blind spots of the liberationists on that score—but I fear that he may be more ambitious for his public theology than is safe or prudent.

It is one thing to note, as he properly does, that all areas of life— "politics, law, science, sexuality, technology, medicine, art, business"—carry theological implications. It is something else to suggest, as he may or may not be doing (he does not fully spell this out), that for every activity of life we need or can usefully construct a "theology of . . . ." What, after all, do we require of a public theology? That it offer distinctive motivation for Christian activity, set limits on behavior, and, above all, provide a transcendent perspective that will judge and relativize all contingent human activity. A proper public theology will teach us to avoid demonic or utopian temptations; but as for offering the comprehensive guidelines for action that Stackhouse seems at points to be suggesting, I would need to be persuaded. Theology helps to set boundaries in our public life, to tell us what we must not do, to warn us against the grandiose; but Stackhouse seems to expect from it a more positive and directly practical assistance than it may be capable of providing.

Programs of public theology tend to say either too little or too much; they either proceed at an unhelpful level of abstraction or specify more than Scripture or tradition allows. We risk, on the one hand, banality, and on the other hand—and this risk is far the more dangerous—the appropriation of religious symbols and discourse for programs arrived at from other than religious sources and for other than religious purposes. The latter danger may take less dramatic form: we may simply place upon public-policy agendas or cultural prescriptions a theological weight they do not require and in any case cannot bear. (And in a pluralistic society like ours there is the further problem that programs offered in the public square framed in specifically Christian language may be either meaningless or offensive to non-Christians. We need to translate, which is to say we need some version of common natural-law discourse.)

Public-theology proposals become particularly problematic when they come armed with the official sanction of the Church—that is, when church bodies take specific and official positions on controversial issues of the day. We must keep in mind the very wide range of questions on which reasonable and faithful Christians can reasonably and faithfully disagree. My own modest proposal on the matter—which I have not the space to elaborate here—has, if nothing else, the virtue of simplicity: Where it is not necessary for the Church to speak, it is necessary for the Church not to speak. To do otherwise is to risk the terrible sin of dividing the body of Christ unnecessarily. In at least this aspect of public theology, the minimalist injunction applies: Less is more—or at least better.

2. PAUL E. SIGMUND

I have only two major points to make about Max Stackhouse's excellent essay, and both involve questions of history rather than his overall argument.

First when we refer to Leo XIII's encyclical *Rerum Novarum* as an important advance in papal social thought, it is important to note that, while it marks the beginning of European Social Catholicism,—i.e., the Church's concern with the social question, defined as the plight of the working classes—it does not move forward in the area of politics towards the acceptance of Christian Democracy, i.e., parties of Christian inspiration that fully accept the modern religiously pluralistic democratic state. Such parties already existed, and many more would be founded in the ensuing century, but it was not until after World War II—and in the case of religious pluralism, until the Second Vatican Council—that the papacy accepted the moral and religious legitimacy of the modern democratic state, notably in the encyclical *Pacem in Terris* (1963) and the conciliar document *Gaudium et Spes* (1965). Thus the social question was addressed in an early and timely fashion, but there was a regrettable delay in addressing the political question of the most desirable form of government from a Christian point of view.

My second criticism concerns what I consider to be the flawed view of John Locke as solely an apologist for capitalist property relations—in Macpherson's words, a theorist of "possessive individualism." In fact, other parts of Locke's theory placed serious limits on absolute rights of property. He believed in the consent of the majority as the only valid legitimation of government, and used that consent to justify laws that imposed taxes to support the institutions of government, including provision for the needy (since one of the purposes of the social contract was the protection of life, and it made no sense to enter a society that would let you starve to death). Thus, as Willmoore Kendall and others have pointed out, the Lockean state was not the capitalist paradise that some have made it out to be. Locke is more religious and less obsessed with

Paul E. Sigmund is a professor of political science at Princeton University.

57

property relations than Stackhouse implies. We are first of all God's property, and we have obligations to one another that limit the property right, although the specifics of those limitations are to be worked out by representatives whom we have elected either directly or indirectly. And that relationship to God is so sacred that with few exceptions (atheists and Catholics) it cannot be regulated by government.

3

The Scandal of Evangelical Political Reflection

MARK A. NOLL

THE evangelical *Rerum Novarum* was a speech. It was given five years and fifty-five days after Leo XIII's promulgation of his encyclical, in response to a social crisis that, in its broad outlines, was remarkably similar to what the pontiff had addressed. As the encyclical summarized the wisdom of Roman Catholic experience, so the evangelical *Rerum Novarum* recapitulated prominent social themes from the history of English-speaking white Protestants in America. Although the evangelical speech did not launch an on-going tradition of Christian social philosophy as Leo's encyclical did, in form and emphases it was every bit as typical of what would come later in evangelical political thought as the pope's pronouncement was typical of subsequent Catholic political thought.

The scene of the speech was the platform debate of the Democratic National Convention in Chicago in 1896. The speaker was William Jennings Bryan from Nebraska, already at age thirty-six an ex-congressman. Bryan had been addressing political crowds for a long time, but not as long as he had been preaching to congregations as a lay Presbyterian.[1] Although the speech in Chicago did

---

Mark A. Noll is McManis Professor of Christian Thought at Wheaton College in Wheaton, Illinois. He is the editor of *Religion and American Politics: From the Colonial Period to the 1980s* and the author of *Princeton and the Republic, 1768–1822*.

not have a text, it too was a sermon. Its character as an evangelical exposition of political thought was manifest in the metaphors of its unforgettable conclusion:

> If they dare to come out in the open field and defend the gold standard as a good thing, we will fight them to the uttermost. Having behind us the producing masses of this nation and the world, supported by the commercial interests, the laboring interests, and the toilers everywhere, we will answer their demand for a gold standard by saying to them: You shall not press down upon the brow of labor this crown of thorns, you shall not crucify mankind upon a cross of gold.[2]

Why Bryan's "Cross of Gold" speech might be considered an evangelical equivalent of *Rerum Novarum* is the first theme of this paper. By examining its historical circumstances, however, we are also in a position to understand twentieth-century evangelical political thought more generally. In particular, this kind of analysis shows why fundamentalism, with which Bryan is often associated, represented not only a massive repudiation of Bryan's specific political principles but also a disastrous abandonment of political philosophy as a whole. It will also be important to see why fundamentalism, which was so utterly scandalous in abjuring responsible political thought, was—and continues to be—politically scandalous in another sense of the term, in the distinctly religious sense that the Christian message of a crucified God is a scandal to those who cannot believe.[3]

The Meaning of "Evangelical"

Before we consider Bryan and the fate of his politics at the hands of fundamentalist successors, we must pause to pin down the term "evangelical." This effort is especially important when the subject is evangelical *political* viewpoints, for here there is considerable variety arising from a wide range of evangelical experiences and convictions. It is especially important not to assume that the most visible expression of evangelical political reflection at any one time represents the political thought of all evangelicals.

During this century, four forms of political thought have dominated evangelical political thought: (1) for the first quarter of the century, Bryan's populist democracy and its variants; for the next half century, (2) in the North a politics shaped by the convictions of premillennial dispensationalism, (3) and in the South a politics shaped by the sectarianism of Southern Baptists, Pentecostals, and Restorationists; and (4) for the last two decades, the politics of the New Christian Right. Yet in each of these eras, evangelical political thought reflected diversity, since evangelicalism was never just Bryan's kind of populism, never just dispensationalism in the North or sectarianism in the South, never just the religion of the televangelists. Moreover, some of the self-conscious evangelical attempts to discover distinctly Christian norms for politics have come from what might be called the penumbra of evangelicalism, from individuals or groups that share some but not all of the traits associated with the most visible evangelicals.

Two Defining Characteristics

Within the minor industry now devoted to the problem of defining "evangelical," the tendency has been to stress either the dynamics of social movement or the principles of Christian theology.[4] A better way—better, at least, if we are to make coherent comments about twentieth-century developments—is to combine the two. So I am classifying as evangelicals those who share two things.

First, as a historically defined movement, American evangelicals are the descendants of the eighteenth-century Anglo-American revivals associated with George Whitefield, John Wesley, and Jonathan Edwards. From this angle, evangelicals are: revivalist Calvinists and their descendants (including dispensationalists), Methodists and their descendants among Holiness and Pentecostal bodies, Baptists in their many varieties, low-church Episcopalians, and independent congregations shaped by influences from these various traditions.

To this historical definition must be added, however, a second defining characteristic made up of beliefs and practices. Evangelicals are, from this angle, people who believe in the truth of the Bible interpreted along commonsensical lines, who seek conversions as the natural outgrowth of the meaning of the gospel, who practice their faith actively in obedience to divine law, and who stress the death of Christ on the cross as the key to human well-being.[5] Adding in these religious standards means that not all descendants of the eighteenth-century revival movements are evangelicals, for some of them among Methodist, Presbyterian, Episcopal, Baptist, or Restorationist denominations no longer hold to those beliefs. On the other hand, there are American Christians who are not heirs of the eighteenth-century revivals—such as some Lutherans, Continental pietists, Anabaptists, and charismatic Catholics—who do hold those beliefs in almost the same form that they are embraced by descendants of the revivals.

What we might call "core evangelicals," then, are descendants of the eighteenth-century revival movements who maintain traditionally evangelical beliefs and practices. Liberal Protestants, by contrast, are those who have laid aside the heritage of pietistic revivalism or have seriously qualified the evangelical beliefs. (The overlap between "evangelicals" and "the mainline" is great and very confusing.) Southern Baptists, the country's largest Protestant denomination, figure as "implicit evangelicals" in this scheme because, although they have maintained an almost closed religious world for over a century, their history can be traced back to the eighteenth-century revivals and their beliefs are quite similar to the evangelical core.

Protestants of non-British origin—like Lutherans, Mennonites, Christian Reformed, or Scandinavian free churches—are among the most important groups in the evangelical penumbra. For the purposes of historical analysis, they do not count as evangelicals (however much their beliefs resemble the evangelical core) so long as they remain entities unto themselves. When, however, they begin to interact significantly with self-consciously evangelical groups, then they may be regarded as evangelicals for the purposes of historical analysis. For example, Missouri Synod Lutherans, even though they embrace evangelical beliefs, would not, in this scheme, count as American evangelicals because they have remained so determinedly isolated from other religious communions. On the other hand, throughout the twentieth century, Mennonites and the Christian Reformed have been journeying from isolated positions that once resembled the Missouri Synod's to positions of meaningful involvement with broader evangelical (and also mainline) constituencies.

Black Protestants are the hardest to classify. While they often share the core religious beliefs of white evangelicals, and while revivalism has powerfully shaped their history, that history is also significantly different from the experiences of white evangelicals. Black Protestants often sound like evangelicals when they speak, but the interaction between them and white evangelicals has been marked by struggle more than cooperation. The result is an extraordinarily complicated relationship that makes African Americans, for the purpose of political analysis, both the most and the least evangelical of all American Protestants.[6]

PARALLELS BETWEEN THE TWO STATEMENTS

Having made our way through this conceptual thicket, we can now return to William Jennings Bryan and his speech at the Chicago Democratic Convention in 1896. Leo XIII was the nineteenth century's most influential voice of Catholic social philosophy, and *Rerum Novarum* was the key document encouraging twentieth-century Catholic political thought. Similarly, a good case can be made, as Garry Wills does, that William Jennings Bryan was "the most important evangelical politician of this century" and the "Cross of Gold" address "the greatest speech at any political convention."[7]

There are some similarities in form between the speech and the encyclical. Each reflected its author's immersion in Scripture, the encyclical through numerous direct quotations, the speech through such allusions as the "cross" of the peroration and the adaptation of First Samuel 18:7, "If protection has slain its thousands, the gold standard has slain its tens of thousands."[8] Leo XIII summed up a long history of Catholic theology and Catholic moral philosophy; so too did Bryan sum up the public witness of a nineteenth-century Protestantism that had, in the words of Leonard Sweet, "created a de facto establishment of evangelicalism whose security lay in a common ethos, a common outlook on life and history, a common piety, and common patterns of worship and devotion."[9] Leo was moved to prepare the encyclical by a sense of "the momentous gravity of the state of things now obtaining"; Bryan felt that "never before in the history of this country has there been witnessed such a contest" as that taking place over monetary policy.[10] Finally, Leo's encyclical was a creative effort to apply historic Catholic theology to the needs of the moment; so also was Bryan's speech a creative attempt to apply treasured evangelical traditions to the crisis of the hour.

The encyclical and the speech also exhibited striking parallels in more explicit assertions. Both authors appealed to principles transcending the details of current circumstances.[11] More substantially, both championed ordinary people. What Leo affirmed by arguing that "the members of the working classes are citizens by nature and by the same right as the rich," Bryan asserted more elaborately: "The man who is employed for wages . . . , the attorney in a country town . . . , the merchant at the cross-roads store . . . , the farmer who goes forth in the morning and toils all day . . . , [and] the miners who go down a thousand feet into the earth . . . are as much business men as the few financial magnates who, in a back room, corner the money of the world."[12] Where Leo began by stating that "some opportune remedy must be found quickly for the misery and wretchedness pressing so unjustly on the majority of the working class," Bryan rose to speak on behalf of "the struggling masses . . . the toilers everywhere."[13]

Bryan's speech, because it was a political address, did not fully reveal the Christian superstructure of his political vision. Throughout his public career, however, he made no secret of the specifically evangelical principles that drove his politics.[14] These principles, even if they were still regarded by most observers in the 1890s as the antitheses of Roman Catholic principles, nonetheless yielded points of social analysis very much like Leo's.

At the end of *Rerum Novarum*, for example, Leo summarized a set of careful discriminations he had drawn between what was important in this world and what was important for eternity by saying that "the main thing needful is to re-establish Christian morals, apart from which all the plans and devices of the wisest will prove of little avail." Time after time throughout his career, Bryan delivered a speech entitled "The Prince of Peace," in which he made the same distinction between the everlasting value of the Golden Rule and the relative value of political action.[15]

To both Leo and Bryan, moreover, the greatest danger from modern secular theories was not the challenge to this or that particular of Christian doctrine but the demeaning of the person that these secular theories entailed. In the encyclical, Leo summed up his defense of private property by arguing that "the main tenet of socialism, community of goods . . . , is directly contrary to the natural rights of mankind, and would introduce confusion and disorder into the commonweal." For his part, Bryan opposed evolution with growing fervor, not so much because it threatened traditional interpretations of Genesis 1 as because evolution was "an insult to reason and shocks the heart. That doctrine is as deadly as leprosy; . . . it would, if generally adopted, destroy all sense of responsibility and menace the morals of the world."[16]

On the specific matter of strikes by workers against their employers, Leo and Bryan, with a common concern for the broader health of the community, made almost the same analysis. "Such paralyzing of labor," said Leo, "not only affects the masters and their work people alike, but is extremely injurious to trade and to the general interests of the public." For Bryan, it was the same: "The strike and the lockout are to our industrial life what war is between nations, and the general public stands in much the same position as neutral nations. The number of those actually injured by a suspension of industry is often many times as great as the total number of employers and employees in that industry combined."[17]

Both Leo XIII and Bryan were compassionate and creative communicators. They both thought that traditional Christian faith had an answer to contemporary public crises, not as the faith was reinterpreted by the conventions of the moment, but as its hereditary truths were redirected to encompass modern situations. Both also felt that the resources of traditional Christianity were especially necessary for redressing the grievances suffered by ordinary people because of economic modernization.

DIFFERENCES BETWEEN THE TWO STATEMENTS

If there is much that links *Rerum Novarum* and "The Cross of Gold," there is also much that divides them. Those points of difference reveal what was most deeply characteristic of nineteenth-century evangelical public thought and most directly anticipatory of evangelical politics in the twentieth century.

Writing vs. Speaking

The most obvious of these differences—that one was a written document and the other a speech—may also be the most significant. American evangelicalism as it had developed since the revivals of the mid-eighteenth century did include a tradition of serious written reflection. But that reflection tended to be concentrated fairly narrowly on theological and biblical topics. Political persuasion and experiential religion, for evangelicals, were primarily matters of public speaking.

Puritan experience, with its central focus on the sermon, pointed in this direction.[18] Even more, although public evangelicalism bore the strong imprint of John Wesley's perfectionist spirituality and Jonathan Edwards's mystical conversionism, it was defined much more by the sermonic power of George Whitefield.[19] Evangelicalism became a tradition in which its greatest speculative theologian, Jonathan Edwards, would be best known for a sermon, "Sinners in the Hands of an Angry God." Evangelicals have no exclusive claim to the religion of Abraham Lincoln, whose faith seems to have been as generally Hebraic as it was specifically Christian. But it is nonetheless significant that the most profound statement of Christian, or at least theistic, political theology in the evangelical nineteenth century was Lincoln's Second Inaugural Address.

After the sermon, nineteenth-century evangelicals looked next to the popular press for their inspiration, instruction, information, and guidance on public issues.[20] It was thus entirely in keeping with American evangelical tradition that the most impressive statement of evangelical political sentiment at the end of the century came from the "Boy Orator of the Platte," who, when he was not speaking on the road, earned his living as a newspaper editor.

As it was in the days of Whitefield and Wesley, Charles Finney and D. L. Moody, so it has been in the century of Billy Sunday and Billy Graham, Oral Roberts and Kenneth Copeland, Jimmy Swaggart and Jerry Falwell, John Stott and Martyn Lloyd-Jones. The most visible evangelicals, with the broadest popular influence, have been public speakers. It was entirely congruent with their past that evangelicals took the lead in exploiting both radio and television for religious purposes.[21] It is also a fitting chapter in the evangelical story that Carl F. H. Henry's *The Uneasy Conscience of Modern Fundamentalism*, a book influential in the awakening of public concern among northern, post-fundamentalist neo-evangelicals, originated in 1947 as a series of talks at a time when Henry was more a journalist than a theologian. While it is true that the place of black Protestants in evangelical history is an ambiguous one, it is still noteworthy that the nation's most profound confrontation with Christian public testimony in the twentieth century was in the sermon/speeches of Martin Luther King, Jr., and his colleagues, in which evangelical themes were prominent.

In general, evangelicals are self-defined by evangelistic urgency. They have promoted a faith, not of Word and sacrament, but of Word preached, Word studied, and Word shared. A tradition of pastoral letters from the popes, addressing specific issues from the standpoint of general Catholic teaching and for the benefit of the whole Church, was well established by the time Leo XIII issued *Rerum Novarum*. Just as firmly established was the evangelical reliance on public speech, in which gathered congregations were addressed on specific issues with the powerful conventions of revivalistic fervor. This emphasis continues to shape the religion and public thought of twentieth-century evangelicals.

Church Action vs. Individual Action

A second obvious way in which Leo's statement and Bryan's differed was that *Rerum Novarum* was issued by the head of a church and assigned the church itself a critical role in meeting the contemporary social crisis, while Bryan's "Cross of Gold" speech was put forth on his own authority and made its strongest appeal to individuals.

The focus on individual action has predominated in the American evangelical tradition since the days of Whitefield. The enduring contribution to evangelicalism of the republicanism of the Revolutionary era was to undermine hereditary trust in institutions.[22] The enduring contribution of the Great Awakenings in the colonial and early national periods was to substitute the voluntary society for the church.[23] The result—with Charles Finney's revivals, Theodore Dwight Weld's abolitionism, Frances Willard's temperance crusade, and William Jennings Bryan's silver movement—was to transform the mechanism of Christian social action. Insight into the public sphere and guidance for political action came, not from authoritative pronouncements handed down from above, but from inner conviction springing up from within.[24] The great men and women of American evangelicalism have been those who recognized this reality and knew best how to persuade.

In his speech, Bryan bypassed the inherited institutions that Leo promoted in *Rerum Novarum* as the agents of change. Rather, he urged on the silver Democrats "a zeal approaching the zeal which inspired the crusaders who followed Peter the Hermit."[25] A call to symbolic battle took the place of the renovation of institutions.

Sometimes the evangelical ecclesiology and the voluntarism with which it is associated are called democratic.[26] Although there is certainly a democratic element, more precisely the situation is not a democratic one as such but one in which authority has been transferred from heredity to charisma, from a power commanding assent to a power eliciting assent. Bryan's speech and the more general evangelical tradition of public political reflection have been, in other words, not just Protestant, but dissenting or congregationalist Protestant. (During the last fifteen years of his life, the Presbyterian church became more important for Bryan, but primarily as one more arena in which to campaign for votes.[27]) Not only American convictions about the separation of church and state but also an entire tradition of voluntary organization kept Bryan from saying what came naturally to Leo XIII, that "no practical solution of this [economic] question will be found apart from the intervention of religion and of the Church."[28]

A Different Use of History

Bryan's use of history in the "Cross of Gold" speech marked a third difference with *Rerum Novarum*. Where the encyclical made careful use of ancient authorities, especially Thomas Aquinas, both to define a proper method for examining public issues and to provide answers to specific economic questions, Bryan's history was ritualistic and mythic. His evocation of "the hardy pioneers who braved all the dangers of the wilderness" was effective but not analytical. Although he knew the importance of the past, he recognized that for his audience that importance was mostly emotive. So he took time to enlist history—"the pioneers away out there [pointing westward], who rear their children near to Nature's heart, where they can mingle their voices with the voices of the birds— out there where they have erected schoolhouses for the education of their young, churches where they praise their Creator, and cemeteries where rest the ashes of their dead." But it was a picture drawn for the purpose of moving rather than instructing: "these people, we say, are as deserving of the consideration of our party as any people in this country."[29] Bryan referred to historical authorities, but these references were mythic—to Thomas Jefferson, who opposed the political influence of banks, and to Andrew Jackson, "who did for us [what Cicero did for Rome] when he destroyed the bank conspiracy and saved America."[30]

In using history in this way, Bryan was extending an evangelical tradition. The American Revolution had taught evangelicals that the past was corrupt and that ardent effort in the present might even usher in the millennium.[31] An intense surge of religious primitivism in the early republic re-energized Puritan motifs, created several new Christian denominations like the Disciples of Christ and the Churches of Christ, powered the new religion of Joseph Smith, and had an effect upon almost all American denominations (including the Catholics).[32] This primitivism sought to set aside history almost entirely in its effort to recapture the pristine glories of New Testament Christianity.

Because it draws strength from evangelicals' devotion to the Bible and to the illuminating examples of the New Testament, the primitivist influence in American evangelicalism remains very strong. For evangelicals, what history teaches is dim at best, corrupting at worst. Responding to the crises of the moment, therefore, requires, as in the example of Bryan, an application of absolute principles (often derived from the New Testament, the more static of the two) along with a fervent appeal to millennial possibilities. The eon between the first coming of Christ to the world and the future second coming has never been the object of systematic evangelical attention.[33] For evangelical commentary on public life there has been no Thomas Aquinas, no deference to a tradition such as Aquinas represented for Leo XIII, and no felt need for such deference.

FOUR MARKS OF EVANGELICAL POLITICAL REFLECTION

An examination of the major themes of Bryan's career yields a portrait of evangelical political reflection. The most important thing a historian can say about the nature of that reflection is that it mirrors the characteristics of evangelical life.[34] Evangelical political reflection has depended upon an a-ecclesiastical or anti-ecclesiastical moralism because evangelicalism in America has been a movement, stressing moral activism without providing a major role for the Church. Evangelical political reflection is oriented in a populist direction because evangelicalism has been a populist movement. Evangelical political reflection has drawn upon intuitive conceptions of justice because evangelicals in general have trusted their sanctified common sense more than formal theology, the systematic study of history, or the pronouncements of formal moral philosophy. Evangelical political reflection is nurtured by a commonsensical biblicism for the same reasons that a "Bible only" mentality has flourished among evangelicals.

This, then, has been the common evangelical framework for political reflection, as well as for political action, in the twentieth century: *moral activism, populism, intuitionism,* and *biblicism.* But to say that there is a common framework is not to suggest that evangelical political action has been entirely uniform or predictable. Twentieth-century evangelicals have differed widely among themselves over specific political actions and principles. These differences sometimes arise when particular aspects of the common evangelical framework are given special prominence at specific times or in response to specific crises; for example, *Roe* v. *Wade* called forth a resurgence of traditional moral activism, whereas in the 1930s an intuitive uneasiness about the evils of politics nurtured a widespread evangelical quietism. Sometimes special emphases in the theologies or religious practices of groups making up the evangelical mosaic lead to political differences, as we shall soon see. Differences also result when the voices of new groups—for example, the Mennonites or the Christian Reformed after World War II—begin to be heard more generally, or when a formerly quiescent group begins to look outward from its own concerns, as Southern Baptists have done in the last two decades.

Bryan's Agenda Today

The magnitude of these differences is suggested by the fate of William Jennings Bryan's specific political agenda among his evangelical successors. Bryan was a populist who favored measures like the direct election of senators and the enfranchisement of women that gave as much power as possible directly to the people; but at least some prominent evangelicals since Bryan have been much more solicitous than he was of constitutional checks on democratic power. Bryan was a progressive who championed the income tax, prohibition, and other measures that dramatically increased the role of the central government in the lives of individual citizens; but while evangelicals favored prohibition and so gave tacit support to increasing the authority of the federal government in that respect, they have tended more generally to argue against growth in centralized power. Bryan's defense of silver coinage put him at odds with later evangelicals who describe inflation as a moral evil. Bryan was also a near pacifist who in 1915 resigned as Woodrow Wilson's secretary of state when he thought that Wilson's policies were needlessly pushing the nation into the world war. And of course Bryan was a Democrat. For much of the twentieth century, the descendants of the eighteenth-century revivals were much more likely to be Democrats than Republicans. Sometime in the 1960s, however, one of the century's most dramatic shifts in political allegiance occurred as hereditary evangelicals moved to the Republican party.[35]

What political positions would Bryan take if he were active in our day? The constituency that makes up evangelicalism as a block discernible to survey researchers is still similar to what it was in Bryan's day—much more southern, somewhat more female, less educated, and less wealthy than comparative groups of mainline Protestants and Roman Catholics. (See the tables on pages 92 and 93.) But today Bryan probably could not speak as generally for evangelicals as he did in 1896.[36] Today he might be likely to be found with Jimmy Carter and Mark Hatfield on the Gulf War, with pro-lifers on abortion, with Democratic rhetoric and Republican practice on the budget deficit, with the fence-straddlers on an Equal Rights Amendment, and with those who appeal for massive federal action against drugs and for inexpensive housing. It is as near a dead certainty as such speculation can be that Bryan would have been a dedicated opponent of Reaganomics and would have gone into orbit over the savings-and-loan catastrophe.

If this speculation is anywhere near accurate, it means few contemporary evangelicals would share the full range of Bryan's positions. But very likely Bryan would have promoted his political convictions in the same way that evangelicals have always pursued politics—activist, intuitive, populist, and biblicistic. That evangelical framework has been remarkably constant throughout the twentieth century. To be sure, hints of alternative approaches have appeared. Yet the set of characteristics inherited from the nineteenth century has been the dominant shaping force on evangelical political reflection to the present day.

FIVE PERIODS OF POLITICAL REFLECTION

A tentative division of twentieth-century evangelical political reflection into five periods reveals how the common framework has been sustained through shifting theological emphases and a changing public landscape. It shows that the intuitive and populist elements in the framework have been the most constant. Only in the last two or three decades have these been challenged from within evangelicalism, and with as yet only minimal results. The elements of activism and biblicism have varied more dramatically. Shifts in what they meant and how they have been applied account for the most important changes in the nature of political reflection.

1. The Age of Bryan

The Age of Bryan, 1896–1925, witnessed mostly a continuation of nineteenth-century themes. Evangelicals were not as yet distinguished clearly from mainline Protestants. American Protestants produced very little reflection on politics, but their actions implied a full freight of theory from the nineteenth century. To summarize an excellent survey of the period by Robert Handy, Protestants in the progressive era relied instinctively on the Bible to provide their ideals of justice. They believed in the power of Christ to expand the Kingdom of God through the efforts of faithful believers. They were reformists at home and missionaries abroad who felt that cooperation among Protestants signaled the advance of civilization. They were thoroughly and uncritically patriotic. On more specific issues, they continued to suspect Catholics as being anti-American, they promoted the public schools as agents of a broad form of Christianization, and they were overwhelmingly united behind prohibition as the key step toward a renewed society.[37]

The more self-consciously evangelical groups within American Protestantism had begun to distinguish between the application of the gospel to society and a gospel defined by the social needs of the period. They were, that is, beginning to be suspicious of what Walter Rauschenbusch would call the Social Gospel. But, as Norris Magnuson has shown, they were by no means withdrawing from social activity such as the promotion of prohibition and other reforms.[38] In the United States, and even more so in Canada, leaders with deeply ingrained evangelical convictions continued to promote a social agenda for the churches.[39]

Evangelical reflection of the period also took for granted the propriety of active political involvement. Bryan never doubted for a moment that a career in politics was a fitting Christian vocation. Woodrow Wilson, who in the phrase of George Marsden was "as Puritan as any New Englander who ever held the office" of president, just as easily carried Christian instincts over into public service.[40] The ease with which the realms of evangelical faith and political activity could merge for Wilson is indicated by an address he gave on the Bible to a Denver audience of twelve thousand in May 1911 as he prepared the ground for seeking the Democratic nomination for president. Wilson closed the address by urging his listeners to "realize that the destiny of America lies in their daily perusal of this great book. . . . If they would see America free and pure they will make their own spirits free and pure by this baptism of the Holy Scripture."[41]

In sum, evangelical political reflection in the Age of Bryan was intuitive in its reliance upon the Bible, its confidence in reform, and its assumptions about a Catholic threat. It was also intuitive in its extraordinarily Whiggish use of history: even when written by a professional like Woodrow Wilson, the history of the West in general and of the United States in particular functioned primarily to illustrate the ideals of American Christian civilization. Evangelical political reflection of the period was also populist, as the prominence of Bryan and Wilson indicates (although there are evangelical echoes also in the pronouncements of Republicans like William McKinley and Theodore Roosevelt). Its activism was of a piece with the kind of biblicism that Timothy Smith has described as such a powerful agent for reform in the nineteenth century.[42] Evangelicals expressed that biblicism passionately but also vaguely in a theology that was Reformed in outline, Methodistic in practice, and perfectionistic in piety.

2. The Age of Fundamentalism

Distinct changes appeared in evangelical political reflection when the Age of Bryan gave way to the Age of Fundamentalism, 1925–41. Although 1925 was the year of the Scopes trial (a largely symbolic event that has been more useful for historians interested in finding a turning point than it was for participants battling over whether and how to teach evolution in the public schools[43]), it is more important to our story as the year of the death of Bryan, the last great exemplar of nineteenth-century evangelical political activism. The third decade of the century also marked the emergence of a more self-conscious evangelicalism (at least in the North), when Baptist and Presbyterian defenders of traditional evangelical beliefs were marginalized by denominational inclusivists, or driven out altogether. It was also the decade when a pair of theological influences—premillennial dispensationalism and a concentrated emphasis on Holiness—that had been active among evangelicals for some time gained a new prominence. These developments pushed evangelical political reflection into a new era.

If in what follows I distort the picture of fundamentalism in this era, the fault is mine, for generalizing from my own experience of growing up in a world dominated by the fundamentalist assumptions of the 1930s and 1940s. It is in no way attributable to the superb studies by George Marsden and Joel Carpenter that are my main academic resources for the period.[44]

Still Intuitive, Still Populist

In terms of the hereditary evangelical framework for political reflection, evangelicals continued to be as intuitive and as populist as ever. Among evangelicals of all varieties, there was in this age of Reinhold Niebuhr little evidence of any felt need for systematic theoretical reflection, for a theology applied self-consciously to politics, or for critical historical studies in aid of political theory. And evangelicalism was still overwhelmingly a religion of the people. In the North, fundamentalism was flourishing because William Bell Riley, Mark Mathews, T. T. Shields, James Gray, Will Houghton, and a host of other dynamic leaders could attract crowds by making good sense face to face. Preachers/editors like Donald Grey Barnhouse, Arno Gaebelein, and Charles Trumbull successfully expanded the influence of their popular periodicals. And on the airwaves, pioneers like Charles Fuller discovered how to adapt the old-time religion to newfangled mass communication. In the South, Southern Baptists, Churches of Christ, and other sectarian evangelicals grew measurably throughout the darkest days of the Depression.

What changed in the framework for political reflection was the relation between biblicism and activism. As the 1920s progressed, evangelical biblicism became increasingly dominated by a form of theology known as premillennial dispensationalism. This theology had been brought to America in the mid-nineteenth century by John Nelson Darby, an early leader of the Plymouth Brethren, and it developed a large following alongside other forms of evangelical biblical theology. With the publication of C. I. Scofield's annotated edition of the King James Version in 1909 (a second edition followed in 1917), premillennial dispensationalism came to dominate those northern evangelicals who had left the mainline denominations and to exert a growing influence among evangelicals north and south who remained in the historical denominations.

As dispensationalism spread, so too did evangelical attachment to a form of piety known as "victorious living," or "the consecrated life." This piety had descended generally from the nineteenth-century emphasis on Holiness. But it was also shaped by influences from Keswick, the popular British religious retreat center that by the 1880s had spawned several imitations in the states. Where Holiness emphases had often provided a spur to a reforming activism in the nineteenth century, twentieth-century forms were more quietistic, more concerned about inward spiritual states than about external ecclesiastical practice or outward social action. Influenced by these two movements, evangelicals became far less active politically.

A Closer Look at Dispensationalism

It is worth pausing to look more closely at dispensational premillennialism, because—as witnessed in 1991 in the flurry of apocalyptic publications attending the Iraqi war—its influence is still strong in some evangelical circles.[45] Dispensationalism is an understanding of the Bible that divides God's relationship to humanity into sharply separate epochs. Scripture is taken to provide explicit divine interpretation for these epochs, or dispensations, that succeeded one another from Adam to the end of the New Testament, as well as for the dispensation foretold in Scripture for the end of the world. The intervening "age of the church" is sometimes treated as a parenthesis, where the ebb and flow of events serves primarily to prepare believers for God's final in-breaking into human history.

The method of dispensationalism is a biblical literalism heavily dependent upon nineteenth-century notions about the goals and systematizing purposes of science. Scriptural passages function like building blocks for the construction of comprehensive doctrines and fully realized scenarios depicting the end of the world.[46] The main reason for the popularity of dispensationalism is that it makes the prophetic parts of the Bible seem understandable to ordinary people and applicable to current circumstances.

Theologically, dispensationalism stresses the decline or apostasy

of institutional churches, the consequent degeneration of civilization, and the need for Christians to separate from institutions of
ungodliness. Dispensationalists view their task in the present epoch
as rescuing unbelievers from sin and keeping themselves unspotted
from the world. The supernaturalism of dispensationalism is intense. The unmediated agency of God is thought to lie behind all
wholesome activities on earth; the mediated agency of Satan is
perceived behind all natural and human evil.

Dispensationalist emphases have interacted powerfully with the
Holiness themes of "personal consecration," "the higher life," and
"victorious living." They share a stress on the dangers of the world,
the assurance of separated piety, and the centrality of evangelism.
To adherents, these are matters of simple biblical truth. To alienated
former adherents, they can appear as the products of bad faith,
social irresponsibility, or heresy.[47] To those with no personal stake,
they may appear as internally logical responses to American conditions in the first decades of the century,[48] as delusions produced by
immature religiosity, or as a mystery from God knows where.

Moving Away From Optimism

The impact of these tendencies on evangelical politics was unmis-
takable. Under their influence, William Jennings Bryan's optimism
about reform and his support for active government gave way to
cultural pessimism and a fear of governmental encroachment. Concern for political involvement was replaced with an almost exclusive
focus on personal evangelism and personal piety. Current events
evoked interpretations of prophecy instead of either a reforming
activism or political analysis.

So it was that James M. Gray, president of Moody Bible Institute
from 1925 to 1935, analyzed the League of Nations and the
Interchurch World Movement primarily as signs anticipating the
end of the age.[49] When in the 1930s Gray watched the rise of
dictatorships in Italy and Germany, he took comfort from the fact
that biblical prophecy gave the assurance that humanity's "darkest
hour" would come "just before the dawn." In 1939 Donald Grey
Barnhouse, a popular pastor, editor, and radio speaker in Philadelphia, reassured the readers of his periodical, *Revelation*, that they

should not be surprised by the rush of current events since they "know the general lines of Bible prophecy." Because they had studied the book of Ezekiel, they knew more about what was going on around them than did the *Saturday Evening Post*. Barnhouse wrote a regular column in *Revelation* entitled "Tomorrow: Current Events in the Light of Bible Prophecy."

Because of dispensational teaching concerning the importance of a ten-nation Roman federation for the last days, evangelicals of many sorts, including speakers at Moody Bible Institute and writers for the *Sunday School Times*, conjectured that Mussolini might be the Antichrist, or at least a stalking horse for him. More than one evangelical saw the Blue Eagle of the National Recovery Administration as related in some way to the sign of the beast described in the book of Revelation. Charles Trumbull, editor of the *Sunday School Times* and leader of the American Keswick movement, regarded the world-shaking events of the 1930s as "signs" of the End. He once wrote that, after one's personal salvation, the most important thing in life was to gain "a knowledge of God's prophetic program."

A few evangelicals, inspired by dispensationalism's focus on the role of the Jews in the latter days, were easy prey for conspiratorial anti-Semites. Many more were enthusiastic proponents of the Zionist movement. In both cases, however, the stance toward the Jews arose from prophetic interpretation much more than from contemporary analysis or from general theological reflection on international justice or the recent history of the Middle East.

The above illustrations have to do with self-conscious fundamentalists in the North, but they are representative of the most visible political commentary of any sort from evangelicals during the 1930s.

Undermining Political Reflection

The combination of "victorious living" Holiness and premillennial dispensationalism may actually have yielded a few insights that escaped the period's more respected political observers. But for the promotion of political reflection it was a disaster. It was a disaster because of the adherents' gnostic supernaturalism, because they pushed analysis away from the visible present to the invisible future, and because they almost totally replaced respect for creation with a contemplation of redemption. When hereditary evangelicalism passed through dispensational premillennialism, the result was a fundamentalism that passionately defended the Book, the Blood, and the Blessed Hope.[50] Fundamentalist contention for these doctrines took a common form that, as a by-product, doomed political analysis. In each case, fundamentalists tried to read experience from the divine angle of vision. They tried to understand the contemporary world as the divinely inspired authors of Scripture had understood their experience. And they denied that historical processes—networks of cause and effect open to public analysis by all and sundry—had anything significant to contribute.

Thus, when dispensational fundamentalists defended the Bible, they did so by arguing for the inerrancy of Scripture's original autographs, an idea that had been around for a long time but had never assumed a central role for any Christian movement. This belief had the practical effect of rendering the experience of the biblical writers nearly meaningless. It was the Word of God pure and simple, not the Word of God as mediated through the life experiences and cultural settings of the biblical authors, that was important.

Likewise, fundamentalist convictions about the miraculous character of redemption through the blood of Christ reflected age-old Christian beliefs, but expressed them with a heightened concern for non-historical elements. When fundamentalists spoke of the new birth, they stressed the unmediated activity of the Holy Spirit. Although in practice they employed a wide variety of "means" to encourage conversion—family worship and nurture, earnest preaching, the example of holy lives—in theory they continued to stress the immediacy of the Holy Spirit's action. This too reflected a negation of historical process.

Finally, the fundamentalist fixation upon the end of the world treated current global history with a similarly cavalier spirit. If current events were important primarily because they fulfilled biblical prophecy, then the relationships that people in general could study between contemporary cause and contemporary effect paled into insignificance. Again, fundamentalists were reading history as if they were inspired as the authors of Scripture had been inspired, rather than as believers whom God had commissioned to participate in the ongoing nurture of the Church in a time between the times.

Fundamentalist belief in the supernatural, and in the extraordinary power of God at the present moment, was by no means unique in Christian history. But the way in which premillennial dispensationalism concentrated its energies upon the transcendent at the expense of the natural was distinctive. With such a biblicism, not only was political *action* suspect, but every possible barrier had been erected against the possibility of systematic political *reflection*. Thus a long evangelical tradition in which biblicistic forms of theology undergirded both political activism and a rough-and-ready intuitive political reflection gave way to a period in which a new form of biblicism undermined both activism and reflection.

"Staying Out of Politics"

In the South, where fundamentalism of the premillennial dispensational type had not advanced as far, another set of circumstances worked against political reflection. Southern evangelicalism in Baptist, Methodist, Restorationist, and Pentecostal varieties was always very much a social phenomenon. But only rarely, after the early decades of the nineteenth century, was it a self-consciously political phenomenon. A doctrine of "the spirituality of the Church," which held that bodies of believers in their corporate life should eschew political involvement, also had the effect of discouraging reflection on politics. The doctrine as a theological principle may have offered interesting possibilities for political thought. But in the actual outworking of events it was, in the words of John Leith, "corrupted by the pressures of racial and economic issues into an escape from social responsibility."[51]

Southern evangelicals could mobilize for specific political causes like prohibition, but they did so without elaborate theoretical justification and as part of populist crusades. The general attitude toward Christian political activity, and by implication, political reflection, was illustrated by the words of a Methodist spokesman who in 1844 defended the creation of a separate southern church by claiming that the "peculiar mission of the Methodist Episcopal Church, South, is that it alone stands for the Christian principle of staying out of politics."[52]

Political activism went into eclipse among evangelicals during the 1930s at the same time that political reflection reached an absolute nadir. But there were also qualifying facts and mitigating circumstances. A few evangelicals did remain active politically. Most unhappily, conspiratorialists like Gerald Winrod were able to enlist some of their fellow evangelicals for their anti-Semitic campaigns of the 1930s.[53] More ambiguously, a dispensational premillennialist radio preacher in Alberta, Canada, William Aberhart, overcame the inactivism implied by his theology to mount a populist campaign that led to his service as premier of Alberta from 1935 to 1943. And throughout the country, countless unnoticed acts of kindness were being done in rescue missions, soup kitchens, and settlement houses by Salvationists, Pentecostals, Baptists, Brethren, independents, and other evangelicals.[54]

If exceptions existed to the general turn by evangelicals from political action, there were few, if any, exceptions to the turn from political reflection.[55] But mitigating factors must be taken into account. First, the evangelical substitution of apocalyptic speculation for serious political analysis was no more irresponsible and considerably less dangerous than the swooning for Stalinism that infected large swaths of the American learned culture in the 1930s. Second, it can be said in defense of the premillennial dispensationalists that they were not entirely wrong. The tumults of the 1930s did, in fact, reflect momentous spiritual realities; they could not, in fact, be analyzed satisfactorily if the spiritual character of human beings was neglected. Third, whatever damage an excessive supernaturalism exerted upon evangelical political reflection, that same supernaturalism did keep alive an awareness of transcendence and so passed on to succeeding evangelical generations the critical starting point for meaningful Christian thought. Fundamentalist docetism began to fade at least slightly in the 1940s. When it did, outside observers, like Nels Ferré, recognized how important the preservation of transcendence actually was. "Fundamentalism, as the defender of supernaturalism," Ferré wrote in 1948, "has . . . a genuine heritage and a profound truth to preserve. . . . We shall some day thank our fundamentalist friends for having held the main fortress while countless leaders went over to the foe of a limited scientism and a shallow naturalism."[56]

3. The Age of Beginnings

The significant changes that followed the era of fundamentalism must be treated more briefly. Even in short compass, however, it is possible to observe several general trends in political reflection among evangelicals from about the time of World War II. First, a return to the more traditional relationship between activism and biblicism has taken place in which evangelical theologies overcame the legacy of dispensationalism to support involvement in politics once again. Second, evangelicalism has remained a deeply populist movement, and so the most visible forms of political reflection are still intuitive—carried on without serious recourse to self-conscious theological construction, systematic moral philosophy, thorough historical analysis, or careful social-scientific research. At the same time, however, from the 1940s there have been a growing number of exceptions to the intuitive character of evangelical politics. For several reasons having to do with the evangelical mosaic itself, significant, if still preliminary, steps have been taken toward self-conscious, critical, and theologically informed political thought.

The year in which the National Association of Evangelicals was established is a convenient signpost to mark a transition from the Age of Fundamentalism to an Age of Beginnings. From 1941, that is, until the re-emergence of evangelical activism, which might be marked by *Roe* v. *Wade* in 1973, a number of subterranean stirrings began to redirect the political energies of evangelicals. Two of these are most important.

The New Evangelicals

In the first instance, young preachers, scholars, and journalists raised as dispensational fundamentalists in the North frankly rejected the dispensationalism of their heritage.[57] They had had enough of second-degree separatism, apocalyptic biblicism, and social passivity. Led by such persons as E. J. Carnell, Charles Fuller, Harold John Ockenga, and Billy Graham (a southerner who became the visible leader of this mostly northern movement), these self-defined "neo-evangelicals" sought better education, better theology, and better cultural analysis.[58]

The key figure in reawakening a concern for social and political thought was Carl F. H. Henry, who not only roused the troops with his *The Uneasy Conscience of Modern Fundamentalism* in 1947 but, first as a theology professor and then as founding editor of *Christianity Today* magazine, urged evangelicals to a much more reflective engagement with the modern world. With such works as *Christian Personal Ethics* (Eerdmans, 1957) and *A Plea for Evangelical Demonstration* (Baker, 1971), Henry provided a mandate for political engagement rooted in traditional evangelical themes of regeneration and sanctification by the Holy Spirit.

The reference works Henry edited, like *Baker's Dictionary of Christian Ethics* (Baker, 1973), contributed still more. For that volume, as an example, Henry enlisted the Orthodox Lebanese diplomat Charles Malik to write on "International Order." Malik told his mostly evangelical readers what they already knew when he said that the visible political world was but a reflection of the truly substantial realm of Christ's eternal rule. Yet he went on immediately to show how important, and Christian, it was to study "the visible international order."[59] Henry's own political thought may have been more straightjacketed by the social reflexes of fundamentalism than he realized,[60] but he nonetheless exerted an extraordinarily positive influence toward the recovery of an evangelical politics.

Influence of Mennonites and Dutch Reformed

The second important development of the post-war period was the first steps undertaken by hitherto isolated bodies of conservative Protestants toward greater involvement with evangelicals at large. The new engagements, especially by Mennonites and the Dutch Reformed, would eventually yield important political results. Mennonite associations with evangelicals were spurred by the general turmoil of World War II, which brought these Anabaptist pacifists into much fuller contact with Americans in general. Networks of educational and pastoral relationships developed between Mennonites and evangelicals. For the Dutch Reformed, it was the publishing houses of Grand Rapids that led toward integration, with Eerdmans, Baker, and Zondervan acting as brokers between the previously insular world of the Christian Reformed Church and the younger, more academic cadre of British and American evangelicals.

The result was a productive cross-pollination. Mennonites and the Dutch Reformed began to sound a little bit more like American evangelicals.[61] And at least some American evangelicals were being confronted with new, and sometimes disconcerting, social theories. Evangelicals could recognize that these theories were rooted in biblicistic theologies, but it was also clear that they were neither conventionally intuitive nor traditionally American in anything like the form to which evangelicals had been accustomed.

The black civil-rights movement of this period had less of an immediate effect on white evangelicals than one might expect, given the substantial contribution to that movement of biblicistic and evangelical themes. The cultural distance between black activists and white evangelicals north and south was simply too great for the whites to recognize how much revivalistic evangelicalism contributed to the civil-rights movement. Early evangelical responses, even in the moderate *Christianity Today*, were so flustered as to think that the evil hand of Communism might be glimpsed in the movement. But soon a more discriminating stance prevailed. For most evangelicals, the civil-rights movement remained extrinsic to their most basic concerns; but it did provide a rallying point for a few young evangelicals, and in only a few years' time it became a model for political engagement by evangelicals eager to agitate on behalf of other causes.

In short, the post-war decades were moving evangelicals in two directions politically—back toward a traditional balance between activism and biblicism, and out toward a more thoughtful engagement with political thought itself.

4. The Age of the New Right

Evangelical reponses to *Roe* v. *Wade* in 1973 may be said to have ushered in the Age of the New Right, which extended at least until the dissolution of the Moral Majority in 1989.[62] During this period, the central story was certainly the reassertion of moral activism in response to the perceived crises of the day. With the New Christian Right we have returned, *mutatis mutandis*, to William Jennings Bryan. If the podiums had become electronic, still the main actors were once again dynamic public speakers like Jerry Falwell and James Kennedy. If injustice to the unborn had replaced injustice to debtors, nonetheless campaigns for at least some classes of unrepresented oppressed were again respected as Christian service. If the political party of choice for restoring Christian morality was now the GOP, it was nonetheless clear that evangelicals had returned to the fray. If mass mailings and mass demonstrations had replaced the whistle-stop tour as the preferred means for enlisting the public, still evangelical politics depended as much on mobilizing the masses in the 1970s and 1980s as ever it did in the days of Bryan.

An intriguing variant to this main story was the rise of a "New Christian Left," which, with nearly the same stock of evangelical phrases and emotions, promoted a public agenda almost completely opposed to the platform of the Christian Right.[63]

For this main story, whether the large right or the small left, it was the old-time evangelical politics brought back to life in virtually the same form as in the days of William Jennings Bryan. It was a biblicistic politics that (despite lingering effects of dispensationalism) vigorously supported a broadening activism. It was a populist politics whose leaders could mobilize the hinterlands most effectively. And it was still largely an intuitive politics, in which the mythic virtues of an Edenic past and the self-evident responses of a born-again people were the bases for argument.

Toward Theologies for Politics

On this last score, however, the recent past may not be exactly the same as the more distant past. At least on the margins there appeared, perhaps for the first time in the entire history of evangelicalism, a self-conscious attention to political reflection resting, not simply on instinct, but on serious theology and systematic social analysis. In typically evangelical fashion, some of this prompting toward a less intuitive politics arose as a by-product of activism. Evangelicals who picketed abortion clinics alongside Roman Cath-

olics were less prone to perpetuate the anti-papal instincts indige-
nous to their tradition. Incongruous political phenomena—like the
evangelical interest group JustLife, which campaigned against both
abortion and nuclear arms, or a pure-bred evangelical congressman
like the GOP's Paul Henry (son of Carl Henry) who did not
subordinate all else to the pro-life cause[64]—have promoted thought
as well as merely scorn or admiration. The evangelist and popular
apologist Francis Schaeffer also urged, in the midst of his own
activism, more careful reflection on the theological meaning of
general cultural developments.[65] Perhaps the most notable example
of evangelical activism resting on sturdy conceptual foundations
was the effort by James Hunter, Os Guinness, and their associates
to formulate a Williamsburg Charter promoting a mediating practice of religious liberty.[66]

These first steps toward self-conscious evangelical political reflection also received direct theoretical support.[67] From the early
1970s, at least some evangelicals worked hard at developing theologies for politics and politics informed by theology. On the more
directly theological side, evangelicals harvested the fruits of their
own broader connections. John Howard Yoder's *The Politics of Jesus*,
published in 1972, was a book by a Mennonite but directed toward
a non-Mennonite audience. Its advocacy of uncompromising Christian pacifism has by no means carried the day among evangelicals,
but it was a landmark effort that has led to much more serious
consideration of Jesus' own life as the norm for political behavior.
Much the same may be said for the work of Ron Sider in promoting
an Anabaptist political economy.[68] Sider's books have not established a new evangelical paradigm, but their push toward a practical,
instead of merely formal, allegiance to the New Testament has
certainly enriched political discussion among evangelicals.

Similarly, Richard Mouw's *Political Evangelism* in 1973 and *Politics and the Biblical Drama* in 1976 were examples of a self-
consciously Reformed literature that was speaking from the Dutch
heritage of Abraham Kuyper, but out to the wider evangelical
world. The message that it and similar Kuyperian works conveyed
has not revolutionized evangelical politics any more than Yoder's
work did; yet its concern for transnational norms of justice rooted

in the great acts of salvation history has added a thoughtful new element to evangelical political life.

A political theology of a very different sort has also been advanced by the network of theonomists or reconstructionists who have tried to extrapolate the theological vision of Rousas Rushdoony, itself based on the philosophical theology of Cornelius Van Til, into practical proposals for public life.[69] Whatever its Dutch or Armenian roots, theonomy sounds a good deal like populist libertarianism. Yet by insisting on carefully formulated theological foundations for political action, it pushes toward a more self-conscious political reflection than is customary in the evangelical tradition.

Toward Politics Informed by Theology

Alongside these theologies for politics came also new attention to politics informed by theology. Since the early 1970s a growing number of mostly younger evangelicals have striven self-consciously for a more realistic assessment of contemporary political situations, a more thorough attention to the bearing of human nature on political possibilities, and a more systematic analysis of politics itself. The most thorough of such proposals, like advocacy of a principled pluralism from James Skillen, Rockne McCarthy, and the Center for Public Justice, still depend upon sources from outside the American evangelical tradition.[70] But other voices schooled by American traditions of political realism have also contributed significantly. The work, for example, of Mark Amstutz, Doug Bandow, Alberto Coll, and Dean Curry is marked by a desire, not altogether universal among evangelicals, to think first before leaping into action.[71] In somewhat the same category is the political thought of Harold O. J. Brown, which, drawing upon warnings from Continental precedents, has also striven toward a self-consciously Christian political theory.[72]

These recent examples of evangelical political theology and theologically informed politics no more constitute cohesive political reflection than the various segments of the evangelical mosaic constitute a cohesive religious movement. Yet they may be straws in the wind. Along with the populist re-pristinization of the politics of Bryan, the Age of the New Christian Right also witnessed at least a mini-renaissance of evangelical political thought.

5. The Post–New Right Age

If commentators are correct in concluding that the Age of the New Christian Right is past,[73] we are then in the early stages of a fifth era, which, for now, is simply the Age After the New Christian Right. What it holds is anybody's guess. The uncertain future for evangelicalism as a whole, as well as more specifically for evangelical politics, means there can be no assured predictions. For every specific contingency, contrasting outcomes are conceivable. For example, it is conceivable that intramural evangelical differences over the specific character of biblical authority, the precise role of women in the Church, or the exact nature of God's creation of the world could further fragment evangelicalism to the point that it loses even the vestiges of theological cohesion. Or a renewal of commitment to the Bible and the cross of Christ might lead to a new era of spiritual insight. It is altogether probable that the Southern Baptist Convention, which has been much more the evangelical sleeping giant than the leader its numbers and wisdom qualify it to be, will become ever more influential among evangelicals. But whether that influence will come from the exporting of Southern Baptist squabbles or through inspiration from Southern Baptist vitality, no one knows. It is also not out of the question that the Pentecostal/charismatic surge will come so to dominate the evangelical mosaic as to give the inner spiritual dynamic of evangelicalism an entirely new shape.

In the political sphere, the forces of the New Right could regroup and go on to more influential political action, or they could sputter and die out. Evangelicals could be coopted by Republican leaders with their own agendas, or could come to influence Republican strategy and maybe even begin to be heard once again among the Democrats. Evangelicals might be able to convince more Americans of the need for pro-life policy and other evangelical concerns, or they might not. On the specific question of social thought, it is possible that the push toward self-conscious Christian theorizing on the nature and ends of politics will move from the margin to the center of evangelical consciousness, but just as possible that it might be thoroughly swamped by new waves of pietistic anti-intellectualism.

Whatever happens to the issues, the leaders, or the partisan allegiance of evangelicals, they will almost certainly continue to exhibit, in one form or another, the activism, biblicism, intuitionism, and populism that have defined evangelicals for more than two centuries. If they repeat the imbalances of their history, their political action may be destructive and their political reflection nonexistent. If, for example, evangelicals remain loyal to biblicisms like dispensational premillennialism, there is little hope for fruitful political reflection.

The problem at this point is twofold. Dispensationalism, first, has a track record that simply cannot inspire confidence as a basis for political analysis. Historian Dwight Wilson has expertly summarized a dismal tale:

> The current crisis was always identified as a sign of the end, whether it was the Russo-Japanese War, the First World War, the Second World War, the Palestine War, the Suez Cris, the June War, or the Yom Kippur War. The revival of the Roman Empire has been identified variously as Mussolini's empire, the League of Nations, the United Nations, the European Defense Community, the Common Market, and NATO. Speculation on the Antichrist has included Napoleon, Mussolini, Hitler, and Henry Kissinger. The northern confederation was supposedly formed by the Treaty of Brest-Litovsk, the Rapallo Treaty, the Nazi-Soviet Pact, and then the Soviet Bloc. The "kings of the east" have been variously the Turks, the lost tribes of Israel, Japan, India, and China. The supposed restoration of Israel has confused the problem of whether the Jews are to be restored before or after the coming of the Messiah. The restoration of the latter rain has been pinpointed to have begun in 1897, 1917, and 1948. The end of the "times of the Gentiles" has been placed in 1895, 1917, 1948, and 1967. "Gog" has been an impending threat since the Crimean War, both under the Czars and under the Communists.[74]

In practical terms, the other-worldly biblicism of dispensational apocalypticism has read everything out of and nothing into contemporary political analysis. The theological problem is even worse. Dispensationalism's artificial exaltation of the supernatural at the expense of the natural makes it nearly impossible to look upon the political sphere as a realm of creation ordained by God for serious

Christian involvement. The same tendency also makes it very difficult to search for norms in this life that combine reverence for God with respect for the variety of human beings and political institutions that God has ordained.

Inadequacy of Intuitionism

Even with less gnostic forms of biblicism, the strength of the evangelicals' traditionally intuitive approach to politics holds out only mixed prospects for the future. Evangelicals may continue to exert a modestly beneficial influence. But if they insist upon maintaining the anti-intellectualism, the God-and-country reflexes, and the denial of contemporary American pluralism that have regularly attended evangelical intuitions about the political sphere, they may contribute sporadically to political action, but they will not assist political reflection.

Hope for evangelical political reflection lies first in the evangel itself. If the Spirit of God continues to dwell among evangelicals, then it is always possible for the life implanted by the Spirit to quicken political reflection along with all other worthy human endeavors. More specifically, if the evangelical community can tolerate the first steps recently taken toward self-consciously theological political analysis, still better and more compelling second steps may follow. If evangelicals can listen carefully to one another (Southern Baptists respecting a word from the Christian Reformed, Mennonites heeding the counsel of the charismatics, evangelical left and evangelical right talking to rather than past each other), then it is possible to imagine that a way will be cleared to benefit from even broader Christian discussions, drawing in Roman Catholics, other Protestants, and the Orthodox, and still more expansive conversations including "men of good will" at large. If evangelicals can retain a faith shaped by numinous events of the eighteenth and nineteenth centuries while addressing realistically the religious pluralism of the twentieth century, they may find that the norms of their faith offer untapped resources for contributing in the present as well as for recovering the past.

To make such an advance, evangelicals must, however, modify the political intuitionism that has been their stock-in-trade. It would no longer be evangelicalism without the direct apprehension of spiritual realities and the dynamic populist simplicities of their expression. But unless that intuition can be modified by a better theological way, evangelical political reflection will never make a contribution living up to the dynamism of evangelical faith.

Learning From Others

It is not clear to me who the best teacher for evangelicals might be, but there are several possibilities. Lutherans, with Luther's own principle of similitude, might be able to show American evangelicals how to look upon the sphere of politics as at once fallen and sanctifiable. Or the same sort of instruction might come from Calvinistic notions of concursus, expressed by Abraham Kuyper as a balance between "antithesis" and "common grace," or from Catholic notions of natural law, which Leo XIII put to use so effectively in *Rerum Novarum*. Evangelicals might even be able to resuscitate an idea from their own heritage, "the spirituality of the Church." Once shorn of the passivity that the defense of slavery forced upon it, this doctrine offers intriguing possibilities for a way of proclaiming the particular truths of the gospel within the congregation while yet acting outside the congregation according to norms acceptable in the world at large.[75] The absence of some kind of dual vision, the inability to speak at the same time with a common vocabulary both inside and outside the community of faith, has been a besetting weakness of evangelicalism and a particular problem of fundamentalism. Yet any of the alternatives— whether the "spirituality of the Church," or insights from Lutherans, Reformed, and Catholics—could be adopted without doing violence to basic evangelical convictions.

Evangelicals, who have a lengthy tradition of political action that includes a generous mix of the noble and the ignoble, can contribute to being Christian in America today simply by replaying the activism of William Jennings Bryan. They will be able to contribute even more, however, if they can expand their recent forays into political reflection and if they can incarnate in thought what William Jennings Bryan incarnated so powerfully in deed.

The first great truth about the Incarnation is that the Son of God *became flesh*. But a truth nearly as great is that the Word became flesh and *dwelt among us*. The condemning scandal for evangelicals is that they have neglected this second truth and all it implies for the possibility of a just political order. Their redeeming scandal is that they have not yet forgotten the first truth.

EVANGELICALS IN THE 1980S
Social-Demographic, Political, and Racial Positioning

These three tables compare evangelicals in a survey sampling with other Protestants, Catholics, Jews, and persons of no religion. The religious affiliations claimed by EVANGELICALS in the survey are: Baptist (including Southern Baptist), Restorationist (Christian Churches, Disciples, Church of Christ), Pentecostal, "non-denominational," Holiness (Church of God, Nazarene, Free Methodist), Reformed, Seventh-day Adventist, Brethren, European evangelical (Mennonites, Evangelical Free, Covenant), "fundamentalist," and, for blacks, AME and AME Zion. The religious affiliations claimed by OTHER PROTESTANTS in the survey are: Congregational, Episcopal, Lutheran, United Methodist, Presbyterian, and "Protestant."

In all but the last line ("Numbers") of each, the tables show percentages within the groups. Except as noted, these percentages are averages of two surveys, done in 1980 and 1988 by the Center for Political Studies, University of Michigan.

TABLE 1: Social-Demographic[1]

	Evangel- icals	Other Prot.	Catholics	Jews	No Relig.
Female	57.7%	60.5%	57.1%	39.5%	39.8%
In South	52.3	21.1	18.6	12.8	16.0
High School +[2]	30.0	45.6	39.8	62.2	48.0
$30,000 +[3]	35.8	47.8	46.7	84.0	39.9
Numbers[4]	346/498	466/522	350/451	50/31	117/153

1. All groups are whites only.
2. More than a high school education.
3. Income over $30,000 (1988 survey only).
4. Number of respondents in 1980 and in 1988 (approximate).

TABLE 2: Political[1]

	Evangel-icals	Other Prot.	Catholics	Jews	No Relig.
Reagan 80	63.1%	67.8%	55.9%	44.0%	63.8%
Bush 88	70.3	64.1	48.4	27.3	41.0
+ / − [2]	+7.2	−3.7	−7.5	−16.7	−22.8
GOP I.D. 80	34.6	48.0	30.7	10.2	26.3
GOP I.D. 88	48.0	54.6	40.3	25.8	37.0
+ / − [3]	+13.4	+6.6	+9.6	+15.6	+10.7
Increase def.[4]	60.8	52.1	51.6	26.4	51.6
No abortions[5]	16.1	6.0	14.9	NA	4.0
Women's rights[6]	52.9	67.7	66.8	77.8	81.0
Numbers[7]	346/498	466/522	350/451	50/31	117/153

1. All groups are whites only.
2. Gain or loss for Republican nominee 1980 to 1988.
3. Gain or loss for identification as Republican 1980 to 1988.
4. Favors increased defense spending.
5. Favors prohibition of all abortion without exception.
6. Favors full equal standing and rights for women.
7. Number of respondents in 1980 and in 1988 (approximate).

TABLE 3: Racial

	Evangel-icals	Other Prot.	Catholics	Jews	No Relig.
Blacks	26.5%	5.4%	3.7%	1.0%	10.2%
Numbers[1]	474/720	380/566	369/473	51/31	130/177

1. Number of respondents in 1980 and in 1988 (approximate).

Responses

1. PAUL R. HINLICKY

What if this "nation with the soul of a church" may no longer be expected to act like a church? What if, then, the churches must come together to act as the Church? To explore the public witness of Christian faith in the United States requires attention to questions of this sort, as urgent as they are difficult, and inevitably controverted.

Behind the first of my questions is, not merely the disestablishment of the cultural hegemony of Anglo-Saxon Protestantism, but the de-Christianization of American public life. With a nod to one of my mentors, I think that today the public square is not so much naked as occupied by another story than that of the Scripture, a story with almost equally deep historical roots in the nation. It is the Promethean story that may claim such founding patriots as Thomas Jefferson and Thomas Paine in its cloud of witnesses, and it runs something like this:

The human being has been held back by priestcraft, superstition, and the spiritual tyrannies of organized religion. Mystification and obscurantism have kept him from gaining knowledge of his world and technical power over it. Antiquated moralities have infantilized her, robbing her of her freedom to make choices and so to realize her own unique potential. The senseless quarrels of religion are rooted in no more than the envy and resentment of hegemonists and have multiplied fanaticism, persecution, and bloodshed. But now this human animal is ascending from the mire of his sloth, and in becoming aware of the uniquely human freedom to transcend his origins, he seizes his fate. With the new "spirituality," she recognizes the spark of divinity within. With the new science, he gains mastery over nature, even over biologically rooted constraints,

Paul R. Hinlicky is the pastor of Immanuel Lutheran Church in Delhi, New York, and the editor of *Lutheran Forum*.

so that the awful accidents of disease, infirmity, and heterosexuality to which the human animal is yoked may be mitigated, and perhaps someday even eliminated.

The "gnosticism" of which Mark Noll writes appears in several forms today, but the one I have just described is the predominant one. It is certainly the aggressive spiritual force impelling de-Christianization. It is certainly aspiring to cultural hegemony. I wonder, therefore, whether true progress toward a more united public attestation of the Christian gospel at its redemptive core is possible if we do not face the depth of the conflict we are in.

Given the trenchant, indeed devastating critique Noll provides us of the bad faith invested in, and the crippling role played by, premillennial dispensationalism in evangelicalism since the time of the fundamentalist/modernist controversies in the 1920s, it is possible to miss the double-sidedness of his thesis and the affirmation it contains, namely, of evangelicalism's—shall I say, lonely?—public witness to "the Christian message of a crucified God," to "the Son of God [who] became flesh," that is, despite all other failings, to the *redemptive* core of the Christian faith. Reinhold Niebuhr, to be sure, from within the liberal tradition in America of Anglo-Saxon Protestantism, drew upon his roots in the old German Evangelical Synod to tell forcefully again that Christianity is not in the first place some simple exhortation to human moral and political possibilities but the message of God's act of redemption on behalf of a lost humanity. But Niebuhr's theology was a brief and passing moment, it seems today, in the general history of the antipode of evangelicalism, liberal Protestantism. Noll therefore calls this public witness of evangelicalism to Jesus as Redeemer its "redeeming scandal" in a fully Pauline sense, and rightly so.

If evangelicalism has been tempted to abandon creation, just as surely has much of that other stream of Anglo-Saxon Protestantism virtually collapsed redemption into creation, as Phillip Lee has shown in his polemical treatise *Against the Protestant Gnostics* (Oxford University Press, 1987). What the more catholic streams of Christian tradition (where the centrality of the Eucharist *necessarily* connects creation and redemption) have kept hidden in the chancel, partly no doubt out of a seemly reverence toward the mysteries of the faith and a horror at the easy profanizing of them in the

Jacksonian carnival that is our culture, evangelicalism has shouted from the rooftops. Evangelicalism has insisted on the necessity of Jesus Christ as saving Lord for the nation, the American people. For that witness, it has won the enmity of this nation's cultured despisers, as an evening's viewing of television, which misses no opportunity to belittle evangelical Christianity, is likely to show.

To be sure, evangelicalism has brought some of this cultural disdain upon itself, and Noll has been properly modest. He has expended his energies in what seems to me to be a fruitfully self-critical fashion. He has asked about the failure of evangelicalism to achieve a dogmatically authentic, historically informed, and socially responsible witness. He has—rightly, in my view—located sources of these failures: theologically, in the aforementioned "gnostic" supernaturalism that severs creation from redemption and, in its premillennial dispensationalism, leaves creation to the devil; historically, in the deeply rooted mood in America of "Protestant primitivism" that disallows to evangelicalism the sobering elixir of historical self-awareness; and socially, in that "cultural pessimism" born of the plight of the poor and laboring classes who have been evangelicalism's core constituency. This latter factor may of course be changing before our eyes, as a new generation attains greater prosperity and aspires to cultural influence, though I am not at all certain that some new "cultural optimism" is the answer. After all, premillennial dispensationalism was a protest against, not some pluralistic neutralization of public life (the "secularization" thesis), but a positive paganization of it. Was that altogether wrong?

While Noll thinks it highly probable that evangelicals will "continue to exhibit, in one form or another, the activism, biblicism, intuitionism, and populism that have defined [them] for more than two centuries," he believes that for evangelicalism to transcend "the anti-intellectualism, the God-and-country reflexes, and the denial of contemporary American pluralism" and become a full-fledged ecumenical partner, it must "modify the political intuitionism that has been [its] stock-in-trade." I think, of course, as a *Niebuhrian* Lutheran, that this is true; sanctified Scottish common-sense realism turns out, on examination, to be too often only the religious justification of unexamined, parochial prejudices—if not bigotries. Likewise powerful religious impulses, chiefly Arminian in origin, have kept American evangelicalism from appropriating the original evangelical insight (with all its hermeneutical and epistemological implications as well in the "theology of the cross") that a Christian is at the same time righteous and a sinner. Historical study, as Ernst Käsemann somewhere wrote, disillusions. Yet such self-knowledge proves to be an embarrassment only in the sense that any kind of naïveté turns out to be an embarrassment. Evangelicalism today, I quite agree, is engaged in the painful process of growing up. As a Niebuhrian *Lutheran*, however, I do not quite agree with Noll that this is the salient truth. And I would like to say why.

Noll writes of "growing up in a world dominated by the fundamentalist assumptions of the 1930s and 1940s," an atmosphere, presumably, in which the Blessed Hope of the rapture at any moment seemed to vindicate a principled abstinence from the affairs of this world; Noll himself, however, represents an irreversible process of intellectual maturation in evangelicalism. And while I do not want to minimize the battles still to be fought on this front, I do want to say that, apart from a full-scale retreat to the 1930s, there is no going back to that Eden now that the fruit of the tree of knowledge has been tasted. What may be occurring in evangelicalism today is new only in the sense that the issue of modernization can no longer be avoided. But that very issue has ample precedents in American religious history going back to the rise of Unitarianism and the decline of Puritanism, and the movement from abolitionism to the post-bellum rise of liberalism. We ought to inquire into such chronic processes of internal conflict in Anglo-Saxon Protestantism that repeated themselves with increasing intensity until the virtual divorce in the 1920s between what we today call conservative evangelicalism and liberal Protestantism. What we would find, I suspect, is a Christological failure at the very fonts of Protestant development.

The question then, from this Lutheran's viewpoint, is whether evangelicalism can successfully grow up; whether, in its present self-criticism, it can avoid the syndrome whereby modern knowledge leads to the loss of dogmatic substance. Loss of innocence should not entail loss of faith.

I have suggested that the distinctive contribution of evangelicalism has been its public, if naïve, witness to Jesus Christ, and that the price of its modernization and maturation ought not to be the loss of this substance; that, rather, a maturing evangelicalism might help the other streams of Christian tradition join it in what has heretofore been a lonely office. Then the pressure for change within evangelicalism would be differently focused and, indeed, far more radically articulated theologically. Noll himself hits the nail on the head when he writes, "Evangelical political reflection has depended upon an a-ecclesiastical or anti-ecclesiastical moralism because evangelicalism in America has been a movement stressing moral activism without providing a major role for the Church."

What if there can be no public witness to Jesus Christ that is not the public witness of his earthly body, the Church? That is, not some witness *sponsored* by the Church, but the witness that *is* the Church in its actual corporate life, including, of course, its deliberation of and response to civil and political issues. What if the public witness to Jesus Christ consists not of enlisting him in our causes but of being enlisted in his, which, whatever else it may be, is membership in his body? And what if even that membership depends not on our choosing but on God's, so that being graciously chosen and graciously sustained in the corporate culture of Christian life is precisely the relevant, if the more modest and indirect, public witness to and sometimes against this wonderful and awful nation of ours?

My question to Noll, then, is whether evangelicalism can entertain some truly radical Christological questions, whether it can test the revivalistic, anti-sacramental, and anti-corporate legacies with which it is burdened against the brave witness to Jesus Christ to which it aspires, and which has been its true glory. Strategies of modernization are required of us, as is intellectual maturation. The temptation of the children, however, is merely to be ashamed of their fathers and mothers; if they stop at this, they never grow up but waste their lives, like Absalom, in mere rebellion. How much better if modern evangelicalism were to be proud of its ancestors' loyalty to Jesus, and, freeing that witness to the redemptive core of Christian faith from gnosticizing distortion, were to prosecute contemporary American life with exactly that theological agenda? Redemption, after all, is properly a most anti-gnostic idea, since it speaks not of the transcendence of nature or the superceding of the creation but of its promised liberation from the demonic powers of sin and death—indeed its re-creation.

My question to Noll about evangelicalism also implies my question about the larger matter of the Church's public witness. It is, in my view, an illusion to think that attention to natural law, in and of itself, can satisfy as the Church's public witness, since that begs the truly critical and genuinely cultural-political questions of the uses and end of the law, as well as the question Jesus addressed, in the parable of the Good Samaritan, about who counts as a member of the human community under the safeguard of law and why. I would affirm such attention to natural law and the art of moral reasoning in the Pauline spirit that the "law is written on the human heart." But I hasten to add that neuralgic questions and answers about the uses and end of the law cannot be narrative-free; for Christian faith, the indispensable limits and the true possibilities of secular life under the law are defined by the Church's public attestation of Him who died accursed by the law in solidarity with sinners and was raised again by God for their free justification.

We cannot anymore, and theologically we should not, expect this nation to act as if it were the Church, as if the public use of power, however democratically done, proceeded on this evangelical basis. That has been, I judge, the illusion of Protestant primitivism, that America really is a *novus ordo seclorum*. But against this, I hold with Paul, Augustine, and Luther that the justification of political power *qua* power is negative and properly limited; it consists in the restraint of private violence by lawful and public means. The Constitution of the United States did not transcend this universal human condition; its true achievement lies elsewhere, and in this, I think, I have Madison, though certainly not Jefferson, on my side. But the belief that America has in fact transcended the humanly ambiguous situation of enforcing the right has been the source, not only of all sorts of awful crusades, but also of the failure to use power decisively for the right.

We can, then, view the de-Christianization that proceeds apace, at least in the apparatus of the state, with some equanimity. But we should feel an equal discomfort about Christianity's forfeiture of cultural hegemony. It is time for America to grow up and see itself as one nation alongside others, deeply troubled like others, and without some messianic mission. It is also time for the churches in America to come together to act as the Church—the Church of Jesus Christ.

The public witness to Jesus Christ, that is, to the order of redemption, is the responsibility of the churches, a responsibility for which they must draw together. And they may draw together to the very extent that they ask Christological questions radical enough to meet this responsibility. In actuality, the limitation of the claims of secularity and the liberation of its true and natural possibilities are generated anew and anew by the corporate experience of God's free and redeeming grace: where those whose consciences are troubled find pardon and peace, where the misfits of this world find welcome, where human personhood is secured without regard to intrinsically attractive qualities or visible achievements of virtue. As radiance from the sun, that light of grace penetrates the order of power and law with the wisdom both to limit secularity's all-encompassing aspirations and to use its powers for the service and care, rather than the enslavement, of humanity.

2. PAUL V. MANKOWSKI, S.J.

Not long ago I found myself in west Texas at a Protestant house of prayer giving a weekend retreat to two Southern Baptist churches on praying with Scripture. I think it's safe to say that even twenty-five years ago the premeditated connivance of Baptists and Jesuits in a religious venture would be a rarity, and it is surely cause for rejoicing that Catholics and evangelicals are willing to listen to each other on subjects of central importance to both. (I was gratified to find also that, in contrast to many of my Cambridge co-religionists, Southern Baptists by and large don't regard the current pope as Antichrist.)

It is a consequence of constraints of space rather than limits of appreciation that I will comment on only one point in Mark Noll's rich analysis. In detailing the chief differences between the enterprise of Catholic social teaching and the American evangelical tradition, Noll makes a striking observation: "The enduring contribution to evangelicalism of the republicanism of the Revolutionary era was to undermine hereditary trust in institutions. The enduring contribution of the Great Awakenings in the colonial and early national periods was to substitute the voluntary society for the church." What I'd like to suggest is that this view of religious association as a "voluntary society" as distinct from a "church" not only has been the prime strength of evangelical political action but, ironically, has worked in recent times to diminish the impact of all Christian corporations (churches, universities, publishing concerns) on American political life.

Noll is surely right that voluntary societies by their nature are well equipped to galvanize and focus individual political enthusiasm—"the inner conviction springing up from within." But surely the will, the *voluntas*, that forms the voluntary society is the human will, the individual will. In the Enlightenment mentality, this was (and to the liberal mind it still is) a truism of free association. A church, on the other hand, an *ecclesia*, understands itself to be brought into existence and sustained by God's will, and the mem-

Paul V. Mankowski, S.J., is a doctoral student in comparative Semitic philology at Harvard University.

101

bers of a church characteristically understand their allegiance as more than a pure act of self-constituting choice. Allegiance is owed to a church; a church deserves allegiance in a way quite different from the loyalty and support we offer to other "special-interest associations" in which we are involved.

Now of course American evangelicals see themselves as members of a church—the Church founded by Jesus Christ—as well as members of a voluntary society; but in the dominant political imagination of the day the voluntary society is the only form of religious association that is seen to be truly American (and thus, legally tolerable). My point is not that this notion doesn't work but that it has worked too well, and that as a consequence the idea of a church has almost no positive place in public discourse about political goods. By "church" I am here referring not to any particular denomination but rather to the understanding of religious community as something that exists independent of contingent human decisions; that provides a conspectus of human destiny and human society that is universally binding and, in its essentials, always and everywhere valid; and that has certain unique prerogatives, including government of the lives of its members in certain areas and the protection of its members from the pernicious effects of the societies in which they find themselves.

One consequence of the belief that churches are tolerable to the extent that they are voluntary societies is the widely held conviction that religious bodies are entitled to speak only to their own members, who associated with them by individual choice. Of deeper concern is the corollary conviction that the activities of religious bodies should be limited in their *effect* to the members of those bodies, since only they have freely covenanted to accept the discipline that goes with membership. But the political decisions of majorities affect all citizens, of course, including those who have no stake in the purposes of the majority. As a result, for a religious community to require disciplined political action of its members is, in this view, a violation of its own nature: individual choices should have reflexive consequences only; but governing majorities are potentially created by these arbitrary, personal, and perhaps irrational loyalties that make up religious identification.

The upshot is that the emphasis on the centrality of inner conviction that gave evangelicals their political impetus now provides the ground for the suspicion in which their political initiatives are held—at least by the cultural elite and that part of the citizenry that shares its values. The irony has often been noticed that, in the last thirty years, it has been the "free churches" that have exploited the power of electronic mass communication for evangelization, while the concept of base communities has arisen within the Catholic Church, or at least in its intellectual suburbs. In both cases, I would argue, these decisions indicate a retreat from the ecclesiology in which primary Christian allegiance is offered to the believer. By the same token, the exaltation of freedom of choice that has sustained them now threatens to muzzle evangelicals, and not only evangelicals, in the political arena.

The notion of a voluntary society has also rebounded upon the churches' understanding of their own mission. To put it bluntly: if you can't find in your idea of religious association the authority to call other Christians to certain theological doctrines, by what authority do you call them to embrace canons of Christian citizenship? Let me stress that here I am not speaking exclusively, or even primarily, of the evangelical churches. No major denomination in America has been unaffected by this scruple. The Catholic bishops of my home state of Indiana issued election guidelines in 1990 that, after much hand-wringing, encouraged Catholics to (1) familiarize themselves with the issues and (2) exercise their right to vote—a telling but not atypical example of contemporary ecclesial diffidence. I do not mean to imply that what was said was wrong. But the fact is that Bucky Badger made precisely the same appeal to the Badger Boosters at halftime of the Wisconsin-Iowa game earlier in the season. We might have expected from our episcopacy guidance that was somewhat more . . . apostolic.

Noll speaks of two "scandals" associated with evangelicalism. The first, which he is clearly working to remove, is an irresponsible abandonment of political philosophy. The second is, simply, the scandal of the Cross, the scandal Christians are *supposed* to give: the proclamation of the message of a crucified God. Perhaps the time has come to ask whether Christians in America, if we continue to allow ourselves to be publicly defined in terms of an Enlightenment notion of churchmanship, can continue to give this second scandal, the scandal of allegiance to one who, before his death, assured his disciples, "You did not choose me; no, I chose you."

4

Protestants and Natural Law

CARL E. BRAATEN

FOR much of the history of Christianity, some type of natural-law theory has been used as a bridge to connect the Christian faith and culture, the Church and the world. But in recent times, an opinion deeply entrenched in churches and theology is that Protestantism rejects natural law and thereby distinguishes itself from Roman Catholic moral theology.

The body of Roman Catholic social teaching—on labor, industry, and society—is impressive, and in the essays in this book we commemorate one of the greatest examples of this teaching, *Rerum Novarum*. That body would lack a spinal column without the recurrent appeal to natural law. Modern Protestantism, by contrast, has no coherent body of social teaching of comparable value and stability. The Dutch Reformed theologian Abraham Kuyper said, on the occasion of the publication of *Rerum Novarum* in 1891: "It must be admitted to our shame, that the Roman Catholics are far ahead of us in their study of the social question. Indeed, very far ahead. . . . The action of the Roman Catholics should spur us Protestants to show more dynamism. . . . The Encyclical of Leo XIII gives the principles which are common to all Christians, and which we share with our Roman Catholic compatriots."[1]

At the core of that encyclical is an appeal to reason and human

---

Carl E. Braaten is a professor of systematic theology at the Lutheran School of Theology at Chicago, and the executive director of the Center for Catholic and Evangelical Theology, Northfield, Minnesota.

nature, but not, of course, without a sure grasp of faith and revealed truth. Natural law is the bridge category used to appeal, beyond those who share an *a priori* commitment to sacred Scripture and the Christian creed, to people of all races, classes, cultures, and religions. There is said to be one universal law to which all people have access by their natural reason, no matter where or when they happen to live.

In much of modern Protestant theology, doubt prevails about this appeal to reason and natural law in the construction of Christian social ethics. The bridge has been shattered. So what the churches say on social issues has no way of reaching the other side, and they end up in dangerous isolation from society, speaking only to themselves.

H. Richard Niebuhr's classic *Christ and Culture* depicts five models of relationship between the Church and society.[2] At one extreme are those who set Christ Against Culture, which leads to a sectarian strategy of withdrawing from the world into separate Christian communities. At the other extreme—Christ of Culture—are those who collapse their Christian identity into the cultural *Zeitgeist*, thus becoming culture-conforming Christians. The middle three models represent the typical Catholic, Lutheran, and Calvinist ways of relating Christianity and culture. While Catholics have held firmly to natural-law thinking, the modern representatives of the two branches of the magisterial Reformation, Lutherans and Calvinists, have not. They swing wildly between utter rejection and conditional acceptance of natural law, almost never conceding as much to it as we find in modern Catholic social teaching.

In this essay, I want to tell the story of the Protestant struggle over natural law, from complete rejection in Barthian covenant theology to qualified acceptance in a Lutheran theology that draws a proper distinction between law and gospel, creation and redemption. I will conclude by proposing that Protestant social ethics reappropriate natural law, placing it carefully within theological brackets defined by principles articulated in the Reformation tradition (particularly the Lutheran branch, which I know best), with an added twist of eschatological theory.

My interest in this project is ecumenically motivated. For more than a quarter of a century, Lutherans have officially engaged in dialogues with Roman Catholics on such doctrinal topics as ministry, baptism, the eucharist, authority, the papacy, Mary and the saints, and now Scripture and tradition. I suggest that social ethics is another challenging area in which we should explore differences, some of them actually as divisive as the better-known doctrinal ones. If we do this, the tradition of natural law will necessarily become a focal point.

PROTESTANT REJECTION OF NATURAL LAW

Karl Barth rejected every form of natural theology and thereby pulled the rug out from under natural law. But among the early dialectical theologians, only Barth and Edward Thurneysen remained consistent and radical in their repudiation of natural law. Others, such as Emil Brunner, Friedrich Gogarten, and Rudolf Bultmann, opened the door to some new version of natural theology by incorporating philosophy into the theological enterprise. Brunner took the lead in calling for a return to natural theology and natural law, though Barth was able to show that Brunner's position was shot through with ambiguity.[3]

The controversy between Barth and Brunner did not settle anything. Some followed Barth in holding that Christian ethics has no use for natural law, which concerns itself with universal principles inscribed in human nature and ascertainable by reason. Instead, ethics is based directly on the command of the living God, which Barth said "is always an individual command for the conduct of this man, at this moment and in this situation; a prescription for this case of his; a prescription for the choice of a definite possibility of human intention, decision and action."[4] Here we have the root of Protestant situation ethics, later popularized by Joseph Fletcher, reduced to the absurd in a more humanistic framework.

Although Barth never provided a systematic treatment of the matter, throughout his various stages of thought he battled against every appeal to natural theology or natural law. Theological ethics that bases itself on the Word of God alone, he said, "will not, then, make the disastrous, traitorous use of 'natural' theology, which is the only use that can be made of it."[5] Barth saw natural law as the self-assertion of autonomous humanity and natural religion. For this reason, he felt he had to speak an irreconcilable "no" to every attempt to derive ethical norms from the orders of creation, as Lutherans did, or from nature, as Catholics did.

Barth recognized that there is such a thing as natural law, of course, in the same sense as he recognized that there is human religion. At best, in his view, natural law is the quest for order on the part of the state and of non-Christians, who have no other source of knowledge, inasmuch as they do not derive knowledge from divine revelation in Christ and the Bible. Barth's refusal to find common ground or an apologetic bridge on which Christians and non-Christians could walk and talk together was not convincing to other theologians. How, then, can Christians go public with their ethic in a pluralistic world, they asked, where the majority does not accept the Christian source of revelation? Some Protestant theologians resumed an interest in natural law, though seemingly with something of a bad conscience on account of Barth's strictures.

Christology and Natural Law

Barth was not alone in rejecting natural law. Perhaps his most faithful follower in this matter was Jacques Ellul, professor of jurisprudence at the University of Bordeaux and the author of almost as many books as Barth himself. Ellul wrote a little book called *The Theological Foundations of Law* in which he based all of law and justice on Christology.[6] The whole world and the entire human situation have changed on account of God's revelation and redemptive act in Christ. Law too must be affected by this event, if it is indeed true. Both Christians and non-Christians are objectively in a new situation, since Christ died for all and was raised for the world's justification. Whatever has been called natural law henceforth loses its ideological character and is relativized by justification.

The problem with this thoroughgoing christological basis of natural law is that it is derived from a source not shared by non-Christians. Hence, there is no bridge, no common ground, no basis for cooperation between Christians and non-Christians in the public orders of life. We are left either with a triumphalist theology of glory in which Christians must conquer the public space, or with sectarian withdrawal into ghetto-like communities alongside the world. The hermeneutical issue becomes a burning one. If everything bearing on law and justice is derived from Christ and the Bible and is known exclusively by the community of believers, then how is it possible for non-Christians to do what is good and right?

The Protestant rejection of natural law has found expression in American theology in the ethics of Paul Lehmann and Stanley Hauerwas. Paul Lehmann, my professor of ethics at Harvard Divinity School, renounced natural-law theory in the name of his "koinonia ethics." Following Barth, he rejected the idea "that there is a common link between the believer and the non-believer grounded in the nature of human reason which enables both believer and non-believer to make certain ethical judgments and to address themselves in concert to commonly acknowledged ethical situations."[7] Stanley Hauerwas flatly asserts that "Christian ethics theologically does not have a stake in 'natural law' understood as an independent and sufficient morality."[8] Ethics stands exclusively on the story about God that Christians learn from the Bible within a covenant community.

Legal Positivism and Natural Law

Why did the tradition of natural law fall on hard times in Protestant theology? One might guess that the reason lies deeply embedded in the Reformation theology of Martin Luther and John Calvin. However, John T. McNeill, the Reformation historian, reached this conclusion:

> There is no real discontinuity between the teaching of the Reformers and that of their predecessors with respect to natural law. Not one of the leaders of the Reformation assails the principle. Instead, with the possible exception of Zwingli, they all on occasion express a quite ungrudging respect for the moral law naturally implanted in the human heart and seek to inculcate this attitude in their readers. Natural law is not one of the issues on which they bring the Scholastics under criticism. With safeguards of their primary doctrines, but without conscious resistance on their part, natural law enters into the framework of their thought and is an assumption of their political and social teaching. . . . For the Reformers, as for the Fathers, canonists, and Scholastics, natural law stood affirmed on the pages of Scripture.[9]

The pressure to abandon the teaching of natural law did not stem from the Reformation so much as from post-Enlightenment developments in philosophy, especially utilitarianism and positivism. There was a loss of belief, not only in a special divine revelation through Scripture and the Church, but also in the ability of reason to discern a natural moral order in human affairs. The way was prepared for law to become an instrument of power. Might makes right. The positivistic attitude toward law and its validity rendered people impotent in the face of the lawlessness of law. The totalitarian state could successfully manipulate law as a mere function of absolute power, with the collapse of the religious and metaphysical foundations of justice. Thus there was no other criterion of validity for the law than the will of those who had the monopoly of force.

The twentieth century has paid a heavy price in legalized atrocities and crimes against humanity as a result of the ascendancy of legal positivism in classrooms, legislatures, and courtrooms. And after World War II, it seemed as though many people had had enough. Protestant theologians were invited to conferences to reconsider the relation between Christian faith and law. Churches gained a renewed sense of responsibility for the process and quality of law in social life. The World Council of Churches and the Lutheran World Federation sponsored conferences to discuss the proper theological response to legal positivism. They debated whether Christian ethics and natural law are necessarily antithetical or perhaps, in fact, complementary.

The conferences and new publications in Christian ethics showed that Protestant theologians were in a quandary about natural law. Theologians like Helmut Thielicke[10] and Walter Künneth[11] moved away from Barth's absolute rejection of natural law but still were most concerned to reiterate the theological objections to it. Natural law came to be seen as a kind of necessary evil, or as an illegitimate child that could not be completely abandoned but whose rights must be severely restricted.

The Twofold Protestant Criticism

The common criticism that Protestant theologians make of Roman Catholic natural-law theorists has two parts. First, as Catholics, in distinction from the Protestant Reformers, they do not take sin seriously. Second, as Romans, they are bound to a medieval philosophy—namely, Aristotelian Thomism—and thus cannot take history seriously.

Natural law seems to suggest that the order of being in the original creation has not been totally disrupted by the fall of man and by sin, and that human reason is not so blinded as to be incapable of reading the will of God in the natural structures of creation. Natural-law theory is guilty of elevating reason above revelation as the standard of what is right and wrong, true and false. But in our fallen world, say Protestants, the *imago dei* is fully destroyed so that there remains only a negative relationship to God. There are no absolute laws and immutable orders untainted by sin. Thielicke says that, since the fall, we confront at best "orders of preservation." Künneth speaks of "emergency orders" through which God is working to sustain human life in a fallen world. Natural law also totally lacks the eschatological perspective, which relegates all orders of life to provisional status, always ambiguous and incomplete, moving along in history in the realm of contingency and novelty.

Despite such criticism, theologians like Thielicke and Künneth could not really dispense with natural law. They saw that it has abiding significance as the sign of the human quest for justice and right. It functions as a goad to the pursuit of justice in an imperfect world. The Church needs to respect the common search for justice and law and promote cooperation between Christians and non-Christians in all spheres of public life.

Still, with half-hearted concessions of this sort, Protestant theologians cannot make significant contributions to the renewal and furtherance of natural law in society. They write with an uneasy conscience, as if natural law were forbidden fruit. Catholic theologians rightly complain that, when Protestants write about natural law, they always take the worst-case scenario, as though there were no history of revision of natural-law theory. They complain that Protestant theologians write about natural law as something fixed, always and everywhere the same and always perceptible as such, as though it existed above and beyond history in a static world of eternal principles.[12] Such caricatures of natural law abound in Protestant textbooks on social and political ethics.

The works of Jacques Maritain and John Courtney Murray are evidence enough that the caricatures do not match the actual representations of natural-law theory in modern times.[13] Who would wish to argue that these Catholic intellectuals are out of touch with the changing factors that historical development imposes upon church and society? Their commitment to natural law did not make them medieval philosophers who would depreciate historical particularity and historical process, or would ignore the imperative that the uniqueness of each situation or decision or action be attended to.

Counterattacking Deconstruction

An ecumenical dialogue on the place of natural law in Christian social ethics is particularly necessary, in my opinion, as a kind of counterattack against the wholesale deconstruction of the classical moral and legal principles on which Western culture is founded. Deconstructionists generally believe that readings of texts and events produce meanings, but that these readings are misreadings because we can never arrive at truth. The pursuit of truth and justice is increasingly spurned in the academy and replaced with the pursuit of a politically correct ideology. Moral relativism joins with political activism to sabotage the standards needed to implement a societal system ordered by principles of justice and truth.

When the normlessness and the nihilistic effects of the deconstructionist mindset are no longer confined to academia but invade the wider public, the way is prepared for the moral collapse of all social institutions, or for the enthronement of the totalitarian state. The love affair of some of the founding deconstructionists with the Nazis has been widely reported and has not been refuted by their disciples.[14] Perhaps it's time to expose deconstructionists' relativist and nihilist theories as the underside of totalitarian ideologies and political authoritarianism.

Some might object that this call to revive interest in natural law is pointless, like rearranging the deck chairs on the Titanic. The role of Christians is to be with the chaplains consoling the passengers on their way down, or to look for a lifesaver and abandon ship.

REVELATION AND NATURAL LAW: A CORRELATION

As we have seen, there was in early dialectical theology an extreme antithesis between biblical revelation and natural law. Those following Barth felt they had to say an absolute no to every form of natural theology. There followed, in the name of faithfulness to biblical revelation, a kind of contempt for natural theology, natural law, and natural reason. While some Protestants allowed a limited role for natural law in the construction of social ethics, that role was mostly to serve as a symbolic sign of the human quest for justice in the social order. We have noted also that natural law is the only available basis of morality for non-Christians, people who do not live within the covenant community and do not share its history and memories.

There is no necessary opposition between evangelical faith that focuses on the justification of the ungodly through Christ and the Catholic doctrine of natural law with its appeal to a universal justice and morality to which people have access through their reason and conscience. An eclectic band of Protestants, from the Lutheran Paul Althaus to Reformed theologian Emil Brunner and philosophical theologian Paul Tillich, has held to a more positive view of natural law. Wolfhart Pannenberg also comes down decidedly on the side of finding an anthropological foundation for asserting a common core of justice and law accessible through reason and conscience. The particulars of that common ground are provisional, relative, and always ambiguous under the conditions of our finite human experience; Pannenberg keeps the eschatological horizon in focus at all times.

Rehabilitating Reason

An approach open to a new affirmation of natural law would also seek a rehabilitation of reason. Reason has suffered a tragic history, and often Protestants have derived a certain *Schadenfreude* from every report of its demise. When reason is discredited, theology seems justified in retreating to the safe haven of fideism. Faith becomes overloaded, its wires overheated. One consequence is direct sorties of faith into the public realm, without benefit of any rational accountability. We may call this the Ayatollah Khomeini phenomenon in the political realm, equally dangerous no matter in whose god's name the crusade is undertaken.

The widespread assumption that Reformation theology allows no access to natural law—that its view of Scripture, revelation, Christ, salvation, and faith bars the door to every kind of natural theology, natural law, and rational morality—needs correction. But evangelical theology can never hold other than a highly circumscribed view of natural law, one that places it within theological brackets so that it does not function apart from the whole of theology.

Edmund Schlink, my professor of systematic and ecumenical theology at Heidelberg University, spelled out the conditions under which an evangelical theologian can take up natural law. Natural law cannot establish the rights of humankind before God, for human beings have no rights *coram*—in the presence of—*deo*; they have rights only *coram hominibus*. Because of the fall into sin there is no ontological continuity between the original creation and the new creation, which is apprehended through faith alone.

The Church's primary task is to proclaim Christ to the nations for the world's salvation.[15] Nevertheless, the Church does have a political responsibility during the time between the first and the final advent of Christ, and here a limited but necessary role of natural law must be maintained. Lutherans need not have any confessional scruples about affirming such a role. It is necessary only to observe the proper distinction between the *coram* relationships. *Coram deo*, human beings are not capable of doing anything right, anything on the basis of which God would be required to set them in a right relationship with himself. Sin disrupts the right relationship between God and humanity. But human beings *are* capable of doing what is good and right *coram hominibus*, in the order of human relationships. Natural law has no theological significance in the sense of providing a basis for human salvation, and so natural law will always seem barely to limp along in Reformation theology. But the negative verdict on natural law in the vertical dimension, *coram deo*, need not entail a rejection of natural law in the horizontal dimension, *coram hominibus* and *coram mundo*.

Varieties of Natural Law

A concept of natural law in correlation with evangelical theology need not retain the particular metaphysical foundations that natural law received in the medieval Thomistic-Aristotelian synthesis. The idea of a law rooted in the nature of humanity and the world and discoverable by reason has been traced back to the "dawn of conscience," and the history of natural law shows a wide variety of interpretations and applications.[16] The Protestant polemic against natural law has been directed primarily against the medieval Thomistic conceptions; the Protestant mind need not be closed to all other varieties.

The "nature" referred to in natural law can mean different things. It can mean the immanent structure of human reason, that which all human beings share by virtue of being human. Its theological correlate would simply be the *imago dei*. Or "nature" may refer to an ideal state in some past Golden Age, uncorrupted by civilization, as in Rousseau's "return to nature." Or it can refer to the fallen condition of humanity, as in the familiar words of the confession: "We confess unto thee, O Lord, that we are by nature sinful and unclean."

"Law," too, can vary in meaning. It can refer to a moral principle written into human hearts by God and, therefore, universally valid. Or it can mean a principle imposed on human beings from the outside, by the authority of God or the state or some other power. It can refer to the Ten Commandments, the Torah, or the Sermon on the Mount. "Law" can also refer to the inalienable rights of human beings that all nations are morally bound to acknowledge.

When we put "nature" and "law" together, then, we confront a legion of possible meanings. We cannot *a priori* foreclose on the possibility that a concept of natural law is fully compatible with a theology faithful to the confessional writings of the Reformation. We cannot agree with Jacques Ellul when he writes: "The doctrine of natural law as a Christian doctrine is thus ruled out at every point."[17]

TOWARD A REINTERPRETATION OF NATURAL LAW

The following principles can help us place natural law within brackets determined by basic principles of evangelical theology.

1. We have to begin with the fact that none of the confessional

documents of the Reformation, neither those of the Lutheran tradition nor those of the Calvinist tradition, rejected the notion of natural law. In fact, those documents acknowledged that Scripture teaches that the Gentiles, though outside the scope of God's special revelation to Israel, are able to know something of God's law through the works of creation by means of conscience and reason.[18] To be sure, the Reformers, as biblical theologians, were primarily concerned to draw the proper contrast between the old law and the new on account of Christ. But, at the same time, they acknowledged that the biblical authors do to some degree recognize elements of the law of God among the Gentiles, a law that in some way must be related to the law of creation that reaches its perfection in Christ.

2. An evangelical theology will interpret the role of natural law in light of the hermeneutical distinction between law and gospel. In light of this distinction, it is possible to develop a Christian understanding of the world and all secular institutions. "Gospel" refers to the absolute particularity and uniqueness of the message concerning God's coming into the world in the person of Jesus Christ. This places all law in a new light: its legalistic character is contrasted with the creative freedom of the gospel.

3. Along with the particularity of the gospel, which rests on *solus Christus*, evangelical theology will want to insist on the other *solas*, such as *sola gratia*, *sola fide*, and *sola scriptura*. But evangelical theology will assert that these *solas* are also good Catholic theology, as Karl Rahner has vigorously argued in *Foundations of Christian Faith*:

> For a Catholic understanding of the faith there is no reason why the basic concern of Evangelical Christianity as it comes to expression in the three "only's" should have no place in the Catholic Church. Accepted as basic and ultimate formulas of Christianity, they do not have to lead a person out of the Catholic Church. . . . They can call the attention of the Catholic Church again and again to the fact that grace alone and faith alone really are what saves, and that with all our maneuvering through the history of dogma and the teaching office, we Catholic Christians must find our way back to the sources again and again, back to the primary origins of Holy Scripture and all the more so of the Holy Spirit.[19]

With such clear provisos, much of the passionate criticism of Protestant theology directed against the place of natural law in Catholic moral theology might be deflected. The Reformation *solas* serve to relativize natural theology, natural law, and the orders-of-creation theology so that they cannot be used as an independent approach to the knowledge of God with any salvific potential. The law is not a way of salvation; at best, it is a way in which God's preserving grace is effective in ordering the world.

4. The doctrine of original sin must be taken seriously. The fundamental structure of reality, including the rational and social nature of humanity, is deeply affected by sin. We live in a fallen world; demonic forces have been let loose upon the world, distorting everything, including human reason. The image of God in humanity is not totally destroyed; rather, it is disoriented, and this puts humanity in a wrong relationship with God and the world he created.

If original creation is thought to be totally depraved, the *imago dei* totally destroyed, the result is a kind of pessimism that places all ethics within the order of redemption and the new creation. This partly accounts for the fact that Protestant ethics has tended to be purely personalistic and voluntaristic, relying on discrete commands announced by God now and then, in this situation or that. Protestant ethics shows a marked tendency to fall into pure occasionalism, actualism, and situationalism. The ontological givens are either denied altogether or ignored, so that the ethical decision is made existentially in each moment and each situation. With the loss of general rules and enduring principles, it is difficult to find a bridge to the public orders of life on which Christians and non-Christians can work side by side.

5. An evangelical social ethics will integrate the eschatological perspective into its ethical theory. The eschatological kingdom of God's love is communicated through the gospel as the justification of the ungodly and sinners on account of Christ, but it is communicated through worldly structures of power and justice under the conditions of a sinful world. This is the basis of Luther's distinction between the two realms or two kingdoms, and correlates with the two states of believing existence in the world, as *simul iustus et peccator*.

6. The proper work of love is expressed by the gospel as the forgiveness of sins and new life in Christ. The strange work of love (*opus alienum*) is expressed by the law as God's instrument to effect justice in a world that does not believe in the gospel. Justice is too important a matter for God to leave to loving persons. Justice can be accomplished in the world in either of two ways: by the miraculous presence and spontaneity of love, or by the pressure and threats of the law. The concept of natural law in one sense is misleading because, when people do what comes naturally, it is neither very just nor very loving. Nevertheless, the idea of natural law is indispensable because it aims to establish a criterion of justice that transcends human conventions or habits and is, in some way, universally intelligible. The love of God is strangely at work behind the back of every human being, seeking justice through law that cannot be identified with mere custom, arbitrariness, power, or interest.

7. Love that expresses itself as justice and by means of law is not at all antithetical to the formulation of principles and rules that can prescribe as well as guide the ethical decisions and moral actions of human beings and institutions. The antinomian idea that love cannot be mediated by rule and principle has sneaked into situation ethics and hides behind the *agape* label, as though there were no way to translate love into the language of moral norms and principles.

8. When the rule of God's love expresses itself through structures of justice and law, rules can be formulated in advance and need not be produced anew for each new situation. For example, rules relating to freedom and equality have been set down in the United Nations Declaration on Human Rights. There could be no World Court to try war criminals if there were no preexisting consensus on what is lawful in warfare. The notion that there are no rules but only situations is an unrealistic appraisal of the human condition this side of Eden. The primary commitment of Christian ethics to the truth and power of love, as manifest supremely in the Christ event, relates to law in a dialectically differentiated way, true to the complexities of the human situation within the fallen world and the new things inaugurated by the inbreaking of God's kingdom in Jesus Christ.

9. An evangelical social ethics will correlate eschatology and natural law, or it will forfeit its right to be considered a biblically Christian viewpoint. One major problem of traditional natural-law theory is that it seems to be more at home in a deistic view of God and the world than in a trinitarian vision that alone can span the whole of reality from creation to consummation.

The final truth of all things is revealed by the arrival of the eschatological future in the person of Jesus Christ. The future of the Kingdom of God is the power that draws all people, whether they know it or not. This power has been revealed in Jesus Christ as the highest good that all people implicitly seek in their quest for fulfillment. Therefore, when people in all societies strive for justice, they are seeking something true and transcendent that for them is still future. From the Christian point of view, this something is the Kingdom of God, which Jesus proclaimed and embodied in his very person. The universal human quest for justice can thus be seen to be the Kingdom of God at work throughout the created order, even under the conditions of sin and estrangement.

Natural law, then, can be viewed as the presence of the Kingdom of God in the universal human striving for what is good and right. It seems to me fortunate that "natural law" has been kept alive in Roman Catholic moral theology, but somewhat regrettable that it has survived in a non-eschatological framework and is therefore generally out of sync with the dynamics of history. The merits of the natural-law tradition can be taken up into the framework of an eschatological perspective.

10. Openness to the tradition of natural law prevents Christian ethics from being totally absorbed with individual personal relationships, which has been the trend in Protestant existentialism. While it is necessary to distinguish between the individual-personal and the social-political dimensions of the Kingdom of God, it is important not to separate them, as though the realm of personal relations were unrelated to the realm of social involvements and political institutions. The non-eschatological form of the two-kingdoms ethic in conservative Lutheranism has tended to dichotomize personal ethics and social ethics.

11. When natural law is baptized by Christian theology, it may be seen as the means by which God is ordering the world on its

way toward the final judgment and consummation. The hope of the world does not lie in optimism about nature and law. The true mission of the Church does not lie in teaching the world about natural law and administering its institutions according to principles of justice and law. It does not lie in patching up the old creation. The mission of the Church is to announce the advent of a new creation in Christ. Even the most splendidly ordered world, a veritable utopia on earth, would still exist in open rebellion against the gospel, counting on a righteousness of works rather than the righteousness of unmerited grace that is a gift from God.

12. The introduction of the eschatological perspective may be disheartening to Christians who dream about a Christian world order and rely on Christian social activism to save the world, or who believe that the Church ought to remake the world after its own image. On the other hand, to link the eschatological perspective to natural law, and thus to provide common ground upon which Christians and non-Christians may share the burdens of maintaining and ordering the world, may appear as a compromise to radical Christians who take the intermediate position and accept for themselves this responsibility for the world. We may think of this in terms of believers' cooperating with God in preserving the world, so that the world may be given time to learn of its true destiny in the Kingdom of God.

It may appear that natural law is so relativized by the eschatological perspective that it hardly deserves to be called law anymore. Our liberties are relative, our rights are relative. There are no absolute laws, no unconditioned principles in this world, a world that from the perspective of God's judgment is passing away and is maintained only by divine patience.

We have set limits to natural law by placing it within theological brackets because, from the perspective of God's final revelation in Jesus Christ, only so much should be expected from human nature and human reason. God does not save the world through natural law; God does not reconcile the world through the pursuit of justice; God does not transform human hearts through the struggles for human rights; God does not create a community of love through our best efforts to order the world for the better.

To know this is to draw the proper distinction between law and gospel, as Lutherans would put it, or between nature and grace, as Catholics have traditionally said it. There is indeed a distinction, but not of the kind or degree that makes it necessary for Protestants to continue to reject natural law for the sake of magnifying the gospel.

Responses

1. ROBERT BENNE

In the quarter century of intellectual companionship I have had with Carl Braaten, he has shown little appreciation of H. Richard Niebuhr's work. Niebuhr, he believed, pressed radical monotheism so hard he wound up with a lamentably low Christology, which made his theology tend toward a Calvinist Unitarianism. I am not surprised, therefore, that in his essay Braaten really doesn't address the main theme of Niebuhr's great *Christ and Culture*—how to be a follower of Christ and live in this fallen, messy world. Instead, he uses the occasion to put forth strong proposals about natural law. His thesis is that Protestants who have disclaimed it should take another look. We need natural law.

Now, to be fair, I must admit that the concern for natural law *is* related to Niebuhr's fivefold typology in *Christ and Culture*. Four types affirm some guidance, such as natural law, for moral life independent of special Christian revelation. Only "Christ Against Culture" is the odd type out. Later I want to say some words of appreciation for the only approach that rejects natural law.

I accept and endorse Braaten's affirmation of generally human sources—reason, conscience, clarified experience, practical intelligence—as epistemological routes to objective moral values and principles that can guide personal and social life. He is willing to press for them in the face of the various kinds of hermeneutics of suspicion, deconstructionisms, and non-ideological relativisms displayed by so many in our day. Indeed, there isn't much in the essay I disagree with.

A good strategy in such circumstances is to change the subject. Here, however, it is only an apparent change of subject. I want to

---

Robert Benne is Jordan-Trexler Professor of Religion and the director of the Center for Church and Society at Roanoke College in Roanoke, Virginia.

speak here of the struggle at my college to introduce a course called "Values and the Responsible Life." Taught by the Religion and Philosophy Department, which I head, the course is part of a new and extensive core curriculum the college has adopted to replace a loose distributional system.

The proposal to reintroduce a required religion/philosophy course taught by Christians was controversial enough. Although the college is related to the Lutheran Church, the vote to proceed was 44–27, not close but certainly not unanimous. Since then the course has been through an intense monitoring process and has been scrutinized more closely than any other new course in recent college history.

Why this close attention? Faculty are worried about *whose* values will be taught and *from whence* those values come. In a diverse faculty we have all sorts of factions concerned about those issues. Our intention to teach normative notions of the moral life has found allies among both Christians and secular people. In the struggle it is very important for us to appeal to the latter group on the basis of commonly shared moral ideas. While we rarely use "natural law" in appealing to this secular group, we could well use that term. And we do find secular allies in the effort actually to commend certain values, not merely to clarify what values students already hold.

At this point I want to return to the forgotten fifth in Niebuhr's typology—"Christ Against Culture." Curiously, in our curricular wars the "against" people—the so-called neo-sectarians—have provided more encouragement for me than those who appeal to natural law. The neo-sectarians, with their skepticism about universal reason, their hostility toward Enlightenment liberalism, and their turn toward the particularity of a living tradition's religious and moral practice, have stiffened the backbone of vacillating mainliners (Protestant and Catholic alike) to put forth with courage the particular claims of Christian faith and ethics. This encouragement has strengthened efforts to reclaim colleges and universities for the Church after years of confusion and retreat. After all, if Christian communities can't maintain a meaningful Christian intellectual witness in their own institutions, how can they be expected to have any serious effect on the larger world?

I am far from Stanley Hauerwas's theology and ethics, and far from the radical historicism of Alasdair MacIntyre, but they have helped me a good deal in thinking through my posture and strategy at an "endangered" Lutheran college. I need their prodding to affirm the particular more than I need Carl Braaten's to prize natural law.

In the struggle surrounding our "Values" course, the neo-sectarians have helped clarify the continuing hegemony, in the academy, of Enlightenment assumptions about religion. So many academics, Christians included, have been convinced by those pervasive assumptions that religion is essentially personal, private, and extracurricular. Too few in the academy welcome Christian views of life and morality in addition to secular ones, and too many continue to hold Enlightenment views that publicly expressed Christian claims will be subjective, coercive, irrational, narrow, rigid, sectarian, and anti-intellectual. In view of all this, they believe, it is better to go as far as possible with a secular ethic. Even Christians may become too embarrassed or intimidated to press their Christian claims, and religion becomes further marginalized. The secular dominates.

However, the relativists in our faculties are not impressed with an "objective" set of values, even if secularly grounded. They rush to demolish the claims of reason and natural law. But in the process they reveal that they have little to offer beyond negation. At best they come up with the minimalist ethic of consent. When it becomes clear how naked they are, they often bow to the historically contingent (to them) fact that the college has promised the Lutheran Church to "honor the Christian heritage" and Judeo-Christian values. Because of this special arrangement with a particular living faith community, there is the weight of sheer, positive "law and custom" on the Christian side. That is helpful to the cause.

James Burtchaell has shown the importance of this empirical connection with a church, and of the provision that a critical mass of the faculty and administration be members of that church. A church gets a big bang for its few bucks if it maintains an ongoing set of promises with its institutions, and uses its moral weight to insist upon fidelity to them.

The approaches of the "against" and "historicist" camps emphasize practice and virtue in a way that is much more effective than the more disembodied reason of the natural-law approach, which relies too much on the guiding and motivating power of reason itself. Several points bolster this preference for a religiously grounded virtue ethic.

First, a religiously grounded ethic flows from a whole vision of life that claims the imaginative, affective, and volitional dimensions of a human being. Such an approach appeals to the whole person and is thereby more persuasive than a merely rational approach.

Second, reason itself may be more historically contingent than earlier figures in the Christian tradition assumed. Paul, Aquinas, and Luther among others thought that reason had access to objective moral truths independent of revelation. The Enlightenment philosophers had similar confidence. Standing at this point in history, however, we are more likely to view those "objective" moral values as rational distillations of settled Christian practice rather than universal truths grasped by the detached person.

I have no desire to come off as a radical historicist, but I do believe there is a good deal of truth in MacIntyre's assertion that tradition—a persisting argument through time—provides the overarching system of meaning in which reason works at making things consistent and coherent.

Finally, reason and natural law may not provide powerful enough limits on human evil, as Braaten hopes they will. Maybe only the strong taboos of a powerful religious tradition can give those. It is usually the rough-and-ready, "primitive" religious groups that have the courage and clarity unabashedly to oppose abortion, pornography, decadent art, and homosexuality. We mainstreamers are much too sophisticated to lift a protesting voice in public.

Philip Rieff, of *The Triumph of the Therapeutic* fame, lends some support to this observation. In a newly collected set of essays entitled *The Feeling Intellect*, he argues that reason freed from its larger religious meaning system becomes merely critical—corrosive of its own guidance system. It meets every taboo—the negative sanction of a sacred order—with the question: "Why not?" Only religion, he avers, can save us from the "abyss of possibilities" by pointing powerfully to a transcendent source of limits.

In view of this great need for more courage and zeal for the particular claims of the Christian vision, my question to Carl Braaten is: What do you really propose to gain by your call for a return to natural law? What place does such a call really play in your theological project?

2. CARL J. PETER

Have confidence in faith, this great friend of intelligence." With these words read in French at the very end of its final liturgy, the Second Vatican Council expressed a conviction in the form of a plea to those who devote their lives to intellectual and scientific pursuits.[1] A quarter of a century has passed since that day in December 1965 when an assembly that had met each fall for four years decided it would not adjourn *sine die* without pouring out its mind and heart in a series of short messages to special groups of human beings throughout the world.

Immediately prior to the reading of the seven texts written with that intent, Pope Paul VI called attention to the convergence of past, present, and future in that brief but historic moment of departure. The assembly would shortly express the desire that those who cultivate the life of the mind continue their search for the light of tomorrow in the light of today until reaching the fullness of the light, which is Christ Jesus.[2] When the pope turned his gaze toward that same future, with quiet simplicity he too expressed the conviction that the future was casting its shadow ahead of itself. It was doing so, he said, in the pressing cry of the world's peoples for more justice, in their desire for peace, and in their thirst (whether recognized or not) for a different and higher kind of life—which the Church belonging to Christ was both ready and willing to offer.[3]

Much of what was future for both Paul VI and the Second Vatican Council is now past. But the pair of tasks they foresaw lays no less claim on those who would be Christian in America today.

Carl J. Peter was a professor of theology at the Catholic University of America until his death in August 1991.

To be more provincial, that pair constitutes a big part of the current and perennial agenda that Roman Catholic teaching and theology cannot give up without losing their soul. Christian faith does not go unchallenged when it dares to claim friendship with a human understanding inclined to be suspicious of any *religious* convictions, and especially of any seeking to have an influence on public life. And as for associating the human needs of peace and justice with the quest for the higher kind of life that the Church belonging to Jesus Christ can offer, such linkage is often held to make the difficult impossible.

Yet, once dismissed to make room for allegedly more pressing issues, the problem of relating critical intelligence to believing Christian faith, and nature to grace, has refused to go away quietly and stay banished. This resilience comes as no surprise to those convinced that Christian faith is missionary in its essence: that it is rooted in particular historical events believed to have universal implications for all that is meaningful, true, and salvific.

Those who are of such a mind are likely to be among the most appreciative of Carl Braaten's revisiting *Christ and Culture* in the context of this centennial commemoration of *Rerum Novarum*.[4] At the heart of this revisitation is a proposal that Protestant social ethics reappropriate natural law by placing it within brackets determined by principles of evangelical theology, together with what he calls "an added twist" of eschatology. This "correlation approach" would seek to rehabilitate reason and help Christian theology overcome the temptation to retreat into "the safe haven of fideism," with the consequent overburdening of faith. There would, as well, be less danger for the "public" or "political" realm from faith bursting in without the "benefit of any rational accountability." An additional benefit might accrue if, for example, Lutherans and Roman Catholics were to take up in dialogue, as they have not heretofore, the use and interpretation of natural law in Christian social ethics. The Church might help in making a reasoned case for the pursuit of truth and justice rather than politically correct ideology. Braaten intends his proposal to contribute to such a dialogue.

In an attempt to treat his fine essay with the seriousness it deserves, I should like to make two fairly extended remarks and then pose two very brief questions. The remarks have to do with what he describes as "the common criticism of Roman Catholic natural-law theorists on the part of Protestant theology": first, that the theorists do not take sin seriously, and second, that, bound to Aristotelian Thomism, they cannot take history seriously either.[5] The caricatures and charges involved in this twofold criticism are, in the words of Braaten, the stuff of serious ecumenical discussion yet to be undertaken. Presumably they indicate the need for a theological bracketing of natural law.

In an attempt to respond to Braaten's ecumenical invitation, I would submit that taking sin seriously is a characteristic of natural-law theory and application in Roman Catholic thought both in principle and at its best moments. Whether *serious enough* I too sometimes wonder. But that the concern is present, and that its presence already suffices to provide a significant theological bracketing of nature, is, in my judgment, undeniable. If this is so, it might enhance rather than diminish the possibility of success in the dialogue Braaten proposes. I share his desire for such a dialogue and hope that it might help achieve the important consequences he has in mind.

Braaten credits Leo XIII with a sure grasp of faith and revealed truth when in the core of *Rerum Novarum* the pope appeals to reason and human nature. That grasp produced a view of human life and destiny that took sin and its consequences with profound seriousness. It would have been curious indeed had things been otherwise. For the thirteenth-century master of theology to whom Leo appealed in 1891 had found the human being unable *because of sin* to will and accomplish even the good to which his or her nature was proportioned. Grace as healing for sin was a theological bracket operative when Thomas considered the good that all human beings by nature might be expected to pursue and accomplish, though in fact they do not.[6] And lest we think these better moments and perhaps even the principle accounting for them have ceased in our century, we should recall Hans Urs von Balthasar's clearly expressed conviction that supernatural reality "only crowns and completes human efforts because it first of all turns them upside down."[7] For his part, Walter Kasper would have us understand the axiom "grace does not destroy but rather presupposes and perfects nature" *christologically*: "God in Jesus Christ assumed and redeemed the moribund, weak, and foolish."[8]

It is in the light of revelation (and not reason) that the sublime calling and at the same time the profound misery that human beings experience find their ultimate explanation.[9] Would that such considerations had become *the* hallmark of Roman Catholic reflections on human nature, its possibilities, and its laws. They did not. Nevertheless, the prominence they have in fact enjoyed shows that the tradition of which they are part has known more than a little of the theological bracketing Braaten thinks necessary if natural law if to be reappropriated in social ethics by sons and daughters of the Reformation.

As for the theological bracketing required because their Aristotelian Thomism keeps Roman Catholic theorists from taking the future seriously, I must respect the constraints of space laid upon me. My second point must be brief: It was precisely the hold of Christian faith on him that led Aquinas to baptize and explode God-ward the notion of human nature he appropriated from Aristotle. Whatever the similarities between their notions of nature, the differences are greater still. As a result, an incompleteness looking to union with the Triune God is characteristic of human nature for Aquinas. That incompleteness is accompanied not only by no demands *coram deo* but rather by a radical creaturely incapacity to take one step toward fulfillment. At the same time it looks to grace and glory as God's work. This looking always to the future gives contingency and historicity an importance not often taken sufficiently into account by those who study Thomas's notions of human nature and its law. It was not missed by Leo, however, when he wrote in *Rerum Novarum*: "Exclude the idea of futurity and forthwith the very notion of what is good and right would perish; nay, the whole scheme of the universe would become a dark and unfathomable mystery."[10] This too provides a theological bracketing that is the potential stuff of ecumenical dialogue.

I end with two questions. First, does a restriction of natural law's relevance to relations *coram hominibus* run the possible risk of separating too much the love of God from that of neighbor, or even the first three commandments from the other seven? And, does the eschatological twist so relativize and de-absolutize all laws promoting justice that their universal applicability is a casualty?[11]

5

The Spirit of Freedom:
To Live Attentively

GLENN TINDER

To reflect on the spirit of freedom is to ask what makes freedom strong and alive. The question arises from the fact that freedom is of utmost value, yet is fragile and cannot be made secure by means of the social and political structures urged by numerous modern philosophers of freedom. The inadequacy of structures compels us to reflect on the spirit. Here is the strength and life of freedom. What is this spirit? I shall argue that it is religious, that freedom is animated by faith. Before considering this thesis, however, we must note why freedom is valuable and why it is fragile; we must note also why structures designed to strengthen and enliven freedom leave it imperiled.

For many thoughtful people today, particularly in universities, freedom is relatively unimportant. It is subordinate to "community," to some idealized form of social solidarity. The ideal of social participation, diversely conceived, serves as a meeting ground for writers of widely differing persuasions, all in some degree neglectful of freedom. Conservatives call us back to traditions and customs originating in earlier times; enemies of moral relativism insist, in Aristotelian fashion, that to live as moral beings we must inhabit

Glenn Tinder is a professor of political science at the University of Massachusetts, Boston. He is the author of six books, most recently *The Political Meaning of Christianity*.

131

an established order of practices and standards; religious writers of varying views look for ways of rendering society "theonomous," thus giving it a communal depth that they believe secularism has destroyed; and of course innumerable reformers, over several generations, have dismissed bourgeois freedom as fraudulent and have concentrated on making society just. Few if any of these proponents of solidarity entirely repudiate freedom. But freedom concerns them only secondarily, and, not uncommonly, they leave unexamined the threats to freedom that the full application of their principles might pose.

The Splendor of Freedom

We should be wary of all visions of social unity. Today intellectual fashion is inducing many to forget certain primal truths in the liberal outlook. One of these truths is that all societies are radically imperfect. Our ability to remove the imperfections so abundantly displayed in history is, to say the least, in doubt. It is doubtful that any society can be so reliable a moral order that a moral person can dispense with a capacity for personal independence and social defiance; that the social system in our industrial and pluralistic times can be one in which a devout religious mind can feel altogether at home; that there can ever be a society entirely free of poverty, unfair privilege, and racial prejudice. And if these things are doubtful, so is the assumption that freedom need not be our foremost concern. If society is stubbornly imperfect, freedom is vital. It allows us to pursue a life not determined completely by the moral derangements, the religious indifference, or the injustices of the society we happen to inhabit.

Beyond this, even if societies were always morally superior to the individuals within them, individuals would still need freedom; they would still need the possibility of living in conflict with society. Freedom is an opportunity to be human. Vital to humanity is choosing personally, under the risks inherent in finitude and moral imperfection. When rulers have absolute power and the people have no freedom, pain and oppression are not the only consequences: rulers think of themselves as more than human, while those under them think of themselves as less than human. The former forget their finitude and fallibility, indulging in illusions of divinity; the later lay down the burdens of personal responsibility and in that way live as animals. On both sides humanity is lost. Even if despotic government could be pleasant and efficient, it would be incompatible with our lucidly and responsibly accepting our humanity. Granted, there are individuals who have realized their humanity under despots—but only by being defiantly and self-sacrificially free, in spite of the despot. Few have the strength to face the risks this involves, and society cannot justly impose such risks. A free society renders freedom less terrifying and costly. It institutionalizes the truths of human nature that despotism denies.

If we are fully to apprehend the worth of freedom, however, it is not sufficient to speak only of the imperfection of society and the essential freedom of man. It is necessary also to speak of values. To be *authentically* human we must do more than choose. We must choose to enter relationships that make us more than we are when we are merely *spontaneously* human. This fact is obscured by politicians who flatter the voters in their ordinary and unexamined lives and by advertisers who encourage consumers to indulge unhesitatingly all whims and desires. People are invited to abandon self-criticism and self-discipline and to think highly of themselves just as they are. Humanity is tacitly treated as though it were as natural to everyone, in the sense of being as easily acquired and as normally attached to every representative of the species, as the power to stand upright and walk. But the greatest spiritual figures tell us something very different: that spontaneous humanity is worth little or nothing, that true humanity depends on striving and discipline, and that the object of our striving and the authority behind all discipline—that is, the source of our humanity—is something beyond humanity. Thus Plato and Aristotle present a severely hierarchical view of human society; those at the peak of the hierarchy have ascended through sustained intellectual and moral training, and their dignity lies in their knowledge of the truth and value at the center of all reality. For Paul and Augustine, being human in the way urged by modern politicians and advertisers is to risk falling into utter nothingness, or hell.

Human beings are truly human, then, because they are fitted to be media of transcendence. They can be mirrors of a grandeur not naturally and effortlessly in every member of the human species. In cultural terms, through human beings truth is discovered and expressed, artistic beauty comes into existence, and moral rectitude is achieved. In biblical terms, a human being is created in the image and likeness of God and possesses the visible form of one in whom God became incarnate. The intrinsic correlation of humanity with transcendence is not entirely strange to any of us. In everyday love, when one person places on another a value beyond all measurement, a human being is recognized as a medium of transcendence; love sees realities invisible to objective scrutiny.

The relationship between an individual and transcendence, however, is free, and the discipline required by this relationship presupposes choices constantly renewed. This is why we can say that the splendor of freedom is the splendor of transcendence—of truth and beauty, of moral goodness, ultimately of God. To be sure, society at its best affirms and teaches such values. But these values are always brought to light by particular thinkers, artists, saints, and prophets. Such figures may reflect the beliefs and standards traditional in their societies, but it is normal for them to be more or less spurned during their lives. Rarely does a society show great or unambiguous spiritual capacity; spiritual figures are compelled to carry on lives intensely personal and free, or to perish. It goes without saying that the spiritual capacities of society should be guarded and cultivated. But those who treat society as a spiritual order divert our attention from the supreme imperative of collective existence: that room be made for the uncoerced lives and actions through which the glories of transcendence become present in history.

To see that freedom is properly glorious, however, makes us aware that it is ordinarily not what it ought to be.

The Fragility of Freedom

The fragility of freedom is due to a single fact: that human beings are inclined to turn away from transcendence. Where they are free they are usually devoted to power, money, and pleasure. The prolonged and systematic effort required by artistic creativity, philosophical thought, moral righteousness, and religious devotion appears onerous and unattractive. In a society where people can live as they please, and there is wealth enough so that pleasant alternatives to spiritual discipline are always available, moral relativism is almost bound to develop. The idea that no one else can rightfully stop you from doing as you like, but that often you should stop yourself, thus submitting to the inaudible commands of transcendence, will sound too doubtful and too paradoxical for many people to accept. Illustrative is the air of moral relaxation (to use no stronger a phrase) that prevails in America today. Also illustrative is the intellectual frivolity and disorder present in American universities. Here we see that among people who are highly trained, economically secure, and legally free, people whose major professional obligation is only to seek and teach the truth, the air is filled not with the light of truth but with the clouds of diverse fashions and illusions; the very idea of universal truth comes under attack. If freedom survives, despite the distractions of entertainment, physical pleasure, and intellectual fashion, it is only as one of life's many amenities; it survives ingloriously.

From a religious standpoint, the fragility of freedom consists in the near-certainty that freedom, at least in the context of industrial prosperity, will bring secularism. This assertion may seem in conflict with polls in which Americans today claim overwhelmingly to be religiously devout. But the pervasive American concern for pleasure, convenience, and security makes it difficult to take such claims at face value; it seems that Americans sometimes create for pollsters images of what they think they ought to be rather than pictures of what they actually are. Moreover, that we are apt to deny transcendence whenever free to do so is implied by the Christian conception of man as deeply and stubbornly a rebel against God. We are speaking, of course, simply of original sin; human beings have set their faces toward world and self.

The human impulses that deprive freedom of its splendor are not curbed or weakened by existing institutions. Rather, they are encouraged. This is exemplified by capitalism. At the moment, capitalism is esteemed more highly than ever before in this century. There are good reasons for this. The Communist experiment produced results jarring to those who most enthusiastically welcomed the experiment. It proved that free markets are essential not only to economic efficiency but to freedom itself; it invalidated much of the socialist case against capitalism. As a result, unqualified opposition to capitalism is no longer an intellectual option.

We should not forget, however, that capitalism is morally ambiguous. Certainly it encourages various forms of self-discipline and cooperation; but it also cultivates a competitive ethos, a love of money, and, through advertising, "the passion for physical gratification"—a characteristic Tocqueville found widespread in America even in the Jacksonian era. Capitalism also is ambiguous culturally. Capitalists do provide indispensable support for symphony orchestras, art museums, and universities; but also, with a relentless and nearly exclusive concern for profits and popularity, they finance whatever television shows, magazine features, and recorded music people happen to like. They refuse almost altogether to exercise cultural authority, and there is little doubt that they break down cultural standards. These ambiguities are vividly manifest in America, with its abundant vitality and liberty, and also its urban violence, moral corruption, and spiritual emptiness.

The impulses corrosive of freedom are nurtured also by democracy, in the sense of popular rule. Democratic politicians are like capitalists in having little to gain from calling on people to exercise discipline or sacrifice personal advantage. Power is gained through popular support, and that support is gained most readily by indulging popular weaknesses and flattering national pride. Thus democracy naturally, if not inevitably, produces majorities more or less indifferent to moral and cultural standards. And such majorities may be uniquely effective in enforcing their will. This was emphasized by Tocqueville in his discussions of the "tyranny of the majority." The majority is dominant not only in all political institutions but everywhere in society. And its power, working not alone through elections and pressure groups and public-opinion polls but also (and far more subtly and pervasively) through censorious glances and silent disdain, may be greater than the power of a single despot. Through equalization, Tocqueville believed, democracy may dissolve the connections among individuals, increasing in this way their economic vulnerability and intellectual uncertainty, and predisposing them toward conformity. Tocqueville thought that the tyrannical tendencies of democracy had been considerably moderated and curbed in America. Nonetheless, he regarded freedom in America as more frail and limited than most Americans realized; he knew of no other country in the world, he declared, where there was so little true independence of mind.

Such observations perhaps are impressionistic. They are intended, however, only to illustrate my principal claim: that freedom is apt to be inglorious, in spite of its potential glory. This is due primarily to the character of human beings, who are spontaneously worldly and self-seeking, hence more or less closed toward transcendence.

There are ways, of course, of counteracting such tendencies. Society can be called to the support of freedom. Indeed, it must be, or else freedom of a kind that has moral substance and is widely enjoyed could neither be born nor survive.

The Structures of Freedom

Freedom can be real and valuable only within social forms that give it moral and communal substance. This principle was worked out by major political thinkers—Rousseau, Burke, and Hegel the greatest of them—during the eighteenth and nineteenth centuries. In a variety of ways, all said that freedom can be vital and authentic only in a setting of social disciplines and legal restraints. Scarcely anyone today would deny that there is truth in these claims.

One aspect of this truth is associated usually with the left. Freedom would be only the despotism of the rich unless limits were placed on the uses of private property. Paradoxically, freedom implies economic constraints. In the nineteenth century, one of the grimmest signs of the tendency of freedom to lose its splendor lay in the squalor and destitution suffered by industrial workers. It was a deeply significant development in liberal thought when philosophers such as Thomas Hill Green, borrowing from Hegel, argued that government had the capacity and responsibility to "hinder hindrances" (a phrase from Bernard Bosanquet, an ally of Green's) on personal liberty. Only by limiting liberty could liberty be realized. Today this principle is accepted by practically all parties, as a guide for policy if not for rhetoric, in spite of the controversies swirling about particular salients where freedom of property and governmental power collide.

Other aspects of the truth that freedom depends on structure are linked usually with conservatives. Basic here is the notion that society has the function not only of protecting people from one another but also of sustaining true values. The penal system, for example, while manifestly concerned with public safety, must also reaffirm the right when a wrong has been done. Criminal proceedings are properly retributive as well as preventive: statutory and moral law are not entirely distinct.

The moral functions of society and government are probably less widely accepted today than are the economic functions. As soon as legislators and judges are given the task of making us good, many will say, puritanical regimentation will loom before us. And in any case, morality and immorality are matters of opinion. "Who is to say . . . ?" But a society that wholly refrained from moral judgments would be nihilistic, however secure it might be against the threat of puritanical regimentation. The very assertion that society should protect us from direct, physical harm by others (and do nothing else) is a moral judgment. If that judgment is permissible, why are not others—for example, that pornography encourages people to regard one another as primarily carnal rather than spiritual beings and hence should be outlawed whenever it is practicable to do so? Censorship is often, perhaps usually, crude and ineffective; but the idea that speech and other forms of self-expression are inviolable, regardless of content, is indefensible. Almost everyone admits this in some situations, if not when the issue is pornography, then perhaps when the issue is the incitement of racial hatred. The so-called slippery-slope argument has little force. It ignores the fact that human beings are always on a slippery slope, in the conduct of political affairs, and are saved from sliding to the bottom by virtue and good sense and not by clinging to rigid principles.

The issue of abortion is illustrative of society's proper moral concerns. In light of the principles set forth earlier in this essay — that only through freedom can the glories of transcendence be manifested in history, and that freedom to turn toward transcendence implies freedom to turn away from transcendence—the "pro-choice" argument cannot be completely dismissed. An absolute ban on abortion would unquestionably entail grave intrusions into personal life. Yet the very principle of freedom rests on respect for persons, and such respect cannot but be seriously compromised when abortion is widely accepted and casually practiced. To assert a limitless right of abortion is nearly as extreme and untenable as it would be to assert a limitless right for parents to do as they please with their children. While the precise restrictions that should be placed on the practice of abortion are a matter of prudential judgment, it is clear, nonetheless, that the millions of abortions carried out in Western nations, year after year, in the name of personal choice, constitute a crisis of freedom. Where there is freedom, it is certain that many wrongs will be committed; but those wrongs can reach such a scale that, undermining its moral foundation, freedom eventuates in its own destruction. In the matter of abortion, restrictions of some kind are essential if only as a public affirmation of the value of life and personality.

The general principle that society and government must support freedom, not simply allow it to exist, is widely applicable—to education, culture, and urban environment, for example. There is no intrinsic value whatever in free choice as such; as Edmund Burke asserted, the value of choice depends altogether on what is chosen. Society does not allow people to make bad choices because choosing is worthwhile in itself, but rather because unless people are free to make bad choices, they are not free to make good choices either. Freedom is pathway, not destination. Hence freedom is not achieved merely through an indifferent society and an inactive government. It requires social and economic conditions that reinforce its moral grounds, and society and government have a role in creating such conditions. The political art, properly understood, is an art of freedom.

It is apparent, however, that social structures cannot provide freedom with the strength and vitality needed to withstand the sinful energies tending to degrade it. Social structures can help, indeed are essential; freedom cannot be real in a desert of solitude outside society. But neither can freedom be real where life is confined to social enclosures; this is the point made at the outset of this essay. If freedom must be maintained in opposition to society, society cannot in turn be summoned to save freedom from the weaknesses thus incurred.

The Burden of Freedom

When freedom is equated with conformity and obedience, as was done by Rousseau, Burke, and Hegel, each in his own distinctive way, the truth of freedom is imperiled. This is not a matter of theory alone. Modern Communism arose from Marx's version of Hegelian social solidarity. That Communism was relentlessly destructive of freedom was not a historical accident, stemming, say, from its Russian setting; at least, it was not only that. It reflected the conviction that freedom is realized through obedience and conformity.

To treat freedom as wholly positive, then, is tacitly to deny it. Freedom has an indispensable negative aspect. It means not being interfered with. It implies the possibility of living unrighteously and unwisely, if one so chooses. Even in a perfect society, this would be true; the perfections of the collective order would be morally insignificant unless freely affirmed by particular individuals. John Stuart Mill once suggested that a society in which ultimate truth was known would have to provide "devil's advocates" in order that individuals might stand apart from the truth and approach it anew in freedom. In like fashion, as strange as it may sound, a society structured in every detail by wholly righteous customs and laws would have to leave open unrighteous alternatives in order that individuals might freely choose righteousness. When we take into account, however, that the best societies are radically imperfect, the case for negative freedom becomes overwhelming.

Freedom seen as that of sinful men, outside social and legal controls, takes on an unaccustomed aspect. Respecting the freedom of others is too often regarded as a matter of simple decency. Only an uncritical—and un-Christian—optimism can permit such a view. Respecting freedom requires a patient and forgiving temper, a capacity to bear with the evil free people are bound to do. This can properly be said both to radicals and to conservatives. Radicals must accept the fact that as long as people are free in any substantial measure to accumulate private wealth and to use it at their own discretion, there will be injustice and exploitation. The design of eradicating these entirely is antithetical to freedom. Some will respond, with Ivan Karamazov, "Very well, then; let us have justice even if the price is freedom." But this is a bargain not offered us. As demonstrated in Soviet experience, to choose justice in preference to freedom is to lose both. The splendor of transcendence is swallowed up in the darkness of totalitarian statecraft. Reformist politics should not aim at justice, but simply at social, economic, and political conditions in which freedom is as real and widely enjoyed as possible.

Conservatives must learn a like realism. Just as freedom depends on accepting the fact that private property will sometimes be used selfishly and irresponsibly, so freedom requires a recognition that many people have highly immoral interests—in pornography, in vivid depictions of violence, in illicit sexual practices—and will indulge them unless freedom is extinguished. A free society is certain to be more or less unrighteous.

Freedom is a burden because it implies, in some degree, the emancipation of evil. Society and government can restrain such evil, but they themselves are distorted by evil. Powers that check abuses of freedom must themselves be checked, and they can be checked only by a populace protected from social and governmental interference. The splendor of freedom is thus inseparable from what could be called the squalor of freedom—a strong phrase, but one amply exemplified in many of the manifestations of freedom in America today.

The burden of freedom, let us note, must be borne by individuals alone. Positive freedom is social, but negative freedom is for separate and single persons. Implicit in my argument is individualism of a sort. Today individualism is largely discredited. This is primarily because the ideal of solidarity, so widespread at present in a variety of forms, is not compatible with individualism. Granted, the individualism repudiated by the philosophers of solidarity, such as Hegel, was in some ways false; individuals were thought of as complete in themselves, each one, as it were, a self-sufficient universe. But the correction of this error gave rise to an error as serious as the one destroyed. Community was confused with society. In the former, people are united in the depths of selfhood; in the latter they are united outwardly, but always remain in some measure estranged. Community is act, so to speak, and society, being. To equate community and society is necessarily to lose sight of serious personal existence.

The fact is that one must now, and presumably in all ages to come, decide alone how to live and what to believe; and in living and believing one must find bearable the displeasure of those around. Individualism is one of the primal facts of our fallen condition even though it is not a metaphysical truth. We are strangers in history although not in essence. This is why freedom is a burden that has to be borne largely in solitude. Anyone with the independence of mind Tocqueville missed in America, for example, must be able not only to withstand occasional disapproval of one or two others; such a person must be able to live with the conviction that almost everyone has fallen into serious error. The pain of such a situation is not just that of feeling that I alone am right, hence utterly alone. It is also that of having to wonder, "Can it be that I alone am right? Perhaps I alone am wrong."

Here we see that the burden of freedom is not simply the burden of others' freedom. It is the burden of one's own freedom as well. I too am fallen and in choosing am apt to choose wrongly. Dostoevsky asserted that freedom was "insupportable," and declared that people prefer "peace, even death, to freedom of choice." Dostoevsky believed that human beings would gladly yield their freedom to a Grand Inquisitor who would relieve them of the task of deciding, alone, what is true and right. A despot who provided authority, bread, and "miracles"—spectacles inviting thoughtless acceptance of the dominant ideology—would find the populace gratefully acquiescent. It may seem that present-day America proves freedom less uncomfortable and fragile than Dostoevsky thought. Why is it, however, that Americans find freedom so readily supportable? Do they see its transcendental glory? No doubt some do. But is freedom bearable for many because it has been lightened—reduced largely to the enjoyment of material abundance and mass entertainment? Is it because the uniformities of majority taste and opinion, and the "miracles" conveyed in the mass media, relieve people of the knowledge of their spiritual insecurity and solitude? In other words, has our freedom been subtly nullified by grand inquisitors disguised as communications executives, business leaders, and elected representatives? Let us remember that Dostoevsky's Grand

Inquisitor was a gentle and compassionate servant of popular desires.

To sum up, the position to which these reflections have brought us is as follows. Freedom can be glorious because it is an opening toward transcendence; it is fragile because it is the freedom of creatures having little interest in transcendence. Hence, the values and disciplines of civilized society are essential to freedom; also, however, they are threatening to freedom. Contrary both to the idealized portraits of tradition painted by conservatives and to the prospects of justice and harmony delineated by radicals, a society is always more or less deformed by the practical pressures and selfish inclinations at work among those who have shaped and led it. And a society is always vulnerable to the lure of solidarity, wherein freedom is either openly denied or cunningly deprived of its spiritual substance.

We have come to the point at which it is necessary to look beyond structure to spirit. What enables human beings not merely to bear the burden of freedom but to find therein their humanity and the splendor of transcendence?

Freedom and Religion

I have argued that the creative and righteous acts that give freedom its spiritual substance all come about when human beings become more than mere human beings, when they become media of truth, beauty, and moral order. This happens strikingly through extraordinary people, such as saints, great philosophers, and artists. But it also happens though ordinary people, even if less conspicuously—for example, when they are resolute in difficult circumstances. Freedom is fulfilled by the presence of transcendence and can be strong and alive in various situations. In many different pursuits and activities human beings can be lifted above their everyday humanity. In one pursuit and activity, however, relations with transcendence are explicitly defined and deliberately cultivated. This pursuit is religion. There is a certain logic, then, in the idea that religion is at the source of the spirit of freedom.

Here I shall speak primarily of Christianity—not because I myself am a Christian (although I am), and not because I consider other religions than Christianity necessarily in error (I do not). But Christianity is the form in which the vast majority of Americans encounter the possibility of religious faith. It is thus in Christianity that sustained and conscious relations with transcendence are opened up for most of us. Much that I say about the role of Christianity in a free society might be said, appropriately qualified, of other religions as well. But the common observation that all religions convey the same ultimate message is false, even though the ultimate message in all religions may concern the same God. Thus not only the desirability of dealing with our own religious possibilities, but intellectual precision as well, suggests that Christianity stand for religion as such.

What then, can justify the hypothesis that Christianity contains the spirit of freedom? First of all, the fact that Christianity sustains values. Liberty is significant in that it enables human beings to be media of transcendence; the presence of transcendence in history takes the form of values; liberty is fragile because transcendence, and the values in which it is manifest, are readily forgotten. They are forgotten by free individuals on account of personal failings such as pride and sensuality. They are forgotten by societies because military and economic necessities, and the moral callousness of leaders and masses, often cause values to be suppressed or obscured. Whatever enlivens values, therefore, enlivens freedom. Christianity does this, while secularism, more logically and definitely than is generally recognized, leaves values vulnerable to the forces of erosion.

Consider, for example, the *individual human being* as a value—the principle that every person, without regard to empirical characteristics or social utility, must be treated as an end and never merely as a means. Every individual has infinite value, according to this principle; judgments assigning superiority to some and inferiority to others are inconclusive. The emotional disposition to recognize the value of the individual is the mark of love, and the capacity for doing so invariably is a primary sign of moral goodness. Today we speak casually of "the dignity of the individual"—too casually. It is not clear that this phrase has meaning except on religious grounds. The idea that every person (counting those who are mentally retarded, emotionally unbalanced, physically repellent;

counting every manner of criminal, failure, and misfit) has infinite value has no empirical support whatever. Anyone relying scrupulously on objective observation must conclude that no one has infinite value, that many persons are of negligible value, and that some, being harmful to themselves and others and a burden on public resources, are of negative value.

For Christians, however, regardless of what our eyes and ears may tell us, a human being as such is cast in the likeness of God; and by virtue of destiny, even if not of visible being, a human being shares the form of Christ, of God visibly and audibly present. Such, of course, is a matter of faith. It is a faith, nevertheless, that enables Christians to provide a coherent account of why even those who are dangerous, debauched, or physically disgusting must be respectfully treated. It is doubtful that people whose premises are purely secular can do that. Logically, they cannot evade the conclusions of empirical observation or the hierarchical and exclusive attitudes (found, for example, among the greatest pre-Christian philosophers) to which empirical observation leads.

Consider in like manner the value of *truth*. One reason freedom is degraded today is that serious speech, which is speech in search of truth, is relatively rare. Freedom of speech is most energetically and conspicuously used for advertising and electioneering—for activities based on the assumption that speech is an expedient in the service of profits and power and that truth is an extreme outer limit rather than central purpose. In universities, truth is conceived of normally according to specialties so narrow and standards so quantitative that it becomes merely "academic," unrelated to the life everyone spontaneously knows. Again, it is not clear that a cogent secular response is possible. Bertrand Russell, with a discernment and candor rare among secular philosophers, once remarked that the ultimate truth may not be very interesting; Friedrich Nietzsche maintained that ultimate truth was too terrible for most people to bear. How can anyone whose universe is entirely secular deny such possibilities? Within the bounds of secularity, how can one be anything but a pragmatist of one kind or another, holding truth to be whatever serves our worldly needs?

For Christians, however, truth discloses a universe reflective, in light and sky, sea and dry land, plants and trees, sun and moon and stars, and fish, birds, and animals, of a divine Creator. And the truth concerning human beings discloses a history that mirrors the merciful and humanly oriented character of the Creator. Here, too, we are speaking of a faith. Such a faith, however, gives truth unquestionable splendor.

Consider, finally, the value of *community*—as distinguished from society. Anything deserving the name is in some fashion a common search for the truth and common enjoyment of the truth. In the sharing of the search and the enjoyment, community is a showing of respect for human beings, since the highest mark of respect is the communal act, the offering of serious attention and speech. Community, then, is a fusion of esteem for truth and esteem for individuals.

For Christians, community is the Kingdom of God; it is thus the ultimate goal of history and the ultimate aim, beyond a multitude of more proximate aims, of political activity. Christianity has sometimes been shamefully anti-communal in practice, as in religious wars and doctrinal inquisitions. It is nonetheless filled with communal idealism. By speaking, God created the world ("And God said, 'Let there be light,' and there was light"), and throughout the Old Testament God is depicted as one who speaks and listens. In the New Testament, God becomes incarnate as "the Word"; Christ is divine speech. As for secularism, however, if it cannot uphold the dignity of persons or the worth of truth, can it affirm community? It is fair to ask whether the logical upshot of consistent secularism is not a regimented society, perhaps in the manner of the Grand Inquisitor (a secret atheist), or of Nietzsche, or of Lenin. Since community combines the values that lend freedom significance, where community is not highly valued, freedom becomes trivial.

My argument is not quite that no secular grounds whatever can be found for affirming the individual, truth, and community. If Christ is the Logos, there must be signs and indications of ultimate value throughout reality. The work of a secular philosopher such as Kant is filled with intimations of transcendence. My argument, strictly defined, is only that the secular grounds for value are obscure and questionable. Consequently, a society that is highly secularized, and lacks the provocation and stimulus of religion, easily slips into relativism and pragmatism, and these turn freedom from a moral imperative into, at best, a mere convenience, at worst, an intolerable nuisance.

The Christian Vision of Freedom

It is not only in providing a strong account of the values underlying freedom that religion strengthens the spirit of freedom, however. In addition, it offers a vision of what freedom fully realized means, and it relates this vision to unfolding history in a way that encourages the virtues needed for taking on the burden of freedom.

Let us consider first the Christian vision of freedom. The thinking of modern supporters of "positive" freedom, such as Rousseau and Hegel, arose partly from an intuition that the old liberal idea of freedom—that it meant simply being able to do what you want to do—was inadequate. It did not correspond with the aspiration that made people willing to struggle and die for freedom. According to the old idea, liberty was small and adventitious; according to the aspiration, it was large and fundamental. Hence a new idea was fashioned. Freedom was envisioned as a state of righteousness and understanding—a vital truth, a realization that freedom is found only in the utmost fullness of personal being. But the vital truth was fused with a deadly error. Freedom was envisioned as a product of participation in a good society. The truth brought to light, it might be said summarily, was that when we think of freedom in the deepest fashion, we are thinking of redemption; the error was that of viewing freedom as a possible social and political achievement.

Christianity brings out the truth and avoids the error. The theology of Paul can be largely summarized in terms of liberation—from guilt, from sin, from law, finally from suffering and death. Paul spoke often of the liberty Christians have and can anticipate. Given the authority of Paul in the founding of Christian thought and practice, we may justifiably call Christianity a doctrine and a way of freedom. At the same time, Christianity embodies an acute understanding of the human tendencies that limit historical possibilities. Only in God's order, never in man's, can freedom take on its redemptive proportions.

Christianity thus situates the complete realization of freedom outside the scope of political action. In this way it refrains from challenging the partial realization of freedom in the manner of doctrines that assert the possibility of earthly paradise. There is no suggestion that with sufficient ruthlessness we can conquer the major evils that have always bedeviled mortal existence. In short, Christianity is free of Leninism.

It is also free, however, of Platonism, a name we might give to the kind of philosophy that places an unqualified concept of political perfection in stark opposition to historical conditions forever preventing its realization. In contrast, in the Christian view, all things—all historical developments—work in the direction of freedom even though the fullness of freedom will come only with the end of history. This happens primarily though grace, however, rather than human power. So human beings are deprived of excuses for totalitarian violence but not of hope. The cause of freedom is in the hands of God, and its success, in eternity, is not in doubt. Since God is merciful, the mercy needed for bearing without hatred the evil men do when given freedom becomes a human possibility; and the patience needed for sustaining the anxieties inherent in one's own freedom is given spiritual grounds. These virtues—hope, mercy, and patience—are elements in the spirit of freedom that flows out of Christianity.

The argument that religion is essential to freedom, however, leads to a difficult question. To fulfill its role, what status must religion have in society?

Religion in a Secular Society

Religious people tend naturally to seek official standing of some kind for religion, for example, through prayer in public schools or public displays of religious symbols. They often argue that the Framers intended to bar governmental aid only to particular religions, not to religion as such. In a secularized society, however, public religious symbols that have any color of official sponsorship are more likely to arouse hostility than faith. Moreover, such symbols always bring the danger that the everlasting truths of religion will become tied to the relative and ephemeral truths contained in political ideologies. It was for such reasons that Tocqueville attributed the religious faith he thought so deep and widespread in America to the sharp separation of church and state. It is true that the most uncompromising defenders of the so-called wall between church and state often display more plainly a bias against religion than an ardor for freedom; and the issues that excite them often seem trivial. Nevertheless, it is doubtful that religion has much to gain by opposing them.

Moreover, opposing secular extremists may put Christians in a false position. Religious faith inevitably calls forth the dream of a sacred society, a society in which laws and social forms, and even physical realities, reflect the major articles of faith. But this dream is contrary to intransigent facts: to the impossibility of forcing people to believe; to the mystery of Christian truth, which allows it to be contained only in "earthen vessels," in doctrines that cannot suitably be imposed on people; and to the sinful nature of Christians, as of everyone else, unfitting them for religious empire.

The meaning of these facts is simple: Christians must acquiesce in secularism. They must allow the life about them to flow on, without explicit religious form or direction. This is confirmed in Scripture. According to both Matthew and Luke, at the outset of his ministry Jesus unconditionally repudiated the temptation to impose a sacred order on the world. He refused to assume the authority to impose righteousness; he refused to perform miracles so spectacular that faith would be involuntary and universal; he refused to turn stones into bread. His followers would have to live without moral, spiritual, or material security, burdened by their freedom; they would have to decide for themselves the moral form, spiritual content, and economic bases of their lives. In short, they would have to dispense with the assurances and consolations of sacred solidarity. Thus, prudence and Scripture alike suggest that God does not intend for Christians to live in a world that mirrors their faith. The dualism of ancient times, that of Jews and Gentiles, and later of Judaism and Christianity, is to be further unfolded as the dualism of Christianity and secularism. Never are God's followers to be given uncontested possession of the truth.

And with good reason. Uncontested possession of the truth is not salutary either for the possessors or for the truth. The possessors, in a universe where they hear only their words and thoughts echoing about them, become triumphal and unreasoning. The truth they are supposedly guarding is lost as it is equated with public symbols to which everyone formally assents. The Christian idea is that God's truth was uttered through an archetypal act of humility and suffering. Can such a truth be understood or expressed by people whose historical situation—reigning over a sacred order—spares them humility and shields them from suffering?

If I am right, then, Christians do not ask the inhabitants of the secular sphere to acknowledge in even the slightest and most innocuous ways any allegiance to the universe of Christ. But they ask something far harder of them and something far more important: that the secular-minded accord them attention. Today such attention is almost altogether withheld. The secular-minded sometimes desire from Christian priests and pastors such agreeable and traditional formalities as the performance of wedding ceremonies, but rarely are they interested in what Christians have to say. This attitude is perfectly illustrated by secular intellectuals. Any conscientious professor in the humanities and the social sciences feels obliged to know something about psychoanalysis, Marxism, postmodernism, and other schools of secular thought. To profess indifference to any of them would be unthinkable, to confess ignorance would be highly embarrassing. But indifference to all schools of theology is taken for granted; and in a gathering of academicians one may confess ignorance of Karl Barth or Rudolf Bultmann not only without embarrassment but perhaps even with a note of promethean pride. Yet Christian theology addresses the gravest issues of human life; it has reflected on these issues for nearly twenty centuries; and it is represented by some of the greatest minds of any era (in our time, for example, Karl Barth is certainly in a class with Heidegger and Wittgenstein). By what intellectual right do those who have never granted Christian discourse serious consideration deem it unworthy of attention?

The Christian claim to secular attention, however, is not just a demand for fair-mindedness and justice; nor does it rest on the hope that very many members of the secular universe might become Christians. It arises also from a sense of responsibility for freedom and for the primal values, such as truth, that nourish the spirit of freedom. As I have argued, these values do not find clear and unequivocal support within the bounds of a secular outlook. Yet they are not entirely inaccessible to the secular mind, since God created the universe and gives all people, through natural faculties, some understanding of that universe. In this way, values that are clear to religious insight may be dimly present to secular insight as well. The idea that every individual has infinite worth, for example, even if indefensible on purely secular grounds, may not be utterly incomprehensible to a secular intelligence; as noted earlier, there are hints of the idea in any instance of personal love. I am suggesting, in sum, that Christianity might awaken the world to the deepest values and thus bring to life the spirit of freedom.

When Christians lay claim to secular attention, however, they immediately fall under obligations toward the secular sphere; the latter has rightful claims on Christians. First of all, Christians should speak with integrity and power. The greatest theologians aside, it would be difficult to show that they do this very consistently now. Many Christian voices betray a pathetic willingness to obscure or surrender core Christian doctrines in order to conform to secular intellectual fashions. In doing this, no longer do they speak for authentic Christianity; nor do they command the interest and respect of secular society, for they seem weak and apologetic. If non-Christians listening to Christians hear only words already familiar to them, set to inappropriate theological melodies, they will properly cease listening.

The second obligation Christians incur in claiming the attention of the secular world is to grant that the secular world has a claim on the attention of Christians. There are strong reasons in Christian doctrine itself for asserting that Christians should heed secular minds, however critical and guarded they must be in doing this. Because Christians believe that Christ was the embodied truth of all things, the Logos become flesh, they must also believe that whoever speaks the truth speaks of Christ, whether explicitly or not, and thus speaks in some sense to Christians. Not only, then, is Christian truth not uncontested; it is not exclusive. Christians cannot ignore such writers such as Nietzsche and Camus, nor artists such as Picasso and Matisse; they cannot ignore heroic unbelievers such as Andrei Sakharov. Christians inhabit an illusory universe, and Christian truth surely cannot flourish unless they confess to being outshone at times, in literature, art, and moral conduct, by people who are not religious. That God should permit Christian truth to be in some sense incomplete and imperfect may be puzzling to Christians; yet it is not incomprehensible. Christians who withhold attention from the secular sphere make idols of their doctrines, and they proudly exaggerate their own understanding. Only by steady and universal attentiveness can they be fully cognizant that, even though illuminated by grace, they are still fallible human beings, and their doctrines are human efforts to elucidate a mystery that can never be made objectively plain.

The Attentive Society

For the sake of brevity and simplicity, the two poles of this discussion have been secularism and Christianity. Judaism and Islam have been ignored; highly spiritual expressions of paganism, such as the philosophy of Plato, have been left out of account; nothing has been said about the diversity of Christian denominations. A general statement of my argument does not require, however, that all such distinctions be explicitly made. Very broadly, I am arguing simply that a recognition of our spiritual interdependence is essential to liberty. This applies particularly to the spheres of secularity and religion. These are the alternatives facing us in the most fundamental act of self-definition we are called on to carry out. For people in either sphere to close their minds to the other is to deny our finitude and fallibility.

Where minds are closed, freedom must be constrained and weak. Simone Weil spoke of attentiveness as "the rarest and purest form of human generosity." Attentiveness arises when we recognize our spiritual interdependence. A society in which people listen seriously to those with whom they fundamentally disagree—an attentive society—is the proper historical setting for freedom. In an attentive society, people are free to repudiate religion, and perhaps most of them will. So far as people are truly attentive, however, they are open to the depths of being. From these depths, freedom draws its splendor and strength.

An attentive society would be unlike the consumer society that

Americans inhabit; it would obviously be radically different from the ideological, totalitarian societies America has so often opposed. An attentive society would not be dominated by the doctrinaire secularism prevailing today among American academicians and journalists; but neither would it be officially or coercively religious. An attentive society would provide room for strong convictions, but its defining characteristic would be a widespread willingness to give and receive assistance on the road to truth. It is often thought that secularism is more open and tolerant than religion, and admittedly, so it has often been. But only religion provides the ultimate basis for openness and tolerance of a kind that attains moral significance through attentiveness. Only religion assigns absolute value to the truth and to every individual sharer in the truth; and only religion gives us reason to think that, in spite of all human failings, the truth will be fully known.

For these reasons, an attentive society is a religious and a Christian ideal. It is a secular ideal only so far as secularism is aroused by religion to affirm the value of truth and of individuals and is induced to rely on the destiny in which the future of truth is assured. That there will ever be an attentive society in history is manifestly improbable. It might be said, nevertheless, that by bearing ourselves, in whatever kind of society we happen to inhabit, in the manner of citizens of an attentive society, we live in the true spirit of freedom.

Responses

1. RUSSELL HITTINGER

One of Glenn Tinder's central themes is the contrast between spontaneous and attentive uses of freedom. Tinder argues that freedom must be understood in terms of the human capacity for self-transcendence. Unlike other natural beings whose careers are limited to the spontaneous unfolding of their immanent potentials, human beings can realize their true nature only by standing in relation to others, by knowing the truth, and by acquiring the virtues. Aristotle said that the virtues arise in us neither by nature nor contrary to nature; they are acquired by intelligent, free action.[1] In short, human development requires the acquisition of a kind of second nature. As Gerard Verbeke affirmed in his recent study *Moral Education in Aristotle*, "ethical behavior is far from being a natural gift; it is the result of much effort and training."[2]

Virtually none of the great religious and humanist traditions in Western culture has keyed its ideas or institutions exclusively to our "first nature." However gifted we may be by nature, becoming human in a moral sense requires toil on the part of both the individual and the society that summons forth the natural endowments. In *The Spirit of the Laws*, for example, Montesquieu wrote:

> Man, as a physical being, is governed by invariable laws like other bodies. As an intelligent being, he constantly violates the laws God has established and changes those he himself establishes; he must guide himself, and yet he is a limited being: he is subject to ignorance and error, as are all finite intelligences; he loses even the imperfect knowledge he has. As a feeling creature, he falls subject to a thousand passions. Such a being could at any moment forget his creator; God has called him back by the laws of religion. Such a being could at any moment forget himself;

Russell Hittinger is an associate professor in the school of philosophy at the Catholic University of America and, in 1991–92, an adjunct research fellow at the American Enterprise Institute.

philosophers have reminded him of himself by the laws of morality. Made for living in society, he could forget his fellows; legislators have returned him to his duties by political and civil laws. [I.1, 5]

While I certainly agree with Tinder's point that exclusively secular accounts of human freedom have often proved to be reductive and inadequate without religious faith, we should recognize that, until very recently, religious and secular thinkers alike have assumed that human nature needs to be tutored.

Tinder gets to the nub of the contemporary problem when he declares:

> To be *authentically* human we must . . . choose to enter relationships that make us more than we are when we are merely *spontaneously* human. This fact is obscured by politicians who flatter the voters in their ordinary and unexamined lives and by advertisers who encourage consumers to indulge unhesitatingly all whims and desires. People are invited to abandon self-criticism and self-discipline and to think highly of themselves just as they are. Humanity is tacitly treated as though it were as natural to everyone, in the sense of being as easily acquired and as normally attached to every representative of the species, as the power to stand upright and walk.

The contemporary social and political world is preoccupied, accordingly, with human *rights*, which are keyed to untutored human nature and are possessed in the same way one possesses hands and feet. Americans especially inherit an all-purpose moral, political, and legal rhetoric of natural rights that claims individuals have inherent and inalienable rights antecedent to government and positive law. In what other legal culture besides ours can an ordinary litigant mount, and often win, a legal argument based on natural rights?

Those holding this view of the human world expect both religious and secular institutions merely to ratify one or another natural trait of selfhood: the capacity for free choice, the capacity for sexual pleasure, the fact of gender, or race, or even physical disability. Our public discourse concerns issues of status and value that can be described without resort to any particular moral or religious specification. Attentiveness, then, is one-dimensional, invariably expressed in the language of dignity and respect for rights. These rights are based on those natural properties found in, and spontaneously enacted by, human beings—provided, of course, that one has crossed the threshold of live birth. Institutions that aspire to educate, discipline, and prune such natural properties are regarded as inhumane.

Every major religious body in our culture has, to some observable extent, yielded to the notion that religion's chief task is to ratify, rather than discipline, human spontaneity. The historical background of this conception is complex and includes various modern forms of religious personalism, as well as the Enlightenment's project to isolate the phenomenon of natural religion. One book that clearly announces this view is William James's *Varieties of Religious Experience* (1902). Like Schleiermacher a century earlier, James certainly believed that he was not subverting religion but rather defending it against its cultured despisers. Be that as it may, we find in James the broad outlines of the position that religion is valuable precisely insofar as it is spontaneous and unchurched.

James argued that religion is not to be defined either in terms of churches or in terms of any particular idea of God.[3] Rather, it is a matter of individual experience, to which institutions are related as secondary and entirely derivative phenomena. James defined religion in contrast to morality, on the one hand, and to the mind's assent to propositional truth, on the other. Moral duty and science, he remarked, require toil, method, and discipline; whereas authentic religious experience is mystical, exuberant, and joyful. Religion, he said, makes the necessary "easy."[4]

James went on to argue that America's unique contribution to religion is what he called "healthy-mindedness" or the "gospel of relaxation."[5] Whereas Wesley and Luther maintained that the individual is saved by virtue of Christ's atonement, American therapeutic religion responds by saying, "You *are* well, sound, and clear already, if you did but know it."[6] Whereas traditional religious moralists urge the self never to cease from duty and discipline, the new religion recommends giving the "private, convulsive self a rest, and finding a greater Self is there."[7] In this vein, we recall Timothy Leary's remark about the great benefit of LSD: "You can be a convict or a college professor. You'll still have a mystical, transcendental experience."[8]

. Because there is, at least arguably, a kind of natural capacity for religious experience, we should expect that some people will try to develop that capacity with little or no fuss about churches, creeds, or even a fully transcendent being. In America, perhaps more than in Europe, this form of religion has always been recognized and even socially approved. What should worry us, however, is churchmen's attitude that religion must be spontaneous, blandly therapeutic, and politically correct to be of any value whatsoever, and that churches, creeds, and religion based on propositional truths are to be regarded as guilty until proven innocent. They cannot be proved innocent, of course, until they are shown to make no disciplinary claims on—but rather, only ratify—the spontaneous, rights-bearing self. On these terms Catholicism, in particular, stands guilty as charged.

I agree with Tinder that this malignant attitude should not be traced to the doorstep of secularism or, for that matter, to our Supreme Court's peculiar conception of what the Constitution requires in the way of church-state jurisprudence. The vice of inattentiveness is no longer a secular attack on religious faith or religious institutions; nor is it a matter of an overly stringent understanding of the so-called wall of separation between church and state that makes religion something merely private. The same criticism mounted against traditional religious bodies is also leveled against school systems, the family, hospitals, and even the Constitution insofar as they are perceived to be inimical to the rights-bearing spontaneous self.

In its stand against such institutions, this self does not want to be educated, or even loved. For that matter, I am not sure that it is in search of freedom. What it clearly does want, like Rodney Dangerfield, is *respect*. Unfortunately, respect is the one thing that none of our traditional institutions, whether secular or religious, can give it.

Whether the churches can still contribute to a public discourse about liberty in terms of natural law has been discussed at length. Surely the churches have as much of a stake in the history and public deployment of this concept as do secular institutions. After all, the first natural-law treatise in the North American colonies was written by John Wise, a Congregationalist minister.[9] Catholic theorists such as John Courtney Murray have argued that natural-law theory can, in the American context, serve as the point of connection between ecclesial and public discourse.

The problem with trying to recover and rehabilitate natural-law discourse from the shackles of contemporary legal and political rhetoric is that the "spontaneous" society is quite happy with, and indeed addicted to, natural-law theories. One or another natural-law theory of rights is commonly used to immunize individual liberty against public conceptions of morality, and against those very institutions that aspire to discipline and to tutor freedom. Individual rights are equated with certain human needs or wants that any individual, regardless of his or her religious or moral deficiencies, must claim. Natural-law theory, then, focuses on certain basic goods that are not conceived of in terms of natural teleology, perfectionist moral directives, or covenantal projects. It traces out no particular educational or institutional tasks other than respect for individual rights claims.[10]

This kind of natural-law theory would seem to corrode what Tinder means by the "attentive society." The churches are faced, therefore, with a double problem. They must both recover natural-law discourse and recover it in a way that does not simply reinforce the current preoccupation with individual rights. Their task today is to make natural-law discourse more difficult, and to prevent it from slipping back into the lazy man's moralisms concerning rights.

2. WILLIAM H. WILLIMON

In wanting so desperately to help America today, we Christians may be unhelpful. Glenn Tinder takes on a daunting task when he argues that the spirit of freedom arises from religion. Except for American presidents going to war to bring freedom to emirates, few can speak of the glory of freedom today without severe philosophical qualifications. What does religion do for freedom that cannot be done as well by philosophy?

Because we live in a radically imperfect world, Tinder is right to

William H. Willimon is the dean of the chapel and a professor of Christian ministry at Duke University, Durham, North Carolina.

insist that we must be free to change our societies. As Christians in a non-Christian society, we certainly have a stake in a liberal democracy's being as free as possible. No one wants change more than Christians, and we are convinced that Christ is quite able to enlist followers without coercion or violence.

But change for what purpose? Freedom for what? Such questions about freedom spring almost immediately to a Christian mind. As a Christian, I agree with John Howard Yoder that, in discussions of freedom, "what for" matters more than "what from." Christians are given some peculiar notions of freedom. One wonders why Tinder utilizes so few of them.

"Freedom is an opportunity to be human," Tinder asserts. That statement accords with the Christian assessment of freedom. For Christians, freedom is only a means of better obeying God, which is our idea of being human. But elsewhere one suspects that Tinder's idea of freedom is not peculiarly Christian.

Tinder is profoundly uneasy—as well he should be—with what modern American society has done to degrade "freedom." He laments that "people are invited to abandon self-criticism and self-discipline and to think highly of themselves just as they are." Unfortunately, the combined languages of liberalism and natural theology fail to give him adequate means of addressing freedom's fallacies. He says that we are "authentically human" only when we become "media of transcendence" and can exercise our "spiritual capacity." This could move us to some interesting qualifications of the notion of "freedom."

Tinder refers to our creation in "the image and likeness of God." He defines the "image of God," however, in Augustinian terms of free will rather than in the images of stewardship and dominion found in Genesis 1 and 2. His reference to "original sin" implies wrongly, as does Niebuhr, that the biblical idea of sin is empirically self-evident to everyone, even those who do not know God. A *Christian* idea of sin is related to our belief that the world is the creation of a jealous God.

I liked Tinder's critique of our society's current glorification of "community" or "society" at the expense of the individual—though I wish it had included the story of the gospel, which well explains why Christians should know that "community" can be as demonic as the "individual." His candid admission of the terrible toll our society has taken on the "glorious" philosophical ideal of freedom is blunted, however, by his continuing, almost wistful desire that our society somehow create structures that give freedom "moral and communal substance." Perhaps sensing that this is impossible in a society with as questionable a philosophical foundation as ours, he finally opts for the Aristotelian necessity of "virtue and good sense."

From whence do these requisite virtues come in a world that demonstrates the "squalor of freedom" so much more vividly than the "splendor of freedom"? A shopping list of qualifiers follows, but none suggests any real means of resisting "inglorious" freedom. Openness toward "transcendence" cannot counteract the corrosive acids of a society that has demonstrated, for perhaps the first time in history, why the classical liberal conception of freedom is uninteresting. Tinder's utilitarian appeal to the values of amorphous "religion" is too vague to be helpful in resuscitating the notion of freedom.

My uneasiness with Tinder's discussion was solidified by his statement that "the theology of Paul can be largely summarized in terms of liberation." This is not so. Paul's theology is about Jesus as the Christ, Jesus Christ as Lord. Paul's confrontation with Christ led him to a wonderful reconsideration of many of his former notions, including his notion of freedom. After his baptism, Paul said that he was a better slave to Christ than anyone else: "that is why I boast."

Paul was a good enough Pharisee to know that the faith of Israel was not about liberation. It was about obedience to a God who gave the Torah. Christ represented for Paul, as the Exodus did for Israel, a movement not from slavery to freedom or from obligation to individual autonomy, but from one form of servitude to another. As the Midrash puts it, God took Israel "from the yoke of iron to the yoke of Torah, from slavery to freedom" (Exodus Rabbah 15:11). Slavery to the Torah, as rabbis never tire of saying, equals freedom.

Why Jews believe this about the Torah or why Christians believe this about Christ and his Church cannot by explained by qualifying or shoring up philosophical ideals. Service to the truth begins and ends in submission to God. True tolerance comes not, as Tinder suggests, from trying to be humble about our claims to the truth. It comes instead from holding steadfastly to our claim that we are not God but rather the recipients of God's salvation in Christ.

Tinder concludes his paper with a plea that "inhabitants of the secular sphere" give us some attention. I believe that as long as Christians continue to discuss ideals like "freedom" in a way that can be heard elsewhere without all the baggage of residual Christianity, the world is quite right to ignore us. We really do have something quite interesting to say about what is wrong with our society's freedom and what is needed for true freedom, but we do not know how to say it without saying "Christ." Tinder urges Christians to prove they are worth listening to and rightly laments, "Many Christian voices betray a pathetic willingness to obscure or surrender core Christian doctrines in order to conform to secular intellectual fashions."

I am convinced that orthodox Christian faith has more of interest to say than does resuscitated natural theology filtered through classical liberalism. As Tinder so well demonstrates, our society does not know what "glorious" freedom is, having perverted and demeaned the economic, sexual, individual, and political freedom we have. What he fails to explain is how we can tell the world Paul's message—"For freedom, Christ has set us free"—without mentioning either Israel or the Church. Only when "public theology" includes religion will it command anyone's attention.

6

Abortion: Moralities in Conflict

JEAN BETHKE ELSHTAIN

WE live in a society marked by moral conflict. This conflict has deep historical roots and is reflected in our institutions, practices, laws, norms, and values. The abortion debate taps strongly held, powerfully experienced moral and political convictions that are linked to complex concerns about what sort of people we are and aspire to be. The abortion debate will not "go away," nor should it. We are, after all, talking about matters of life and death, freedom and obligation, rights and duties: none of us can dispute that, and none of us can be nonplussed when we face the dilemmas the abortion question poses.[1]

To jog our thinking on abortion, values, and the family, I want to show how a pair of contrasting images of the human community—and of the nature and good of that community and the human beings who compose it—shape the positions we hold. After some general observations on language and the abortion debate, my remarks on abortion and the family will focus on two alternative frames, the social contract and the social compact. Finally, I will proffer a few mordant reflections on the "clear and present dangers" we face if we remain tied to a perspective that exalts choice and control over obligation, human interdependency, and caretaking.

Jean Bethke Elshtain is Centennial Professor of Political Science and a professor of philosophy at Vanderbilt University. Her books include *Public Man, Private Woman: Women in Social and Political Thought*, *Meditations on Modern Political Thought*, and *Women and War*.

LANGUAGE AND THE ABORTION DEBATE

The resources of ordinary language are supple, and they are available to all within a linguistic community. Language importantly constitutes social reality and frames available forms of action. We are all interlocutors in a language community and hence participants in a project of theoretical and moral self-understanding, definition, and redefinition. We can never leap out of our linguistic skins. Our ideals are not icing on the cake of social reasoning but are instead part of a densely articulated web of social, historical, and cultural meanings, traditions, rules, beliefs, norms, actions, and visions. In a society bereft of moral consensus, such as ours, the differences that emerge in the language of moral debate take us to the heart of competing understandings of social life. A way of life is a complex, if fractious, whole. One cannot "seal off" attitudes toward the unborn and their fate from other features of the culture. Abortion does not exist apart from everything else.

It is difficult to assay whether the language and the terms of discourse we are using help us to see clearly, or blind us to, important features of moral existence. Language inadequate to its task may creep up on us unawares as social norms evolve or as terms drawn from one sphere—law or medicine, for example—are deployed to "cover" broad areas of moral and political life ostensibly ill-served by our ordinary linguistic resources. Especially problematic and troubling in the abortion debate is the recourse to morally distancing language, particularly on the part of those who might be called "extreme" or "ultra" liberals or pro-choice absolutists.

A few examples strongly suggest that the implicit aim of many pro-choice analysts and philosophers is to sever our stance on abortion from our moral reactions altogether. They construe human emotions as irrational, serving only to muddy the waters.[2] References to the fetus as a "parasite," a "tenant," an airborne "spore," or "property" erect a linguistic barrier between us and the reality and conflict of abortion. The biologically human status of the fetus is covered up. To prevent adult humans from recognizing in the developing fetus some shared humanness, the fetus must be dehumanized. In reviewing the arguments of extreme pro-choice advocates Michael Tooley and Mary Anne Warren, Philip Abbott notes that these philosophers, and others, never base their cases on everyday human social existence. They never make contact with ordinary life, language, and moral conflict. Abbott writes:

Sixteen examples (and there are variations) are used to analyze the morality of abortion. But what examples! The world of the philosopher is filled with people seeds, child missile launchers, Martians, talking robots, dogs, kittens, chimps, jigsaw cells that form human beings, transparent wombs, and cool hands—everything in fact but fetuses growing in wombs and infants cradled in parents' arms.[3]

When challenged, such pro-choice philosophers respond that we cannot confront the human condition directly because our minds are too muddled by emotional debris. As proof of this debility, Tooley cites our revulsion to infanticide, seeing it as an irrational taboo "like the reaction of previous generations to masturbation or oral sex."[4] Philosophers Elizabeth Rapaport and Paul Sagal note that this extreme liberal position is highly vulnerable; if one accepts it, one also endorses the right to infanticide. Tooley's position, they declare, "permits unrestricted infanticide."[5]

With Abbott, Rapaport and Sagal, and other critics, I reject easy solutions that strip our language of moral evaluators. Jane English, a feminist thinker, was correct in claiming that "anti-abortion forces are indeed giving their strongest arguments when they point to the similarities between a fetus and a baby, and when they try to evoke our emotional attachment to and sympathy for the fetus." The 24-week-old aborted fetus, for example, is so much like a premature infant that "no one can be asked to draw a distinction and treat them so very differently."[6] I shall avoid, therefore, all the euphemisms deployed to avoid thinking clearly about what is going on when abortion is going on. I shall not supplant images of the unborn with medical talk of "fetal matter" or "products of conception." One must be wary of attempts to constrict the vitality of moral discourse in any area of human life. Once benumbed in one area, one's emotions may continue to be suppressed, and a pervasive and unreflective mode of denial and suppression may evolve as "normal."[7]

The opposing side, however, is not entirely blameless. The hyper-emotional language used by some right-to-life proponents and activists—calling all cases of abortion "murder," the woman who aborts a "murderer," and those who abort her "accomplices to murder"—is too strong. Language of this kind also washes out all ambivalence.

My minimal point, for now, is that words matter. The words with which we characterize our daily lives and our moral conflicts count for something. Were our language to be stripped of its moral dimension, as in extreme positions that grant the fetus no moral weight nor even a human reality, we would be denied our power to reflect on, or even to see, what is going on. But an absolutist moral language also blinds us to ambivalence and complexity. I shall try to steer between these alternatives by staying on the ground of practical reasoning and eschewing fanciful and extreme examples.

ALTERNATIVE VIEWS OF ABORTION AND FAMILY

An intrinsic feature of our moral life is the pervasiveness of moral conflict. In our attempts to resolve these conflicts, some stress particular ties of obligation; the rest stress abstract right and individual free choice. Debates on abortion and the family are situated inside the universe constituted by these two moral poles. Unless one has opted fully for abstract right and individualism or, alternatively, for the individual's absorption in a web of obligations to others, the overlap and tension between these broad frameworks will affect one's perspective. Less interesting than the way in which these frameworks shade into each other are the distinct postures and possibilities that each nourishes, sustains, or denies.

The atomistic turn of much pro-choice social theory makes explicit an important truth about our society: the current order of things tends increasingly to perceive its members as sovereign selves or consumers—our contemporary variant of the abstract "individual" of classical atomistic theory.[8] Atomistic theory provides the foundation for the notion of a social contract. In the contract model, which has its historical roots in seventeenth-century social-contract theory, society is constituted by individuals for the fulfillment of individual ends. "The term is also applied," writes Charles Taylor, "to contemporary doctrines which hark back to social contract theory, or which try to defend in some sense the priority of the individual and his rights over society, or which present a purely instrumental view of society." The central feature of this tradition is an "affirmation of what we could call the primacy of rights."[9] Rights, rather than any principle of belonging or obligation, are primary and fundamental.

Primacy-of-rights theory has been one of the most important formative influences on the political consciousness of the West. Indeed, we are so immured in the world this notion has wrought that most of us, most of the time, grant individual rights *prima facie* force. By insisting on human self-sufficiency and on the absolute centrality of "freedom to choose one's own mode of life," atomism makes the primacy-of-rights doctrine plausible.[10] It also exalts the human capacity for choice, demanding that we rise to the level of self-consciousness and autonomy where we can exercise choice well. We must not remain mired through fear, sloth, ignorance, or superstition in some code imposed by tradition, society, or fate that tells us how we should dispose of what belongs to us.[11]

From Contract Theory to Choice

These presuppositions underlie pro-choice arguments grounded in the language of rights, including those that advance ultra-liberal positions for abortion "on demand" and for a woman's "absolute right" to "control her own body." There is, however, a difference between modified arguments from rights and an extreme ultra-liberalism. Classical liberalism affirmed rights and choice. It envisioned a person freed from nature and from the irrational constraint of tradition, a person free to construct a new order. This bracing vision of the free individual can readily dissolve, however. As Rapaport and Sagal pointed out, "Simply to employ the language of moral and legal rights . . . is to inherit all the ambiguities associated with this language."[12] These ambiguities project a somewhat different vision—the vision of the "possessive" individual.

C. B. Macpherson contends that seventeenth-century liberal contract theory conceived "of the individual as essentially the proprietor of his own person or capacities, owing nothing to society for them. The individual was seen neither as a moral whole, nor as part of a larger social whole, but as owner of himself."[13] Society is an aggregate of contracting, proprietary persons. Fusing such liberal argumentation with market images suggests that individuals are merely means to one another's ends, or barriers in their way. In both social protest and self-advancement, the point is to "get yours." Any constraint on individual "wants" or "demands" is seen as coercive. The language of want and demand in our time signifies the particular shape that liberal discourse takes within a consumerist order. Individuals are denuded of a social matrix, and questions of the responsibility that freedom entailed in classical liberal doctrine are lost. Evocations of choice conjure up images of social atoms getting, acquiring, and keeping.

These images permeate the ultra-liberal arguments for abortion, placing those arguments squarely inside the contract framework. As Rapaport and Sagal note, arguments for abortion couched exclusively in the language of rights focus "on individual persons" and neglect relationships involving family, class, race, and human-kind—relationships that might prove crucial to resolving a problem like abortion. Even if it were conceded that the fetus is a non-person, obligations involving other social relations would still require careful attention and might suggest restrictions on the extreme liberal position.[14]

Under the tacit terms of atomistic and contract doctrine, abortion is cast as the right of a possessing and choosing self. Some even claim it is an absolute right having *prima facie* force. In choosing to abort, the woman demonstrates her freedom from the chains of nature and tradition and, like a man, remains true to her rational self. Accepting the devolution from "rights" to "wants," the ultra-liberal position grants all the weight of moral argumentation to a particular understanding of the "self alone."

How does the family fare within this scheme of things? Many popular pro-choice arguments are based on the same presumptions, less abstractly couched, that one finds in the work of well-known abortion philosophers. Radical feminist Ti-Grace Atkinson, for example, defines the fetus—along with what she calls the woman's "reproductive function"—as a woman's property.[15] Recalling Mac-pherson's notion of possessive individualism, within which the individual is construed as the sole proprietor of self, Atkinson claims that a woman may decide to permit her special function to operate on her raw-material gift or she may decide to stop the process—to have the embryo destroyed. Only when the fetus ceases to be the woman's property can it be interfered with.[16]

Atkinson uses proprietary and market language in the abortion debate to confer or to deny "personhood." Jane English challenges this ultra-liberalism because, as she puts it, "you cannot do as you · please with your own body if it affects other people adversely." Even if one decides that the fetus is not a person in the full-blown, legal sense, "that does not imply that you can do to it anything you wish. Animals, for example, are not persons, yet to kill or torture them for no reason at all is wrong."[17] But the hard-line version of atomistic contractualism allows no such constraints or brakes on absolute choice.

The "Value" of the Unborn

The fusion of "rights" with "wants" and market language is also evident in Garrett Hardin's justification for abortion. He argues that the "unwanted" should not be brought into the world because "they are more likely than others to be poor parents themselves and breed another generation of unwanted children."[18] Hardin conjures up the image of a society overrun by the "unwanted," most of them poor. He makes us fearful of the threat posed by the unwilling pregnant woman—just as Thomas Hobbes, in his classic *Leviathan*, aimed to make us so fearful of our fellows that we would choose a political world of absolute, authoritarian controls. Lawrence Lader goes on to compound these fears by warning that "unwanted children"—most, again, belonging to minority groups—threaten the social order. He writes, "Above all, society must grasp the grim relationship between unwanted children and the violent rebellion of minority groups."[19]

Equally vulgar are pro-abortion arguments based on "value" theory, a spin-off of neoclassical market economics. For Hardin, the fetus's value is "entirely dependent" on the social value attributed to it by society. Daniel Callahan has pointed out that the implications of arguments from value, within the contractual frame, are straightforward and dire: the fetus has no value; "it awaits someone's wanting it"; then, and only then, "is it of moral interest or human worth."[20] Hardin's insistence that the fetus is entirely dependent on social "value," on the value attributed to it by the market at the going price, preserves consumer sovereignty and untrammeled choice but ignores all questions of moral evaluation.

The narrow rationalism implicit in the atomist ideal—an ideal that defines us as so many choice-making Robinson Crusoes on disconnected islands—emerges in Lader's arguments for liberalized abortion. He stigmatizes women without the "abortion option" as creatures stuck "at the level of brood animals." Human birth at this level, he insists, is often "the result of blind impulses and passion"; the children born are "little more than the automatic reflex of a biological system."[21] Lader's fear of impulse and passion is instructive, for the ultra-liberal rationalist can see passions and emotions only as bestial or potentially anarchic. The answer to what is seen as woman's animal-like and irrational state—the "one just and inevitable answer"—becomes abortion, "the final freedom."

Lader quotes approvingly an associate editor of *Harper's* magazine who, speaking of Aid to Dependent Children, notes, "It is a bitter irony that here in New York, where some of the most enlightened efforts of the Planned Parenthood movement are based, hundreds of thousands of mothers still live in as dark ignorance as the peasants of a remote Pakistani village."[22] Those holding a position grounded in rationalist choice-making can see others who do not fully share that position only as unenlightened, ignorant, or backward—as pure victims either deliberately or through no fault of their own.

These crassly reductionistic arguments call to mind an earlier generation's fear of being overrun by the feeble-minded. Indeed, the "science" of eugenics came into being on the presumption that the germ plasm of "social defectives" might soon overtake that of hardier stock. Now discredited studies of "degenerate families" (remember the Jukes and the Kallikaks?) fueled eugenic and birth-control fervor in the late nineteenth and early twentieth centuries. This paranoia culminated in the now notorious 1927 decision by the United States Supreme Court that upheld a case of "eugenic sterilization" on the grounds that the woman in question, Carrie Buck, was a product and carrier of "degenerate germ plasm."

The U.S. Supreme Court's 1973 decision in *Roe* v. *Wade* eschewed eugenics reasoning, relying instead on the notion of an autonomous self having the right to privacy and fusing that ideal with state interest. The decision was pitched to the unequally matched poles of the sovereign individual and the sovereign state, and ignored entirely mediating social relations, institutions, ideals, and practices. By denying that husbands or anybody else had any say in the matter of deciding the fate of fetal life in the first six months of that life, the court declared that family and community considerations could and should be stripped from the adjudication of the rights of a sovereign self.

The Family's Fate

This decision indicates fairly clearly how the family fares in the world of atomism and the social contract. The family is an anomaly within a world bounded by the sovereign self, the primacy of rights, and "free choice," a world in which contract is the only acceptable form of obligation. Historically, strong liberal voluntarism has never mixed easily with ties of family, kin, and community. The woman's legal subordination to her husband, for instance, always posed a serious problem. It simply did not square with the terms of the liberal public sphere. While questions of women's continued immersion in the familial web still haunt feminist discourse and color approaches to the abortion debate, today the tension between *particular* ties and *abstract* right encompasses children as well. Not surprisingly, one hears arguments for children's liberation cast in ultra-liberal terms.

Such arguments eliminate childhood as a distinctive and dependent period in the human life cycle, seeing that dependency as being imposed by illegitimate adult authority. Children are urged to take their place in society as atomistic individuals, liberated from oppressive parents and supported by a paternalistic welfare bureaucracy. According to Abbott, all this is yet another manifestation of the rights model, which is based on self-sufficient, rational human beings. No matter that this category excludes a good portion of humanity at any given moment—the bulk of which is made up of children and those who are about to become children. Of no consequence either is any notion of solidarity among human beings.[23]

Women and children are to join ranks with males as sovereign, free, rationally choosing moral agents. The extreme atomist sees in women's links to biology, birth, and nurturing only the vestiges of our "animal" origins, the residues of our pre-enlightened history. Women, long suspect as overly emotional beings, can become "persons" only if they embrace and act on sovereign choice—and sever their links with nature.

Within this frame of argument, abortions are not cast as the occasionally necessary but regrettable, even tragic, responses by particular women to desperate situations; instead, they become essential to women's freedom. In the extreme individualist scheme of things, abortion is turned into the technological resolution to what might be called the woman's control deficit—her lesser capacity to control all aspects of life, given her continuing ties to nature. The "final freedom" increases that control, and control is by definition a good thing. This line of reasoning, of course, presumes that absolute control is an appropriate response to interdependency. If something is within our power—the fetus, for example—we have the right to control it. Humanity is defined by self-sufficiency. A very different sensibility links dependency with care and responsibility rather than with control.[24]

This form of theoretical and moral argumentation has an interesting sociological footnote, particularly for the feminist analyst. Polling data from the early 1970s through the present show that men favor abortion-on-demand more highly than do women. The single group most consistently supporting an extreme rights position on abortion is composed of white, upper-middle-class males. In trying to explain this phenomenon when it first appeared in the early 1970s, Judith Blake concluded that "upper-class men have much to gain and very little to lose by an easing of legal restrictions against abortion."[25] For such men, relaxed abortion promises fewer restrictions on sexuality and lowers financial responsibility and dependency.[26] Feminists who contend that the abortion issue pits men seeking to keep women enchained against women demanding liberation refuse to see the complexity of the picture.

The country's most recent data show that a majority rejects "a constitutional amendment that would categorically prohibit abortion. . . . Almost consensually, Americans would permit abortion to save the mother's life." On the other hand, again almost consensually, "Americans oppose abortion as means of birth control." In a survey conducted by the Wirthlin Group in late 1990, over 70 per cent of the respondents disapproved of nearly all abortions performed in the United States. Fewer than 30 per cent endorsed abortion for non-medical reasons. A "clear majority" is also opposed to "having abortion legal in all circumstances, and about half the public is willing to have its legality limited to very restricted circumstances." Large majorities "endorse laws that would require counseling about alternatives to abortion, and that would mandate parental notification and parental consent before a woman under eighteen can have an abortion."[27] Although male and female views on abortion have become more similar in the past decade, with more women moving towards a modified pro-choice posture, women remain queasier than men about many aspects of abortion and the new eugenics.

The Social-Compact Model

The second broad frame, the social compact, entails a quite different understanding of the human self and the family. The issues dividing the more rooted social and historical beings of the social compact from their atomistic opposites are serious and very deep. Beings who see themselves primarily through the lens of the social compact do not find at all self-evident the primacy of rights and choice informing the atomist position. In contrast to the thin self moored in modern individualism, the compact self is "thick" and more particularly situated—a historical being who acknowledges the "variety of debts, inheritance, rightful expectations, and obligations" that "constitute the given of my life, the moral starting point."[28] Compact beings believe that cutting themselves off from the past, as required by the ultra-individualist mode, deforms their present relationships. While not totally embedded within and defined by particular ties and identities, the compact self recognizes that without that beginning there is no beginning at all.

The world of the social covenant or compact is in tension with the dominant ultra-liberal surround, and it must be supple enough to provide for rebellion and dissent from within. Tradition is not monolithic; the past is a living embodiment of vital conflicts. Rebellion against one's particular place is one way to forge an identity with reference to that place.

The compact frame, however, allows little "space" for rebellion to take the form of an identity that excises all social ties and relations as the individual "freely" chooses. The familial base of the social compact cannot be understood from the standpoint of contract theory. In the contract model the family gets bracketed or severed, and women's traditional roles and identities are, and have been, devalued. Within the social compact, by contrast, women's identities as wives, mothers, and community benefactors—and the social activities associated with these identities—are not sealed off and are less likely to be devalued.

Sociological theorist John O'Neill argues that only a new anthropology grounded in a robust and self-conscious view of social embodiment can correct the excesses of "neo-individualism and statism." He contends that "maternalism and feminism" are not at odds but rather are proper "defenses of the family against the state." In practice this means that human life is recognized as fragile and vulnerable and the human family as "the first cradle of intelligence, common sense, love, and justice."[29]

The contract model dismisses those contributions of women that have been linked to the human life cycle, to the protection and nurturance of vulnerable human existence. Women's partial contributions cannot stand, symbolically, for social regenesis as a whole. They do not get writ large on the social screen because the ontology of the contractual world projects images of extrinsically sundered selves rather than intrinsically linked beings.

Within the compact vision, on the other hand, what women do, or historically have done, can be seen—there is at least the possibility—as helping to make human society a caring society. By a caring society, I mean one that renounces a technological politics in favor of a sense of history and community; that repudiates a narrow rationalism contemptuous of the values of diverse forms of life; and that promotes a respect for nature and its limits rather than its continued despoilment.

Any ongoing way of life must have in an important segment devoted to the protection of vulnerable human existence. Historically, women have fulfilled this mission. The pity is not that women have reflected this ethic of social responsibility but that the public world of ultra-liberalism has, for the most part, either repudiated it or offered us distorted versions in welfare-state bureaucracies.[30] I am convinced that moves to detach women altogether from this compact world and its animating ethos jeopardize both feminism and family. In the past, of course, family and community have been enormously constraining and burdensome for women in particular ways. What I shall here call the modern traditional family cannot be the family of old that placed all the responsibility for nurturing on women. But before we look at this modern traditional family, I want to explore the historical roots of my image of a world governed by a social compact within which obligations and duties have great, at times overriding, force.

Visions of Community

One historical root is the Christian vision of community. Early Christians viewed the Church as an artificial kin group. Its members "were expected to project onto the new community a fair measure of the sense of solidarity, of the loyalties, and of the obligations that had previously been directed to the physical family."[31] While no final resolution of the tension between the individual and the community is ever possible, the early Church, seen symbolically as mother (*pia mater communis*), exerted a powerful influence that strengthened community. Most important, Christians radically re-defined the classical city: "It included two unaccustomed and potentially disruptive categories, the women and the poor."[32] As members of this new community, women assumed a vastly ex-panded public role—documented by the historian Peter Brown—as they visited the sick, gave alms, founded shrines and poorhouses in their own names, participated in religious ceremonials, and so on. The classical political division between citizen and non-citizen was supplanted with a model that embraced rich and poor, male and female, and made it the duty of the rich to support the poor.

From such beginnings flowed centuries of by-no-means-consis-tent institutional growth and change. The emergence of the atom-istic doctrine that I have already examined privatized the link between women and an ethic of caring, succor, and endurance. Devalued in the dominant public sphere, this ethic went underground, as it were, and persisted in submerged discourse. While the historic accretion of all those images of goodness surely bore heavily on women, and sometimes quashed them or forced them into self-abnegation,[33] the historical and symbolic link of women to notions of empathy and compassion lingered and animated generations of female activists and reformers.

Women's worlds and identities could not remain untouched by liberal individualism and the triumphant market. I suggested above a few of the problematic effects, as well as the promises, of these developments. In the face of the continuing pressure put on the traditional family, community, and female identity by individualist, rationalist presumptions, the idea of the social compact offers one locus of resistance to our technocratic, "throwaway" society; but it must make room for women's rightful claims as individuals. The social compact cannot, in our time, be composed of innocent do-gooders who sentimentalize the old ways. There can be no assent, without ambivalence, to a single scheme of things. We are all marked by the moral conflict of our age. "My body, myself" is a necessary corrective when communities overwhelm the individual and stifle the self. But that obsession with an abstract self, which is one defining feature of ultra-liberalism, meshes all too perfectly with obsessive consumerism.

As more and more areas of social life are subjected to decisions made along the lines of a narrowly construed policy science, families and the remnants of traditional communities may help preserve social relations not reducible to instrumental terms. In the world of the social compact, human beings are ends in themselves, not means. No one is in a position to arbitrarily or capriciously assign value to the human life of another, for that value is a given; it is the starting point, the foundation of things.

Do any communities approximate this vision of the social compact? Pieces of such communities exist in small-town and rural America, in working-class communities, in inner-city neighborhoods, or wherever people organize to preserve their way of life against the dissolving force of many current trends. Harry Boyce, a populist, observes:

American history and tradition, like that of any nation, embodies contradictions between rapaciously individualist, democratic, and authoritarian elements. To reclaim the best in America's traditions and history is to rediscover the popular democratic heritage: our nation's civic idealism, our practices of mutual aid and self-help, our religious wellsprings of social justice.[34]

What political theorist Sheldon Wolin calls rejectionism—a form of rebellion that defies the terms of the wider system—pervades our society. We see such rejectionism, Wolin notes, in community fights against toxic waste, in rent-control movements, in environmentalism, in civil rights, and, I would add, in grass-roots aspects of the right-to-life movement.[35] Inspired by the social compact, such movements are local, bounded, and grass-roots; they are anchored to a community, not a state, and their ethos is preserving, not acquiring. Such communities know they cannot change the society writ large. Instead, they are organized to defend and sustain what remains of a way of life not permeated by the forces of atomism, consumerism, and technological forms of control.

The Catholic Contribution

The modern social encyclicals of Leo XII, Pius XI, John XXIII, Paul VI, and John Paul II "affirm much more strongly the importance of the individual and, as [St.] Thomas never did, of his or her rights."[36] But these rights are not

spoken of primarily as individual claims against other individuals or society. They are woven into a concept of community which envisions the person as a part, a sacred part, of the whole. Rights exist within and are relative to a historical and social context and are intelligible only in terms of the obligations of individuals to other persons.[37]

This understanding of persons steers clear of the antinomies of individualism and collectivism. Catholic social thought does not offer a "third way": it does not hack off bits and pieces of the individualist and collectivist options and meld them into a palatable compromise. Rather, Catholic social thought begins from assumptions fundamentally different from those of individualism, on the one hand, and statist collectivism, on the other—assumptions that

provide for the individuality and rights of persons within a community, together with the claims of social obligation.

Pope John XXIII argues that society must be ordered for the
good of the individual and that good is achievable only in solidarity
with others, in cooperative enterprises tailored to an appropriate
human scale. This version of individuality makes possible human
unity as a cherished achievement and acts as a brake against coercive
uniformity.[38]

The U.S. bishops' pastoral message on the economy sounds a
similar note: "The dignity of the human person, realized in community with others, is the criterion against which all aspects of
economic life must be measured." All economic decisions must be
judged "in light of what they do for the poor, what they do to the
poor and what they enable the poor to do for themselves."[39]
Drawing on the principle of subsidiarity, the bishops speak of the
"need for vital contributions from different human associations";
to assign to a greater and higher association what a "lesser"
association might do disturbs the "right order" of things. In this
way institutional pluralism is guaranteed, and "space for freedom,
initiative and creativity on the part of many social agents" is made
possible.[40] David Hollenbach calls this "justice-as-participation,"
noting that the bishops' contribution to the current, deadlocked
"liberal/communitarian debate" lies in the way justice is conceptu-
alized "in terms of this link between personhood and the basic
prerequisites of social participation."[41]

Summing up subsidiarity, Joseph A. Komonchak lists its nine
basic elements: (1) the person has priority, being the origin and
purpose of society; (2) the human person is essentially social and
achieves self-realization through social relations (the principle of
solidarity); (3) social relationships and communities exist to help
individuals and the "subsidiary" function of society augments
rather than supplants self-responsibility; (4) "higher" communities
exist to perform the same subsidiary roles toward "lower" communities; (5) communities must enable and encourage individuals to
exercise their self-responsibility, and larger communities must do
the same for smaller ones; (6) communities are not to deprive
individuals and smaller communities of their rights to exercise self-

responsibility; (7) subsidiarity serves as a principle to regulate interrelations between individuals and communities, and between smaller and larger communities; (8) subsidiarity is a formal principle that can be embodied only in particular communities and circumstances; and (9) subsidiarity is a universal principle, grounded in a particular ontology of the person.[42] Subsidiarity thus favors Tocqueville's associative version of democracy at its best and works to enhance the "construction of society 'from below up.' "[43] Subsidiarity is a theory of, and for, civil society that rejects the stark alternatives of individualism and collectivism.

Family Ties

And what is the role of families? While hesitating to use the term "traditional family," I wish to convey by my reference to a modern traditional family the image of a set of human relations that exist in tension with the full sway of atomism. From the standpoint of the dominant ultra-liberal discourse, traditional families are sites of the unfree and the suppressed. Yet it is such families that gave birth to generations of female activists, reformers, and social benefactors. And it is such families that come to mind when I consider what Stanley Hauerwas has called "the moral meaning of the family."

Ideally, the family is an entity whose adult members have come together to create a mutual order. These adults acknowledge and accept the new identities that this coming-together forges, making them social beings of a particular kind. They take on a responsibility for the future, either through rearing their own children or through other generative activities that link them to past and future beings. A collection of persons who happen to be under one roof at the same time does not make this family. Within such a family the animating ethos is to nourish humanity—not to "fulfill" an insatiably pleasure-seeking self. This family is first and foremost an intergenerational institution, not first and foremost an interpersonal association.

We seem to lack a descriptive vocabulary that would aptly and richly distinguish the modern traditional family, which exists in tension with the wider surround in which it is situated, from families thoroughly suffused with contractualism and "non-binding commitments" that allow their members to remain "free." This latter family cannot transcend the point of contract. The intergenerational family must do so if it is to be true to its ethic and its purpose. The ties of the modern traditional family help to constitute us as historical beings. "Set out in the world with no family, without a story of and for the self, we will simply be captured by the reigning ideologies of the day," Hauerwas writes.[44] We do not choose our relatives—they are given; and as a result, Hauerwas continues, we know what it means to have a history.

> We do require a language to help us articulate the experience of the family and the loyalty it represents. . . . Such a language must clearly denote our character as historical beings and how our moral lives are based in particular loyalties and relations. If we are to learn to care for others, we must first learn to care for those we find ourselves joined to by accident of birth.[45]

In a transformed traditional family, women are equal partners and helpmeets, as well as necessary and respected community members. A precise parity of wage-earning power is not required for marriage partners to achieve such a balance, because this family is neither defined exclusively by economic relations nor ground down in a ceaseless struggle for power. Each person has a wide berth within a supportive communal surround for his or her activities. Dependency in the compact frame entails responsibility, not control.

The expectation that such families can be mandated, however, is faulty. One cannot gerrymander structures in a way that guarantees that Institution X or Y will pop up to perform Function Z. Institutions do not come into being like that; they are not designed by some rationalist artificer. The family I have sketched will very likely unfold if the disintegrative pressures of the wider culture, and the often sterile surround in which mothering currently takes place, are eased or made more humane. We can trust human beings to do the rest, for we are social and bonding creatures.

None of this will convince the hard-nosed power realist or the committed individualist whose suspicions are raised by the mere suggestion of anything traditional. And I have not yet even addressed the matter of social compact and abortion. Though I hope to undercut some disapproval in the rest of my argument, one point needs to be stated clearly: To anyone wedded to the image of a world dominated by force and infused by power relations that can be curbed only by counterforce, my social compact will look like the concoction of a starry-eyed optimist. I can only insist that this compact does speak to personal and political realities, as the current "gender gap" and women's reported understanding of political and social life indicate.[46] My vision of mutual respect, moreover, is not merely an abstraction. I grew up in such a family, and I have seen others struggling to create and to sustain such families. I am constantly struck by the uncommon, quiet heroism of ordinary people who trust themselves enough—and have sufficient hope— to bear and raise children under the strains that contemporary society imposes.

Family loyalty, devotion, constraint—all are unacceptable if one's model is atomism. One recalls Aldous Huxley's prescient warnings in *Brave New World* that as political and economic freedom diminishes, sexual freedom may well tend to increase. He concluded that a dictator would do well to encourage such freedom. To the extent that abortion advocates embrace this ideal of freedom, they worship at the altar of that modern idol, scientific fundamentalism: if we can do it, we should do it. This is unthinking secular fideism at its worst.

The compact order cannot readily support radical forms of individualism. Persons who believe that positioning themselves *against* the community is essential to their own identities create tensions. But ideally, this community would have sufficient elasticity to allow individual expression and rebellion, which can, after all, be creative and need not be destructive. More importantly, it would exert pressures and constraints on men and women with similar force—though women, who labor under a greater historical density and weight as communal beings, would undoubtedly be more affected. But none of this should be inflexible. One cannot and should not ignore the force of feminist concerns, nor can one undo the self and the world that liberalism has wrought—even if one wanted to, and I do not.

Abortion in a "Compact" Society

What are the implications for abortion? The social compact world cannot be an "easy" abortion society. Because it derives its moral identity from a non-contractual, non-atomistic ethos—one that repudiates instrumental rationality and technological fixes and that promises reconciliation rather than domination, mutuality rather than power politics—the order must sustain the human being at each stage of the life cycle. Abortion-on-demand, which conforms to the atomized contract world, would represent an anomaly within this world. In this world, abortion would become what many supporters of liberalized abortion claimed all along it would be—a reluctant response to a desperate situation.

If the compact community succors and forgives rather than punishes and condemns, it would have space for the woman who determined that an early-stage abortion was her only possible recourse. But abortion-on-demand through the sixth month of pregnancy would present too sharp a moral disjuncture within an order that construes its members as communal rather than consuming. Its reigning symbols are those of mutuality and fructification, rather than of technologically engineered "equality" embodied in abortion-on-demand without qualification, the ultra-liberal stance.[47]

The irony of the moment may well be that women, caught in the grip of rationalist fideism, wind up endorsing the image of freedom from nature that, historically, has invited insidious forms of domination—of women and of whole ways of life. It is a technocratic prejudice, not a liberating or democratic ideal, that we are somehow most "human" when we are in absolute control. Translated into the atomistic argument for abortion-on-demand, this dictum makes the human body, in microcosm, mirror a controlling macro-order. As that order manipulates nature, the body controls human nature. What this controlling body-self fails to see is that she, too, is controlled by her own putative "power." With reference to the wider social body, she becomes self-policing, while that order can appear to sustain liberationist imperatives and to be responding to radical demands.[48] But as long as these demands are to free the self from all the old shackles and to gain control over all areas of human existence, the social order is confirmed in its deepest structure.

The covenant or compact frame puts pressure on this language of control by nourishing a vision of commonalities and attempting to realize some ideal of a shared human good. Abortion is not disallowed, but it is "problematized." Pro-abortion arguments must occupy the same linguistic terrain as other, partially countervailing convictions. As a result, the easy, ultra-liberal abortion arguments of the social-contract frame are chastened, even as the absolutist claims that give no weight to individual choice are called into question. Clearly, though, the compact image does give great weight to the moral status of the fetus, as well as to the adult woman, and does insist that a social network be brought into play in making abortion decisions.

Some might argue that my social-compact ideal is too good to be true. But that is part of the point of an ideal of any sort: it sets up a standard toward which an individual or a whole people may strive. I am not persuaded by suggestions that we must wait for the full victory of a "socialist" or "feminist" morality before we can begin to think in more social and interconnected ways; that we cannot "transcend . . . the more individualist elements of feminist thinking" until we get the right historic conditions.[49]

To continue to act and to think—whether about abortion or any other matter of deep importance and moral concern—wholly within the language of control, atomism, individualism, and so on derails even the possibility that we might attain a more egalitarian future. We cannot use the excuse of not yet living in the new world to sever men from any say whatever in the fate of their unborn children, and then presume that they will, in the future, be transformed into beings with some involvement. Current presumptions widen a gulf between present and future until it becomes unbridgeable—unless one clings to an implicit teleological faith.[50] Indeed, we had best tend to many present danger signals if we mean to keep alive some alternative to atomism. It is to these alternatives that I now turn.

MORAL AND POLITICAL DANGERS

I shall be both mordant and brief. My intent is to alert us to those clear and present dangers embedded in the technocratic, utilitarian faith. This ethic holds that nothing is of intrinsic value; hence, there are no intractable barriers to social engineering and experimentation. Individuals and society do not embody "good in themselves"; instead, good becomes a calculation of aggregate consequences. In our time the toting up of social "good" or "bad" is largely determined by cost-effectiveness and efficiency. One can find many examples.

First, the same ethic underpinning those pro-abortion arguments that stress "wants" and measure the differential "value" of lives (presuming that one being can confer "value" on another) can also be used to justify claims for making all moral adjudications along cost-benefit lines. Some children's lives become more valuable, others more expendable. How readily one can envisage state-financed systems, established under the cover of such utilitarian formulas, that mandate amniocentesis, genetic screening, subsequent compulsory abortion, and so on. Fortunately, many feminists who favor even the extreme liberal position on abortion also oppose such possible compulsions in the name of freedom.

The technocratic worldview also buttresses human arrogance regarding the possibility of being able to produce the perfect child. All less-than-perfect models, as revealed through a panoply of tests, could be aborted. Parent-child relations would suffer, of course, if the perfect child turned out to be less than perfect. More important, our human capacity for risk-taking, spontaneity, and welcoming would be very much jeopardized. The new reproductive technologies, coupled with our throwaway ethos, reinforce our yearnings for absolute certainty and 100 per cent control.

In former times, when deliberate choice and rational control ranged over only so much of human existence, and when contingency and the unexpected played themselves out in other areas, our demands for order and our hubris were bounded and chastened. That is less and less true. My concern is not just with what will happen to families as this technocratic ethos spirals onward and upward but with what will happen to democratic politics. Given current cravings for order and control, as well as the technocratic world's apparent capacity to satisfy these cravings in ways that feed rather than sate the hunger, will our compulsion to control shift to the wider public sphere? Democracy is a chancy, unpredictable enterprise. Our patience with its ups and downs, its debates and compromises, indeed its very anti-authoritarianism, may wane as we become inured to more and more control—all in the name of freedom.

More sophisticated control over reproduction opens the door to a third danger. Foreknowledge of the sex of the fetus combined with the right to abort could lead to a future in which the natural balance of females to males will be undermined as more and more couples, in a society that remains male-dominated, choose male offspring. An article in the *Boston Globe* of July 20, 1982, reported the results of a nation-wide poll done by the Princeton University Office of Population Research. Asked what the sex of their firstborn would be if they were able to choose, 45 per cent of the respondents said male and 20 per cent female. All the respondents were women.[51] These figures continue to hold.

The New Eugenics

The fourth danger is simply stated in one word: eugenics. This is a covert concern in much of the abortion debate, pro and con. We appear to be moving in this direction as more and more of the "imperfect" unborn and newborn are destroyed, the most dramatic example being the increased number of Down's-syndrome babies who die lingering deaths when nourishment is withheld. A much celebrated "success" was signaled by the following *New York Times* headline a few years back: "Twin Found Defective in Womb Reported Destroyed in Operation." The case, the "first successful surgery of this kind in the country," risked the lives of twin fetuses in order to kill a defective one while it remained in the womb. Matter-of-factly, the *Times* reported, "The abnormal fetus was killed by withdrawing about half its blood through a hollow needle inserted in its heart, which then stopped beating."[52] This once startling procedure—"fetal reduction"—is now routine. Even if we refuse, as I do not, to extend our understanding of community to include the developmentally disabled, why should we assume that the targets of eugenics efforts—state-sponsored as well as private—will remain "only" the defective? How liberally will we begin to define "defect"?[53]

By intervening in, and disrupting, what might be called the "natural lottery"—the fact that no human being can control whether he or she is white or black, male or female, Down's-syndrome victim or musical prodigy—we undermine the basis of human equality. Human equality rests on the fragile insistence that there is about each and every human being an ontological givenness that he or she did not create and over which no society has control. Sustaining such equality requires acceptance and welcoming of life in all its variety.

Once we claim we do in fact have such control—that we can insure more males and fewer females; that we can prevent the appearance of the Down's-syndrome child and maybe, in the braver new world to come, manipulate genes to get the musical prodigy—we pave the way for a nightmarish biological totalitarianism. For at that sorry point, some among us will have been selected for a top ontological priority. Some will be ontologically inferior, having been lower on the preference list. Others will be disallowed life altogether, and should "their sort" sneak through, there will be no moral basis to insist on their decent treatment. If the controls had been working right, after all, they would not be here in the first place.

It is important to note that the dominant media have signed on with the new eugenics. The *Wall Street Journal*, for example, extolled the Human Genome Project, a piece of extraordinary scientific hubris aimed at mapping the human race genetically, by claiming that those fretting about the ethical implications were dour reactionaries "who are fearful of or hostile to the future."[54] The Office of Technology Assessment of the U.S. Congress dispenses neatly with ethical considerations raised by the Genome Project in these words: "Human mating that proceeds without the use of genetic data about the risks of transmitting diseases will produce greater mortality and medical costs than if carriers of potentially deleterious genes are alerted to their status and encouraged to mate with noncarriers or to use artificial insemination or other reproductive strategies."[55]

Euthanasia bears a close relationship to the eugenics effort, for it aims to "rationalize" our approach to the old and dying and sever it from intergenerational ideals. The elderly, like the unborn and the disabled, are to be treated one way or another depending on the "social costs" involved. To these concerns one must add those of blacks and other minorities in the matter of abortion and birth-control policy. Such fears arise from historical practice and from proposals "floated" from time to time concerning mandated abortion, sterilization, and so on.[56] One black writer has claimed that Planned Parenthood's policies have been those of upper-middle-class whites, who often express "a fetish about controlling the reproductive capacities of others, those who are poor and black."[57] The feminist argument for "reproductive freedom," construed as the absolute right to abort as well as freedom from coerced or enforced abortion or sterilization, does not seem a sufficiently reliable brake should our social ethos move further in the atomistic direction.

On the Slippery Slope

How powerless our words seem as we confront great social forces and tendencies. Nevertheless, if I am correct in saying that our language of self-description, understanding, and moral evaluation does help to shape those social forces and tendencies, it is important to articulate some possible *via media* between atomism and control, on the one hand, and some long-gone communal past, on the other.

More and more prevalent, it seems, is the view that human suffering is bad and can never be a source of strength or a lesson in grace. It follows that suffering should be prevented at all costs. Families should not suffer, so retarded children must be allowed to die. The handicapped suffer, so they should not be allowed to live. Old people suffer, so we should find ways to kill them humanely. There is also "wrongful life": those who should never have been born should not be forced to live; they have "the right to die." And if one's birth was wrongful, that right is exercised by others on one's behalf. The possibilities in this direction are limited only by our capacity to conjure up yet more problems that can be solved by eliminating people or by not allowing them to be born.

Should a politics of technological control and an ethos of consequentialism grow apace, as I fear they will, what might be the results for the family and the wider society? Minimally, as some have already noted, there will be an erosion of the ethic of stewardship, care, and trust—an ethic that respects the richness, the diversity, and the intrinsic value of life and that sees the person primarily as a caretaker rather than an aggrandizer. Our acquiescence to each new restriction of the concept of humanity numbs our moral sensibilities. Such restrictions never enhance "a respect for human life"; they always threaten to erode that respect. They did not, Philip Abbott proclaims, "enhance the rights of slaves, prisoners of war, criminals, traitors, women, children, Jews, blacks, heretics, workers, capitalists, Slavs, Gypsies."[58]

When we concurred, as a society, in almost fully redefining fetal life so as to place it altogether outside the bounds of moral consideration, we suffered a deep if subtle moral corruption. Daniel Berrigan writes of "the mystery of the silence of the unborn." Dr. Seuss concludes that "after all, a person's a person, no matter how small." I think of others once hidden from view so that we were not required to see them. We seem more and more incapable of truly seeing what we are doing. By acting unthinkingly, by simply accepting the dominant terms of discourse of our age, we may one day tip the balance toward a society whose reigning symbols are violence, death, and expendability. "Life is cheap in Casablanca," says Sidney Greenstreet to Humphrey Bogart. Life is getting cheaper in the United States of America.

Note: The author is grateful to Richard Hatchett for drawing her attention to several helpful sources. She dedicates this essay to her daughter Sheri, who says she herself "thinks different."

Responses

1. JAMES T. BURTCHAELL, C.S.C.

Jean Bethke Elshtain has written a modest proposal—a "mordant" one, as she calls it—addressed primarily to feminist pro-choice advocates in the abortion debate. She identifies the ideology beneath pro-choice doctrine as a devolution of classical liberalism: absolutizing individual wants allows those in power to confer on the vulnerable only such rights as it pleases them to give. Elshtain commends instead personal and social relations that make moral realities and obligations matters for discernment and deference rather than of decision and domination. In such a community, fundamental moral claims arise from bonds of kinship rather than from autonomous concessions made by us to strangers. A morality of binding solidarity is more life-giving than a morality of wary individualism.

As one already unpersuaded that the unborn ought be exposed to their mothers' preference to destroy them, I find that Elshtain's mordant moral proposal has a sharp bite to it. It is, however, her desired outcome that most invites our scrutiny. If women were to accept her account and feel themselves as sufficiently bound by consanguinity and fellowship to accept their unborn offspring—if, in a word, a pregnant woman did not face a *decision* of whether to welcome or to extirpate her fetus but instead a *duty* to accept that she is already a mother and must foster the child whose life depends uniquely upon her—then what result does Elshtain foresee? Abortion would become "problematic," not unquestioned. It would be an "anomaly," not a typical outcome. It would become "a reluctant response to a desperate situation." Abortion would be allowed and not condemned, but not in just any circumstance. There would, for instance, be fewer late abortions for the convenience of the mother.

James T. Burtchaell, C.S.C., is a professor of theology at the University of Notre Dame.

This is what Elshtain aspires to with "starry-eyed optimism." It is not clear, however, what change it would represent. It hardly seems to describe a society that has undergone a moral conversion forceful enough to transform its members from capricious, consuming individualists to communal philanthropists who exhibit "caring, succor, and endurance." For a mordant proposal, one would have to say that its desired yield is mighty modest, so modest that it is not significantly different from what we already behold.

Still, I will take what is offered here, or what is hoped for, concerning abortion provided that it is extended to child abuse, wife-battering, and enforced labor. These too, while not disallowed, would then find acceptance provided they were reluctant and untypical responses to desperate situations.

But the feminist pro-choice movement has never defended these actions. What do they possibly have in common with abortion? I will remind you. By their own testimony, mothers, fathers, and live-in boyfriends who bash, burn, and choke their infants are women and men with disordered lives whose children have failed to satisfy their hopes. They are desperate people at the end of their tether. Men who beat their wives are, by all professional accounts, driven by the mad indiscipline of their own impulsive lives to inflict injury that they themselves deplore. Employers who crowd sweat-shops or fields with undocumented aliens or long-unemployed parents with children to feed—and deny them hygiene, health care, social security, workmen's compensation, a living wage, and the possibility of collective bargaining—operate at the margin of the economy where their tenuous fingerhold drives them, reluctantly but desperately, to sacrifice those subject to their power to insure their own survival.

These stories are pages from the same book that tells the sad tale of contemporary American abortions. In each of these sad acts of violence, a threatened, incoherent, unresourceful loser makes a troubled, desperate decision to pass on his or her grief to an even more vulnerable human being. For all of them, passing on violence is what, to accept Elshtain's account of the aborting mother, seems to be the "only possible recourse." If abortion is allowed not at will but only in some specified conditions, then child abuse, wife-battering, and the exploitation of laborers should be as easily tolerated: not on demand, but as a last recourse.

I am, of course, suggesting that the new moral perspective proposed here is mortally compromised. Elshtain says more than once that abortion-on-demand through the sixth month of gestation is unacceptable—indeed, perhaps not allowable. If this reference is intended to characterize the present legal situation, then it is in error, since the *Wade* and *Bolton* decisions of 1973 authorize abortion-on-demand up to the moment of birth. But Elshtain may be making a moral rather than legal point. Her proposal suggests that late-stage abortions "would present too sharp a moral disjuncture," whereas the abortion of a younger child could be abided.

For Christians in America today, the most radical moral disjuncture between their convictions and the proclivities of this brawny country's moral order stems from the Christian belief that the frailest and least self-sufficient should have greater claim to our vigilance than do those more equipped to fend for themselves. I would have thought that the more one human being lies within the power of another, the more morally imperative it would be that the powerful party act to safeguard the survival of the weak one rather than to follow his or her own preferences.

In the suggestion that the youngest of our children are the most expendable, I hear terrifying echoes. I hear echoes of the call to close our borders to helpless boat people fleeing from chaos and violence. I hear echoes of the advice that it would be merciful to send off the elderly when they can no longer feed themselves or relish life as well as we do. I hear echoes of the disdain for whatever substandard people we are bombing this year, because the earth cannot abide the way they bully their neighbors. How am I, trying to be a Christian—and committed to the belief that there is no human being on this earth who is not my brother or sister (a belief as burdensome to us as it was to the prophet Jonah) and forbidden to gainsay this teaching by excluding the weak or the handicapped or the unwanted or the burdensome or the enemy—to take the idea that, in a new spirit of unselfish solidarity, only the most vulnerable and voiceless will continue to be eliminated, albeit reluctantly?

The Elshtain proposal lacks the force of its own convictions. A woman who considers her child as a possession to be accepted for

her own satisfaction can have no serious obstacle within her conscience to abortion-on-demand (nor to perfection-on-demand). For
such a woman to be moved by the Elshtain appeal to consider her
child as entitled to her devotion, she would have to experience a
conversion of conscience that obligated her to rearrange her own
preferences on behalf of her child's needs. What Elshtain wishes to
propose is a moral conversion, but she seems unready to believe
that it might succeed and portrays instead an outcome whereby
consciences would be disturbed but not transformed. That does
not take the ruthlessness from our hearts; it merely makes the
ruthlessness more troubled. And much savagery in this world is
excused by people whose only moral claim is that they are unsettled
by what they do.

2. MARY ANN GLENDON

Jean Bethke Elshtain's paper on abortion and moral conflict in
America puts me in mind of George Santayana's description of
Catholicism as a religion that, having taken shape amid the ruins of
a dying empire, was "full of large disillusions about this world and
minute illusions about the other."[1] James Burtchaell's comments on
the paper are addressed mainly to Elshtain's "minute illusions"
about what might be done to ameliorate the dismal state of affairs
she describes. Mine are primarily concerned with her somber
diagnosis.

I am in such complete sympathy with Elshtain's observations and
general approach that I can do little but embroider the edges of the
design she has created. I will throw out a few more ideas for further
reflection along the three lines she has suggested: the role of
language, the frameworks for most discussion on abortion and the
family, and the "clear and present dangers" that Elshtain associates
with certain linguistic practices and habits of mind.

Elshtain has made an impressive argument that in America public

Mary Ann Glendon is a professor of law at Harvard Law School. Her
most recent book is *Rights Talk: The Impoverishment of Political Discourse.*

deliberation about abortion and the family is profoundly but silently affected by several unconscious or unarticulated assumptions about human beings and society. Her description of how language has been deployed in the abortion debate to dehumanize the unborn child and to deprive the act of abortion of any moral quality reminded me of a similar process that seems to be at work in recent debates about the family. The "culture struggle" currently being waged in the United States includes what Brigitte and Peter Berger have called "the war over the family"—"a vociferous debate over the history, the present condition, the prospects and, most important, the human and societal value of the family."[2] In the political arena, one might say this war is mainly an air war, with gas as the weapon of choice on both sides. It is not laughing gas, but it's not lethal gas either. On the legal front, however, the conflict is more serious. There is intense ground fighting, with considerable territory at stake.

What is being contested in various legal skirmishes about zoning, adoption, succession to rent-controlled tenancies, and so on is the very definition of the family. The strategy of the cultural left moves along two lines. The first seeks to abolish the term "family" altogether. One must either say "families" to emphasize the variety and equal moral status of family forms, or, better yet, emulate the Swedes and the Danes by treating the individual, for all legal purposes, as the basic social unit. A second strategy is required, however, to deal with the fact that legislatures still perversely attach a number of benefits and privileges to family status. Here, a favored technique is to expand the term "family" to include so many different types of relationships that the word loses all meaning. These linguistic initiatives have made progress: last year the Supreme Court of New Jersey held that ten male college students, sharing a house under a four-month renewable lease, constituted a family for purposes of their community's single-family zoning laws.[3]

One might be inclined to dismiss these squabbles over naming things as trivial were it not for their overall effect. The campaign of the cultural left means to have parenthood and dedication to child-rearing treated as just one more "lifestyle" about which the state ought to remain "neutral." What needs to be made clear in these disputes—and this can be done without belittling anyone—is that our society does not have to apologize for its special concern about the nurture and education of future citizens.

To supplement Elshtain's observations about the intellectual frameworks that underlie much American political deliberation, I will mention just briefly another connection between what she calls the "ultra-liberal" case for abortion rights and the positions often taken by the cultural left on the family. In both cases, extraordinary emphasis is placed on the centrality of sexual freedom to individual self-realization. Elshtain does well to remind us of Aldous Huxley's warning that sexual freedom may actually increase in inverse proportion to political and economic freedom.

Think of the development of the concept of privacy in constitutional law. In a country like the United States, with a strong tradition of protecting individual liberty, one might have expected that, as governments and corporations began to acquire the ability to collect, store, correlate, and exchange vast amounts of data concerning individuals, the privacy idea would become a legal bulwark against these unprecedented means of invading, manipulating, and controlling personal life. Yet we Americans receive remarkably little legal protection from governmental, journalistic, and corporate prying.[4] At the same time much solicitude is accorded, in the name of privacy, to our sexual practices. What vision of the human person and what vision of the polity can it be that informs Justice Blackmun's statement in his dissenting opinion in *Bowers* v. *Hardwick* that the "heart"—the very heart—"of the constitution's protection of privacy is the right of an individual to conduct sexual relationships in the intimacy of his own home"?[5] Elshtain rightly points out that it does not augur well for the future of the American democratic experiment if unlimited polymorphic sexuality is to be our consolation prize for the loss of liberty in other areas.

Finally, let me turn briefly to Elshtain's warnings concerning the dangers we now face when we frame institutions, laws, and policies on the basis of assumptions that human beings are best understood as autonomous, self-seeking individuals; that relations between them are naturally competitive; and that political association is founded on contract for the sake of self-preservation. Her chilling admonitions about what effects such a "technocratic, utilitarian faith" may have on abortion policy are not at all far-fetched.

Recently, the idea of aborting the less-than-perfect child has made alarming gains in legislation and has been lent what some will consider intellectual respectability by the current incumbent of a chair in jurisprudence at Oxford University, Ronald Dworkin. A 1991 Maryland statute provides, astonishingly, that an unborn child may be aborted even after viability if it is found to possess a serious defect.[6] This means presumably that the life of a child with Down's syndrome may be terminated at any time right up to birth, provided only that a doctor can be found to do the deed. Dworkin, in his 1990 Holmes lecture at Harvard Law School, seemingly gave his approval to such procedures. In a lecture curiously titled "The Sanctity of Life," Dworkin stated his view that there are some circumstances where abortion is not only permitted but morally demanded.[7] These circumstances are, he said, those where there is strong evidence that the fetus is "seriously physically deformed"—as where the mother has taken thalidomide—or where evidence suggests that the fetus would have a "stunted, frustrating, incapacitated, and perhaps very short life." Dworkin twice insisted that, in his view, it would be morally wrong to bring such a life into the world. Even among Dworkin's predominantly pro-choice audience, some were shocked at what seemed to be his essentially aesthetic criterion for determining what life is worthy to live—especially those old enough to remember National Socialism.[8]

The irony is that all that ultra-liberals profess to hold dear—their particular understandings of liberty, equality, privacy, and technological progress—rests on the invisible support of certain social understandings, chief among which is respect for the dignity and worth of each and every human being. To Elshtain's list of differences between "social contractors" and "social compactors," I would add the apparent inability of the former to grapple with the question of where those qualities upon which their enterprise so heavily depends are supposed to come from. What is it that makes people willing to view others as valuable in themselves, as entitled to respect and concern? This inability to take the long view, to discern the cultural foundations of the habits and practices that are indispensable to the maintenance of any meaningful form of liberty, entails serious consequences.

The differences in basic assumptions to which Elshtain points are not merely of interest to philosophers and political theorists. For if we frame institutions, laws, and policies as though human beings were a certain way, we may look around someday and find ourselves surrounded by human beings as we have imagined them to be.

7

The Lay Vocation:
At the Altar in the World

CHRISTA R. KLEIN

THE 1970s Italian movie *The Garden of the Finzi-Contini* leaves
the indelible memory of two Jewish families whose lives are
increasingly circumscribed and finally destroyed by the racial laws
of fascism. This modern parable evokes one dilemma the "world"
poses whenever Christians seek to define life beyond the communion rail. Does the so-called public sphere or the private sphere
define reality? Vittorio DeSica's film does not equivocate: the
primary purpose of the political order is to sustain and encourage
families in caring for one another, pursuing their daily work,
celebrating holy days, and building their future through love and
friendship.

The moral of DeSica's tale also goes one step further. The
boundaries between the private and public worlds are far more fluid
than the difference between business suits and tennis attire, or
between Ferrara's public streets and the Finzi-Contini garden,
would lead us to believe. "All of Italy has a family," cries young
Giorgio to the apologetic university library administrator who has
just evicted him and who claims that he must enforce the state's law

Christa R. Klein, an American church historian, is an independent
scholar and consultant. She is a program consultant to the Lilly Endow-
ment and a research affiliate with Yale University's Program on Non-Profit
Organizations.

197

if he is to provide for his family. The complicity of families contributed to the corruption of the Italian political order, which in turn crushed Jewish families and tainted Christian ones. Not only is the separation of public and private spheres an illusion—it is an evil because it contributes to the undoing of both.

"Fragmentation," the conventional term for human disconnect-edness in the modern West, in effect becomes a belief system that helps spawn the very phenomenon it describes. In response to this interpretation of reality, the Christian vocation must try to unify without oversimplifying the variety in human experience. The God who has created and redeemed us provides a wholeness that transcends any fragmentation we may experience. Christians should live, therefore, as if all aspects of life are interconnected and as if their own lives have integrity.

This truth is conveyed by the best in Christian social teaching, and it certainly permeates Pope Leo XIII's *Rerum Novarum*. The encyclical's affirmation of private ownership, for example, empha-sizes that the "power of disposal" belongs not simply to the individual but to the individual with responsibility for the family. And the family "has at least equal rights with the State in the choice and pursuit of the things needful to its preservation and its just liberty." The encyclical goes on to argue on behalf of labor unions and, by extension, other voluntary associations: "If the citizens, if the families, on entering into association and fellowship, were to experience hindrance in a commonwealth instead of help, and were to find their rights attacked instead of being upheld, society would rightly be the object of detestation rather than of desire."[1]

Beneath all the papal letter's implications for the behavior of workers and capitalists lies a fundamental assumption: traditional Christian resources for interpreting the social order should inform the lives of Christians, can be understood by others, and provide norms for sustaining a more humane society. The centenary of *Rerum Novarum* recalls these resources, the same ones evoked a decade ago when Alasdair MacIntyre insisted that our individual lives are intelligible only when seen as embedded in various inter-secting historical narratives. Those narratives give moral meaning to our identity and describe our accountability within our historical circumstances. MacIntyre's reminder of the narrative sources of personal integrity provides an important key to exploring the meaning of lay vocation.[2] But first we must consider how a Christian understanding of the unity of life and the integrity of the individual becomes established among the Christians themselves.

The Making of the Laity

Social teachings, to be teachings, depend on far more than the structure of their argument or the intent of the teaching authority. They require a receptive audience, a gathered people who can hear and be enlightened by the teaching. Christian social teaching presumes a great deal: it presumes the vocation of the laity.

One must begin, therefore, with laicization, the making of God's peculiar people. Technically, "laicization" refers to the return of a priest to the laity, but I'm appropriating the term to emphasize that the laity must be *turned into* the laity. Orthodox Christianity understands baptism as the way natural-born creatures first enter this peoplehood. Such a view is itself, of course, a post-baptismal perception that recognizes the whole created order and all creatures in it as God's. Our redemption in baptism brings our personal history into the history of God's saving acts and, most particularly, into the triumph of Jesus of Nazareth over sin, death, and the devil. Thus incorporated, our stories become more than accounts of single, genetically determined human beings who are culturally defined by family heritage and all the historical experiences, insights, and parochialisms of gender, ethnicity, class, geography, and nationality.

How do we come to understand what it means to belong to a new people? Only in time and only partially. Because God himself is its final author, our own narration must necessarily be limited by our finitude and sin. We must even concede that our salvation depends on grace rather than on our comprehending our vocation. Infancy, senility, insanity, psychological disability, retardation, and other incapacities are not conditions that deprive the reborn of grace.

To live as part of this people, those of us with able bodies and discerning minds must identify ourselves with the biblical narrative of Israel, Jesus, and the Church. God has already completed that identification. Over time we must be enlightened viscerally by the Holy Spirit through Word and sacrament. The liturgy consistently exposes us to God's larger narrative as well as to the meaning of our own. Year after year, through repentance and absolution, the lectionary, preaching, reception of the sacrament, and hymnody, the risen Christ comes to us and claims us. Within the framework of the liturgy, we come to see and understand our lives—some days more clearly than others—as belonging to a communion of saints that extends across space and to times past, present, and future.

The call to be God's people comes from the Holy Spirit, "who calls, gathers, enlightens, and sanctifies," as Martin Luther explained in discussing the third article of the Apostles' Creed. To speak of the laity as having a vocation, then, is virtually a tautology: to be the people is to have the call; to have the call is to be the people. Knowing and living the implications of that vocation becomes the narrative of the Christian's life and includes a daily dying to sin and rising with Christ, a path marked by the liturgy.

Sustaining the Laity

My emphasis on the nature of peoplehood is a Lutheran's reaction to much contemporary "theology of the laity" that measures the laity's worth according to its commitment to particular behaviors and reforms. Historically, many attempts by ecclesial bodies and revival movements to define the Christian life have been plagued by legalisms, rationalizations, and indifference to consequences. Yet, even when such efforts are proven wise and just, they do not by themselves provide the basis for Christian life. In fact, as Mark Noll has noted in a book that describes American Protestantism's nineteenth-century reforming movements and their secular extensions in the late twentieth century, such efforts are riddled with ultraism, perfectionism, and utopianism—evidence of a failure to reckon with sin and the interconnections of human reality.[3]

Noll's forceful argument poses a challenge that goes beyond the evangelical Protestant community. The singular weakness of this reforming tradition, Noll claims, arises from the great personalism of the Puritan strain of American Christianity that moves in "a straight line from personal belief to social reform, from private experience to political activity." According to this understanding of the lay vocation, Christians are "to work out their salvation, and the salvation of everyone else, through the restructuring of public life." For Noll, "a theory of government transcending the values guiding the self" is needed to counteract this view. He notes that theologically Catholics, like Lutherans, have such resources—they acknowledge that God exercises his sovereignty through different instrumentalities in the Church and the public sphere—but they squander their riches. American Catholics have tended to follow the reformed model while, in the past at least, Lutherans have tended toward political quietism.[4] But now Lutherans, too, are rapidly appropriating the secularized version of the reformed model.

Pushing Noll's critique yet further, I would argue that the individualism of American revivalism and social reform has evolved not only at the expense of a corporate sense of the social order, which includes a corporate sense of the family's role. It has also evolved at the expense of a corporate sense of the Church and of salvation. When the laity is identified as a potential political lobby, or even as politically correct leaven, its call to peoplehood by God is demeaned. Such characterizations of the laity are neither defining nor constituitive. What is defining or essential is baptism. Through baptism we are introduced to the realities of our vocation—to both the creaturehood and the sinfulness of the people, the otherness and the allness of God, and the historical difference made by Christ Jesus. That difference restores us to the interconnections of the new creation, freeing us to work within the old creation in all spheres of human life through continual repentance.

Such a sense of peoplehood can be sustained only through corporate worship. Only there are we forced to feed on the Word with others whom we have not chosen and whom we cannot control. Only there—and by extension in our private and family devotions—are we able to glimpse the oneness of the Church, the interconnections of reality, and the sources of our own integrity. That glimpse, however limited in the neighborhood congregation, is advanced by the memory of the saints who have gone before us. Members of a worshiping community who are continually confronted by the Word will be led to bear one another's burdens in love and, charged with a vision of the new creation, inspired to work with hope amid the brokenness all around them. The clergy are the stewards of the Word that calls the laity into being and nourishes it for life in the broken world.

The liturgy invites us to deepen our understanding of the Christian tradition by studying the Scriptures and Christian doctrine, history, music, and art. The hunger for such study and reflection continues to surprise the clergy and to place demands on them that they are not always prepared or able to meet. This appetite for solid preaching and teaching, probably always prevalent among the laity, has intensified in an age in which it is harder to see things whole and to maintain personal integrity.

Study of the biblical narrative is essential to the vocation of the laity. That narrative proclaims, above all, that God is a God of history. Those who are his people know that telling their story in their time is telling the truth. From our forebears in the Old Testament, we know that the call to peoplehood entails excruciating accountability. In Israel's story we witness incredible faith and scandalous faithlessness. God sends prophets to address the rebellious, to remind them of their identity, and to call for repentance. After Israel's identity is forged through repeated repentance, God continues to rescue and discipline her. The history of the Church is more of the same—a story of faith and unfaith and of the continual call to repentance.[5]

The Laity Within the Wider World

The laicizing of the reborn, the declaring and shaping of them as a people, is the primary work of the Church. But how shall this people live among other peoples? Through the practices of truth-telling and repentance that mark its history, the Church helps to shape this response to others. This generalization fits all known times, but what about these particular times? What truths need to be told today to elicit repentance and reformation?

Catholic and other Christian social teachings enlighten the laity's life among other peoples by acknowledging the provisional structure of all societies in the old creation. They argue for the interconnection of all human activity and for the integrity of human practice. The isolating and individualizing tendencies of contemporary life pose the greatest temptations to the laity. We live in a culture that has settled on a naïve notion of human agency. On every front we are tempted to deny the accountability implicit in our own narratives. Most of all we are tempted, like the bigamist, to keep more than one narrative going, as if our experiences were unrelated and we had no one to answer to but ourselves and our own sense of personal comfort. We are encouraged in our self-deceptions by institutions and practices that are conducted as if they had no prior history nor any responsibility for their connection to the whole of human society.

As we follow our lay vocation in family, work, and voluntary association, we are tormented by the disconnections and discontinuities that now seem to be acceptable practice—the jettisoning of spouses and unborn children, the abandonment of family and the aging, the callous dismissal of our communities' underclasses and unemployed. A false belief in the autonomy of persons underlies these tendencies, as do the increasing number of choices that are now technically possible and socially acceptable. We are also confronted with practices outside the realm of historical experience or even developed ethical reflection. Because the number of choices appears to increase with each passing decade of the twentieth century, moreover, the divisions between the generations seem to be growing.

For the laity these conditions require fortitude, strength of character, and a capacity to unite with others in the exercise of virtue that defies isolation. To challenge and fracture our isolation, we must converse with others, examining the narratives of our own lives in connection with theirs. Thus engaged, we must tell the truth about our human gifts, limitations, and sinfulness. Truth-telling restores vitality to our moral lives and, for Christians, is always modeled on the biblical story of people, God, and God's law. These rudimentary conversations have tremendous formative power and undergird our participation in all spheres of life, including the political.

Sharing this quest for truth enables us to build the resolve that becomes courage and to develop the wisdom that makes us just. At the same time, we are preparing to repent for our shortsightedness and complicity. When our conversation partners are others in the family of the laity, we can be especially open about acknowledging this latter means of renewing integrity.

Church teaching, which also arises out of conversation, should promote and enrich these moral conversations. The best teachings make the tradition accessible, clarifying particular problems and practices. Catholic social teaching includes a form of argumentation that can be especially helpful: it moves from the certainties known in the biblical witness, and the Church's experience with that witness, to the more provisional reading of changing circumstances. And it does so while encouraging responsibility and reminding us of our capacity for both creativity and sin.

All too often in recent years, many American denominations have squandered their tradition, primarily by interpreting the condition of isolation and moral confusion as quietism. They have sought to rouse people without fostering conversation. Their remedies amount to cooperative activism, often promoted by a social statement on a particular social ailment. Such responses tend to be short-lived because they avoid arguments over ends and what constitutes the common good. Individuals are left either angry that their views have not been affirmed or jubilant that the Church is on their side. But their isolation continues. There is no common quest for truth and no renewal of moral life. Moreover, the rest of society yawns because the Church is offering nothing different from what other institutions in society are offering.

This squandering of tradition also occurs when, even in the good name of what James Gustafson has called "moral deliberation," all viewpoints receive equal weight without the expectation that participants will know and value the tradition over which they argue. To be a faithful member of a religious community, one must continually debate the meaning of that community's tradition and practice. But one must also recognize that his or her own life becomes more, not less, intelligible within the larger and longer history of the tradition.[6]

Some Opportunities for Social Teaching

By focusing on the settings in which we live and work rather than on particular political issues, churches could help shape the narratives of the laity and influence the social order. I repeat one of the morals from *The Garden of the Finzi-Contini*: the purpose of the political order is to enable the vocations of private citizens in family, work, friendship, and religious community to flower.

Looking to the future of moral conversation and social teaching, I would like to look briefly at three instances of conversations in which social settings desperately in need of attention have begun to take precedence over social issues. (1) Within the sphere of family life, *twelve-step programs* constitute an increasingly powerful movement. (2) Within the world of corporate business, *theories of leadership* are expanding the concept of responsibility. (3) Finally, among the dramatically increasing number of voluntary associations, the moral role of a legal necessity, *the board of trustees*, is attracting growing interest.

In each of these spheres of human experience, roles are being examined and practices are being proposed for the exercise of virtue. If the American churches were to join these conversations, they could offer needed resources and insights. In each, the laity is already well represented and principles drawn from the Christian tradition are influencing discourse. Nevertheless, the Church's truth-telling about human gifts, limitations, and sinfulness could serve to push these conversations to deeper levels. It could further strengthen the laity's resolve and humanize structures within the social order. By becoming engaged in these movements, the churches would be returning to a place that has been held for them by courageous lay people living out their vocation.

The Family and the Twelve-Step Movement

By the late 1980s the twelve-step movement had emerged as the major source of therapy for people seeking to overcome addictive behaviors. Begun fifty years ago with Alcoholics Anonymous, this movement has spread and established groups for many other troubled individuals and for family members who themselves have become addicted to the experience of crisis and abuse. It has paralleled, benefited from, and informed the emerging field of family-systems research and therapy. Yet, even more than family therapy, twelve-step programs represent a frontal assault on the well-entrenched tradition of Freudian psychoanalysis. People who join twelve-step groups are treated not as autonomous individuals but as family members who must face the relational aspects of addiction. Healing comes not from a private reassessment of a victim's past griefs but from hearing and speaking, at weekly public meetings of the anonymous, about the daily struggle to be truthful and live with integrity.

Anyone who has read the twelve steps cannot fail to recognize their Christian roots. The confession of powerlessness and of faith in a higher power, the call to conversion and the commitment to taking moral inventory, the prayer for forgiveness and healing, the resolve to make amends to those who have been hurt, the pursuit of continuing spiritual renewal, and the promise to share the message with others are all reminiscent of Anglo-American revivalism. The influence of the Oxford Movement, later called Moral Rearmament, has been documented. The meetings are often housed in church basements, moreover, and participants are frequently Christians or former Christians, some of whom bear scars because their own pastors participated in the deception that fueled ongoing abuse.

The efficacy of twelve-step meetings is well known, but the program has had at least one unfortunate side effect. The language of addiction and recovery increasingly is being used as a substitute, rather than as a crude analogy, for sin and grace and as a means of defining all social ills. While more sophisticated—and therefore more cogent—than the program promoted by the Women's Christian Temperance Union at the turn of the century, the twelve-step movement nevertheless faces many of the same pitfalls documented by Mark Noll. For example, does the healthy family becomes the savior of society, one day at a time? Surely for all that is right in such a hope, the possibilities of utopianism and perfectionism also remain rife.

Social teaching among Christians should explore, however, one of this movement's central insights—one that has repercussions for other institutions in society. Theologically, the cumulative effect of twelve-step meetings may have less to do with the grace of the gospel than the grace of truth-telling. Learning to speak the truth destroys any delusion that individuals are either god-like in their ability to control destiny or subhuman in their inability to conquer their lack of control. Such grace bestows a recognition of creaturehood, of membership in the human race. The power of the twelve-step movement may indeed be that it teaches what dysfunctional families, and even churches, rarely teach effectively: the humbling yet comforting sense of finitude that is essential for recognizing both the power of sin and the nature of human giftedness.

Leadership in the Business World

Reports from the world of corporate business are also encouraging. They indicate that its leaders are entering a widening conversation about how to make organizational life more humane. Two recent books, one by a practitioner and the other by a business academic, show a renewed emphasis on the importance of personal responsibility within particular social structures.

The Herman Miller furniture company, a business with one thousand employees in Zeeland, Michigan, has been recognized for its remarkable performance for decades. It scores high on every test: return on investment, employee productivity, investment in research and design, and product excellence (for example, the Eames chair). Observers of the company are most amazed by the style of leadership and employee interaction that became its trademark long before the more cooperative forms of Japanese management became popular here.

When Herman Miller's second-generation chairman and chief executive, Max DePree, chose to publish his ethics in 1987, he found a ready audience. His book, *Leadership Is an Art*, makes clear that the best of Calvinism pervades DePree's thinking: his company shares a covenant.[7] A leader with integrity, one with a "fine sense of one's obligations," owes the corporation "a new reference point for what caring, purposeful, committed people can be in the institutional setting." The art of the leader is to liberate people "to do what is required of them in the most effective and humane way possible." All Herman Miller employees are stockholders and receive the benefits of their contributions to productivity. In perhaps his most interesting chapter, DePree describes how "tribal storytellers" are needed to maintain the values that have arisen through the company's history and customs. DePree presides over an organization designed to encourage enduring and inclusive conversation about life and work.

Last year, M.I.T. professor Peter M. Senge published *The Fifth Discipline: The Art and Practice of the Learning Organization* in which he also decries the individualistic notion of leadership. He delineates a theory in which leaders perform as designers "of the institutional embodiment of purpose"; teachers "who help people achieve more accurate, more insightful and more empowering views of reality"; and stewards "of the people they lead" and "for the larger purpose or mission that underlies the enterprise." In each role the leader must manage responsibly the "creative tension" between "seeing clearly where we want to be, our 'vision,' and telling the truth about where we are, our 'current reality.' "[8] Senge's theory draws on the experience at Herman Miller and other enlightened businesses. The leader is one who hosts conversations that foster the exercise of virtue in the workplace.

Both books offer inviting and refreshing glimpses of moral leadership in the economic order, and remind us that values rooted in the Christian tradition are finding expression in the lives of remarkable lay people. Accountability in profit-making institutions seems to have been a source of moral creativity. For those in the churches who see little good in capitalism, the location of these emerging moral practices is, of course, laden with irony. In fact, truth-telling in those corporate settings contrasts favorably with the way business is conducted in many church bureaucracies and agencies. The Church can enter this conversation only if it will insist upon moral audits within its own institutions.

Trusteeship in the Volunteer Sector

No part of American public life has expanded more dramatically in the last fifty years than the non-profit sector. From 1967 to 1987 alone, the number of charitable, tax-exempt, religious and secular organizations has mushroomed from 309,000 to 907,000.[9] Trusteeship has entered the limelight by virtue of both the increased legal apparatus defining fiduciary responsibility and trustee liability and the sheer demand for volunteer expertise and participation on governing boards.

Trusteeship, once largely limited to a recognized Protestant and northern European ethnic cadre, increasingly is spreading to other, less-experienced social groups who bring their own cultural values to the boardroom. Keeping contemporary non-profits focused on their mission, professionally managed, and financially viable, moreover, requires considerable sophistication. These developments are generating greater concern about trustee recruitment.

Those who serve as trustees in the voluntary sector have wonderful opportunities to debate issues of the common good in concrete settings and on a scale that enables them to evaluate and improve their work. Governing boards set policy on issues central to the identity of their institutions. Trusteeship offers entrance into conversations about how to tend such mediating institutions as congregations, schools, youth-serving agencies, hospitals, museums, symphonies, and civic groups that embody long traditions. Through staff and budget decisions, governing boards have the power both to maintain the vitality of tradition and to contribute to its corruption. Institutions are the everyday settings in which people live their lives. Along with the family, they are the settings in which people have more or less opportunity to become adept at practicing the virtues. When trusteeship is construed as the stewardship of such settings to preserve certain practices and the exercise of virtue, then trustees are actively participating in God's ongoing work of creation. Trustees must tell the truth and be courageous and devoted to justice if the institutions they serve are to remain true to their purposes.

Trusteeship remains one of the unsung roles of the laity for the care of the social order. Social teaching that does not address these institutions, or those who are stewards of them, misses an important opportunity to encourage the laity in gaining wisdom about how the world works. It consigns itself to dealing in the ephemeral, not the structural, in society.

The Church, through its congregational, diocesan, and other boards, has its own means of exploring trusteeship and of drawing lay people into governance. But it must face squarely issues of authority and of teaching. Much will be at stake in such a discussion. Through conversation about particular practices within discrete settings, virtue is discovered and the capacity for its exercise expanded. Recognizing this fact can only strengthen the nature and purposes of social teaching in the churches.

The American experiment continues to pose new challenges to American churches. Pursuing vocations located at the point where the liturgy intersects with the family, the economic order, and the voluntary sector, the American laity have opportunities to build their personal narratives in concert with one another and as part of God's sustaining work in creation. Truth-telling—rooted in Israel's experience with God's revelation through the law and prophets, and in the Church's experience with confession and absolution—may be the characteristic virtue of Christians in the social order. The baptized are freed to acknowledge the worst about themselves, their institutions, and the public square; to repent; and to continue as God's creatures charged with the burden and wonder of creation in a fallen world.

Rather than discussing political issues, I have emphasized the underpinnings of the created order and the sources of integrity for God's people. I believe that American churches can achieve their greatest impact on the American experiment in two ways: first by feeding God's people on Word and sacrament, and then by opening, joining, and nurturing conversations that encourage the baptized to know the good and to exercise the virtues in the many settings that connect human experience.

Responses

1. ALBERTO R. COLL

Christa Klein's thoughtful essay concludes with an apt challenge: "American churches can achieve their greatest impact on the American experiment . . . by opening, joining, and nurturing *conversations* that encourage the baptized to know the good . . . in the many settings that connect human experience." The key word is *conversation*. Churches face a major problem because, as Klein points out earlier,

> they have sought to rouse people without fostering conversation. Their remedies amount to cooperative activism, often promoted by a social statement on a particular social ailment. Such responses tend to be short-lived because they avoid arguments over ends and what constitutes the common good. Individuals are left either angry that their views have not been affirmed or jubilant that the Church is on their side. But their isolation continues. There is no common quest for truth and no renewal of moral life. Moreover, the rest of society yawns because the Church is offering nothing different from what other institutions in society are offering.

The failure to nurture authentic moral dialogue prior to launching activist enterprises has been costly for both the churches and the rest of society. The churches have not availed themselves of one of their strengths or, to use the language of economists, one of their "comparative advantages." The churches' comparative advantage is, of course, not current policy expertise, or even a high degree of moral righteousness, but a rich tradition of moral reasoning and experience with difficult moral and political questions. Accumulated over the course of two millennia, this resource is

Alberto R. Coll is the principal deputy assistant secretary of defense for special operations and low intensity conflict in the Department of Defense.

211

being overlooked while the churches devote their energies instead
to specific prophetic stances. The churches have missed an opportunity to enrich the moral vitality of what is now a largely uni-
dimensional politicized and ideologized public square dominated
by passion and largely bereft of the skills and modalities of moral
reasoning.

Klein also draws our attention to the degree to which classical
Catholic social teaching, by moving us away "from the certainties
known in the biblical witness . . . to the more provisional reading
of changing circumstances," nurtures private moral conversations
that are truly open and creative. In my view, classical Catholic
social teaching nurtures prudence and prudential reasoning,
whereas today the churches often tend to add to the shrillness and
passion of the voices clamoring in the public square.

The 1991 war in the Persian Gulf dramatically illustrated some
of the problems we face. Denominations that are deeply split over
issues on which Scripture and Christian tradition are quite clear,
such as homosexuality and abortion, showed an excess of certainty
and consensus when the time came to evaluate the morality of U.S.
policy. Bishop Browning of the Episcopal Church, often equivocal
and at times even sympathetic in his attitude towards the ordination
of practicing homosexuals, had no doubts as to what course of
action the United States should pursue. If there was an effort at
initiating a conversation, it came from a layman, George Bush, who
seemed more agonized about the moral dilemmas of American
policy than the self-assured bishop whom he invited to the White
House for a discussion.

It is unfair to single out the Episcopal Church. All other major
denominations were equally confident of their anti-war position,
and equally unwilling to precede their prophetic gestures by an
extended public conversation that would have explored the moral
issues involved with the kind of intellectual openness and modesty
Klein rightly counsels. The churches made up their minds early;
their pronouncements were long on certainty and short on both
deliberativeness and tentativeness. At every step along the way, their
responses to Saddam's stratagems were predictably and uniformly
conciliatory, without a shade of nuance. And unlike some secular
commentators, among whom one might not expect to find large

doses of humility, the churches have yet to admit that some of their judgments on the matter were incorrect or less than balanced.

If the churches are failing to encourage those conversations essential to the moral health of the laity, it may be that lay people will have to take this task into their own hands. Klein suggests that this is indeed happening. The lay vocation in the modern world will be increasingly exercised by Christian men and women who, despite the absence of nourishment from their ecclesiastical leaders, will be moved to responsible moral reflection and action through their involvement in particular Christian communities from which they derive their sustenance. The way was opened by Vatican II's ringing affirmation of the Church as "the people of God" and its concomitant teaching that the laity are the primary sources of Christian wisdom about the affairs of this world.

Indeed, for the foreseeable future, the laity will be more likely than the Church to promote those moral conversations that guide Christian reflection and action. Whether it be a Max DePree in the business world, or a James Watkins or James Woolsey in the world of political and military affairs, these lay people—by virtue of their experience in the world and the challenges such experience poses to their faith—are often in a better position than ecclesiastical leaders to understand what Christian principles really mean in a recalci-trant, often hostile, world. Thus lay people are more comfortable with prudence, deliberation, the weighing of ends and means, and the pondering of consequences than are their church leaders, who seem to favor monochromatic prophetic judgment.

Church leaders will continue, as they should, to comment on political and social questions. But their authority on such matters will be secondary to that of lay experts, and whatever conversation precedes the Church's activism will be largely the result of the probing queries of lay people. It would not be the first time in its history that the Church, confused and exhausted by the meander-ings of its formal leaders, is revitalized and its vision clarified by the insights of the laity.

2. Robert Destro

C hrista Klein sets forth basic requirements for contemporary Christian life. She argues that to be a Christian *church* today, the constituent members must be integrated into a conversation that takes seriously their vocations as preachers, teachers, hairdressers, plumbers, and whatever else God has equipped them to be. Second, she maintains that to be a Christian layperson is to put one's vocation into the service of God and his Church. And finally, to be a Christian in society is to speak the truth, accept responsibility personally, and demand truth and responsibility from others in an understandable, prudent, and principled way. I will focus on how we can encourage the multi-faceted and sometimes intense "conversation" Klein desires.

The moral conversation she proposes sounds quite innocent at first, and those who concern themselves with fidelity to contemporary political etiquette would be likely to dismiss a conversation among church members as largely irrelevant. But they would be wrong to do so.

Such a conversation is politically "incorrect" for at least three reasons. First, it encourages far more than a social ministry for the Church. Second, it does so in explicitly Christian terms. And third, it raises the almost heretical possibility that thoughtful self-restraint, guided by religious ethics, may contribute more to the development of civilized social relations and discourse than just about anything else.

As a civil-rights lawyer, I have been involved in quite a few conflicts over legislative and judicial policy—what Mary Ann Glendon has referred to as cultural "air, gas, and ground" wars and have learned several hard lessons. One is that "politically correct" etiquette seeks to control the content of conversation so as not to offend current sensibilities, however defined. Even if one is the target of a particularly vicious attack in the name of civil rights, one is expected to respond without violating politically "correct" sensibilities about the nature of the discourse itself. The examples are

Robert Destro is an associate professor of law at the Columbus School of Law, Catholic University of America, Washington, D.C.

many, on both sides of the political spectrum. The goal is simple: to stop meaningful conversation before it starts.

The primary goal of political correctness is to recast culture in a mold that reflects what "opinion leaders" deem to be acceptable. While it is perfectly legitimate to identify oneself as Jewish, Christian, black or African-American, Polish, Italian, or Muslim, one must never act or speak, especially in public, as if such identity at all affects one's thoughts. Conventional wisdom holds that highlighting differences in value orientation is politically and socially "divisive." To live in a pluralistic democracy, we must mute differences in worldview, especially those based on religion. The *New York Times* euphemistically describes this self-censorship as a "truce of tolerance."[1] Its practical result, however, is neither a conversation nor anything remotely resembling pluralism, but rather a lecture by those who seek to control the agenda.

A Call for Accountability

Klein calls repeatedly for accountability shaped by faith, familial obligation, and duty to the communities in which we live and work. She defies conventional wisdom by attacking the myth that one can completely control one's life, and she does so in a threateningly unconventional way. She highlights the religiously based wisdom that so often appears as a paradox to the modern, liberal mind: liberation occurs when people are free, as business leader Max DePree has put it, "to do what is required of them in the most effective and humane way possible."[2] In short, our conversations are most productive when we understand our respective roles and feel free to embrace them without reservation. Klein threatens the "truce of tolerance" by pointing out that the Holy Spirit's call demands that we be Christians "beyond the communion rail."

Accepting that call allows us to make our small contributions to God's design—to follow our vocation as the people of God, united in the mystical body that we call the Church, of which Christ is the head. The key issue is duty, and just what it means to be a Christian "beyond the communion rail" is the $64,000 question. Formulating an answer requires careful reflection on who we are as individuals, on our God-given talents and gifts, on our personal strengths and weaknesses, and on the vitality of our faith. Such reflections are at first necessarily internal, but our orientation changes from self to "other" when we approach communal structures such as family, church, work, and society. We must consider our role in God's larger plan while humbly recognizing the limits of our ability to change things beyond our control.

At communion we eat and drink at a common table as members of a single family. Each of us has similar obligations in faith and works. But at home or at work, we are members of unique families, and our obligations become more diverse. Our differences seem more marked "beyond the communion rail," and yet we are obliged to utilize those differences in the service of God.

This brings me to what I consider to be the central question Klein poses: how can Christians contribute to the world "beyond the communion rail"? The short answer is: by living our vocations *as Christians*. But what are these vocations? The metaphorical communion rail separates the lay and the clerical vocations. The weakness of Klein's essay lies in its tendency to combine the two. The Church has much to offer precisely *because* each of us has a different vocation and function within it. If the clergy are, as Klein writes, "the stewards of the Word," and if God made us all different for a reason, the Church can meet its responsibilities only by drawing explicitly on the resources that lie on both sides of the communion rail. A conversation "across the rail" will underscore and amplify the relevance of the Word in the modern world.

The Church needs to divide the work in the vineyard "beyond the rail." Duplication of effort is wasteful, and Scripture reminds us that, in the end, God himself will judge our use of the talents he has entrusted to us as individuals. Like the master in the parable, God will not be pleased if we buried those talents because we were afraid to take our vocations seriously. Klein might call this "vocational" accountability, and I would like to examine it in two concrete situations: in the conduct of moral and civil discourse on civil rights, and in the Church's role in that discourse.

Accountability and Civil Rights

Shortly after I was nominated to be a member of the Civil Rights Commission, I received a letter asking about my position on the

Roman Catholic bishops' pastoral letter on racism.[3] My initial reaction was some embarrassment and surprise that I was unaware of such a document. When I read the pastoral, however, I found I had not missed much. The letter discussed social responsibility at length but shied away from the question of personal responsibility—the manner in which we, as individuals, should deal with personal differences. The bishops decried racism as a social sin and urged that we take our responsibilities as a society seriously. The implicit message was typical of much liberal writing on the topic: we are all responsible for the sin of racism.

I disagree. Not all of us are responsible for causing the devastation that lack of charity and respect for others wreaks in society. Part of my job as a civil-rights lawyer is to find and assign personal responsibility for civil-rights violations. At the root of every valid claim, there are *persons* who bear *individual* responsibility for the damage caused. To assert that "society" is to blame is simply a way of avoiding the always difficult project of judging others' behavior and holding them strictly accountable for it.

The bishops, of all people, should know better. They know that sin is not societal; it is personal. Why didn't they say this in the letter? Had they hammered this message home on a regular basis— from their pulpits—would any church-going Catholic in the country have ignored or missed it? I think not.

During six years of Civil Rights Commission deliberations, I listened with the same skepticism to highly charged moral arguments and countless expressions of "concern" for victims of societal injustice and institutional racism. The commission was preoccupied with *social* sin, and some commissioners even borrowed religious language to anoint themselves the nation's "conscience" on civil rights. But not once did we engage in a searching inquiry about how law can affect the moral behavior of individuals, including that of the officials who make and enforce the law. Individual morality is a "private" matter, it seems, and best left to personal conscience.

For several of my colleagues, looking seriously at accountability would have opened a door they preferred to leave closed. Those who saw rights as claims or trumps protecting individuals from a faceless, uncaring "society" rejected the notion of personal responsibility for behavior out of fear that it might be used elsewhere to "blame the victim." Others, who suspected that even civil-rights law blemished the libertarian ideal, also tacitly agreed that to make societal judgments about individual behavior is taboo. To the libertarians, assigning personal responsibility might interfere with the autonomous self operating in the marketplace. Sermons from both camps blocked all meaningful conversation.

What is needed is a discussion of the duty and ethics (that is, Christian charity) that were the foundation of Dr. Martin Luther King's dream. Today, however, power, not morals, is the issue. Truth-telling, if politically "incorrect," can jeopardize one's career, though truth is essential if justice is to be done. When a well-known civil libertarian can ask, "What does ethics have to do with equal protection?," it is clear that we have turned 180 degrees away from Dr. King's path.

This, of course, is the problem—and the point missed in contemporary civil-rights disputes focusing on power. Civil rights is about *duties*, not claims on others. It is about taking personal responsibility for one's natural inclination to prefer the familiar and fear the unfamiliar, a fear that often leads to ungodly behavior toward those who are different. The only way to counter this is with an unambiguous *moral* message that such behavior is unacceptable. Our seeming inability to provide meaningful remedies for both present and past injustices has the same root: asking the wrong question virtually guarantees a wrong answer. A message based on accountability, by contrast, asks the right question. It directly challenges those who continue to violate the second great commandment— the commandment that directs us to love our neighbor, caring only that he or she is a child of God.

As strange as it may seem to the modern mind, the second commandment is the only "realistic" way to approach the issue. We must ask, for example, whether those in authority exercise their leadership as well as the Herman Miller company's Max DePree. We must ask whether our leaders are willing to take personal responsibility for their failures and resign when they fail or create scandal. And we should suggest that forgiveness plays as important a role in the development and preservation of communities as it does in the lives of families, parents, and children.

Do school boards design policies and adopt curricula to train students in what DePree called "the most effective and humane manner possible"? A look at the conditions in our public schools suggests that the answer is no. We speak of public servants as "trustees" but rarely hold them personally responsible for their policy failures by firing them or voting them out. Until we speak the truth, our language is meaningless and our promises are lies.

We must begin a new discourse and invite others to participate. But how? The trusteeship model to which Klein refers provides a good starting place. Since we were not even born when the evil of racial segregation began in this country, and many of us were children when it was officially abolished, we are not "responsible" for it in the sense of which the bishops spoke.

The first step for Christians, then, is to refuse to participate in conversations about "societal" responsibility. They get us nowhere. Our vocation as Christians is to underscore, for ourselves and others, our *current* responsibilities—responsibilities that exist whether or not we succeed in attaching blame for modern injustices on someone long dead.

We must begin with an awareness of our own ultimate vocation: I am personally responsible for any act that might jeopardize my own salvation. If I take my faith seriously—and that is my first responsibility—I will not demean or injure others by word or action. I will, in short, take the second commandment seriously. I will also recognize that even the best among us will fall short of the ideal, and I will do what I can to remedy the damage caused by my acts, or those of others.

The Church's Role

The Church needs to alter its course as well. Though it will on occasion be vilified for doing so, the Church must elaborate the Christian dimensions of lay trusteeship; it must teach the nation about each person's obligations; and it must state clearly that conversation about rights is secondary to accounting for one's trusteeship of the talents given by God. Without question, these talents must be used for the benefit of those who walk with us on the road to salvation.

Will such guidance from the clergy inhibit or chill our freedom?

Will demands that we do our duty invade our privacy? Yes, if freedom and privacy are understood to be unfettered by civic, familial, professional, and religious obligations. Properly understood, rights end at the demarcation line between the self and others.

When she spoke of the hunger for good preaching and teaching, Klein put her finger on a problem of the clergy as well as the laity. The impact of a good sermon far outweighs the long-term impact of legal briefs or political harangues. The clergy have pulpits and should not hesitate to judge individual behavior. They should tell the lawyers, politicians, and judges who go to church something useful. It is, in fact, their *job* to do so. Martin Luther King's sermons were eloquent elaborations not only of the moral foundations of public policy but, more importantly, of the moral foundations of good living. They changed us forever.

Klein emphasizes that "the call to peoplehood entails excruciating accountability," but I believe she is far too kind when describing our shortcomings. When Christians who have much to offer the modern world acquiesce in the *New York Times*'s "truce of tolerance," they are untrue to their vocation. Political correctness is an unacceptable price for us to pay for admission to the policy debates taking place in the public square.

The vocation of the laity is to bring the light of Christ into every dark corner of the world. Knowing that it will often not be possible to convert the unbeliever, and that it is inappropriate in many situations even to try, we must recognize that we teach most effectively by example. If we accept the universal ethics of Scripture in our lives as clergy, lawyers, philosophers, auto mechanics, hairdressers, and plumbers, our vocations on either side of the communion rail will bear witness to the truth every day. We need only to give and demand in our own lives respect for standards of conduct and accountability that are consistent with the Christian vision of community.

The "truce of tolerance" is inconsistent with that vision, and with the realization of our vocation. We must reject it whenever justice and the common good—as well as the First Amendment—require it. If the result is another skirmish in the ground war over values, so be it: the territory is important and should not be ceded without a fight. Part of our task "beyond the communion rail" is to remind our fellow citizens that actions have consequences and that somebody will pay for them. If that somebody is us, then part of our vocation is to see that the appropriate payments are made.

Another part of our vocation as laity is to remind guardians of the public trust that their actions must be consistent with their duty. And as we speak to the clerical trustees of the Word, our task as laity is no less difficult: to get clerics, and their lay employees, to take the gifts God gave his lay people more seriously. We can contribute much to the conversation and ongoing life of the Church. As parents, workers, and professionals, we live on the cutting edge of society. Each of the myriad roles of daily living has its moral dimension, and it is the vocation of the teaching church to shape and declare moral parameters in conversation with those who appreciate the practical ones. The conversations must not be conducted in abstract terms, as was the bishops' letter on racism. They must be heard everywhere people live and work, on television and in the newspapers.

All this is possible—and in our lifetimes. *Rerum Novarum* and its progeny demonstrated that morally grounded conversation about policy questions can indeed change history. It can give moral meaning to our identity as lay workers and a moral reason to change our behavior for the good.

8

Christians and
New World Disorders

J. Bryan Hehir

THE centenary of Catholic social teaching prompts one to think about the public life of the United States from a Christian perspective. In discussing politics among nations in the 1990s, I will draw on both the Catholic tradition and a second tradition of empirical analysis of international relations influenced by Hans Morgenthau. I will try to reflect a mix of empirical, normative, and contemporary concerns in analyzing—consecutively—the world, the Church, and policy choices confronting the United States.

The world scene today is marked by change. In the last decade of this century—a century scarred by two world wars, fifty years of cold war, and over 150 other conflicts—an understanding of the depth and dimension of change that occurred in 1990 is prerequisite to any analysis of international relations. This year stands with 1648, 1815, and 1945 as one of the fault lines in the study of world politics. It necessitates the hard work of changing our conception of international affairs.

While there is solid consensus that the Cold War is over and has virtually no prospect of resurgence, there is little consensus about how the post-war order should be shaped. The "America and the World 1990/91" issue of *Foreign Affairs* offers striking testimony to

J. Bryan Hehir is a professor at the Kennedy Institute of Ethics, Georgetown University, and an advisor to the United States Catholic Conference.

223

the range of opinion: Charles Krauthammer asserts, with the confidence of one stating self-evident principles, that ours is now a "unipolar" world in which the United States is the only superpower; in the next article William Pfaff argues that the term "superpower" no longer fits anyone.[1] In trying to sort out both the events that made 1990 decisive and the debate that has followed those events, we need to focus on two issues: the source of the change in 1990 and the emerging structure of power in world politics today.

The Source of Change

Two different kinds of change—revolutionary and evolutionary—produced the fault line of 1990. The intersection of these two distinct processes in the late 1980s created the decisive shift in the world of the 1990s. Revolutionary change—deep, systemic, and rapid—was best symbolized by the destruction of the Berlin Wall, the starkest symbol of the Cold War for three decades. But the breaching of the wall was only one short act in a wider drama composed of four major elements.

The first was Mikhail Gorbachev's introduction of *decisive changes in the Soviet Union* beginning in the mid-1980s. Whatever lies ahead in his own future will not erase the role Gorbachev played in ending the Cold War. His program was a mix of *perestroika* and *glasnost* at home and "New Thinking" abroad. Early in the Gorbachev era, Professor Seweryn Bialer wrote: "New Thinking as a process of profound reassessment of the Soviet approach to international relations has only started. It holds the promise of further evolution and long-term change in Soviet international behavior".[2] In subsequent years, the currency of both *perestroika* and *glasnost* plummeted, but the policy of "New Thinking" persisted, as was visibly evident during the Persian Gulf war.

The second element of revolutionary change was *the effect the Gorbachev policy had in Eastern Europe*. Here, however, we need to distinguish between the *causes* of revolutionary change and the *catalytic* role played by the Gorbachev policy. The principal agents of change in Eastern Europe were the long-suffering people of the region. They became the architects of the revolution through their drive for political freedom, their demand for full public expression of their faith, and their hope for economic security and well-being. These three distinct roots of revolution varied in significance from country to country, and among groups within each country, but together they affected developments in all nations under Soviet control since the 1940s. Gorbachev's policy was catalytic in two ways. His advocacy of change *within* the Soviet Union legitimated the call for change *beyond* its borders. Then, in the face of an uprising he may not have fully expected, he chose not to use military power to repress it. Once it was clear that 1956 and 1968 would not be repeated, the client regimes of Eastern Europe were swept away in a matter of weeks.

The logic of revolution extending from Moscow to Warsaw, Budapest, and Prague quickly moved into Central Europe as well, transforming "the German question" in a way no one expected.[3] While the division of Germany was ritually lamented for decades, both analysts and statesmen had seemingly come to terms with it. In a matter of months, however, *German unification*—the third element of revolutionary change—progressed from an unlikely possibility to a necessity that neither superpower could resist or even regulate.[4] Analysts' fears and diplomats' modulated plans were simply pushed aside in 1989–90. By the time the Conference on Security and Cooperation in Europe met in Paris in November 1990, both the Cold War and the unification of Germany—the issues that had defined European politics for fifty years—were consigned to the historical record.

The fourth element of revolutionary change was *the impact all these events had on the U.S.-Soviet relationship*—from strategic arms negotiations and conventional arms reductions, to the dissolution of the Warsaw Pact and the recasting of NATO, to the redefinition of superpower interests in the world outside Europe. Not without historical significance is the fact that the first chapter of the new U.S.-Soviet interaction was written in the dangerous arena of the Middle East.

The many consequences of revolutionary change, both in Europe and in the wider international system, are yet to be well defined. In trying to understand them, however, we must link the analysis of revolutionary change with the study of evolutionary change. The latter study has been largely limited to the domain of international-politics specialists, but such change has been under way since the mid-1960s and is a staple of the literature of international-relations theory and policy.[5] Risking intellectual life and limb, I will attempt to reduce this argument about evolutionary change to three elements: change in the actors on the stage of world politics, change in the nature of their relationships, and change in the understanding of foreign policy and domestic politics.

Contrasting a "classical" view of international relations with a "contemporary" one helps explain these changes. The classical view adequately accounts for the Westphalia system from the seventeenth century well into the twentieth century: the *actors* were sovereign states; world politics was about the interaction of states. The *relationships* among the actors were defined in terms of political-military power; power had a univocal meaning—military power that presumably could be translated directly into usable political influence. The single meaning of power defined, in turn, a single hierarchy among states, which were ranked according to their military status. Finally, *domestic politics* was regarded as a separate realm from *foreign policy*; indeed, one could define the role of foreign policy as protecting the domestic polity and population of a country from outside influences.

Contemporary international politics requires shifting the definition of each of these elements. Since 1945, new factors—including, primarily, the impact of the nuclear revolution and the increasing economic interdependence of states and people—have altered the meaning of the terms. In addition to states, the *actors* in the arena are now transnational institutions, the product of what Samuel Huntington has called the transnational revolution in world politics.[6] States remain the dominant, but no longer the sole, architects of world affairs. Their interaction is complemented, contested, and contradicted by a variety of transnational organizations.

The *relationships* among the actors occur, moreover, on two chessboards: the political-military and the political-economic. The former competition is dominated by states following the zero-sum logic of win/lose. In the latter game, states, transnational entities, and international institutions share an arena in which interests and outcomes (win/lose, win/win, and lose/lose) are more mixed. When states try to use political-military logic in the political-economic arena, they can threaten the entire framework of economic exchange. The dual chessboards also multiply the hierarchies in the international system. Because power today takes many forms, several actors are dominant. Military powers without economic significance interact with economic giants devoid of military might.

Lastly, the logic of interdependence obscures the distinction between foreign and domestic policy. *Linkage* now describes how purely foreign-policy issues feed back directly into domestic politics, and traditionally domestic issues have immediate international implications.

These evolutionary processes were at work in world politics for twenty years before the advent of revolutionary change. To some degree they moderated the Cold War and were already transforming relations within the U.S.-European-Japanese alliance. They affected as well the relationship of both superpowers to the developing world. But now, in the 1990s, this evolutionary change is intersecting with revolutionary change to create a new structure of international order.

The Emerging Power Structure

To move from describing sources of change to defining the new system's power structure is to pass from consensus to dissonance. Clear, concise—and, in my view, premature—predictions are being offered, but they do little more than help draw the lines of the public argument. Because the international order is changing so rapidly, they generate critique, negation, and complementary proposals. Two leading descriptions of what is occurring in the international system give me an opportunity to dissent from both without having to formulate my own thesis.

As we have seen, Charles Krauthammer has stated unequivocally that the bipolar structure of the Cold War world order has been superceded: "The most striking feature of the post–Cold War world is its unipolarity. No doubt multipolarity will come in time. . . . But we are not there yet, nor will we be for decades. Now is the unipolar moment."[7] With equal certitude, Henry Kissinger had earlier predicted a different shift in the 1990s, from bipolarity to multipolarity: "You will have the United States, Soviet Union,

China, India, Europe. All of which will be simultaneously economic, political, and military powers."[8] These two stark predictions
could then be contrasted with the alternatives of Robert Tucker,
Samuel Huntington, Joseph Nye, and William Pfaff; the debate
about the structure of power is a buyer's market.[9]

In my view, neither Krauthammer's vision of unipolarity nor
Kissinger's of multipolarity can be taken as a guide to the future.
Krauthammer is right that Cold War bipolarity, the political-
military competition that the United States and the Soviet Union
carried on across the global stage for so many years, is gone. But
an end to strategic, nuclear bipolarity will require deep cuts in arms
that have not yet occurred. So Krauthammer is half-correct; the
political threat of the Soviet Union has disappeared, but limited
bipolarity exists.

The Kissinger prediction has much to commend it; the "decline"
of the superpowers creates the setting for a multipolar world. But
Stanley Hoffmann's correction of the multipolar thesis is useful:
The old model of multipolarity presumed that each "pole" possessed the same kind of power—military power; but the poles of
the 1990s will reflect diverse forms of power.[10] To determine who
has power in the 1990s, we must define the meaning of power.
Multipolarity undoubtedly lies ahead, but there will be several
multipolar worlds. No single hierarchy will exist.

In staking out such clear-cut positions, both Krauthammer and
Kissinger omit some of the complexity of reality. Both ignore,
moreover, another salient feature of the current system. In his
analysis of the emerging system, Stanley Hoffmann moves beyond
traditional concerns to discuss "people power" or "citizens say"—a
highly visible phenomenon in the Philippines, Iran, and Eastern
Europe in the 1980s. Its consequences for the foreign-policy
agenda are, in Hoffmann's view, long-term and fundamental:

> The notion, inseparable from Realism, that this agenda is "objec-
> tively" set by the map of geography and by the map of alignments
> dictated by the "security dilemma" is obsolete. The agendas are
> either dictated by domestic imperatives or delicate attempts at
> reconciling these with external constraints.[11]

These contending views of power and structure in the emerging system incline me toward an eclectic view. I see the stage for U.S. policy as a world in which bipolarity is not dead but is of limited significance and a complex form of multipolarity is its likely successor. The logic of force will have to accommodate the logic of commerce; alliances are likely to differ on differing issues; and states and transnationals will need to attend to "citizens say." As Joseph Nye has observed, even the most sophisticated models of changing power dimensions show the United States as the one actor that fits somewhere near the top of every hierarchy.[12] But for all its clout, it will have to deal with constraint and restraints from other actors and forces. The United States will need a sense of limits, as well as a sense of possibilities, to choose wisely and effectively in a world greatly altered by revolutionary and evolutionary change.

RESOURCES FOR A CHRISTIAN RESPONSE

In the face of the changing international system and the rising saliency of religion in world politics, what resources can be used to shape a Christian response? For an answer to this question, I will draw from one part of the Christian tradition, while trying to illustrate that alternative approaches would have yielded different insights. A more integrated ecumenical analysis of foreign policy, one incorporating several voices in the Christian Church, would require more space and greater capacities than I have. As an alternative, I have fallen back on a popular conception—which is partly a misconception—that Protestant theology can be understood in terms of personalities, while Catholic thought belongs to a more impersonal tradition.

Following this fragile distinction, I will devote most of my assessment to Catholic teaching. But I wish first to acknowledge three Protestant thinkers—Reinhold Niebuhr, Paul Ramsey, and John Yoder—who set high standards of scholarship for anyone seeking to join the Christian tradition to the world of foreign policy.

Reinhold Niebuhr occupies a unique position. In this century no other Protestant or Catholic theologian so effectively demonstrated the resources of a religious tradition for illuminating the world of power and politics.[13] Undoubtedly, his influence can be attributed in part to how well his message fit the needs of the post-war moment in America—a characteristic he shared with Hans Morgenthau—but no post-mortem has undercut or even eroded his accomplishment.[14] In essence, Niebuhr still calls others to be as confident of the power and truth of Christian theological reflection as he was, and to use it as he did in shaping realistic goals of justice and international community.

Paul Ramsey was a disciple of Niebuhr who strayed from his teachings.[15] While Niebuhr appreciated Catholic social thought, he was skeptical of what John Langan has called the style of Catholic rationalism.[16] Catholic use of natural law, its variegated distinctions among forms of justice, and its multiple categories of just-war analysis did not appeal to Niebuhr. All reflected too much certainty about the ability of the human mind to identify the right, the good, and the equitable in a world marked by sin, interest, and power.

Ramsey, however, was attracted by the very characteristics that made Niebuhr skeptical. He neither left Niebuhrian thought behind nor wholly embraced Catholic moral analysis. But in both medical ethics and international affairs, he took hold of Catholic categories and gave them new analytical power.[17] At a time when many Catholics and Protestants found just-war issues uninteresting, Ramsey almost single-handedly applied the old ethic to the new problems of nuclear strategy, thereby renewing a tradition of thought about political-strategic questions.

Niebuhr and Ramsey represented the strength and influence of mainline Protestant churches as intellectual and religious forces in American culture. John Yoder represents an alternative vision to both mainline Protestant and standard Catholic conceptions of the relationship of religion and politics.[18] His refusal to be categorized as "sectarian" or marginal in the theological or political world underscores his distinctive witness. While holding political and pacifist positions that would seem to make him a perennial outsider, Yoder, with his colleague Stanley Hauerwas, has created a constituency of support for his policy ethics that cuts across both Protestant and Catholic communities. Yoder and Hauerwas have managed to sharpen the policy debate without ever directly engaging the policy world itself.

Catholic social teaching is usually identified with the encyclical tradition of the last century and with the socio-economic themes so prominent in that tradition from the time of Leo XIII through John Paul II. While valid, this emphasis diverts attention from the full scope of the precepts developed during the last century, primarily through the leadership of the popes. Catholic social teaching encompasses church-state issues (Leo XIII and Pius XII), church-society issues (all the social encyclicals), and church teaching on international relations (Pius XII through John Paul II). From 1891 to 1941, the teaching was overwhelmingly concerned with socio-economic issues in a national economy,[19] but from 1941 to 1991, it explicitly shifted gears to address problems on the international stage.[20]

In seeking resources relevant to the contemporary international system, I will focus on four components of this most recent social teaching: the primacy of order, the declining legitimation of resort to force, the rising significance of human rights, and the economics and ethics of interdependence.

The Primacy of Order

Throughout Catholic social teaching, one repeatedly finds the notion that the human person belongs by nature to three communities: the family, the civil society (or, in contemporary terms, the nation), and the human community. Much of the social teaching assesses how these three "natural" communities should be structured to achieve their inherent purposes. While the concept of order applies to each community, however, it is particularly prominent in the treatment of the international community. By contrast, the literature of international-relations theory takes the "anarchical nature" of world politics as the starting point of analysis.[21] Both in realist theory and by those more sympathetic to traditional liberal ideas, this anarchical quality is accepted as a fact. Little attention is given to the possibility of *fundamentally* transforming it.[22]

In Catholic teaching, the lack of any adequate political authority in world politics is an unfortunate and morally significant structural defect that frustrates the normal expectation for the international community. This view accounts for the primacy given to shaping an acceptable international order. In stark contrast to Hobbesian acceptance of international politics as a true state of nature, which is a state of constant warfare, Catholic thought affirms the organic character of the human community, united by common human nature in a society shaped by reciprocal rights and duties among its members.[23] Despite an inadequate political authority, a fragile realm of law, and a minimal consensus on values, Catholic teaching affirms the existence of morally binding reciprocal obligations among citizens and states. These general obligations provide the foundation for more specific teaching about the ethics of war and economic responsibilities.

Catholic teaching on international affairs, therefore, is based on what Hedley Bull calls a Grotian conception of international society—not a society of states in the first instance, but a society of persons who are also citizens of states.[24] In this conception, the sovereign state has real but relative moral value. As John XXIII made clear in *Pacem in Terris*, the state is situated in a structured framework that places constraints upon it from above and from below. From below, the citizens of the state, who are also members of the wider human community, possess a spectrum of human rights that restrict the demands the sovereign state can make on them. From above, the demands of international order contain and restrain the claims of the sovereign state.

Pacem in Terris systematically enumerates these limitations. Its second chapter, which analyzes the citizen-state relationship, develops a structure of restraint within a state that can be called on to contain the scope of state power. As a result, while there have been innumerable examples of states abusing the rights of their citizens in the years since *Pacem in Terris* was published, moral, legal, and political norms existed that could be invoked to indict those states for their behavior. In chapter four, John XXIII turns to the international order to seek means of restraining states from above. Here the pope acknowledges the inadequacy of the political authority available to meet the needs of the international common good.[25]

Such stress on the primacy of order has characterized papal teaching ever since Pius XII attempted to highlight and close this gap in the international community. The emphasis on moving beyond the "anarchical order," on finding at least incremental methods of restraining the claims of sovereignty, and on creating strong international institutions has been noticeably greater in Catholic teaching than in most international theory. Pius XII devoted himself to shaping the political-legal order of the international community. Reflecting the traditional concerns of Vatican diplomacy, Pius XII in his writings had the ring of an international lawyer with a well-honed moral sense.

Pacem in Terris went beyond this moral-legal emphasis to discuss the political structures necessary to shape a community of states. John XXIII particularly focused on the new political-military questions of the nuclear age. In 1967 Paul VI wrote the complementary piece to *Pacem in Terris*; in *Populorum Progressio* he set forth a normative conception of the political-economic dimensions of international order. In both these encyclicals of the 1960s, the conception of order went far beyond the specific possibilities envisioned by the empirical literature of the time. John XXIII argued that the demands of the international common good *required*, in moral terms, some immediate movement toward centralized international authority; he also pressed for much larger negotiated cuts in nuclear weapons than anything achieved over the next twenty years. Paul VI urged some form of international taxation on industrialized countries, to be used for developing countries. His encyclical foreshadowed the proposals of the developing countries in the 1970s.

The need to address the systemic framework of international affairs as a first priority because of the structural defect in the existing order has been a constant theme in Catholic social thought for fifty years. The interesting point to note here is that, for most of those fifty years, empirical literature regarded such talk of international order as a vague demand beyond the pale of the possible. But in the 1990s the profound changes—revolutionary and evolutionary—that color the horizon of world politics make any less sweeping conception seem inadequate. The 1990s may see the normative concerns of Catholic teaching on order converge with the empirical concerns of both analysts and actors in world politics.

The Declining Legitimacy of War

In papal teaching the moral evaluation of war has always rested on the recognition of the structural defect in international order. Because of the absence of any political authority capable of protecting the basic rights of individuals and states, a limited but morally legitimate right to resort to war exists. The just-war ethic provides a moral framework, or set of standards, by which to judge the legitimacy of resort to force.

Catholic teaching is the institutional setting in which the just-war ethic has been most prominently cultivated and used, and I support the ethic as the best means available for assessing the morality of war today. A review of Catholic teaching on war in the 1990s, however, demands delineation of a clear theme of papal teaching reaching back to Pius XII and continuing to John Paul II: a growing skepticism about the use of force. This skepticism even extends to the long-term viability of the just-war position.

I will cite three examples of this theme. First, Pius XII, perhaps the strongest exponent of the ethic among twentieth-century popes, changed the traditional teaching on just cause. As John Courtney Murray noted in 1959, Pius XII restricted the just-cause arguments to self-defense or defense of others.[26]

Second, in *Pacem in Terris* John XXIII shifted the focus of analysis from cause to means, an area largely untouched by Pius XII. While more ambiguous than Pius XII's argument, John XXIII's controversial questioning of whether the resort to war could pass rational moral standards in the nuclear age had more far-reaching implications.[27] Even if John XXIII's position is conservatively interpreted as posing a question rather than making an assertion, the encyclical illustrates the increasing pressure exerted on just-war teaching in the very institution that has most systematically developed its argument.

Third, John Paul II has also shown some doubt about the ethical argument even though he has reaffirmed its fundamental logic. In a series of statements reaching from Drogheda, Ireland, in 1979, to Lesotho in 1988, John Paul II strongly supported non-violence as a method for resolving disputes.[28] While his remarks applied primarily to conflicts within nations, the force of his position was notable. Perhaps to dispel the impression that he was invalidating any claim to a legitimate use of force, however, John Paul II used his 1982 World Day of Peace message to reaffirm the right of states to defense, including the possible use of force.[29]

The tension between these two earlier positions became manifest in the practical case of the Gulf War. In a series of statements, the pope seemed to be saying that he judged resort to force a mistake. While some of these statements could be classified as exhortation rather than moral analysis, the letter that he sent President Bush on the eve of the declaration of war exhibited a clearly structured argument. The pope acknowledged the existence of "just cause" without using the term, and reiterated his previously stated view that Iraq's invasion of Kuwait constituted a serious evil, a violation of law and morality. But in the face of this objective evil, John Paul II recommended against war: "I wish now to restate my firm belief that war is not likely to bring an adequate solution to international problems and that, even though an unjust situation might be momentarily met, the consequences that would possibly derive from war would be devastating and tragic."[30] After this and other critical statements about the war generated Italian opposition to his position, however, the pope included in a wartime address the elliptical statement—similar to the one he had made in 1982—that "we are not pacifists."[31]

Neither the cumulative weight of the positions taken by Pius XII, John XXIII, and John Paul II nor the explicit record of any authoritative statement yields the conclusion that the teaching authority of the Catholic Church has judged the just-war ethic inapplicable to modern war. But the direction of papal teaching has clearly enhanced the capacity of the moral doctrine to restrict resort to force and reduced its capacity to legitimate war. Using James Childress's suggestion that the just-war argument be understood as a presumption/exception mode of reasoning, one could say that the thrust of papal teaching has reinforced the presumption against war and made more stringent the tests a justifiable exception must meet.[32]

The Enhanced Role of Human Rights

In the evolution of Catholic social teaching over the last century, the appeal to human rights has moved more and more toward center stage. While the encyclicals of Leo XIII and Pius XI are noticeably reticent about human rights, Pius XII's *Christmas Addresses* of the early 1940s initiated a shift toward a more expansive use of human rights, one situated solidly within a natural-law framework. Even more decisive were *Pacem in Terris* and Vatican II's *Dignitatis Humanae*, which located the right to religious liberty within a spectrum of basic human rights. Since the Council, human-rights concerns have been critical in shaping both Catholic teaching and Catholic social ministry.

Not least among the influences that have increased the significance of human rights is the teaching of John Paul II. He has both built on the post-conciliar human-rights emphasis—particularly the emphasis on religious liberty—and made the boldest statement in Catholic thought about the relationship of human rights and international order. In an address to the United Nations in 1979, John Paul II examined an extraordinary range of contemporary political and economic issues through the prism of the U.N. Declaration on Human Rights.[33] This address highlights the centrality that the once sparsely used category has assumed in Catholic thought. If the concept of order is the primary theme in Catholic teaching on international relations, human rights now defines the content of that order.

The Economics and Ethics of Interdependence

In its early history, the Catholic social teaching of Leo XIII and Pius XI focused on issues of economic justice arising out of the Industrial Revolution. The nation was the assumed unit of analysis; the criteria of social justice were meant to shape a just economic system within a national community. Since Pius XII began the process of internationalizing the social teaching in response to World War II and the post-war emergence of an interdependent international economy, Catholic teaching on justice has changed both in scope and in depth.

The change in scope begins with Pius XII but finds its symbolic statement in Paul VI's encyclical *Populorum Progressio*. When Leo XIII wrote the first social encyclical in 1891, he did it as a response to "The Social Question"; in 1967 Paul VI said, "The social question has become worldwide."[34] The papal dictum was the product of several forces: the post-war decolonization that increased the number of sovereign nations in the world from fewer than 50 to more than 150, the growing technological, communication, and socioeconomic bonds that developed in the 1960s and 1970s; and the continually expanding integrated economy that defies the notion of sovereign states. Both markets and productive processes are now joined in a complex web of dependence and interdependence.

Faced with this new "social question," Leo XIII's successors have widened the scope of their moral analysis. At least since *Mater et Magistra* in 1961, their moral teaching has recognized that the analysis of justice in any single economy must take into account the relation between national and international economic forces. John XXIII suggested that the traditional Catholic concept of the common good now be understood in terms of the national and international common good. Paul VI's *Octogesima Adveniens* (1971) pointed out the moral significance of ever-stronger transnational actors, which academics were beginning to study in the 1960s.

John Paul II's teaching in *Sollicitudo Rei Socialis* is the most striking example of how the scope of Catholic economic teaching has expanded. He asserts that national and local issues of justice must be examined within the framework of international socioeconomic forces.[35]

While changing the *scope* of Catholic teaching was a conceptual move, the development of the teaching in *depth* was a product of pastoral experience. The universal teaching authority has reached down into the experience of local churches to incorporate themes for the whole Church. The influence on Catholic teaching of Latin America's theology of liberation is the clearest example of this process, which has a long, complex history but an easily described result.

Since the Medellín conference of Latin American bishops in 1968, a dominant theme in the theology and ministry of the Church in Latin America has been "the option for the poor."

Although the phrase arose after Medellín, it symbolizes a movement with roots in the 1960s. John Paul II both used and modified the term during his 1979 trip to the Latin American bishops' meeting at Puebla, Mexico, which marked the beginning of the dialogue between the theology of liberation and the Magisterium.[36] In 1984 the Congregation for the Doctrine of the Faith produced a quite critical assessment of key themes in Latin American theology,[37] but in 1986 a document by the same body actually showed how the focus on the poor and some other elements of liberation theology were being accepted in wider church teaching.[38]

John Paul II's own contributions to Catholic social teaching on international economic issues illustrate this development in both scope and depth. In *Sollicitudo Rei Socialis* he turns explicitly from the primacy-of-order theme to the adverse effects that both the political superpowers' competition and the economic patterns of interdependence have had on the life of poor nations and individuals.[39] Many in the United States were dismayed that the papal critique seemed to treat the two superpowers equally; they seemed to misunderstand that John Paul II was focusing on the similar *consequences* that superpower policies often had despite their differences. The pope was examining the dynamics of the international system as a whole through the lens of the life of the poor. In this sense, he followed the logic of the option for the poor.

Precisely because discussions of the international system rarely adopt this perspective, John Paul's efforts were discounted by many in the United States before they were analyzed on their own terms. His goal was to redefine the debate and to view the adequacy and justice of the existing order from the edge of international economic life. That goal has yet to be achieved.

CHRISTIANS AND U.S. POLICY CHOICES

How can these resources of recent social teaching be applied to the changed context of international politics? I will concentrate on three issues in the U.S. foreign-policy debate to show how a creative Christian response might be developed from this one part of the Christian tradition.

Wars and the Ethic of War

Since 1945 three kinds of war have been evident in world politics, and each has provoked a major political and moral debate in the United States. The threat of nuclear war—and the nature of nuclear deterrence that evolved from the policies of the United States and the Soviet Union—posed the dominant problem. But standing at the other end of the spectrum of force was the most visible form of war since 1945: internal war, civil war, and the problem of big-power intervention in local and regional conflicts.

The post-war order has managed to avoid nuclear war while failing to handle satisfactorily over 150 wars of the internal/inter-vention variety. Between these two extremes of nuclear and uncon-ventional war, a limited number of wars between states have fol-lowed a "conventional" pattern: they have involved aggression across boundaries and been fought with conventional means and methods. The Korean War fits this model. After Korea, the conven-tional conflicts that have occurred have been fought almost exclu-sively in the Middle East: 1956, 1967, 1973, and 1991.

The moral arguments surrounding both the Vietnam War and the nuclear debate of the 1980s focused on means. While such scholars as James Turner Johnson and George Weigel have criticized this emphasis on means for its tendency to neglect or exclude issues of purpose—the ends or threat being opposed—I believe their critique is more appropriately directed to the problems of internal-war-with-intervention than to the nuclear question.[40] Now that there is no longer superpower competition in the developing world, U.S. intervention needs to be stringently contained. Johnson and Weigel's idea of giving the *ius ad bellum* issues more attention can help to reduce the justification for intervention.

In my view, however, the nuclear debate of the 1980s was properly focused on an ethic of means for two reasons. First, the nature of the U.S.-Soviet competition provided a clear-cut "just cause" for designing a strategy to deter Soviet attack on the United States as well as on those nations the United States was pledged by treaty to defend. Unlike the cause in Vietnam, the cause question in the nuclear issue did not seem problematic. Second, while the cause was clear, the risk posed by the range of nuclear arsenals and the strategy of deterrence did raise authentically new issues of means for the traditional moral teaching. The intensive focus on means was appropriate and helped relate moral and strategic issues not just in the churches but in the wider American policy argument.[41]

Where do issues stand after the nuclear debate of the 1980s? The extensive public discussion cut across government, the academy, and the churches, and installed the principles governing the debate in the vocabulary and thinking of the press, the military, and, to a less well-defined degree, the citizenry. The contrast between the reception accorded Fr. John Ford's classic essay on obliteration bombing in 1944 and the implicit and explicit use of just-war categories during the Persian Gulf debate indicates a higher level of public sophistication.[42] The distinctions made between "civilian and combatant" targets, and between "direct and collateral" damage, did not solve the moral issues of the Gulf war, but they did help to structure the policy argument in a way not achieved during World War II, Korea, or Vietnam.

The nuclear debate of the 1980s also contributed, I believe, to specifying the central questions of the nuclear argument and to reinforcing the nuclear taboo. The questions of use vs. deterrence, of the moral character of "first use" (not first strike), and of the merits of defensive nuclear strategies have been examined at length. The debate both narrowed the differences among distinct positions and illustrated what moral and strategic burdens one assumed by choosing one option over others. In sum, it effectively raised the moral threshold against resort to nuclear weapons, even among those who support some moral possibility of using them.[43]

What the 1980s debate did *not* do was to prepare either moralists or strategists for the questions of the 1990s. While the nuclear issue remains a fundamental political-moral challenge for Christians and citizens generally, the radically changed post-1990 world places it in a new context. The nuclear debate will not command the central role in the policy debates of the 1990s because the threat of a major nuclear war has declined substantially. Nevertheless, the possibility of nuclear use—now most likely to result from the problem of proliferation—guarantees the issue's permanent place on the U.S. policy agenda.

Given this new context, I would suggest that Christian analysts and advocates first turn their attention from strategic ethics to political ethics. Reducing the nuclear danger will require deep, stabilizing cuts in the nuclear arsenals of the United States and the former Soviet Union, and a recasting of the strategic doctrine to lessen the possibility of war by miscalculation, accident, or the catalytic choice of a third power. Second, the theme of political ethics should be extended to respond to the contention of non-nuclear states that non-proliferation is simply another form of international discrimination. Lastly, Christians should try to buttress the nuclear taboo by resisting any blurring of the line between nuclear and conventional weapons, pressing for no-first-use pledges, and emphasizing qualitative forms of arms control to phase out vulnerable systems.

It will take time to draw lessons about political-moral discourse from the Persian Gulf debate, but American Christians should reflect on the visibility of the moral arguments. The recourse to moral discourse to defend and to criticize U.S. policy was substantially greater than during World War II, Korea, and even Vietnam. Two reasons seem to account for this: the almost measured pace of the August-January debate, and broad public awareness of the categories for moral assessment (cause, last resort, proportionality, and discrimination), which was the legacy of the Vietnam and nuclear debates.

A second point Christians should keep in mind when considering the Persian Gulf debate is the interest it renewed in the just-war ethic. After two decades of moral argument about the "extreme cases" of war—revolutionary war and nuclear strategy—the Iraqi invasion of Kuwait once again raised "the standard case" that compelled attention to both *ius ad bellum* and *ius in bello*. Indeed, the public argument from August to January, even when people were not explicitly invoking ethical categories, moved from *cause*, to *conditions* for using force, to the *means* debate after the war began. The means debate was less fulsome than I would have hoped, but it was still substantial.

Turning to specific just-war criteria, I am sure we need a more clearly articulated hierarchy of tests for proportionality. We must be able to make proportionality judgments *before*, *during*, and *after* a war. The quite impressive concern with avoiding direct targeting of civilians in the Gulf war may have left the debate about proportionality limits for combatants unfinished. While holding fast to the vital distinction between civilians and combatants, we must not allow ourselves to become too cavalier about combatant casualties. On the basis of the limited information available, I would question on the grounds of proportionality both the repeated strikes against legitimate targets in Baghdad and the bombing of retreating Iraqis. The strikes near densely populated civilian areas lost their justification, in my view, as they were multiplied, and the problem posed by the retreating forces did not justify the style of bombing to which they were subjected. These are, of course, initial judgments that will need to be reviewed as more complete information becomes available.

Human Rights and Democracy

Since the mid-1980s the changing horizon of international politics has been marked by a movement toward democratization in Latin American, Asia, and—most dramatically—Eastern Europe. Often reversing decades of history, popular pressure and some remarkable personal leadership have created embryonic but real democratic polities. Many of these new democrats have openly acknowledged their debt to American sources of democratic philosophy and practice.

Both the trend toward democracy and the role of the United States as an example of democratic governance raise the question of whether fostering democracy abroad should be a specific objective of U.S. foreign policy. In the 1990s the consensus, supported by commentators across the political spectrum, is resoundingly affirmative. The churches are part of the broader coalition, although Protestants have a stronger track record on this issue than Catholics do. In Catholic teaching clear support for democratic principles did not surface until Pius XII and more particularly Vatican II.

Philosophical support for democratic principles does not make me the least bit uneasy, but I am concerned about the design of policies meant to implement those principles. Unfortunately, in recent years, the distinction between human rights as a policy objective and democracy as a policy goal has become somewhat blurry. Human-rights policy should not be collapsed into democratization policies. While democratic polity *is* the best soil and support for the protection of human rights, the more modest pursuit of human rights should not be entirely sacrificed to the larger and more complex goal of building democratic institutions. The human-rights policies of the 1970s and 1980s served as a restraint and a guide for the United States, as well as a source of pressure on governments that relied on the United States but were found wanting on human-rights grounds.

In the 1990s the United States should continue a human-rights policy based on the legislative framework established in the 1970s, and it should design a complementary set of objectives and policies to foster democratic institutions. But these objectives should be kept distinct. U.S. policy should actively address the protection of human rights of individuals and groups in societies where democracy may be hardly conceivable for years to come. If we focus exclusively on the states that seem ready for democracy, we may not notice the human suffering caused, at times, by some governments that receive military and economic assistance from the United States. The creation of democratic institutions—and the cultural context needed for democratic polity—is also a far more complex task than seeking to establish minimum human-rights guarantees. The United States should pursue the larger goal but not at the expense of a human-rights policy already installed in U.S. law and practice. Neither should the United States ignore the opportunity offered by the end of the Cold War to return to some of the United Nations' original goals and build multilateral institutions focused on human rights.[44]

In brief, I think the United States should follow a two-track policy: support for a basic minimum of human-rights guarantees through bilateral agreements and multilateral institutions, and support for democratic institutions where they are feasible.

The International Order

Today, as we have seen, the concept of international order is commanding new attention in policy debates. While these discussions are not usually cast in the normative terms of Catholic social teaching, the concept of order has intrinsically normative dimensions and can easily be related to normative themes. John Paul II's writings and addresses are particularly useful in this regard. From the 1979 U.N. address to the 1987 encyclical *Sollicitudo Rei Socialis*, the pope has been urging the development of a conception of order for world politics that is adequate in terms of both its *scope* and *structure*.

The *scope* of the international system refers to who is included when decisions are made about patterns of power, distribution of resource, access to decision-making, and determination of the issues that will receive primary attention in world politics. *Sollicitudo* underscores Paul VI's contention that the social question is now global in scope. John Paul II, the pope so associated in the public mind with "East-West" issues and the revolutions in Eastern Europe, has effectively and pointedly used this reputation to call the world's attention to problems and peoples falling outside the East-West framework. His repeated assertions in *Sollicitudo* that "the South" had been a casualty of the East-West competition are part of his argument for addressing anew the problems of debt and development.

In many ways the empirical assumptions of *Sollicitudo* have been dated by events: the "East" as a geopolitical concept has been largely emptied of meaning, and the "South" is too general a term to encompass sub-Saharan Africa, Central America, and the "NICS" (Newly Industrializing Countries) of East Asia. But certainly the moral standard for any conception of order has continuing relevance.

The persistent regional conflicts of Central America and southern Africa, the devastating debt of Latin America, and the disastrous droughts and internal wars of sub-Saharan Africa neither threaten vital interests of the "North," as Middle East oil supplies do, nor command world attention. The decision to give political and economic priority to these issues—and to the people and nations whose fate depends on their resolution—is one that the "North" will have to make consciously, for normative and empirical reasons. It is not clear at the outset of the 1990s that such a decision has widespread support. John Paul II's lasting message in *Sollicitudo* is that a just international order must effectively address these questions. This pope from the "East" is determined not to let the world forget the "South."

The question of the structure of power in the emerging order is only indirectly addressed by John Paul II, but Charles Krauthammer's "unipolar" thesis strikes me as just about opposite to the pope's vision of the future. Krauthammer argues,

> We are in for abnormal times. Our best hope for safety in such times, as in difficult times past, is in American strength and will—the strength and will to lead a unipolar world, unashamedly laying down the rules of world order and being prepared to enforce them.[45]

John Paul II, by contrast, has often appealed for a devolution of the role of the superpowers and the opening of space in the international system so that others might play a more controlling role in their destiny and development.

The Krauthammer proposal, which can easily be enhanced by drawing the wrong lessons from the Persian Gulf, calls for a world role that is beyond one country's wisdom, resources, or right. One can reject Krauthammer's vision, however, without denying that American strength—wisely, justly, and proportionately used—will be a central factor in determining how the emerging international order develops.

In the short run, the United States is uniquely endowed to fulfill some important tasks. But unilaterally laying down the rules and enforcing them is not what it should be trying to do. It should aspire instead to contribute, in conjunction with others, to a pluralistic world order designed to accommodate multiple needs and mediated by institutions in which the United States is neither the sole architect nor the primary guardian of order. A unipolar world would not be good for either the United States or the rest of its inhabitants. The U.S. posture should be neither to retreat from the world nor to try to run it. Wisdom—moral and political—lies in finding a middle way between these two dangerous options.

Response

JOHN P. LANGAN, S.J.

Near the end of his excellent essay, J. Bryan Hehir urges us to avoid a unipolar conception of the world when thinking about America's future international role. Warning against "unilaterally laying down the rules and enforcing them," he suggests that the United States can best contribute "in conjunction with others" to a world "mediated by institutions in which the United States is neither the sole architect nor the primary guardian of order." In my opinion, the policy of the Bush administration in the Persian Gulf came reasonably close to fitting these norms, but also demonstrated the range of options and policy disagreements that a general call to pluralism and multilateralism may conceal.

The often-repeated claim that the United States should not act as "the policeman of the world" usually elicits ritual consent. Hehir, though he does not use the policeman image, clearly shares this sentiment. I want to challenge it by exploring some of the implications of the image.

What does a policeman actually do on the beat in a city like New York or Washington? He or she has to be ready to intervene in conflicts in which there may well be uncertainty about who is in the right and who is ready to submit to the decisions of a court of law. He or she has to find a way through emergencies in which acknowledged guideposts are few and resistance unpredictable. At the same time, the policeman introduces the rule of law in dangerous, lawless places; protects the innocent; and arouses hostility in people who have reason to be anxious about having their activities examined.

These observations suggest two points: first, that such a role is

---

John P. Langan, S.J., is Rose F. Kennedy Professor of Christian Ethics at the Kennedy Institute of Ethics and a senior fellow of Woodstock Theological Center, Georgetown University.

an honorable and necessary one in dangerous times and places, one that contributes to the common good and requires several important virtues; and second, that this image comes reasonably close to conveying the morally significant aspects of what the United States did in the Persian Gulf. This does not mean that the role is one the United States should insist on playing when the need is not so grave, or that such a role will always yield the best results. Being an honest broker or a non-violent preacher may bring better results in other situations. But I do think we should recognize the possibility that the policeman's role, far from being contemptible or inappropriate, may be both beneficial and praiseworthy.

In a somewhat more serious but still tentative vein, I want to sketch briefly four types of moralism that, in my view, color contemporary discussions of ethics and international affairs, including Hehir's essay. I call these tendencies "moralisms," not to belittle or condemn them, but to convey the point that they are incomplete clusters of moral considerations or aspirations. They can influence our moral arguments, but they do not constitute anything like a comprehensive morality.

The first of these moralisms often presents itself as a renunciation of morality, though usually for worthy or weighty ends. It is what I call *realistic moralism*. Despite its professed determination to avoid the language of morality, realism often has a significant moral agenda and style of its own. It takes existing patterns of international behavior as a reliable indicator of what is morally possible and actually obligatory, and tends to dismiss departures from these patterns as impracticable and dangerous. Stressing the importance of limited objectives and denouncing the perils of utopianism, it acknowledges the limited resources available to decision-makers and to the country. It is concerned about the risk of imperial overstretch and is ready to accept President Bush's rueful remark that we Americans have "more will than wallet." Realistic moralism is concerned with order; it generally takes interests and institutions more seriously than ideas.

The second type of moralism at work in our deliberations is *church moralism*. This sort of moralism aims at greater impartiality and favors policies that will be less interest-driven. In military crises it commends talk over war, negotiation over confrontation. While seeing the future role of superpowers as quite limited, it argues for a more benevolent response to the needs and cries of the Third World—for more generous aid and for transfers of technology and resources. It is also concerned about order, but it understands order mainly in terms of protecting the sovereignty of more vulnerable states, strengthening international organizations, and avoiding war. For historical, doctrinal, and political reasons, it refrains from endorsing pacifism; but it is made more uncomfortable by American military success than by Third World despotisms.

The third type of moralism, which expresses the public idealism of American political discourse, has been particularly influential in shaping U.S. foreign policy in this century. While secular in its program and much of its language, this *idealistic moralism* touches on religious and even messianic themes and aspirations. The public rhetoric of Woodrow Wilson, Franklin Roosevelt, John Kennedy, Jimmy Carter, and Ronald Reagan reflected the conception of America's central task according to idealistic moralism: to foster the key American political values of democracy, freedom, and human rights around the globe. In this quest it has been willing to fight extended wars and to bring significant economic and diplomatic pressure to bear on other states.

This idealistic moralism has held the high ground in American public rhetoric, even though some would dismiss its language as a cover for cynical and manipulative projects of America's rulers. Its strong conception of world order overlaps to a large extent with the internationalism favored in church moralism. Serious problems of consistency present themselves, however, when its key values, which are happily conjoined in the United States, come into conflict with one another in less favored parts of the world. The tangled situations in Iraq and Yugoslavia, as well as in the former Soviet Union, illustrate how difficult it can to be promote all the objectives of idealistic moralism simultaneously. Nonetheless, this is the form of moralism that has the strongest hold on the hearts of the American people. Its view of international order can stress both ideological issues and institutional factors such as the United Nations and security alliances.

A fourth type of moralism is what I call *sectarian moralism*, which can be found in both religious and secular forms. It is concerned

JOHN P. LANGAN 249

above all with the problem of dirty hands in the United States'
international dealings. Even when not explicitly pacifist, it is uncomfortable with policies that seem likely to require force, deception, or manipulation. Often drawing on America's strong isola-
tionist streak, it alternates between confidence in America's moral
superiority to the devious proceedings of lesser states, and despair
over America's corruption, self-righteousness, and episodic brutal-
ity. While tending to agree with realistic moralism about the costs
and actions required to manage international conflict successfully,
it finds these morally unacceptable.

Anyone who regards some actions as morally unacceptable even
when they would be politically advantageous or ideologically attractive has to sympathize, to some degree, with sectarian moralism.
Sectarian moralism can also be vividly renewed when people react
to suffering in the international arena. Particularly in the age of
television, when it is easier to exhibit catastrophes than rationales,
the occurrence of such non-systematic reactions has to be taken
into account.

All these types of moralism influence both individual thinking
and the wider foreign-policy debates in the United States, but none
adequately addresses the demands of theoretical understanding or
can serve as a sufficient guide to practical rightness.

9

Culture First:
The Democratic Capitalist
Revolution Transformed

MICHAEL NOVAK

I N announcing one of the many worldwide conferences convoked
in 1991 to mark the centenary of Pope Leo XIII's social
encyclical *Rerum Novarum*, a brochure from St. Edmund's College
in Cambridge, England, spoke of "Four Revolutions": the industrial revolution, the liberal-capitalist revolution, the socialist revolution, and a yet-to-be-seen "Christian transformation of society."
The same brochure contained the following description of the
present situation: "In the century since [1891], capitalism seemed
to go into decline, while socialism was in the ascendancy. In the
last twenty years, however, capitalism has regrouped and risen
again; now Marxism and socialism seem to be in decline."[1]

This thumbnail sketch of recent history, while broadly acceptable, raises certain serious questions. First, why did Marxism and
socialism fail? Correlatively, as the American Marxist Robert Heilbroner recently asked, why did so few intellectuals or academics,
particularly of the center and the left, predict this failure?[2] On these

Michael Novak holds the George Frederick Jewett Chair in Religion and
Public Policy at the American Enterprise Institute, Washington, D.C.
Among his books on Catholic social thought are *Catholic Social Thought
and Liberal Institutions*, *Free Persons and the Common Good*, and *Will It
Liberate?*

251

points, much can be learned today from those who have lived under Marxist and socialist systems. Their accounts stunningly confirm the predictions made by Leo XIII in 1891.

Second, how are we to understand the capacity of the "liberal-capitalist revolution" to renew itself? Part of the answer to that question may lie in the marriage of capitalism to a democratic political system, which opens it to the religious and humanistic ideals, habits, and aspirations of a Jewish and a Christian people. Besides that, though, what exactly constitutes the inner dynamic of capitalism and its ability to change? The dictionary definitions of capitalism and the descriptions of it proffered by its ideological opponents seem oddly wide of the mark.

Third, supposing that most of the human race will now be "stuck" with the capitalist model for the foreseeable future because it seems the most practical and liberating social ideal, how can these capitalistic societies be brought into closer accord with Jewish, Christian, and humanistic criteria?

Each of these questions must be faced in turn.

WHY DID SOCIALISM FAIL?

The *Socialists*, therefore, in endeavoring to transfer the possessions of individuals to the community, strike at the interests of every wage earner, for they deprive him of the liberty of disposing of his wages, and thus of all hope and possibility of increasing his stock and of bettering his condition in life.

What is of still greater importance, however, is that the remedy they propose is manifestly against justice. For every man has by nature the right to possess property as his own. This is one of the *chief points of distinction* between man and the animal creation. [*Rerum Novarum*, 3]

We are talking here about "real existing socialism," meaning Eastern European and Soviet socialism and the socialism of those elsewhere who admired and supported it. Socialism in this sense has a broader meaning than is intended today by Western social democrats and democratic socialists. The pope in 1891 was using the term "social-ism" in this very broad sense, easily understood by ordinary Catholic parishioners throughout Europe and elsewhere. Socialist labor unions and parties had been spreading the word, sometimes under the name of socialism, sometimes under the name of communism.[3]

In *Rerum Novarum*, Leo XIII listed at least ten reasons why the program of socialism would prove futile. A hundred years later his words seem remarkably prescient. At the same time, Pope Leo attacked many beliefs, customs, and abuses he observed in liberal capitalist nations (then relatively few in number). He severely criticized capitalism, although not by that name, which never occurs in the encyclical. But his approach to socialism was not at all symmetrical. He did not criticize socialism or recommend its reform; he condemned it. He condemned it because it is against natural justice, against nature, against liberty, and against common sense. To get beyond the liberalism of the day and to reconstruct the social order, the pope judged it especially necessary to distinguish his own ideal of a reconstructed order from that of the socialists.

Among the good factors in capitalist and pre-capitalist societies that Leo XIII thought socialism violated were the principles of private property, personal initiative, and natural inequality. Commenting on *private property*, the pope writes, "Nature confers on man the right to possess things privately as his own" (10). He adds, "In seeking help for the masses this principle before all is to be considered as basic, namely, that private ownership must be preserved inviolate" (23). "To own goods privately is a right natural to man, and to exercise this right, especially in life in society, is not only lawful but clearly necessary" (36).[4]

On *personal initiative*, *Rerum Novarum* is equally forthright: "Clearly the essential reason why those who engage in any gainful occupation undertake labor, and at the same time the end to which workers immediately look, is to procure property for themselves and to retain it by individual right as theirs and as their very own" (9). "Would justice permit anyone to own and enjoy that upon which another has toiled? As effects follow the cause producing them, so it is just that the fruit of labor belongs precisely to those who have performed the labor" (16). "If incentives to ingenuity and skill in individual persons were to be abolished, the very fountains of wealth would necessarily dry up; and the equality conjured up by the socialist imagination would, in reality, be nothing but uniform wretchedness and meanness for one and all, without distinction" (22).

On *natural inequality*, Leo XIII writes:

> Therefore, let it be laid down in the first place that in civil society the lowest cannot be made equal with the highest. Socialists, of course, agitate the contrary, but all struggling against nature is vain. There are truly very great and very many natural differences among men. Neither the talents, nor the skill, nor the health, nor the capacities of all are the same, and unequal fortune follows of itself upon necessary inequality in respect to these endowments. And clearly this condition of things is adapted to benefit both individuals and the community; for to carry on its affairs community life requires varied aptitudes and diverse services, and to perform these diverse services men are impelled most by differences in individual property holdings. [26]

To which he later adds, "While justice does not oppose our striving for better things, it does forbid anyone to take from another what is his and, in the name of a certain absurd equality, to seize forcibly the property of others; nor does the interest of the common good permit this" (55).

Among the nearly one dozen serious charges that Leo XIII then levels against socialism (in paragraphs 8–23) are the following: Socialism "violates the rights of lawful owners," "perverts the functions of the State," and "throws governments into utter confusion" (8). Socialism is "openly in conflict with justice inasmuch as nature confers on man the right to possess things as his own," and its partisans "abolish the freedom to dispose of wages" (10). Socialists injure the farmer inasmuch as they "absolutely deny him the right to hold as owner either the ground on which he has built or the farm he has cultivated" (16). Further, "inasmuch as the Socialists disregard care by parents and in its place introduce care by the State, they act *against natural justice* and dissolve the structure of the home" (21). Socialism abolishes "incentives to ingenuity and skill in individual persons," which causes "the very fountains of wealth" to dry up (22). Socialism "contravenes the natural rights of individual persons" and "throws the function of the State and public peace into confusion" (23).

Experiencing the Flaws of Socialism

This is a pretty devastating list, and it is not hard to match it against the testimony of those who have lived under socialism in the USSR and Eastern Europe for the last several decades. Kevin Acker compiled such testimony in *Policy Review*, and many others have also been collecting quotations.[5] From Acker we glean the following:

> Several German intellectuals and politicians had hard words for the fellow citizens who flung themselves on the West German shops as soon as they could. . . . These could only be the words of people who have forgotten, or never knew, the personal humiliation inflicted by the permanent lack of the most elementary consumer goods: the humiliation of silent and hostile lines, the humiliation inflicted upon you by sales people who seem angry to see you standing there, the humiliation of always having to buy what there is, not what you need. The systematic penury of material goods strikes a blow at the moral dignity of the individual. [Bulgaria][6]

> For fifty years it was said that this was public property and belonged to everyone, but no way was ever found to make workers feel they were the co-owners and masters of the factories, farms, and enterprises. They felt themselves to be cogs in a gigantic machine. [USSR][7]

> We cannot talk of freedom unless we have private property. [USSR][8]

> How can you say you have a motherland when you don't own a single square meter of land which you can leave to your grandchildren? [USSR][9]

> We are consciously limiting the role of the state in the economy. It is no longer the supermanager of a superfactory, the main boss and the main controller, the main storekeeper and the main distributor of goods and services. Several dozen years of costly experience have shown that the state cannot do this well, and, in particular, cannot inspire energy in people so that they may work productively, efficiently, and economically. [Poland][10]

> When people are compelled to look only one way, when they are deprived of information and the possibility to compare things,

they stop thinking. Well-informed people, ones who have access to versatile information, inevitably begin to think. The very system invites lies. [USSR][11]

We categorically favor the concept of private initiative. The economic foundation of totalitarianism has been the absolute power derived from the monopoly on property. We shall never have political pluralism without economic pluralism. But some of those who still have Communist leanings try to equate private initiative with "exploitation" and maintain that the emergence of rich entrepreneurs would be a catastrophe. In the same way they try to play on the feelings of those who are lazy and would therefore envy the wealthy, and those who—having once enjoyed the privileges of the Communist system—are afraid of the effort of working. [Romania][12]

The totalitarian system has a special bacterial property. The system is strong not only in its repressive police methods but, more, in the fact that it poisons people's souls and demoralizes them. [Czechoslovakia][13]

In a totalitarian situation people conform outwardly to the prevailing morals and isolate themselves in microsocieties where they live, work, and die. People act according to moral double standards, an unwritten social contract that everyone knows. Workers are allowed to idle and steal, as long as they come to party meetings and applaud. Only a small mafia of party bosses and enterprise bosses took it seriously; the rest of the people cut themselves off. [Czechoslovakia][14]

Listen again, with these texts in mind, to two of Leo XIII's extended predictions about socialism:

The *Socialists*, working on the poor man's envy of the rich, endeavor to destroy private property, and maintain that individual possessions should become the common property of all, to be administered by the State or by municipal bodies. They hold that, by thus transferring property from private persons to the community, the present evil state of things will be set to rights, because each citizen will then have his equal share of whatever there is to enjoy. But their proposals are so clearly futile for all practical purposes, that if they were carried out the working man himself would be among the first to suffer. Moreover they are emphatically unjust, because they would rob the lawful possessor, bring the State into a sphere that is not its own, and cause complete confusion in the community. [4–5]

A few paragraphs later, after some further jabs, the pope once again opens up with both fists:

The Socialists, therefore, in setting aside the parent and introducing the providence of the State, act *against natural justice*, and threaten the very existence of family life. And such interference is not only unjust, but is quite certain to harass and disturb all classes of citizens, and to subject them to odious and intolerable slavery. It would open the door to envy, to evil speaking, and to quarreling; the sources of wealth would themselves run dry, for no one would have any interest in exerting his talents or industry; and that ideal equality of which so much is said would, in reality, be the leveling down of all to the same condition of misery and dishonor. Thus it is clear *that the main tenet of Socialism, the community of goods, must be utterly rejected*; for it would injure those whom it is intended to benefit, it would be contrary to the natural rights of mankind, and it would introduce confusion, and disorder into the commonwealth. [11–12]

This prediction, one hundred years later, seems inspired.

Irrational Rationality

Nonetheless, there is one major criticism of socialism that Leo XIII did not make; Ludwig von Mises discerned it some thirty years later.[15] Perhaps a market system's most important function is to communicate information vital to everyone. Without market systems, economic actors are blind. They cannot know what people want, or how much of it they want, or how much they are willing to pay for it; and they cannot know the costs that lie behind raw materials, labor, and goods or services.

A "planned" system is an exercise in pretense. Its prices are arbitrary; someone just makes them up. In the Soviet economy, Heilbroner reports, the State Committee on Prices had responsibility for setting prices on more than 24 million items.[16] A "planner" charged with setting prices had to determine the value of hundreds of items in a certain sector each day. It proved impossible to deal

with so many prices even monthly. Individual planners or function-
aries were reduced to blind guesswork. Nothing related rationally
to anything else, except in the mind of the planner. Left out of the
equation were the sweat, the desires, and the effort that real human
beings attached to their purchases or sales. The joke was, "We
pretend to work, and they pretend to pay us." The whole economy
was based on make-believe, pursued in the name of "rationality."

As Hayek has pointed out, the "fatal conceit" of socialism lies in
its mistaken view of reason.[17] In the name of rationality, socialism
misconstrues the nature of practical intelligence as it actually operates in society. Socialism imagines that society works from the top
down, like a pyramid, and through a more-or-less geometric form
of reason. From a few goals or premises, a planner is suppose to
deduce practical directives, which in turn will guide every individual
action. This indeed is a form of rationality. But, as Aristotle
remarked, there are several kinds of rationality, and it is a sign of
wisdom to choose an appropriate kind for each field of inquiry. In
the practical affairs of society, one must allow for the contingency
inherent in temporal events and also for the liberty of individual
human agents. In such a field, the appropriate form of rationality is
prudence (practical wisdom, *phronesis*), not geometry. This is why
so many writers rebelling against socialist rule, such as Dostoevsky,
Orwell, and Zamyatin, protested against the "2 x 2 = 4 man."[18]

Freedom is a necessary condition for the exercise of practical
wisdom, since individuals must activate their own capacities for
practical reasoning and make their own choices. Regarding ideas,
individuals need freedom of inquiry and discourse. Regarding
economic choices, they require a free market. Reflections of this
sort lay behind Leo XIII's arguments in favor of private property,
long-term family incentives, and the limited state.

The Importance of a Free Market

Leo XIII neither defended nor attacked the free market. He
neither described its many important functions nor pointed out
why it is necessary to a free society governed by practical wisdom
and charity. As A. M. C. Waterman has pointed out, the Catholic
environment in which Leo XIII worked missed out on the argu-

ment for market systems that had agitated British intellectual life for a century prior to 1891; its main points had simply not been considered.[19] While Leo was especially concerned about the condition of workers and the poor, he did not seem to grasp how much they suffered from the lack of competition in markets. He saw the excessive power of a relatively few employers but saw no cure for such monopoly except in government.

While he dwelt little on markets, Leo's grasp of the fundamental importance of private property to the free society was admirable. A regime of private property is, as Eastern European reformers see clearly, indispensable to limiting the power of the state. But so also is a regime based on market exchange. For the alternative to market exchange is an authoritarianism so vast that it overpowers every exchange of private property. Indeed, most Eastern Europeans have learned to dread total political control over markets. In 1989 Václav Klaus, finance minister of Czechoslovakia, stated unequivocally:

> We want a market economy without any adjectives. Any compromises will only fuzzy up the problems we have. To pursue a so-called third way is foolish. We had our experience with this in the 1960s when we looked for socialism with a human face. It did not work, and we must be explicit when we say that we are not aiming for a more efficient version of a system that has failed. The market is indivisible; it cannot be an instrument in the hands of central planning.[20]

A market economy is important not only for political freedom; it is also important for morals. A market economy inculcates a type of mentality quite different from that of a command economy. In place of passivity and obedience, it awakens the life of active virtue. The mayor of Leningrad in 1990 put the alternative quite clearly:

> For decades in our country, we have fostered a beggar/consumer mentality: the state will provide and decide everything for you— poorly, perhaps, but provide equally for everyone, give you all the basic necessities. And this parasitic mentality is very widespread here. Yet a market economy, in order to function, requires a very different type of mentality: enterprise, initiative, responsibility, every person solving his own problems. The government does nothing more than create the conditions in which one can

employ one's initiative and enterprise; the rest is up to the individual.[21]

If markets are to serve liberty and morality in this way, competition within each market area needs to be insisted on, not narrowed. Access to markets must be universal, legally accessible to all. By not fully exploring the ways in which markets may be used as tools, especially for ameliorating the lot of the poor, Leo XIII deprived himself of an important argument against socialism—one that would prove decisive in history.

Why Predictions Failed

Returning to Heilbroner's question—why writers of the left and center were so remiss in failing to see the impending failure of socialism—the most direct answer is that most have shared in the rationalistic conceit. To many, it once seemed almost intuitively obvious that an economy under political control from above would be more "rational" than one in which every person simply thinks and chooses for himself. There would be, so it was thought, less duplication, less wastage, less concern with what some saw as trivialities, and more concern with basic needs. Intellectuals were especially tempted by the proposition that members of their own class, given authority, would fashion a more rational and more moral social order than would free citizens alone, left to their own choices. Once theoreticians of the left and center succumbed to this conceit—particularly in an intellectual environment driven by the left, in which the center merely moves more slowly than the left but in the same direction—it was exceedingly difficult for them to predict their own failures. Those who rejected this conceit root and branch, by contrast, were more likely to spot the inevitability of failure.

But why were such persons, the scholars of the "right" named by Heilbroner (Hayek, von Mises, Friedman, and others), treated so dismissively by their leftist peers? Those who knew which way history was moving—toward greater rationality from above—could dismiss such dissenters as malcontents who preposterously wanted "to set the clock back." They seemed to assume that history moves forward as rigidly as a clock's inner mechanical wheels. In other words, the rationalistic conceit disallowed challenge from the outside. Those who embraced it claimed to have rationality all to themselves. Their consciences were not uneasy, therefore, when they accused those to their right of irrational and unworthy motives, such as protecting the interests of the rich. They never imagined that their own motives might be suspect, and that they might be protecting the interests of the politically powerful. Their consciences were clean, and their core conceit was untroubled by doubt. That is why the sudden collapse of the moral prestige of socialism surprised them. One must credit Heilbroner for his honesty in admitting it.

THE RESURGENCE OF LIBERAL CAPITALISM

It is a paradox that in the twentieth century the ideas of socialism have not been realized in the socialist countries, but in other countries, the capitalist countries. In the countries which call themselves socialist, socialism has been distorted to the degree where it causes disgust.[22]

The reasons for socialism's failure are many. What are the reasons for capitalism's success in reforming and refashioning itself from within? "Progressives" are not the only ones who hold capitalism in low regard. Down through the ages, aristocrats have shown considerable contempt for persons of commerce.[23] Aristocrats could afford to be concerned with things "for their own sake," and could look down on grubby utilitarian efforts requiring sweat. More generally, especially in Latin cultures, traditionalists have thought of capitalism as crass, vulgar, and uncivilized. In Latin America, there is even a saying that "liberalism is sin." From both the left and the right, there were many reasons for misjudging capitalism.

From the point of view of *Rerum Novarum*, by contrast, the European economy of 1891 had two or three saving features, even though it was in need of reconstruction. The saving features were these: liberal capitalism allowed for private property, the *sine qua non* of a society of personal self-determination; it allowed for, even insisted on, the limited state; and it created a significant degree of "civic space" within which free associations could thrive.

Nonetheless, Leo XIII judged that the liberal capitalist society of 1891 was founded on at least two serious errors. Liberalism misunderstood the human person, thinking that each was radically individual and isolated from others, except through artificial social contract. Second, it assumed that all human beings are equal, paying insufficient heed to the weakness and helplessness of many who could not be expected to compete with others on equal terms. In this respect, the new liberal order left too many at the mercy of too few: "The present age handed over the workers, each alone and defenseless, to the inhumanity of employers and the unbridled greed of competitors" (6).

Karl Marx built his concept of exploitation on his theory of class conflict, his labor theory of value, and his theory of the expropriation by capitalist owners of the "surplus value" of the labor of workers. In a more subtle way, as Stephen T. Worland has demonstrated, Leo XIII also worked from a theory of "exploitation" different from and deeper than that of Marx.[24] Leo XIII rejected the theory of class conflict, the labor theory of value, and the theory of surplus labor. In his view, each class "needs the other completely: neither capital can do without labor, nor labor without capital" (28). The exploitation Leo feared was of a different order. He feared that the concrete pragmatism required by capitalism would inculcate habits of instrumentalist thinking at the expense of other habits, from the religious to the aesthetic, necessary for full human development. Everything might come to be judged according to a calculus of profit and loss, which would induce hard-heartedness among powerful persons in society, truncate their humanity, and warp their souls. In one sense, such tendencies in humans are an old story; the Bible recounts many tales of hard-heartedness, callousness, and cruelty. In another sense, though, liberal capitalism might inculcate such habits more systemically and more broadly throughout the population.

This was a serious charge. It rested, however, on the hidden premise that liberal capitalism is a one-sided system, subject to no checks and balances from the political and moral-cultural systems, for example. This premise *does* hold for pre-modern regimes and for socialist regimes. The rationalistic conceit at the heart of socialism leads to authoritarian, monistic social structures because all three powers—moral, political, and economic—are concentrated in one set of institutions and one set of hands. The economy is controlled by political power, and both realms are under ideological or moral control. In the classic texts of Marxism and socialism, accordingly, there is little or no discussion of the separation of systems, the separation of powers, checks and balances, and the "auxiliary precautions" of which, at the very founding of the American constitutional order, James Madison spoke so eloquently.[25]

The socialist vision in most of its forms has been caught up with the vision of shaping "the new man," a man perfect in justice and thoroughly imbued with the spirit of equality and comradeship. This rationalistic conceit led to considerable optimism concerning man, once he could be freed from the evil structures of capitalism. No such illusion is likely under democratic and capitalist presuppositions.[26] The liberal capitalist order was brought to birth, at least in the United States, within an ethos thoroughly aware of human weakness, fallibility, and vice—of what in Christian theology is called original sin. On this point the work of James Madison and Alexander Hamilton echoed that of the Puritan divines.

The Limits of Capitalism

As contrasting social visions, therefore, socialism and capitalism are not symmetrical. Socialism is a unitary system. It *intends* to concentrate all powers in the hands of those who control the apparatus of the state. Even in its more moderate forms, the impulse of socialism is to bring the economy under political control and, in general, to strengthen the hand and enlarge the reach of government. By contrast, liberal theory, even in its most secular forms, retains a healthy fear of Leviathan, a worry about torture and tyranny flowing from the concentrated power of the state.

Liberalism constantly tries to divide social systems, to divide the powers of the state, to divide offices and functions from top to bottom as thoroughly as possible, and to establish checks and balances. One purpose of this pervasive effort to limit and to divide government is to retain as large a civic space as possible for the voluntary action of individuals and their associations. Liberal theory holds the profound conviction that the most creative sources of virtue, intellect, and moral progress lie in spheres of private life protected from state control.[27] The state is granted no right to make any laws restricting the free exercise of religion. Neither is it permitted to restrict the generation or dissemination of information and ideas. The life of the spirit—of religion, science, the arts, morals, and culture—is kept free of state control.

The resulting moral and cultural vigor, in turn, has provided a decisive check and balance to the economic system. Citizens are regarded as moral and cultural agents first and as economic agents only secondly. They are regarded as having moral and religious responsibilities that, at crucial times, take precedence over their economic projects. In the hot blood of its youth, of course, the new capitalist order often ran roughshod over religious and moral energies. But these quietly gathered their force and over the generations have tamed the wildness of capitalism's youth. They could not have done so if they had not been ceded the important role of counterweight throughout the social system as a whole. Through the observance of the Sabbath, through the encouragement of philanthropy and compassion for the poor, through the "social gospel," through activism, and in many other ways the churches continually and steadily disciplined the raw economic passions with which they were confronted. This process took time. But whole generations of clergymen, university professors, social workers, writers, and reformers gradually made their presence felt in the world of public opinion.

They did not have to rely on moral and cultural persuasion alone. A second counterweight was also built into the system: the political power of the democratic state. In a democracy, farmers, workers, and the poor outnumber the rich owners of factories and the captains of commerce by large numerical proportions. Moreover, in a highly diversified society, the interests of citizens cannot be confined solely within the narrow banks of class analysis; this was Madison's point in *Federalist* papers 10 and 51.[28] The many have effective means of slowly but steadily transforming social institutions until those institutions meet their pleasure. As a whole, working people and the poor tend to be socially conservative, not nearly so radical as intellectuals and middle-class reformers. Ordinary people seldom want revolution, since they fear disruption in the patterns of their already-difficult daily lives. What pleases them best is steady but measurable progress, which a pluralistic, democratic order is well suited to provide.

The gradual, systematic change in liberal capitalism, then, owes much to notable creative energies generated from two different directions—one moral-cultural and the other political. Since its founding in the late eighteenth century, capitalism's social system as a whole, which is composed of three relatively independent spheres—political, economic, and moral-cultural—has demonstrated a remarkable capacity for self-reform and internal transformation. Slavery was abolished; a civil-rights revolution was conducted. By practically every measure available, the conditions of daily life were quite considerably improved from decade to decade. Even in the seventeenth century, John Locke had noted that "a king of a large fruitful territory [in a primitive land] feeds, lodges, and is clad worse than a day laborer in England."[29]

Unprecedented Development

As liberal capitalist countries experienced further material progress, their standards for the life and health of the poor rose as well, and their sense of compassion and civil responsibility grew exponentially. Medical care improved dramatically. So did wages, housing conditions, educational opportunity, and other facets of life. Associations of "middle-class reformers" of all sorts flourished. Churches used available civic space to develop a remarkable number of institutions in the social sphere: schools, orphanages, hospitals, musical societies, domestic clubs, athletic leagues, and discussion groups. It is doubtful that any century surpassed the nineteenth in the reach of its social reform, civic responsibility, and voluntarism. Millions who came to America poor soon were poor no longer, just as in Western Europe standards of living reached by 1991 exceeded the wildest fantasies of the Depression of 1931, let alone of 1891.[30]

Today we take for granted much that would have astonished John Locke and Adam Smith. This is certainly true regarding the condition of the poor. In addition to welfare benefits, which are not counted in calculating who is below the poverty line, consider these facts: 38 per cent of the American *poor* own their own homes; the average poor American is more likely to own a car than the average Western European; 95 per cent of the poor have television sets;[31] the elderly poor are eligible for medical care and the younger for Medicaid. Even such trivial indicators as the Reeboks worn by poor youngsters on schoolyard basketball courts are telling. Boris Yeltsin astringently pointed out, "Some of what are, in the United States, called 'slums' would pass for pretty decent housing in the Soviet Union."[32] Never in the history of the North Atlantic peoples have so many been so free and so prosperous. Marx wrongly predicted the poor's accelerating immiseration under capitalism. Instead of collapsing, the liberal capitalist order has experienced one resurgence after another.

The fundamental reason for democratic capitalism's capacity for self-reform lies in the independence of its moral-cultural order and its political order, both of which operate effectively on its economic system. Each of these three systems represents a different aspect of reality, and each of them is moved by certain organic laws that, when violated, exact considerable costs. The system as a whole, then, comes under three quite different reality checks. While such tension regularly produces crises, each crisis becomes an opportunity for fresh restructuring.

Relying on Human Creativity

Underlying this threefold system is a considerable faith in the creative capacity of the human person. Theologically, this faith is well placed. Each person is made in the image of God, the Creator; each is called to be a co-creator and is given the vocation to act creatively and responsibly as a free citizen. Each is expected to show initiative and to assume responsibility.

In this way a new moral virtue is summoned up among such citizens, who are no longer merely subjects of king or emperor but sovereigns in their own right: I mean the virtue of enterprise. Enterprise in this sense is a moral and intellectual virtue that prompts people to be alert, noticing, and discerning with respect to projects to be launched and goods and services to be provided.[33]

Such citizens are taught to act for themselves rather than to look to the state for the things they want and need. They themselves must set in motion procedures to bring about the goals they desire. They are taught to live as free men and women, responsible for their own destiny.

This image of free men and free women in a free society is compatible with the vision of Leo XIII. *Rerum Novarum* encouraged Christians around the world to take responsibility for restructuring the social order. It played a significant role in transforming liberal capitalism.

Within capitalism itself, moreover, lies another source of regeneration: its innovative spirit. Joseph Schumpeter discerned that the dynamism of capitalism lies in the creative impulse.[34] Hayek showed that this creativity appears in practice as enterprise.[35] Israel Kirzner showed that at the heart of enterprise is the act of discovery.[36] In brief, capitalism is a system rooted in mind. The characteristic signs of its presence are innovation, discovery, and invention.

In this respect, capitalism goes beyond all preceding economic systems. The three elements forming the spine of earlier traditional economies—private property, market exchange, and profit or accumulation—are preconditions of capitalism but do not identify its specific difference (although they figure in most dictionary definitions).[37] Such dictionary definitions seem to distinguish capitalism from Marx's idea of socialism but not from traditional, pre-capitalist market systems. They fail to mention the dynamic and creative quality that sets capitalism apart from prior systems of the traditional market type. It is ironic that Mikhail Gorbachev should have grasped the point that so many Westerners miss:

> The Soviet Union is suffering from a spiritual decline. We were among the last to understand that in the age of information technology the most valuable asset is knowledge, which springs from individual imagination and creativity. We will pay for our mistakes for many years to come.[38]

Capitalism has its origin in the human capacity for invention and innovation—the human capacity to create. For that reason, it has a profound interest in freedom of thought and expression. As any visitor to a trade fair may observe, a market functions as an official disseminator of information, skills, methods, and new possibilities. In addition, a market is an efficient instrument for taking useful goods and services from the research laboratory into the public arena. The USSR was not scientifically backward; still, lacking a vital marketplace, it largely failed to make its research serve the common people. Similarly, the public success of the Industrial Revolution depended on the spirit of enterprise and the openness of the marketplace. Abraham Lincoln, who saw in the Patent and Copyright Clause of the U.S. Constitution one of the decisive turning points in the history of liberty, was aware of this dependence, but it has received too little attention from economic historians.[39]

In summary, capitalism is resurgent for two main reasons. First, a capitalist order was early embedded in a powerful moral-cultural system and a democratic political system, which together were able to direct it into fruitful channels and eventually to curb many abuses, real and potential. Second, the dynamic agency at the heart of capitalism is the creative capacity of the human mind, which a capitalist order nourishes by means of a distinctive set of institutions. Among these institutions are universal education, patent and copyright laws, research facilities, and associations for raising venture capital.

WHAT'S LEFT?

I have been to the West and have become convinced that we can use many things from the Western democracies, including the attitude to property, the parliamentary system, and much more. There is no reason to renounce all this because it is capitalist. Why should we do that if it is rational and useful? [Boris Yeltsin, 1989][40]

For many years after *Rerum Novarum*, interpreters of Catholic social thought suggested that since Leo XIII had condemned socialism and was critical of capitalism, the Catholic Church must be propounding a "middle way." But such thinking overlooked the asymmetry between capitalism and socialism. Socialism fuses the moral, economic, and political systems into one; capitalism is only an economic system, which for its full and free development requires a democratic polity and a humanistic and pluralist culture. In a sense, then, the threefold combination of democracy, capitalism, and religious liberty *is* the middle way between socialism and capitalism, narrowly defined. Just the same, after praising institutions of democracy, personal economic initiative, and religious liberty, Pope John II said emphatically in *Sollicitudo Rei Socialis* that the Catholic Church is *not* seeking a middle way.[41]

No doubt the pope recognized that in Central Europe these days, the term "middle way" is spoken of disdainfully. In 1989 Leszek Balcerowicz, finance minister of Poland, declared: "We don't want to try out a third way. We will leave it to the richer countries to try out a third way, and if they succeed maybe we will follow."[42] The finance minister of Czechoslovakia spoke in terms as clear as Bohemian crystal: "We want the market economy without any adjectives. Any compromises will only fuzzy up the problems we have. To pursue a so-called third way is foolish. We had our experience with this in the 1960s when we looked for socialism with a human face. It did not work."[43] The future president of Bulgaria went further: "To speak of any future for socialism in this country is nonsense. . . . Our goal now is to lead Bulgaria to a modern, democratic capitalism."[44]

Some persons in the Church, particularly in Latin countries, have resisted the fact that papal social thinking refuses to endorse either a socialist way or a middle way. Even after accepting the teaching, they are reluctant to conclude that democratic capitalism is the only alternative and that an incarnational strategy must begin with the best materials available, however poor they are. Democratic capitalism is a poor system, but the known human alternatives are worse. In Catholic social thought, the perfect and the good are not enemies. The ethic proper to political economy is an ethic of prudence suffused with charity,[45] of justice tempered with mercy.[46] Nonetheless, Catholic social thought does insist on one principle that some erroneously regard as contrary to the spirit of democratic capitalism.

Pope John Paul II stated "the characteristic principle of Christian social doctrine" quite simply in a single sentence in *Sollicitudo Rei Socialis* (42): "The goods of this world are *originally meant for all*." In the footnote accompanying this text, the pope cites as background Vatican II's decree *Gaudium et Spes* (69), Paul VI's encyclical

Populorum Progressio (22), and St. Thomas Aquinas, *Summa Theologiae* (I-II.66.2). This principle is formally known as "the universal destination of created goods." Vatican II affirms this principle in these words: "God intended the earth and all that it contains for the use of every human being and people. Thus, as men follow justice and unite in charity, created goods should abound for them on a reasonable basis."[47]

"Created goods should abound"—this modern treatment of the ancient principle includes two modern assumptions: first, that the goods of creation do abound in support of human life; second, that human economic creativity can keep ahead of population growth. These assumptions clash with pre-modern views, which stress scarcity, hardship, poverty, and the persistent threat of famine, plague, and demographic decline. In 1776 the earth supported only 735 million persons, for example. Yet by 1990, after experiencing the inventiveness of democratic capitalism, especially in the fields of medicine and agriculture, the earth supported 5.3 billion persons. The assumption that human inventiveness and economic creativity can keep ahead of population to provide abundance "on a reasonable basis" is, therefore, a sound one, but only when democratic capitalist institutions function smoothly. In the non-capitalist countries of the world, poverty and scarcity still prevail.

The modern statement of the "universal destination" in *Gaudium et Spes* and *Populorum Progressio* assumes, then, that abundance may be taken for granted. But in socialist and pre-capitalist (Third World) nations, this assumption does not hold. It only holds in democratic capitalist nations, in part because within them rights to private property are respected by a regime of law. Yet here these documents take a curious turn. Since ancient times—in the Bible, in Aristotle, in Cicero, in St. Augustine, and consistently in the Catholic tradition—statements about the universal destination as final end have led to unambiguous statements about the necessary means to its fulfillment: a regime of private property. Traditional, pre-capitalist moral reasoning highly commended private property. By contrast, appearing near the high tide of Eurosocialism in 1967, *Populorum Progressio* sounded a troubled note about private property: "Private property does not constitute for anyone an absolute and unconditional right. No one is justified in keeping for his exclusive use what he does not need, when others lack necessities" (23). A similar affirmation is found in St. Thomas Aquinas, it is true, but his main argument ran in exactly the opposite direction.

St. Thomas on Private Property

The issue that confronted Aquinas (cited by Pope John Paul II in *Sollicitudo*) was this: "Whether it is lawful for a man to possess a thing as his own" (S.T. I-II.66.2). St. Thomas took the principle of universal destination for granted. Against it he saw the urgent need for a regime of private property. By contrast, recent Vatican passages attempt the reverse: they take the principle of private property for granted and seek to limit its sweep. St. Thomas argued against extreme communitarians; some recent Vatican statements seem to argue on their behalf. This shift in emphasis is altogether legitimate, but it should be noted.

Aquinas begins with three objections against the legitimacy of private property, as raised by the communitarians. The first objection he faced was this: "According to the natural law all things are common property." The second was a criticism by St. Basil of "the rich who deem as their own property the goods that they have seized." The third was from St. Ambrose, who had written, "Let no man call his own that which is common property."

St. Thomas replies to these objections by distinguishing between two kinds of power human beings have over material goods: the power to procure and distribute material goods, and the power to use them.

Regarding the second of these—the *use* of material goods—he says that a man "ought to possess external things, not as his own, but as common, so that he is ready to communicate them to others in their need." In support of this principle, which he seems to hold as a matter of Christian belief, Aquinas quotes from St. Paul's first Epistle to Timothy (6:17-18), St. Basil, and St. Ambrose.

Regarding the *production* and *distribution* of material goods, however, Aquinas gives three reasons why a regime of private property is "necessary." He cites one argument from faith (from St. Augustine) and three based on natural reason. A regime of private property, he writes, is necessary to human life for three reasons. First because every man is more careful to procure what is for himself alone than that which is common to many or to all: since each one would shirk the labor and leave to another that which concerns the community, as happens where there is a great number of servants. Secondly, because human affairs are conducted in more orderly fashion if each man is charged with taking care of some particular thing himself, whereas there would be confusion if everyone had to look after any one thing indeterminately. Thirdly, because a more peaceful state is ensured to man if each one is contented with his own. Hence it is to be observed that quarrels arise more frequently where there is no division of the things possessed.

To those who have lived through the seventy-year experiment with socialism in our time, this threefold reasoning about the necessity of private property must seem painfully vindicated by modern experience. If men were angels, the common ownership of the means of production might work, but human experience has taught us that private property is a practical necessity. Indeed, Pope John Paul II himself, having experienced "real existing socialism" first hand, has taken pains to spell out the commonsense reasoning of St. Thomas on property, much as Leo XIII did.[48]

Clearly, the Ten Commandments take for granted a regime of private property. Neither "Thou shall not steal" nor "Thou shall not covet" makes sense apart from the right to personal property. Beyond this, Aquinas's arguments underline the social functions of private property. A regime of private property encourages social peace, good order, and positive personal incentives. Without peace, order, and incentives, the raw goods of creation cannot be transmuted by human labor into usable goods and services. Creation left to itself does not fulfill human needs. If a man wants to eat, he must work "by the sweat of his brow."[49] Socialism, as Leo XIII emphasized, severs the arteries of economic growth by undercutting family-centered incentives. The resource-rich Soviet Union was a living lesson in the damage a nation can do to itself by abandoning private property. The situation in the Third World is nearly as bad.

In few places on earth today are property rights practiced as "natural rights" in the sense intended by Madison and Jefferson. In most of Latin America, for example, property rights are insecure even where they are respected in principle. Property of the wealthiest has often been subjected to arbitrary confiscations, nationalization, and unlawful seizures; property of the lowliest is even less well guaranteed. Title to property is often uncertain and virtually unverifiable, and huge majorities of the population are property-less with respect to land or home. Wherever property rights are protected across the generations, families of farmers and other laborers find incentives to improve their property. Wherever those rights are not protected, stagnation or even decline is visible.

Traditional Catholic reasoning on the universal destination of created goods as the end and property rights as the means is not exactly identical to that of John Locke and the Anglo-American tradition, but neither is it wholly different. Locke, too, regarded all earthly goods as belonging by nature to the entire human race.[50] He held that without human labor, the earth would hardly support human life, and that human wit and labor are indispensable in improving and cultivating nature. Left to nature alone, a field might yield a harvest only one-tenth to one one-hundredth as large as the same field under human care and cultivation.[51] Human creativity, then, produces the wealth of nations. From experience Locke, like the ancients, concluded that people would not be induced to draw usable wealth out of nature—to improve the land, for example—without a system of laws securing man's natural right to private property. Human creativity needs many social supports, including limited government, the rule of law, monogamous marriage and the family, systems of transport and markets, and a regime of private property.

A regime of private property is a social institution, designed for social purposes with benefits redounding to all. John Stuart Mill even maintained that, because service to the common good provided the justification for private property, a landowner who did not improve his property would lose his claim to private ownership.[52] In other words, the principle cuts two ways: A society that arbitrarily abridges private property will destroy incentives, but individuals who do not use private property to improve the public good undercut their claim to ownership.

How to Help Others

In general, since *Gaudium et Spes*, papal statements on the universal destination of goods have been directed toward persuading rich nations and rich persons to give of their abundance to poor nations and poor persons. They have done less well in persuading the citizens of socialist and pre-capitalist states to reconstruct their inadequate social systems. But this task is also important. Self-reliance—within nations and among nations—is a crucial concept for Catholic social thought, as the Pontifical Commission on Justice and Peace has emphasized for many years.[53] Dependency is not honored. In commending the welfare programs of highly developed (that is, democratic capitalist) nations, for example, *Gaudium et Spes* also includes a prescient warning about problems that would become apparent in all welfare states three decades later:

> In highly developed nations a body of social institutions dealing with insurance and security can, for its part, make the common purpose of earthly goods effective. Family and social services, especially those which provide for culture and education, should be further promoted. Still, care must be taken lest, as a result of all these provisions, the citizenry fall into a kind of sluggishness toward society, and reject the burdens of office and of public service. [69]

In recent years, papal social teaching has also spoken metaphorically of a "gap" between the affluent, democratic capitalist nations and the pre-capitalist and socialist nations. This "gap" is not to be understood arithmetically, of course. If a poor country grew by 10 per cent while a wealthy one grew by only 1 per cent, the bases on which the rates are calculated might be so different that, at the end, the absolute difference between the two Gross Domestic Products might be larger, not smaller. Ten per cent of a $50 billion economy is only $5 billion, but 1 per cent of a $5 trillion economy is $50 billion. Thus, poorer countries might be improving at a faster rate even though the gap does not seem to be diminishing. The "gap" is not the moral issue; the rapid improvement in the lot of the poor is what is morally significant.

The inability of some Third World nations to pay their debts indicates that their economies do not use borrowed money very creatively. If they did, they would make a profit on it, from which interest could be paid. Instead, the money seems simply to vanish, sometimes with little to show for it. It is questionable, therefore, whether even massive infusions of funds from other countries would be of much lasting benefit. Moneys paid into the coffers of governments, bankers, industrialists, and other members of local power elites do not always find their way into uses benefiting ordinary people or even into productive investments at home. On the contrary, amounts equal to half or more of the total debt of Latin America have actually been reinvested in Switzerland, North America, and elsewhere, in a phenomenon known as "capital flight."[54]

For such reasons many scholars oppose "foreign aid" on the ground that it encourages an irresponsible use of others' money.[55] They object particularly to foreign aid granted by one government to another because the corruption of political elites in Third World countries is virtually uncontrollable. A much sounder policy, they argue, is to give aid directly to ordinary people, not as welfare benefits but in the form of education, training, and small amounts of carefully supervised credit for the launching of small local businesses. "Better than to give a man a fish is to teach him how to fish."

A serious Jewish or Christian conscience, even the conscience of a serious humanist, feels the bite of the principle that the world's material goods should ultimately benefit all human beings. A human society is judged morally by how well it cares for the most vulnerable in its midst and for the most vulnerable on the planet. But how best do we care for them? By outright grants? By loans? By the transmission of basic skills? By training in the laws and practices of a sound economy? By good counsel on how to establish the basic institutions of a productive system? By opening the markets of Europe, Japan, North America, and other centers of dynamic economic growth to the products and services of the poorer nations? It is not enough to say that citizens of the commercially successful nations have an obligation to help their less fortunate brothers and sisters. It is crucial to begin asking *how* this obligation can be fruitfully acquitted. Few tasks in life are more difficult than giving truly useful help to the needy without reducing them to servile dependence on their donors.

Democratic capitalist societies must invent practical working methods for helping other nations experience fruitful institutional development. Clearly, even some nations with enormous material resources, such as Brazil and the former USSR, have violated the principle of the universal destination of material or created goods by failing to develop those resources. We need to realize that many of God's precious gifts are not being developed for the benefit of humankind but are lying neglected or abused for want of creative, productive systems of political economy.

Being saddled with a defective system frustrates even a virtuous people, whereas getting the system right helps them mightily. That is why it is crucial for Jewish, Christian, and humanistic thinkers to inquire carefully into which sorts of systems best serve the potentialities of our human nature. It does the poor no good to entrap them further in defective, illiberal, and inhumane systems.

TRANSFORMING DEMOCRATIC CAPITALISM

Given the capacity of democratic and capitalist societies for self-reform, how can we bring them more into harmony with Jewish, Christian, and humanistic ideals? Reform could take many directions. Since no temporal system ever approaches the fullness of the Kingdom of God, a good and realistic conscience and a strong social imagination can always bring to light useful changes. For purposes of brevity, I limit myself to proposing two urgent reforms—first, in the cultural and moral sphere, and, second, with regard to the poor.

Moral and Intellectual Reforms

The moral-cultural system is at once crucial to the health of democratic capitalism and easily overlooked. It is crucial because the primary form of capital is the human spirit, which moves forward by inquiry, enterprise, discovery, and action. It is too easily taken for granted because the habits of the heart are learned in childhood, supplying reasons that reason has forgotten. Each generation lives off the spiritual capital of its inheritance, and may not even notice when it is squandering this treasure. By dint of habits of hard work and attentiveness, for example, men sometimes grow successful only to indulge themselves and to leave their children barren of spiritual instruction. The moral and spiritual life of nations depends, therefore, on sequences of at least three generations. Habits inculcated by the first generation may be significantly abandoned by the second and almost nonexistent in the third. Conversely, we do not always understand the treasures that, all unknowing, we have inherited from the hard experience of several faithful generations. The moral life of any one generation runs deeper than is discernible to the conscious mind.

Tragedy, therefore, always haunts a free society. Precisely because it is free, it is rife with alluring temptations. A generation may not grasp the full implications of altering past traditions until too late. If ever a single generation forgets the principles on which the society has been constructed, citizens may slide into behaviors and ways of thinking that set in motion its destruction. When the founders of the American experiment announced "we hold these truths to be self-evident," they took as a model republican Rome with its civic virtue. But later generations may brush aside this model, forgetting the truths once held to be self-evident and the daily practices that kneaded such truths into civic virtues. A people that abandons the intellectual and moral habits holding its social system together must fly apart.

The specific moral challenges to democratic capitalist systems today are perhaps too obvious to need elaboration. Especially through the new technology of television, the solicitations of popular culture—rock videos, films of violence, sexual license, and the cultivation of passion and desire—have come to occupy unprecedented space in the inner lives of the young. Although counterbalanced by abiding moral seriousness on the part of many, there is considerable evidence of mounting behavioral dysfunction among us: drugs, crime, births out of wedlock, children disoriented by divorce, teenage pregnancy, and a truly staggering number of abortions. All these behavioral dysfunctions result in various forms of social dependency. A widespread loss of moral virtue creates larger and larger numbers both of clients demanding to be supported by society and of un-civic-minded hedonists.

In addition, a profound disorientation of intellectual habits undermines the truths a people once held to be self-evident, until such truths can no longer be intellectually defended. Richard Rorty has propounded a "cheerful nihilism," in which any claim to "truth" independent of social preference is to be joshingly brushed aside,[56] while Arthur M. Schlesinger, Jr., argues that America was founded on "relativism."[57] Rorty urges us to be kind and tolerant toward one another, and to avoid any intellectual or "metaphysical" defense of our system.

By contrast, the conception of "inalienable rights" on which the American experiment rests is intelligible only in terms of truth, nature, and nature's God. Against a background of "cheerful nihilism," this experiment makes no sense at all; it is only an assertion of arbitrary will. Cheerful nihilism would render the American experiment philosophically vulnerable to any adversarial will armed with superior power.

Quite unlike Rorty, others—such as John Courtney Murray, S.J., and Jacques Maritain—have argued that the philosophical background of the American experiment is congenial to the traditions of Christian philosophy and Christian belief.[58] Indeed, a large majority of American citizens still share these traditions today and understand the American experiment in their light. Rooted in a sense of transcendence, what Walter Lippmann has called "the public philosophy" gives individual citizens an intellectual basis for resisting public expressions of arbitrary will and for defending their rights against aggression from any quarter.[59] They believe their rights derive not from human preference, will, or custom but from the intellect and will of God. Parallel to the task of renewing the moral foundations of modern free societies, therefore, is a further task of deepening their intellectual foundations. The Enlightenment's secular philosophers may no longer be sufficient to defend liberal institutions; more ancient arguments, consistent with Jewish and Christian intellectual traditions, may have to be mobilized.[60]

Finally, since democratic capitalist societies encourage new moral and intellectual virtues to complement the classical virtues, some new Aristotle should describe their phenomenology. Many traditional moral concepts—such as person, community, dignity, equality, rights, responsibilities, and common good—are understood quite differently than in the past. Individuals today are citizens, for example, rather than subjects; they are expected to act for themselves, with initiative and enterprise, and not simply to wait for orders. Large and broad markets work through voluntary choice, consent, and cooperation to achieve beneficial outcomes too complex for any one agency to direct, a form of common good quite unlike the simple common good defined by a tribal chief of yore. From infancy our children—erroneously described as suffering from excessive individualism—are immersed in social practices, group activities, cooperative projects, and group memberships of so many sorts that scarcely any human beings in history have been so thoroughly and complexly socialized. Fresh thinking is needed on these and other characteristics of moral life today.

The work of reforming the moral and cultural sphere is immense.[61] And it is connected to both a new way of thinking about helping the poor and a new practical approach to doing so.

The Poor

Among the 165 or so nations of the world, the ones most conspicuous for their poverty lie either in the pre-capitalist, traditionalist parts of the world—Africa, Latin America, and South Asia—or in the socialist world. We have learned recently, indeed, that the "second world" did not exist except as a more heavily armed part of the Third World. The crumbling economy of the former USSR more resembles the economy of India or China than that of West Germany, and even in the newly united Germany, the economic inferiority of its eastern portion is quite pronounced. The promise of economic development, which originated in Adam Smith's *Inquiry into the Nature and Causes of the Wealth of Nations*, seems to have been realized almost exclusively among the relatively few capitalist nations of the world. The economic plight of the poor, moreover, is much harsher in socialist and traditionalist economies than in capitalist economies. As a system, capitalism is better for the poor than any other existing system.

In Latin America, for example, some 90 million youngsters

under the age of fifteen will be entering the work force over the next fifteen years. But scores of millions of older adults in Latin America are unemployed or underemployed. Moreover, by the year 2000, fewer Latin Americans than today will be working in agriculture, since the flight from farm to city is virtually universal; and fewer will be working for transnational corporations. This vast pool of unemployed exists in an area where enormous amounts of work need to be done to improve the daily life of the poor.

By what mechanism shall these two factors—work to be done and workers needing employment—be brought together if not by the rapid generation of tens of millions of small businesses engaged in manufacturing and services? A large proportion of Latin America's poor, however, are excluded not only from employment but also from access to the legal incorporation of small businesses. Notwithstanding this disability, 43 per cent of the houses in Peru have been constructed by *illegales*, and 93 per cent of public transport is provided by them.[62] Further, two-thirds of all the poor in Peru are neither peasants nor factory workers (proletarians); they are entrepreneurs. But their work is considered illegal, even criminal, and no legitimate institutions exist to extend them credit, the mother's milk of enterprise. All these exclusions—from employment, incorporation, and credit—are unjust. So also is the exclusion of the poor from property ownership, whether in land or home or business. Property titles in Peru are in disarray and very unstable.

Much the same situation, *mutatis mutandis*, obtains throughout Latin America. *There is no capitalism for the poor of Latin America.* Nearly all Latin American economies are in the grip of the state, and the state in turn typically serves a relatively few elite families. Neither in Cuba nor in Nicaragua nor in any other socialist experiment has socialism answered the longings of the poor for material progress, creative opportunity, and civic liberty.

In this sense, Heilbroner's famous sentence is true: "Less than seventy-five years after it officially began, the contest between capitalism and socialism is over: capitalism has won."[63] The reason for this victory, which surprised so many, appears to be twofold. First, capitalist institutions nourish invention, innovation, and enterprise—primary catalysts of economic development. Second, market systems better recognize the dignity of individuals and respect their choices, better reward cooperation and mutual adjustment, and attain ever-higher levels of progress. Both in creativity and in cooperative voluntary activities, the capitalist order attains a progressively higher standard of the common good.[64] Nonetheless, the question remains: *Within* capitalist nations, how may the good of the poor be better served?

A long study of poverty in the United States undertaken by the Working Seminar on Family and American Welfare Policy examined both the successes and the failures of the so-called War on Poverty launched by President Lyndon Johnson in March 1964.[65] It found that after twenty years the welfare of the elderly had been dramatically improved, and that both medical and other non-cash benefits had substantially bettered the economic plight of nearly all the poor. In contrast to this success, however, the condition of younger cohorts among the poor, particularly children and single parents, had deteriorated. There were far more births out of wedlock in 1985 than there had been in 1965, and far more single parents, especially young parents. In addition, especially in urban areas, morale among the poor seemed to be worse.

While there was undeniably more money in poor inner-city areas than ever before, there was also far more social dysfunction. Drug use and crime rates were higher than ever; a certain pall of despondency had become visible. Many households seemed trapped in a cycle of welfare, unmarried pregnancy, unemployment (or even unemployability), and inability to cope. Even though schooling through high school is free, many drop out. Even though books are more widely available than ever, many do not learn to read. Even though jobs are so plentiful that immigrants from abroad flock to them, many remain out of the work force, not finding or even seeking gainful employment. Material circumstances in 1985 were at far higher levels than in 1965; beyond their relatively high levels of reported income, the poor—in a separate survey—reported spending three times as much money as they acknowledged in income.[66] Nevertheless, levels of dependency, behavioral dysfunction, and inability to cope were higher than in 1965.

This pattern is not unique to the United States. Other social welfare states face analogous problems. Indeed, a radical dilemma has appeared at the heart of the welfare state. Rates of out-of-wedlock pregnancy in Sweden are even higher than in the United States, and are growing rapidly in most welfare states.[67] In the United States, the granting of material benefits traps a significant proportion of able-bodied adults between the ages of eighteen and sixty-four in more-or-less permanent financial and behavioral dependency. Many recipients remain on-and-off, if not continuous, wards of the state.[68] Their behaviors also affect their children in ways that are not difficult to trace. Birth out of wedlock dramatically increases the rate of infant mortality, and such children have a higher likelihood of poor health, difficulties in school, truancy, unemployment, crime, and involvement in drugs.

From a year's study of the evidence, the Working Seminar decided that the radical problem of the poor in the United States is no longer monetary; indeed, the urban poor often have considerably more disposable income than did the immigrant poor of any preceding generation (or even of today). The radical problem has a far thicker human dimension. It has come to be identified by the unpleasant name "underclass," a term that in the United States is applied to some four million persons concentrated in poverty areas of the nation's one hundred largest cities.[69] Unlike the large majority of the poor, whose poverty is primarily monetary and temporary, member of the "underclass" exhibit many self-destructive habits that keep them in perpetual dependency on others. Instead of living as free and independent citizens in a free society, they live almost as serfs, dependent on the state. Instead of contributing to the common good, they take from it and, in some cases, prey upon it. Even more disturbing is the quasi-permanency of their dependency and the probability of their passing it on to their children.

In fairly sharp contrast, those poor Americans who perform three traditional and relatively simple accomplishments well have almost no probability of remaining long in poverty. Some 97 per cent of those who complete high school, stay married (even if not on the first try), and work full-time year-round (even at the minimum wage) are not poor; nearly all poverty is associated with the absence of one or more of these basic accomplishments.[70] Indeed, the vast majority of the more than twelve million, mostly non-white immigrants who entered the United States in the 1970s and 1980s swiftly moved out of poverty chiefly because of strong family life and diligent work. Not even inadequacy in the English language held them back. They compensated for their lack of a high school education or its equivalent by reliable work, commending themselves to employers by the soundness of their moral habits.

Within capitalist countries, however, the residual poverty left behind by this generally rapid *embourgeoisement* of the "proletariat" seems resistant to traditional anti-poverty techniques. Economic growth alone does not cure this form of poverty because so many afflicted with it work not at all or only for brief stints.[71] It requires humane solutions far more complex than can be reached by monetary grants alone. The rest of the human community has to reach out to these most injured and self-destructive poor, helping them to restore sound behaviors, motivations, outlooks, and habits and to restructure the small, vital "little platoons" of healthy social life. Civic life has broken down among them and needs to be rebuilt, with sympathetic assistance, from within. Perhaps the Christian community will respond, as it has historically, by inspiring new religious congregations to undertake this civilizing mission.

Some commentators stress that, in every society, some percentage of persons will suffer from physical, emotional, or moral disabilities that prevent them from achieving the levels of independence and self-reliance that others do. With the right sort of help, some of these less fortunate persons may be brought into the mainstream. Care must be taken, however, lest programs of assistance seduce even the able-bodied into self-destructive dependency—a powerful accusation against democratic capitalist societies.

To return to a worldwide perspective, much also needs to be done in the non-capitalist world to construct institutions that promote economic development from the bottom up. Critical prerequisites are universal education, institutions of credit and venture capital designed especially for the aspiring poor, easy procedures for the incorporation of small businesses, an ethos of enterprise, and other crucial social supports tailored for the poor. Guy Sorman calls this "barefoot capitalism,"[72] and others call it "popular" or "people's capitalism." Emphasizing enterprise and creativity is consistent with the use of credit unions, cooperatives, workers' ownership, employee stock options (ESOPs), and other techniques. But it is more important than any other single factor.

OUR BEST HOPE

In *Rerum Novarum*, Leo XIII predicted with remarkable accuracy the futility of socialism. His criticism of visible faults in liberal capitalist societies also set in motion currents of reform that ultimately contributed to social reconstruction. Nonetheless, for various historical and cultural reasons, neither Leo XIII nor his successors until John Paul II thoroughly analyzed the sources of regeneration and invention in democratic capitalist societies. These sources notably include the separation of economic, political, and cultural systems—a separation mirrored in the threefold structure of *Gaudium et Spes*. Also pivotal is the internal constitution of capitalism itself, specifically those institutions that add invention, innovation, and enterprise to traditional market economies. Finally, the institutional protection of religious liberty and private property—the *sine qua non* of free civic life and family-based incentives—ensures flexibility.

Even though the poor's best hope lies in the universal spread and development of democratic capitalist systems, fresh thinking is needed to deepen the present intellectual and moral foundations of these societies. Clear thinking is also needed if we are to bring swift and effective assistance to the poor.

On the Jewish and Christian horizon, the road toward an earthly approximation of the Kingdom of God stretches very far into the future, and there is no danger of confusing that kingdom with democratic capitalist societies marked by sin, imperfection, and suffering. For human beings, given their liberty, often do what they should not do and do not do what they should. What can be said, though, is that no existing alternative offers better promise, and none seems more adequately suited both to eliciting human creativity and to deflecting human weakness into watchfulness. Private interest acts as a sentinel to public good.

Note: The author is grateful to Kenneth R. Craycraft, Jr., for the execution of the endnotes, and to Derek Cross for significant editorial and research assistance.

Responses

1. Dennis P. McCann

M ichael Novak's role in shaping the Catholic discussion of political economy over the past decade can hardly be exaggerated. *The Spirit of Democratic Capitalism* (1982), despite its rhetorical excess or perhaps because of it, may assume a preeminence analogous to Schleiermacher's *Reden* (1799). That bold confrontation of the Enlightenment's "cultured despisers" of religion still serves as the fountainhead for liberal Christian theologies. All of us, clearly, are in Novak's debt, even if we feel compelled to criticize and revise his vision of Christianity's constructive engagement with democratic capitalism. In my view, the transformation he envisions in his essay is not yet revolutionary enough.

Novak's argument here consists of three points: (1) Recent events, especially the collapse of "really existing socialism" in Eastern Europe, have vindicated democratic capitalism in its balanced differentiation among the moral-cultural, political, and economic spheres of social interaction. (2) Whatever defects may currently exist in the system can best be remedied, not through any further politicization of the economy, but through a renewal of private and public morality in the moral-cultural sphere. (3) Transforming the revolution means not only focusing on this process of renewal in our own society but also extending the system to the poor of the so-called Third World. Novak proposes constructing "institutions that promote economic development from the bottom up . . . universal education, institutions of credit and venture capital designed especially for the aspiring poor, easy procedures for the incorporation of small businesses, an ethos of enterprise, and other crucial social supports tailored for the poor." This agenda he approvingly refers to as "barefoot capitalism."

Dennis P. McCann is a professor of religious studies and the co-director of the Center for the Study of Values at DePaul University, Chicago.

While I have some reservations about each of these propositions, they are relatively minor. The major issue separating us is the seriousness with which we view the *economic* threats to the ongoing democratic capitalist revolution. I believe the greatest threats to that revolution are primarily internal to the economic sphere, though they do bear enormous consequences for the political and moral-cultural spheres. These threats, now more than ever, reflect the bewildering dynamism of the marketplace.

Some recent symptoms of the problem include the worsening gap between the incomes of the top 20 per cent of American wage earners and the other 80 per cent, the real and imagined consequences of the hostile takeover movement for most business managers, the savings-and-loan debacle and the risks of real-estate speculation, the increasing irrelevance of Wall Street's financial markets as an indicator of the strengths and weaknesses of the real economy, the seeming intractability of the U.S. trade deficit, our inability to respond adequately to the Third World debt crisis, and the collapse of the Bretton Woods institutions governing the world-wide flow of capital. Each of these problems suggests the imminent obsolescence of the national economy if Robert B. Reich's study *The Work of Nations: Preparing Ourselves for 21st Century Capitalism* (1991) is to be believed. Yet these tremors marking the eclipse of the national economy also signal the partial realization of one of democratic capitalism's most revolutionary aspirations: the creation of a truly global economy.

Why doesn't Novak treat these symptoms with the seriousness they deserve? Perhaps his fondness for Adam Smith leads him to underestimate the instability inherent in existing capital markets— what Joseph Schumpeter aptly described as their tendency toward "creative destruction." Smith's influence may also obscure business corporations' constructive role in seeking to compensate for this instability through various market-management strategies. At any rate, though Novak once promised us a theology of the corporation, he has never developed one that breaks the spell of Smith's invisible hand and follows instead the visible hand of business management.

Unlike poets who see only the awesome beauty of a fierce thunderstorm, farmers also have a holy fear of them. They know that the lightning that renews the soil may simultaneously burn their barns down if they are not careful. Novak seems to be a poet; business managers are more like the farmers I have in mind. They must respond to the vagaries of the markets they serve by maximizing creativity while minimizing destructiveness. What business people need today is a new theological approach to the corporation, one capable of renewing their sense of vocation—a vocation now being tested and challenged by the emerging global marketplace.

Such a theology must move beyond the ideal generalizations of Novak, the poet of democratic capitalism, and speak to the unique histories of individual corporations. It must discern the relative ethical merits of the various patterns of organizational development that mark the history of modern business corporations. It must address the ethical possibilities latent in different types of business enterprise—from sole proprietorships, to partnerships, to privately held corporations, to publicly held ones. Finally, it must determine the moral accountability of different industries. Do the markets that McDonald's serves, for example, require them to be more socially responsive than, say, a construction company? The kind of moral support needed in these situations may vary considerably. A theology of the corporation should help us to appreciate such nuances in ways that a theology of democratic capitalism or a theology of economics cannot.

Now more than ever, Catholic social teaching must develop an adequate theology of the business corporation. If Reich's analysis and others like it are at all on target, the conventional focus on questions of *national* political and economic policies will become increasingly ineffective as a means of securing economic justice. *The Work of Nations* confirms what we suspect from reading daily newspapers: national governments are becoming less and less able to determine economic policy on their own, not for a lack of political will but for reasons intrinsically linked to the emergence of a global economy. Global interdependence limits the power of national governments to regulate their own economies.

With these constraints, however, comes a host of new opportunities. Partisans of Catholic social teaching should diligently investigate ways of addressing directly those institutions that increasingly set the tune for the global economy—the corporations that are evolving into what Reich calls "global enterprise networks." Because it has never lost contact with its pre-modern tradition that instinctively views the social order in international terms, Catholic social teaching is better situated than most other perspectives to respond to this challenge.

The tripartite system of democratic capitalism, so provocatively illuminated by Novak on the national level, needs to re-deploy itself on the global level. The vision of the international order found in Catholic social teaching could help establish an appropriate global system of market regulation in which external constraints are combined with the voluntary restraints encouraged by specific corporate cultures. As Novak himself insists, the political sphere's major contribution to the *economic* viability of democratic capitalism is its capacity for institutionalizing an *appropriate* system of market regulation. The work of imagining, building, testing, and continually adjusting such a global system should advance the transformation of the democratic capitalist revolution that Novak envisions, while avoiding any anti-democratic, anti-capitalist conception of a new world economic order.

2. HERBERT SCHLOSSBERG

Michael Novak's 1982 book *The Spirit of Democratic Capitalism* did much to advance the idea that an economic system must be considered not in isolation but in conjunction with its political and cultural environment. Still, most analyses of this three-legged stool remain badly unbalanced, with the cultural leg seldom appearing as more than a stub. When Novak speaks of the destructive ecnomic effects of hedonism, nihilism, and family dysfunction, he is reviving an older tradition of discourse—a biblical one, in fact—that modern commentators have largely abandoned. Most contemporary analysts, not just Marxists, have adopted instead materialistic theses that discount cultural matters as derivative of social conditions.

Novak is surely correct in discussing the long-term effects of cultural dysfunction. His evocation of three successively less reliable generations echoes Gertrude Himmelfarb's analysis of the decline of Victorian culture. She surveys that descent from the vigorous spiritual revival sparked by the Clapham community; through the dull conformity of the next generation that, having rejected its religious roots, could no longer explain its devotion to duty; to the third generation of rebellious Bloomsburyites who gloried in what John Maynard Keynes called their immoralism. This devolution of English society from Lord Shaftesbury to Lord Keynes was a sad decline indeed.

Is it only a coincidence that Keynes, the proud chronicler of his own set's moral decadence, should also have been the architect of the intellectual system underlying so much that has gone sour in twentieth-century economies? "What about the long run?" Keynes was asked when defending the efficacy of his economic expedients. "In the long run we're all dead," was Keynes's famous reply.

The immoralist Keynes devised an economic program that claimed to restore a stagnant economy to health by stimulating demand—the answer to a hedonist's prayer if, indeed, hedonists pray. Interestingly, Keynes knew better. In *Monetary Reform*, a book

---

Herbert Schlossberg is a project director of the Fieldstead Institute, Irvine, California.

he published in 1924, he demonstrated the immorality and futility of solving national economic problems by printing money; and he attributed the health of the British economy in the nineteenth century to the fact that the country's morals, literature, and religion constituted a "giant conspiracy for the promotion of saving."

If the culture is crucial for the development of a healthy economy—a point on which witnesses as diverse as Keynes and Novak agree—then the moral and religious components of the culture are obviously also crucial. It is a curious thing, then, that so much opposition to the arguments of Novak and those who think as he does comes from church leaders, who base their opposition ostensibly on religious grounds. I have heard Novak criticized for being, in effect, a bad Catholic—not because of the religious doctrines he professes or the morality of his actions but because of his economic analysis, which does not support many of the ideas expressed by the bishops of his church. And the leadership of the mainline Protestant denominations show a similar drift. All these church bodies exhibit little tolerance for free-market economies and considerable skepticism about whether such economies can lead to justice.

This tradition in the United States became significant at least as far back as the Social Gospel movement of a century ago, but the Great Depression provided its strongest impetus in the English-speaking world. That calamity set the direction for the early work of Reinhold Niebuhr who, in *Moral Man and Immoral Society*, argued that the best means of promoting economic justice was to increase the economic powers of the central state.

Transferring economic decision-making powers from individuals and businesses to politicians and bureaucrats appealed to ecclesiastical figures across the sea as well. The leader of the Anglican church, Archbishop of Canterbury William Temple, encouraged a host of theorists to look to socialism to bring about a just society. In 1942 one of the clergymen in this group asked, "Does not the greed and self-seeking implicit in the profit motive on which capitalism rests flout the whole substance of Christ's teaching?" He left us in no doubt about his answer: capitalism and greed go together like ham and eggs. Those who produced the last three study papers (1984, 1985, 1990) issued on this subject by my own denomination, the Presbyterian Church, U.S.A., repeated the same theme. Even the collapse of socialism in Eastern Europe and just about everywhere else did not deter them.

If we endorse Novak's contention that a society's moral health will profoundly affect its economic performance, that religion is vital to that health, and that a free-market economy is more productive and more just than a command economy, we must confront the hostility of the most influential—or at least the most visible—Christian bodies in the United States. Why don't they agree with us? The answer lies in the extent to which the mainline churches have been taking their cues for the last generation or so from the ideological forces of the surrounding society rather than from their own heritage. There is hardly an arbitrary, brutal, or destructive idea in the world that someone or other in the churches (sometimes many) has not embraced as a harbinger of the Kingdom of God.

Laszlo Tokes, the reformed pastor in Transylvania whose courageous defiance of Ceauşescu's regime ignited the Romanian revolution, has said that the cowardice and complicity of the World Council of Churches abetted the regime in its repression of the Church. When Tokes called on the council to repent publicly, he got a half-hearted acknowledgment from the general secretary that the WCC could have done better. An accompanying defense, moreover, transformed the statement from an acknowledgment of sin to a self-justification. But Tokes was on the right track. He seemed to be saying that mistakes may not be only intellectual errors but matters of the will. They can arise from moral faults as well as from intellectual limitations. In the former case, the only hope is repentance. A passage in the New Testament makes this point. Paul tells his young disciple Timothy to be gentle in correcting those who disagree with him: "God may perhaps grant that they will repent and come to know the truth" (II Tim. 2:25).

According to polls, church officials with deeply ingrained suspicion of free-market economies have little support among ordinary American churchgoers, who are deserting their denominations in droves. But these officials remain unfazed. Adopting a self-proclaimed "prophetic" role, they denounce the United States with gusto and shake off impatiently any suggestion that they are exceeding their authority in the Church or discrediting their profession of faith. As long as anybody remains poor, they deny the legitimacy of the economic system that has done the most to eradicate poverty. As long as the distribution of wealth does not follow the proportion of each race and gender in the population, they see no justice. Any proposed tax cut is, for them, a plan to engorge the rich at the expense of the poor. In their zero-sum world, forcible transfers of wealth are the only way to help the needy.

The main problem, however, is not that the churches are getting their economics wrong, although they are. The main problem is their failure to become a powerful engine of moral and spiritual reform in the culture. If they were able to do this, they could make a real contribution to economic life and to the transformation of the democratic/capitalist culture. By losing their vision of a transcendent source of moral teaching and pushing instead the larger culture's destructive antinomianism under an exceedingly thin and unconvincing religious guise, mainline church officials are unwittingly working hard to keep poor people in poverty. Even if some of their errors are honest mistakes, the kind that befall everyone, making recommendations that cause damage to others because one has not done one's homework still entails moral culpability.

Finally, I would caution that the democracy leg of Novak's triad is not a panacea. It was the Athenian democracy that killed Socrates. As a graduate student, I came across French writings hostile to the growing absolutism of seventeenth-century kings that contained the saying *Vox populi vox dei*. Two centuries ago the Scottish thinker Alexander Tyler observed that democracies normally do not last long because the people eventually discover they can vote themselves stipends out of the public treasury, which is the beginning of the end. I think that's the basic reason we can't balance a budget. People with their moral blinders removed would not insist on receiving what they do not pay for; they would throw out of office politicians acting as irresponsibly as ours, daring to buy votes by handing out the property of others. They would act out of what Novak calls a "sense of transcendence," something that sets limits beyond which democratic decisions, like all other decisions, must not be allowed to pass. The high calling of being a Christian requires us to tell people that theirs is *not* the voice of God, and that some of their wants are not legitimate.

There is no reason to be as cynical as William Tecumseh Sherman was when he wrote disgustedly to his wife about the fickle public's criticism of General Grant after the heavy casualties at Shiloh, "*Vox populi, vox humbug.*" But we ought to recognize and be willing to declare—on the basis of transcendent truth—that what people say sometimes *is* humbug or worse. Mainline churches will need a powerful renewal before they are able to provide the leadership for Christian people to do that.

Afterword

Can Atheists Be Good Citizens?

RICHARD JOHN NEUHAUS

T HE very question posed by this title is bound to offend. Few concepts are more basic to our civil piety than that of citizenship. Citizenship, the American creed affirms, is open equally to all, regardless of race, color, or creed—and in these latter days it is added, regardless of gender, sexual orientation, age, physical ability, looks, and other differentiae. The question "Can atheists be good citizens?" might therefore seem downright un-American. If it is to be asked at all, it obviously must be asked with great care.

The essays in this volume, for all their differences of viewpoint, assume that there are connections between being a Christian and being a good citizen. While it may be essential for a Christian to be a good citizen, nobody argues that it is essential for a good citizen to be a Christian. Except in terms of demography, with its attendant cultural and sociological implications, nobody here argues that ours is or should be a "Christian nation." Most participants join George Weigel, Mark Noll, and Carl Braaten in underscoring the moral commonalities shared with non-Christian citizens, and join Glenn Tinder in affirming that Christians cannot be entirely at home in even the best of earthly polities. I too join in these affirmations. My title question can perhaps best be understood as an extension of Max Stackhouse's deliberations on a "public theol-

Richard John Neuhaus is the president of the Institute on Religion and Public Life and editor-in-chief of *First Things*.

ogy." Does our Constitution presuppose constituting truths that an atheist, or at least a consistent atheist, is obliged to deny?

Before we can answer the question, we should first determine what is meant by atheism, and then inquire more closely into what is required of a good citizen.

Consider our late friend the philosopher Sidney Hook. Can anyone deny that he was a very good citizen indeed? During the long contest with totalitarianism, he was a much better citizen than the many believers—including numerous church leaders—who urged that the moral imperative was to split the difference between the evil empire and human fitness for freedom.

Although Sidney Hook described himself on occasion as an atheist, I suggest that he might be more accurately described as a philosophical agnostic, one who says that the evidence is not sufficient to compel us either to deny or to affirm the reality of God. Hook was often asked what he would say when he died and God asked him why he did not believe. His standard answer was, "Lord, you didn't supply enough evidence." Unlike many atheists of our time, Sidney Hook believed in reason and evidence that yield what he did not hesitate to call truth. He was not without his gods, though they may have been false gods.

The Early Christian "Atheists"

The Greek a-theos means "without gods." In the classical world this meant the gods of the city or the empire. For his perceived disbelief in gods, Socrates was charged with atheism. The early Christians were charged with atheism for their insistence that there is no god other than the God whom Jesus called Father. In the eyes of the ancients, to be a-theos was to be outside the civilizational circle of the civitas. To be an atheist was to be subversive. The atheist was a security risk, if not a traitor. Christians were thought to be atheists precisely because they professed the God who judges and debunks the false gods of the community. In the classical world, the answer to our title question was negative: no, an atheist could not be a good citizen. But those whom they called atheists then we do not call atheists today.

Those whom we now call atheists think they are denying what

earlier "atheists," such as the Christians, affirmed. That is to say, they deny the reality of what they understand believing Jews and Christians to mean by God. This form of atheism is a post-Enlightenment and largely nineteenth-century phenomenon. It developed a vocabulary—first among intellectuals but then in the wider culture—that was strongly prejudiced against believers. Note the very use of the term "believer" to describe a person who is persuaded of the reality of God. The alternative to being a believer, of course, is to be a knower. A similar usage developed with the categories of faith and reason, the subjective and the objective, and, in the realm of morals, values and facts. Belief, faith, subjectivity, values—these were the soft and dubious words relevant to affirming God. Knowledge, reason, objectivity, facts—these were the hard and certain words relevant to denying God. This tendentious vocabulary of unbelief is still very much with us.

Necessarily following from such distortive distinctions are common assumptions about the public and the private. One recalls A. N. Whitehead's axiom that religion is what a man does with his solitude. Even one as religiously sensitive as William James could write, "Religion . . . shall mean for us the feelings, acts, and experiences of individual men in their solitude" (*The Varieties of Religious Experience*, Lecture 2). In this construal of matters, we witness a radical departure from the public nature of religion, whether that religion has to do with the ancient gods of the city or with the biblical Lord who rules over the nations. The gods of the city and the God of the Bible are emphatically public. The confinement of the question of God or the gods to the private sphere constitutes what might be described as political atheism. Many today who are believers in private have been persuaded to accept political atheism, or intimidated into doing so.

Political atheism is a subspecies of practical or methodological atheism, the assumption that we can get along with the business at hand without addressing the question of God. Here the classic anecdote is the response of the Marquis de Laplace to Napoleon Bonaparte: when Napoleon observed that Laplace had written a huge book on the system of the universe without mentioning the author of the universe, Laplace replied, "Sire, I have no need of that hypothesis." When God has become a hypothesis we have traveled a very long way from both the gods of the ancient city and the God of the Bible.

The Ersatz God

In his remarkable work *At the Origins of Modern Atheism*, Michael Buckley persuasively argues that the god denied by many moderns is a strange god created by the attempts of misguided religionists to demonstrate that God could be proven or known on philosophical grounds alone, as those grounds were delimited by the philosophies of the day.

> The extraordinary note about this emergence of the denial of the Christian god which Nietzsche celebrated is that Christianity as such, more specifically the person and teaching of Jesus or the experience and history of the Christian Church, did not enter the discussion. The absence of any consideration of Christology is so pervasive throughout serious discussion that it becomes taken for granted, yet it is so stunningly curious that it raises a fundamental issue of the modes of thought: How did the issue of Christianity vs. atheism become purely philosophical? To paraphrase Tertullian: How was it that the only arms to defend the temple were to be found in the Stoa? [New Haven: Yale University Press, 1990, repr. of 1987 ed.]

As Nietzsche's god had nothing to do with Christology, so, needless to say, the god that he declared dead had nothing to do with Sinai, election, covenant, or messianic promise.

In his notebook, after his death, was found Pascal's famous assertion of trust in "the God of Abraham, the God of Isaac, the God of Jacob, not of philosophers and scholars." Modern atheism is the product not so much of anti-religion as of religion's replacement of the God of Abraham with the god of the philosophers, and of the philosophers' consequent rejection of that *ersatz* god. Descartes determined that he would accept as true nothing that could be reasonably doubted, and Christians set about to prove that the existence of God could not be reasonably doubted. Thus did the defenders of religion set faith against the doubt that is integral to the life of faith.

The very phrase "the existence of God" gave away the game—as if God were one existent among other existents, one entity among other entities, one actor among other actors, whose actions must conform to standards that we have determined in advance are appropriate to being God. The transcendent, the ineffable, the totally other, the God who acts in history was tamed and domesticated in order to meet the philosophers' job description for the post of God. Not surprisingly, the philosophers determined that the candidate recommended by the friends of religion did not qualify.

The American part of this story is well told by James Turner of the University of Michigan in *Without God, Without Creed: The Origins of Unbelief in America.* "The natural parents of modern unbelief," Turner writes, "turn out to have been the guardians of belief." Many thinking people came at last "to realize that it was religion, not science or social change, that gave birth to unbelief. Having made God more and more like man—intellectually, morally, emotionally—the shapers of religion made it feasible to abandon God, to believe simply in man." Turner's judgment is relentless:

> In trying to adapt their religious beliefs to socioeconomic change, to new moral challenges, to novel problems of knowledge, to the tightening standards of science, the defenders of God slowly strangled Him. If anyone is to be arraigned for deicide, it is not Charles Darwin but his adversary Bishop Samuel Wilberforce, not the godless Robert Ingersoll but the godly Beecher family. [Baltimore: Johns Hopkins Press, 1986.]

H. L. Mencken observed that the great achievement of liberal Protestantism as to make the subject of God boring. That is unfair, of course—Mencken was often unfair—but it is not untouched by truth. The god that was trimmed, accommodated, and retooled in order to be deemed respectable by the "modern mind" was increasingly uninteresting, because unnecessary. Dietrich Bonhoeffer described that god as a "god of the gaps," invoked to fill in those pieces of reality that human knowledge and control had not yet mastered. H. Richard Niebuhr's well-known and withering depiction of the gospel of liberal Christianity is very much to the point: "A God without wrath brought men without sin into a kingdom without judgment through the ministrations of a Christ without a Cross." In the absence of human judgment and redemption, it is not surprising that people came to dismiss the idea of God not as implausible but as superfluous, and, yes, boring. The reality of God apart from sin, judgment, and redemption might be of interest to the philosophically and mystically minded, but it would not be the God of the Jewish and Christian Scriptures.

Attempts to Preclude "God Talk"

It would no doubt be satisfying for Christian believers—and for Jews who identify themselves not by the accident of Jewishness but by the truth of Judaism—to conclude that the God of Abraham, Isaac, Jacob, and Jesus has not been touched by the critiques of atheism. However, while it is true that the god denied by many atheists is not the God of the Bible affirmed by Christians and Jews, there are forms of atheism that do intend to preclude such affirmation, and certainly to preclude such affirmation in public. The more determined materialist, for example, asserts that there simply *is* nothing and can be nothing outside a closed system of matter. This was the position of the late and unlamented "dialectical materialism" of Communism. It is the position of some scientists today, especially those in the biological sciences who are wedded to evolution as a belief system. (Physicists, as it turns out, are increasingly open to, indeed excited by, the metaphysical.)

Perhaps more commonly, one encounters varieties of logical positivism that hold that since assertions about God are not empirically verifiable—or, for that matter, falsifiable—they are simply meaningless. In a similar vein, certain types of analytical philosophers would instruct us that "God talk" is, quite precisely, nonsense. This is not atheism in the sense to which we have become accustomed, since it claims that denying God is as much nonsense as affirming God. It is atheism, however, in the original sense of *a-theos*, of being without God. Then there is the much more radical position that denies not only the possibility of truth claims about God but the possibility of claims to truth at all—at least as "truth" has usually been understood. Perhaps today's most prominent proponent of this argument in America is Richard Rorty of the University of Virginia. Please take note: *This is not the atheism that pits reason against our knowledge of God; this is the atheism of unreason.*

Rorty is sometimes portrayed, and portrays himself, as something of an eccentric gadfly. In fact, along with Derrida, Foucault, and other Heideggerian epigones of Nietzsche, Rorty is the guru of an academic establishment of increasing influence in our intellectual culture. Here we encounter the apostles of a relativism that denies it is relativism because it denies there is any alternative to it: therefore the term relativism is "meaningless." They are radically anti-foundationalist. That is to say, they contend that there are no conclusive arguments underlying our assertions except the conclusive argument that there are no conclusive arguments. They reject any "correspondence theory" of truth. There is no coherent connection between what we think and say and the reality "out there." Truth is what the relevant community of discourse agrees to say is true.

Deconstruction and Self-Construction

The goal, in this way of thinking, is self-actualization, indeed self-creation. The successful life is the life lived as a *novum*, an autobiography that has escaped the "used vocabularies" of the past. This argument (so to speak) has its academic strongholds in literary criticism and sectors of philosophy, but it also undergirds assumptions that are increasingly widespread in our intellectual culture. If personal and group self-actualization is the end, arguments claiming to deal with the truth are but disguised stratagems for the exercise of will and the quest for power. Whether the issue is gender, sexual orientation, or race, we are told that the purpose is to change the ideational "power structure" currently controlled by oppressors who disingenuously try to protect the status quo by appeals to objective truth and inter-subjective reason.

The only truth that matters is the truth that is instrumental to self-actualization. Thus truth is in service to "identity." If, for instance, one has the temerity to object that there is no evidence that Africans discovered the Americas before Columbus, he is promptly informed that he is the tool of hegemonic Eurocentrism. In such a view, the "social construction of reality" (Berger and Luckmann) takes on ominous new dimensions as it is asserted that all of reality, without remainder, is constructed to serve the will to power and self-actualization. Brevity requires that I describe this approach with broad strokes, but alas, the description is no caricature.

Are people who embrace this view atheists? They brush aside the question as "not serious," for the theism upon which atheism depends is, in their view, not serious. As with relativism and irrationality, so also with atheism: the words make sense only in relation to the opposites from which they are derived. Of course, privately, or within a particular community, *any* words might be deemed useful in creating the self. One might even find it meaningful to use the language of the Declaration of Independence in speaking about "Nature and Nature's God." People may be permitted to talk that way, so long as they understand that such talk has no public purchase. Rorty's "liberal ironist" can employ any vocabulary, no matter how fantastical, so long as he does not insist that it is true in a way that makes a claim upon others, and so long as he does not act on that vocabulary in a manner that limits the freedom of others to construct their own realities.

There is indeed irony in the fact that some who think of themselves as theists eagerly embrace deconstructionism's operative atheism. Today's cultural scene is awash in what are called "new spiritualities." A recent anthology of "America's new spiritual voices" includes contributions promoting witchcraft, ecological mysticism, devotion to sundry gods and goddesses, and something presenting itself as Zen physio-psychoanalysis. All are deemed to be usable vocabularies for the creation of the self. The book is recommended by a Roman Catholic theologian who writes that it "turns us away from the 'truths' outside ourselves that lead to debate and division, and turns us toward the Inner Truth that is beyond debate." But theism—whether in relation to the gods of the *civitas* or the God of Abraham—is devotion to that which is external to ourselves in the sense that it is not of our own contriving. Theism posits our dependence upon the Other.

Sometimes "new spiritualities" are more socialized in nature, being focused less on the "Inner Truth" than on the ultimate truth of our sociality. Father Avery Dulles tells of preaching in a parish where a large banner in the chancel declared, "God Is Other People." He says he fervently wished that he had a magic marker so that he could put an emphatic comma after the word "other." However variously expressed, many of the burgeoning "spiritualities" in contemporary culture are richly religionized forms of atheism.

Debunking Autonomous Reason

There is additional irony. Beyond pop spiritualities and Rortian nihilism, a serious argument is being made today against a version of rationality upon which Enlightenment atheism was premised. Here one thinks preeminently of Alasdair MacIntyre, and especially of his most recent work, *Three Rival Versions of Moral Enquiry*. MacIntyre effectively polemicizes against a construal of rationality that understands itself to be universal, disinterested, autonomous, and transcending tradition. Our situation, he contends, is one of traditions of rationality in conflict. MacIntyre's favored tradition is Thomism's synthesis of Aristotle and Augustine. If I read him correctly, MacIntyre is prepared to join forces with the Rortians in debunking the hegemonic pretensions of the autonomous and foundational reason that has so long dominated our elite intellectual culture. After the great debunking, all the cognitive cards will have to be put on the table, and we can then have at it. Presumably, the tradition that can provide the best account of reality will win out.

If that is MacIntyre's proposal, it strikes me as a very dangerous game. True, exposing the fallacious value-neutrality of autonomous and traditionless reason opens the academy to the arguments of eminently reasonable theism. But in the resulting free-for-all it is opened to so much else. It is made vulnerable to the Nietzschean will to power that sets the rules, and those rules are designed to preclude the return of the gods or God in a manner that claims public allegiance. For one tradition of reason (e.g., Thomism) to form a coalition, even a temporary coalition, with unreason in order to undo another tradition of reason (e.g., the Enlightenment's autonomous "way of the mind") is a perilous tactic.

And yet, something like this may be the future of our intellectual culture. In our universities, Christians, Jews, and, increasingly Muslims will be free to contend for their truths, just as lesbians,

Marxists, Nietzscheans, and devotees of The Great Earth Goddess are free to contend for theirs. It is a matter of equal-opportunity propaganda. But—and again there is delicious irony—the old methodological atheism and value-neutrality, against which the revolution was launched, may nonetheless prevail.

In other words, every party will be permitted to contend for its truths so long as it acknowledges that they are *its* truths, and not *the* truth. Each will be permitted to propagandize, each will *have* to propagandize if it is to hold its own, because it is acknowledged that there is no common ground for the alternative to propaganda, which is reasonable persuasion. Of course, history, including the history of ideas, is full of surprises. But I believe there is reason to fear that theism, when it plays by the rules of the atheism of unreason, will be corrupted and eviscerated. The method will become the message. Contemporary Christian theology already provides all too many instances of the peddling of truths that are in service to truths other than the truth of God.

We have touched briefly, then, on the many faces of atheism—of living and thinking *a-theos*, without God or the gods. There is the atheism of the early Christians, who posited God against the gods. There is the atheism of Enlightenment rationalists, who, committed to undoubtable certainty, rejected the god whom religionists designed to fit that criterion. There is the practical atheism of Laplace, who had no need of "that hypothesis" in order to get on with what he had to do. There is the weary atheism of those who grew bored with liberalism's god, created in the image and likeness of good liberals. There is the more thorough atheism of Nietzschean relativism that dare not speak its name, that cannot speak its name, lest in doing so it implicitly acknowledge that there is an alternative to relativism. And, finally, there is the atheism of putative theists who peddle religious truths that are true for you, if you find it useful to believe them true.

Citizenship and a Higher Truth

Can these atheists be good citizens? It depends, I suppose, on what is meant by good citizenship. We may safely assume that the great majority of these people abide by the laws, pay their taxes, and are congenial and helpful neighbors. But can a person who does not acknowledge that he is accountable to a truth higher than the self, a truth that is not dependent upon the self, really be trusted? Locke and Rousseau, among many other worthies, thought not. However confused their theology, they were sure that the social contract was based upon nature, upon the way the world *really is*. Rousseau's "civil religion" was apparently itself a social construct, but Locke was convinced that the fear of a higher judgment, even an eternal judgment, was essential to citizenship.

We may disagree with Locke's argument, but it is important to understand it. On one occasion when I publicly made the present argument about atheism and citizenship, it met with outraged reactions from declared secular humanists, each of whom produced instances of atheists who had made significant contributions to the common good. The militantly secular voice of the left, *The Nation*, took me to task with a full-page listing of all the terrible things that Christians do, citing the outrages reported in the press in only one month. Scandals surrounding television evangelists headed the list, joined by numerous other instances of clergy abusing children, embezzling funds, perpetrating insurance frauds, and doing other things that can hardly count as good citizenship. *The Nation* clearly thought the case conclusive. How dare a theist ask whether atheists can be good citizens when so many theists are bad citizens?

I readily allow that too many theists, meaning mainly Christians, are execrable citizens. I cannot imagine that Locke would for a moment have denied the fact. But it has little or nothing to do with his argument. Locke believed that an atheist, if he truly adhered to such belief, could not be trusted to be a good citizen, and therefore could not be a citizen at all. Locke is rightly celebrated as a champion of religious toleration, but he was highly censorious of irreligion. "Those are not at all to be tolerated who deny the being of a God," he writes in *A Letter Concerning Toleration*. "Promises, covenants, and oaths, which are the bonds of human society, can have no hold upon an atheist. The taking away of God, though but even in thought, dissolves all." Taking away God makes it possible, thought Locke, for every text to become a pretext, every interpretation a misinterpretation, and every oath a deceit.

James Madison in his *Memorial and Remonstrance* of 1785 wrote to similar effect. It is often forgotten that for Madison and the other founders, religious freedom was an inalienable right premised upon inalienable duty. "It is the duty of every man to render to the Creator such homage and such only as he believes to be acceptable to him. This duty is precedent, both in order of time and in degree of obligation, to the claims of Civil Society." Then follows this passage that could hardly be more pertinent to the question that prompts our present reflection:

> Before any man can be considered as a member of Civil Society, he must be considered as a subject of the Governour of the Universe: And if a member of Civil Society, who enters into any subordinate Association, must always do it with a reservation of his duty to the General Authority; much more must every man who becomes a member of any particular Civil Society, do it with a saving of his allegiance to the Universal Sovereign.

State constitutions could and did exclude atheists from public office. The federal Constitution, in article VI, would simply impose no further religious test. In reaction to the extreme secularist bias of much historical scholarship, some writers in recent years have attempted to portray the Founders as Bible-believing, orthodox, even born-again evangelical Christians. That is much too much. It is well worth recalling, however, how much they had in common with respect to religious and philosophical beliefs. While a few were sympathetic to milder versions of deism and some were rigorous Calvinists in the Puritan tradition, almost all assumed a clearly Christian, and clearly Protestant, construal of reality. In the language of contemporary discourse, the Founders were "moral realists," which is to say they assumed the reality of a good not of their own contriving. This is amply demonstrated from many sources, not least the Declaration and the Constitution, and especially the preamble of the latter. The "good" was for the Founders a reality not of their own fabrication, nor was it merely the "conventionalism" of received moral tradition.

The Social Compact

The Founders did not view the social contract as some truncated and mechanistic contrivance of calculated self-interest. They saw it more as a compact, premised upon a sense of covenantal purpose guiding this *novus ordo seclorum*. That understanding of a covenant encompassing the contract was, in a time of supreme testing, brought to full and magisterial articulation by Abraham Lincoln. The Constitution represented not a deal struck but a nation "so conceived and so dedicated."

In such a nation, an atheist can be a citizen, but he cannot be a good citizen. Again, the behavior of atheists may in some cases be morally superior to that of Christians. That is not at issue. At issue is our understanding of the fullness of citizenship. A good citizen does more than abide by the laws. A good citizen is able to give an account, a morally compelling account, of the regime of which he is part. He is able to justify its defense against its enemies, and to recommend its virtues to citizens of the next generation convincingly, so that they, in turn, can transmit the regime to citizens yet unborn. This regime of liberal democracy, of republican self-governance, is not self-evidently good and just. An account must be given. Reasons must be given, reasons whose authority is drawn from that which is higher than the self and is not of the self's creation, from that to which the self is ultimately obliged.

An older form of atheism pitted reason against the knowledge of God. The new atheism is the atheism of unreason. It is much more dangerous because more insidious. Fortunately, the overwhelming majority of Americans—and, I believe, the majority of our intellectual elites, if put to the test—are not atheists of any of the varieties we have discussed. They believe that there are good reasons for this ordering of the *civitas*, reasons that have public purchase, reasons that go beyond contingent convenience, reasons that entail what is just, the laws of nature, and maybe even the will of God.

And so, those who believe in the God of Abraham, Isaac, Jacob, and Jesus turn out to be the best citizens. Those who were once called atheists are now equipped to be the most reliable defenders not of the gods but of the good reasons for this regime of ordered liberty. Such people are the best citizens not *even though* but *because* their loyalty to the *civitas* is qualified by a higher loyalty. Among the best of the good reasons they give in justifying this regime is that it makes a sharply limited claim upon the loyalty of its citizens. The ultimate allegiance of the faithful is not to the regime or to its constituting texts, but to the City of God and the sacred texts that guide our path toward that end for which we were created. They are dual citizens, so to speak, in a regime that, as Madison and others well understood, was designed for such duality. When the regime forgets itself and reestablishes the gods of the *civitas*, even if it be in the name of liberal democracy, the followers of the God of Abraham have no choice but to invite the opprobrium of once again being "atheists."

I am well aware that there are those who will agree with the gravamen of this argument for reasons quite different from my own. They do not themselves believe, but they recognize the importance of religion as a "useful lie" essential to securing public order. It is sad that there are such people—sad because they do not believe, and sadder because they are prepared to use, and thereby abuse, the name of the God whom they do not honor.

But of course they are right about religion and this public order. It is an order that was not conceived and dedicated by atheists, and cannot today be reconceived and rededicated by atheists. In times of testing—and every time is a time of testing for this American experiment in ordered liberty—a morally convincing account must be given. Convincing to whom? One obvious answer in a democracy, although not the only answer, is this: convincing to a majority of the citizens. Giving such an account is required of good citizens. And that is why, I reluctantly conclude, atheists cannot be good citizens.

Note: An earlier version of this essay appeared in *First Things*, published by the Institute on Religion and Public Life.

Appendix

Conference Participants

The conference upon which this book is based, "To Be Christian in America Today," took place in Washington, D.C., April 3–5, 1991. The following persons participated:

Lawrence Adams, Institute on Religion and Democracy
Mark Amstutz, Wheaton College
J. Brian Benestad, University of Scranton
Robert Benne, Roanoke College
Matthew Berke, *First Things*
James H. Billington, Library of Congress
Carl E. Braaten, Lutheran School of Theology at Chicago
James T. Burtchaell, C.S.C., University of Notre Dame
Lynn R. Buzzard, Campbell University
William J. Byron, S.J., The Catholic University of America
Agostino Cacciavillan, Apostolic Pro-Nuncio to the United States
Alberto R. Coll, Department of Defense
Kenneth R. Craycraft, American Enterprise Institute
Michael Cromartie, Ethics and Public Policy Center
Dean C. Curry, Messiah College
David G. Dalin, University of Hartford
Thomas S. Derr, Smith College
Robert Destro, The Catholic University of America
Jude P. Dougherty, The Catholic University of America
Ervin S. Duggan, Federal Communications Commission
Terry Eastland, Ethics and Public Policy Center
Jean Bethke Elshtain, Vanderbilt University
John Farina, author

309

Robert P. George, Princeton University
Mary Ann Glendon, Harvard Law School
Edward R. Grant, Americans United for Life
Kenneth L. Grasso, St. Peter's College
Os Guinness, author and lecturer
Christopher Hancock, Virginia Theological Seminary
J. Bryan Hehir, Georgetown University
Daniel R. Heimbach, Department of the Navy
Carl F. H. Henry, author and theologian
Paul R. Hinlicky, Immanuel Lutheran Church, Delhi, New York
James Hitchcock, St. Louis University
Russell Hittinger, Princeton University
David Hollenbach, S.J., Weston School of Theology
George W. Hunt, S.J., *America*
James Davison Hunter, University of Virginia
Robert Jenson, St. Olaf College
Dean M. Kelley, National Council of Churches
Christa R. Klein, *In Trust*
Diane Knippers, Institute on Religion and Democracy
Thomas C. Kohler, Boston College Law School
Richard D. Land, Christian Life Commission, Southern Baptist
    Convention
John P. Langan, S.J., Woodstock Theological Center, Georgetown
    University
Peter J. Leithart, Reformed Heritage Presbyterian Church, Alabaster,
    Alabama
George Lindbeck, The Divinity School, Yale University
Daniel Mahoney, Assumption College
Paul V. Mankowski, S.J., Harvard University
Dennis P. McCann, DePaul University
Ralph McInerny, Jacques Maritain Center, University of Notre Dame
William Murphy, Archdiocese of Boston
Kenneth Myers, *Genesis*
Richard John Neuhaus, Institute on Religion and Public Life
Mark A. Noll, Wheaton College
Michael Novak, American Enterprise Institute
James Nuechterlein, *First Things*
Thomas C. Oden, Drew University
Mario J. Paredes, Northeast Hispanic Catholic Center

Allan M. Parrent, Virginia Theological Seminary
Carl J. Peter, The Catholic University of America
A. James Reichley, Brookings Institution
Robert Royal, Ethics and Public Policy Center
William G. Rusch, Evangelical Lutheran Church in America
James V. Schall, S.J., Georgetown University
Herbert Schlossberg, Fieldstead Institute
Ronald J. Sider, Eastern Baptist Theological Seminary
Paul E. Sigmund, Princeton University
James W. Skillen, Center for Public Justice
Max L. Stackhouse, Andover-Newton Theological School
Paul T. Stallsworth, Creswell (N.C.) Charge, United Methodist
    Church
Glenn Tinder, University of Massachusetts at Boston
Steven M. Tipton, Emory University
David Trickett, Washington Theological Consortium
Philip Turner, General Theological Seminary
David Walsh, The Catholic University of America
George Weigel, Ethics and Public Policy Center
Robert L. Wilken, University of Virginia
William H. Willimon, Duke University
Elliott Wright, National Conference of Christians and Jews

Note: Affiliations were current as of April 1991.

Notes

CHAPTER 1: "Taking America Seriously"
George Weigel

1. To this traditional listing of key documents might well be added the New Year's Day addresses of Paul VI and John Paul II marking the "World Day of Peace" inaugurated by the former on January 1, 1969. John Paul II has frequently used this vehicle to develop his public theology of religious freedom—most recently on January 1, 1991, where the fundamental human right of religious freedom was explicitly linked to the pursuit of peace through the creation of democratic political structures within nations. The two instructions from the Congregation for the Doctrine of the Faith—the "Instruction on Certain Aspects of the 'Theology of Liberation'" (1984) and the "Instruction on Christian Freedom and Liberation" (1986)—are also significant texts in the emerging social teaching of the Church.

2. Cf., for example, George Weigel and Robert Royal, eds., *A Century of Catholic Social Thought* (Washington: Ethics and Public Policy Center, 1991).

3. Cf. James Davison Hunter, *Culture Wars: The Struggle to Define America* (New York: Basic Books, 1991).

4. "A Modell of Christian Charity," cited in Robert Bellah, *The Broken Covenant: American Civil Religion in Time of Trial* (New York: Seabury, 1975), 14–15. Perry Miller argued that Winthrop's sermon, with its insistence on the covenantal character of the American experiment, "stands at the beginning of our [national] consciousness" (Perry Miller, *Nature's Nation* [Cambridge: Harvard University Press, 1967], 6).

5. Cf. John Courtney Murray, *We Hold These Truths: Catholic Reflections on the American Proposition* (New York: Doubleday Image Books, 1964), 50:

> The Bill of Rights was an effective instrument for the delimitation of government authority and social power, not because it was written on paper in 1789 or 1791, but because the rights it proclaimed had already been engraved by history on the conscience of a people. The American Bill of Rights is not a piece of eighteenth-century rationalist theory; it is far more the product of Christian history. Behind it one can see, not the philosophy of the Enlightenment, but the older philosophy that had been the matrix of the common law. The "man" whose rights are guaranteed in the face of law and government is, whether he knows it or not, the Christian man, who had learned to know his own personal dignity in the school of Christian faith.

6. Cited in John Tracy Ellis, *American Catholicism*, 2d ed., rev. (Chicago: University of Chicago Press, 1969), 151.

7. The full text of the speech may be found in *Public Papers of the Presidents of*

313

the United States: John F. Kennedy, 1962 (Washington: U.S. Government Printing Office, 1963), 470–75.

8. Nor has Kennedy's positivist projection been any more borne out in world affairs. The Islamic revolution of the late 1970s, the democratic revolution in Latin America, and the Revolution of 1989 in Central and Eastern Europe were all massive eruptions on the world-historical scene that had little or nothing to do with the technical-managerial ethos, and a great deal to do with questions of meaning and value.

9. Maureen Dowd, "Bush's Holy War," *New York Times Week in Review*, 3 February 1991, 2.

10. Cf., among many examples, Richard Rorty, *Contingency, Irony, and Solidarity* (Cambridge: Cambridge University Press, 1989). See also Richard John Neuhaus's response, "Joshing Richard Rorty," *First Things* 8 (December 1990): 14–24. It is perhaps significant, and certainly ironic, that Rorty is the grandson of Walter Rauschenbusch, father of the Social Gospel movement.

11. Eschatological themes have been especially strong in the social teaching of John Paul II. Cf. *Laborem Exercens*, sec. 27, and *Sollicitudo Rei Socialis*, sec. 98. Cf. also the "Instruction on Certain Aspects of the 'Theology of Liberation,' " IX-3, X-6; and the "Instruction on Christian Freedom and Liberation," sec. 51, 58–60, 63.

12. Cf. "Telling the American Catholic Story," *First Things* 7 (November 1990): 43–49.

13. Cf., for example, Jay P. Dolan, *The American Catholic Experience* (New York: Doubleday, 1985).

14. Cf. *Sollicitudo Rei Socialis*, sec. 44.

15. On the notion of the Church as a community of disciples, cf. Avery Dulles, S.J., "Imaging the Church for the 1980s," in *A Church to Believe In: Discipleship and the Dynamics of Freedom* (New York: Crossroad, 1982), 1–18. Dulles takes this image of the Church from John Paul II's inaugural encyclical, *Redemptor Hominis*, sec. 21.

16. Cf. Peter L. Berger and Richard John Neuhaus, eds., *Against the World for the World* (New York: Seabury, 1976).

17. Cf. *Lumen Gentium*, chapter 3.

18. "Instruction on Christian Freedom and Liberation," sec. 6, 18–19.

19. For a survey of this evolution, see Franz H. Mueller, *The Church and the Social Question* (Washington: American Enterprise Institute, 1984).

20. And yet there is, to this day, what can only be described as minimal representation by Americans (clerical and lay) on the Vatican councils concerned with these matters.

21. Cf. most recently the pope's 1991 World Day of Peace message, "Respect for Conscience: Foundation of Peace," *Origins* 20, no. 29 (27 December 1990): 472–76.

22. For a fuller treatment of the subject, see Donald Pelotte, S.S.S., *John Courtney Murray: Theologian in Conflict* (New York: Paulist Press, 1975). Cf. also chapter 5, "John Courtney Murray and the Catholic Human Rights Revolution," in my *Catholicism and the Renewal of American Democracy* (New York: Paulist Press, 1989).

23. For a more detailed argument in support of this claim, see "Catholicism

and Democracy: The Other Twentieth-Century Revolution," in my *Freedom and Its Discontents* (Washington: Ethics and Public Policy Center, 1991).

24. Although the current debate over "multiculturalism" clearly bears on this. Cf. Diane Ravitch, "Multiculturalism: E Pluribus Plures," *The American Scholar* 59, no. 3 (Summer 1990): 337–54.

25. Cf. my report on that conference, "Living in the Light: The Copenhagen CSCE Review Conference on the 'Human Dimension,' " *American Purpose* 4, no. 6 (July/August 1990).

26. For recent examples of this work, see Michael Novak, *Freedom With Justice: Catholic Social Thought and Liberal Institutions* (San Francisco: Harper & Row, 1984); Michael Novak, *Free Persons and the Common Good* (Lanham, Md.: Madison Books, 1989); Mary Ann Glendon, *Rights Talk: The Impoverishment of Political Discourse* (New York: The Free Press, 1991); and David Hollenbach, S.J., *Justice, Peace, and Human Rights* (New York: Crossroad, 1988).

27. Philadelphia: Fortress Press, 1981.

28. New York: Simon and Schuster, 1982.

29. In addition to the letter, see Lay Commission on Catholic Social Teaching and the U.S. Economy, "Toward the Future: Catholic Social Thought and the U.S. Economy," and, for representative commentary, Thomas M. Gannon, S.J., ed. *The Catholic Challenge to the American Economy* (New York: Macmillan, 1987).

30. Max L. Stackhouse and Dennis P. McCann, "A Postcommunist Manifesto," *The Christian Century*, 16 January 1991, 44–47. See also the commentaries by Robert Benne, Barbara Andolsen, Robin Lovin, John Cobb, and Preston Williams, and a Stackhouse/McCann rejoinder, in the 23 January 1991 issue of the *Century*.

31. John Courtney Murray, "Things Old and New in 'Pacem in Terris,' " *America*, 27 April 1963, 612. Interestingly enough, the American bishops explored the "world order" question in five remarkable, and now largely forgotten, statements issued during and immediately after the Second World War. For a summary and analysis, see my *Tranquillitas Ordinis: The Present Failure and Future Promise of American Catholic Thought on War and Peace* (New York: Oxford, 1987), 55–67.

32. Cf. Richard John Neuhaus, "Just War and This War," *Wall Street Journal*, 29 January 1991; George Weigel, "The Churches and the Gulf Crisis," in James Turner Johnson and George Weigel, *Just War and the Gulf War* (Washington: Ethics and Public Policy Center, 1991); James Turner Johnson, "The Use of Force: A Justified Response," *The Christian Century*, 6–13 February 1991.

33. "Pastoral Letter of the Third Plenary Council of Baltimore," in *Pastoral Letters of the United States Catholic Bishops*, vol. 1, ed. Hugh J. Nolan (Washington: NCCB/USCC, 1984), 216.

CHAPTER 2: "Liberalism Revisited"
Max L. Stackhouse

1. Carl Braaten's paper struggles with this problem from a Lutheran perspective. Most of ecumenical Protestantism, however, is rooted on one or another branch of the Reformed or Arminian traditions, which I here seek to address.

2. The failure of some of the century's leading thinkers on this point is

responsible for many of Protestantism's present ills. For all their other contributions, Rudolph Bultmann had no discernible interest in social analysis and drew his views of modernity from the quasi-Fascist views of Martin Heidegger, while Karl Barth's radical *Nein* to these themes, plus his embrace of socialism, encouraged some Protestants to adopt anti-religious and finally anti-theological modes of social analysis.

3. The relationship of the Social Gospel to the struggles against slavery and racism has been a matter of some debate in liberal Protestantism in recent decades. Most of the issues have now been laid to rest by Ronald White, *Liberty and Justice for All: Racial Reform and the Social Gospel* (New York: Harper, 1990).

4. See my "Jesus and Economics: A Century of Reflection," in *The Bible in American Law, Politics, and Political Rhetoric*, ed. James T. Johnson (Phildelphia: Fortress Press, 1985), 107–51.

5. For Catholic understandings of this background, see J. A. Zahm, "Leo XIII and the Social Question," *North American Review* 161 (1895): 200–213. Contemporary Roman views of the background of the social encyclicals can be found in David Hollenbach, *Claims in Conflict* (New York: Paulist Press, 1979); William P. Gooley, "Shared Visions: Human Nature and Human Work in *Rerum Novarum* and *Laborem Exercens*," Ph.D. dissertation, Syracuse University, 1987; and Charles E. Curran, "100 Years of Catholic Social Teaching: An Evaluation," Presidential Address, American Theological Society, April 1990.

6. See Walter Rauschenbusch, *The Righteousness of the Kingdom* (Nashville: Abingdon Press, 1968 [written in 1892]).

7. See, for examples, Br. Azarias, "Ethical Aspects of the Papal Encyclical," *International Journal of Ethics* 2 (January 1892): 137–61; and the anonymous "The Policy of the Pope," *Contemporary Review* 62 (1892): 457–77, with subsequent discussion of the article in vol. 63, 663ff. and 899ff.

8. W. J. Kerby, "The Roman Catholic Church and Social Reform," in *The New Encyclopedia of Social Reform*, ed. William D. P. Bliss (New York: Funk and Wagnalls, 1910), 1070–74.

9. See Washington Gladden in John Ireland et al., "Leo XIII, His Work and Influence," *North American Review* 177 (September 1903): 352. I am grateful to Gooley, "Shared Visions," for drawing my attention to this.

10. W. J. Tucker, "Editorial: The Papal Encyclical on Labor," *The Andover Review* 16 (August 1891): 175–76.

11. E. Troeltsch, *Die Sozialehre...*, 1911; and M. Weber, *Gesammelte Aufsätze zur Religionssoziologie*, 1922. I extend this argument in *Creeds, Society and Human Rights* (Grand Rapids: Eerdmans, 1984), especially chapters 2, 3, and 6.

12. It is striking to note the competing interpretations of Locke in discussions about liberalism and its relation to human rights and democracy. Liberal Protestants who know their history view him as one who, when the Puritan, parliamentary revolution was crushed at the hands of the Laudians (who demanded an established church) on the one hand and the anti-religious/anti-parliamentary Hobbesians on the other, wrote a philosophical statement of what Protestants believed their enemies were falsely denying as reasonable *theological* truths. Important sources on the background include: A. S. P. Woodhouse, *Puritanism and Liberty* (London: J. M. Dent, 1938); J. H. Nichols, *Democracy and the Churches* (Philadelphia: Westminster Press, 1951); and Margo Todd, *Christian Humanism and the Puritan Social Order* (Cambridge: Cambridge University Press, 1987).

This view contrasts with that of Roman Catholics who know little and care less about Protestant social thought and wonder why theological language is present in arguments about rights; with that of continental Jewish scholars who doubt that Christians could be serious about tolerance; and with that of secular scholars who are suspicious of theology in any form. Among Catholic disciples of Leo Strauss, these views are peculiarly mixed.

13. Some Catholic scholars acknowledge the Lockean influence on Leo XIII. Thomas Kohler, for example, speaks of the "correction" that *Quadragesimo Anno* made of the "non-Thomistic understanding of private property that was set forth in *Rerum Novarum*. Ironically, the notions that informed the 1891 encyclical were based on the theories of John Locke, which had been incorporated into neo-scholastic thought by the nineteenth-century Jesuit theologian Taparelli d'Azeglio." See George Weigel and Robert Royal, eds., *A Century of Catholic Social Thought* (Washington: Ethics and Public Policy Center, 1991), 33.

14. W. J. Tucker, "Editorial," 177.

15. H. R. Niebuhr, *The Kingdom of God in America* (New York: Harper Bros., 1937).

16. This term was evidently first used in correspondence between John Courtney Murray and Reinhold Niebuhr, and has been subsequently elaborated by Martin Marty, David Tracy, and others.

17. A deep division on this matter was already evident in the movement around Martin Luther King's struggle for civil rights. Some joined because they believed it was an attempt to actualize the higher laws of human rights, as King articulated in his "Letter From a Birmingham Jail." Others joined because they thought "the movement" would carry history from the oppressions of the past to the promises of a new future, as he articulated in his "I Have a Dream" speech at the Lincoln Memorial. In the later anti-Vietnam and counterculture movements, the latter impetus eventually obscured the moral logic of the former emphasis.

18. See Robert Bellah et al., *Habits of the Heart* (Berkeley: University of California Press, 1985).

19. Reinhold Niebuhr, *The Nature and Destiny of Man* (New York: Scribner's, 1939), vol. 1. This great work of modern ecumenical Protestantism is under sharp criticism today. See Beverly W. Harrison, *Making the Connections: Essays in Feminist Social Ethics*, ed. C. S. Robb (Boston: Beacon Press, 1975).

20. See, especially, Paul E. Sigmund, *Liberation Theology at the Crossroads: Democracy or Revolution* (New York: Oxford University Press, 1990). I am grateful to Prof. Sigmund for several comments on this paper.

21. I do not attempt to trace the ways in which these ideas have come to dominate segments of the World Council of Churches, but one might trace similar redefinitions to the impact of Latin American liberation theology on the World Council of Churches since Richard Shaull's appeal to the Conference on Church and Society in Geneva in 1966.

22. Robert Wuthnow, *The Struggle for America's Soul: Evangelicals, Liberals, and Secularism* (Grand Rapids: Eerdmans, 1989).

23. See, as an example of Marxist fundamentalism, Tom Kelly, "Manifestos, Marx and the Christian Century," *Christianity and Crisis*, 18 March 1991, 76–77.

24. J. W. von Goethe, *Faust*, part I, tr. Peter Salm, rev. ed. (New York: Bantam Books, 1985), 77, ll. 1225–37.

25. My colleague S. Mark Heim has just brought out a volume on these matters

for the Faith and Order Commission: *Faith to Creed: Ecumenical Perspectives on the Affirmation of the Apostolic Faith in the Fourth Century* (Grand Rapids: Eerdmans, 1991).

CHAPTER 3: ". . . Evangelical Political Reflection"
Mark A. Noll

1. See especially Paolo E. Colletta, *William Jennings Bryan*, vol. 1: *Political Evangelist, 1860–1908* (Lincoln: University of Nebraska Press, 1964).

2. William Jennings Bryan, "Speech Concluding Debate on the Chicago Platform," in *The First Battle: The Story of the Campaign of 1896* (Chicago: W. B. Conkey, 1896), 206.

3. As the *skandalon* of I Corinthians 1:23.

4. See Donald W. Dayton and Robert K. Johnston, eds., *The Variety of American Evangelicalism* (Knoxville: University of Tennessee Press, 1991); Douglas A. Sweeney, "The Essential Evangelicalism Dialectic: The Historiography of the Early Neo-Evangelical Movement and the Observer-Participant Dilemma," *Church History* 60 (March 1991): 70–84; George M. Marsden, *Understanding Fundamentalism and Evangelicalism* (Grand Rapids: Eerdmans, 1991); and David S. Dockery, ed., *Southern Baptists and American Evangelicals* (Nashville: Broadman, forthcoming) as recent refinements and corrections of earlier attempts at definition, of which the best remains George M. Marsden, "The Evangelical Denomination," in *Evangelicalism and Modern America*, ed. Marsden (Grand Rapids: Eerdmans, 1984). Other "early modern" attempts were Bruce Shelley, *Evangelicalism in America*, which was focused on the National Association of Evangelicals (Grand Rapids: Eerdmans, 1967); George M. Marsden and Ernest Sandeen, "Defining Fundamentalism," *Christian Scholar's Review* 1 (Winter/Spring, 1971): 141–51, 227–33; Donald W. Dayton, *Discovering an Evangelical Heritage* (Peabody, Mass.: Hendrickson, 1988; orig. 1976); David Wells and John Woodbridge, eds., *The Evangelicals*, rev. ed. (Grand Rapids: Baker, 1977); John D. Woodbridge, Mark A. Noll, and Nathan O. Hatch, *The Gospel in America: Themes in the Story of America's Evangelicals* (Grand Rapids: Zondervan, 1979); Cullen Murphy (with Timothy L. Smith), "Protestantism and the Evangelicals," *Wilson Quarterly* 5 (Autumn 1981): 105–16; William J. Abraham, *The Coming Great Revival: Recovering the Full Evangelical Tradition* (San Francisco: Harper & Row, 1984); Timothy L. Smith, "The Evangelical Kaleidoscope and the Call to Christian Unity," *Christian Scholar's Review* 15 (1986): 125–40; and Mark Ellingsen, *The Evangelical Movement: Growth, Impact, Controversy, Dialog* (Minneapolis: Augsburg, 1988).

5. These four are adapted from David W. Bebbington, *Evangelicalism in Modern Britain: A History from the 1730s to the 1980s* (London: Unwin Hyman, 1989), 3–17.

6. A different problem is presented by charismatic or "evangelical" Catholics who share many traits with Protestant evangelicals but who, because of historic divides between Catholics and evangelicals, are not considered in this essay.

7. Garry Wills, *Under God: Religion and American Politics* (New York: Simon and Schuster, 1990), 97, 67.

8. Bryan, "Speech," 204.

9. Leonard I. Sweet, "Nineteenth-Century Evangelicalism," in *Encyclopedia of*

the American Religious Experience, vol. 2 (New York: Scribner's, 1988), 896. Sweet's entire essay is much to be commended, as is his bibliographical *tour de force*, "The Evangelical Tradition in America," in *The Evangelical Tradition in America*, ed. Sweet, (Macon, Geo.: Mercer University Press, 1984).

10. Leo XIII, *Rerum Novarum*, in *The Papal Encyclicals, 1878–1903*, vol. 2, ed. Claudia Carlen (Raleigh: McGrath, 1981), sec. 241, par. 1; Bryan, "Speech," 199.

11. Bryan, "Speech," 199; Leo, *Rerum Novarum*, sec. 241, par. 2.

12. Leo, *Rerum Novarum*, sec. 249, par. 33; Bryan, "Speech," 200.

13. Leo, *Rerum Novarum*, sec. 241, par. 3; Bryan, "Speech," 205–6.

14. On the consistency of Bryan's career from populist politician to fundamentalist champion, see especially Lawrence W. Levine, *Defender of the Faith: William Jennings Bryan, The Last Decade, 1915–1925* (New York: Oxford University Press, 1965).

15. Leo, *Rerum Novarum*, sec. 215, par. 62; Bryan, "The Prince of Peace," in *William Jennings Bryan: Selections*, ed. Ray Ginger (Indianapolis: Bobbs-Merrill, 1967), 148–49:

> Christ has given us a platform more fundamental than any political party has ever written. . . . When He condensed into one commandment those of the ten which relate of man's duty toward his fellows and enjoined upon us the rule, "Thou shalt love thy neighbor as thyself," He presented a plan for the solution of all the problems that now vex society or hereafter arise. Other remedies may palliate or postpone the day of settlement, but this is all-sufficient and the reconciliation which it effects is a permanent one.

16. Leo, *Rerum Novarum*, sec. 244, par. 15; Bryan, *The Last Message of William Jennings Bryan* (New York: Fleming H. Revell, 1925), 51. This is also the conclusion of Levine, *Defender of the Faith*, 261–70; and Wills, *Under God*, 97–106.

17. Leo, *Rerum Novarum*, sec. 251, par. 39; Bryan, *In His Image* (New York: Fleming H. Revell, 1922), 231.

18. See especially Harry S. Stout, *The New England Soul: Preaching and Religious Culture in Colonial New England* (New York: Oxford University Press, 1986).

19. See especially Harry S. Stout, *The Divine Dramatist: George Whitefield and the Rise of Modern Evangelicalism* (Grand Rapids: Eerdmans, 1991).

20. David Paul Nord, "The Evangelical Origins of Mass Media in America, 1815–1835," *Journalism Monographs* 88 (1984): 1–30; and Nathan O. Hatch, *The Democratization of American Christianity* (New Haven: Yale University Press, 1989), 125–26, 141–46.

21. Quentin J. Schultze, "Evangelical Radio and the Rise of the Electronic Church, 1921–1948," *Journal of Broadcasting and Electronic Media* 32 (Summer 1988): 289–306; and idem, ed., *Evangelicals, the Mass Media, and American Culture* (Grand Rapids: Zondervan, 1990).

22. For a summation of this argument, see Hatch, *Democratization of American Christianity*, 5–9.

23. Sidney E. Mead, *The Lively Experiment: The Shaping of Christianity in America* (New York: Harper & Row, 1963); and Donald G. Mathews, "The Second Great Awakening as an Organizing Process, 1780–1830," *American Quarterly* 21 (1969): 23–43.

24. See especially Stout, *The Divine Dramatist*; Hatch, *Democratization of*

American Christianity; and Stout, "Religion, Communications, and the Revolution," *William and Mary Quarterly* 34 (1977): 501–41.

25. Bryan, "Speech," 199.

26. See especially Hatch, *Democratization of American Christianity*.

27. See the sections on Bryan in Bradley J. Longfield, *The Presbyterian Controversy: Fundamentalists, Modernists, and Moderates* (New York: Oxford University Press, 1991).

28. Leo, *Rerum Novarum*, sec. 245, par. 16 (my italics).

29. Bryan, "Speech," 200.

30. Ibid., 203.

31. See especially Ruth H. Bloch, *Visionary Republic: Millennial Themes in American Thought, 1756–1800* (New York: Cambridge University Press, 1985).

32. Richard T. Hughes and C. Leonard Allen, *Illusions of Innocence: Protestant Primitivism in America, 1630–1875* (Chicago: University of Chicago Press, 1988); Richard T. Hughes, ed., *The American Quest for the Primitive Church* (Urbana: University of Illinois Press, 1988); and T. D. Bozeman, *To Live Ancient Lives: The Primitivist Dimension in Puritanism* (Chapel Hill: University of North Carolina Press, 1988). For hints of Catholic primitivism, see the sections on the Enlightenment and Romanticism in Patrick W. Carey, ed., *American Catholic Religious Thought* (New York: Paulist Press, 1987).

33. For further analysis of this situation, see Nathan O. Hatch, " 'The Clean Sea-Breeze of the Centuries': Learning to Think Historically," in *The Search for Christian America*, expanded ed., ed. Hatch, Mark A. Noll, and George M. Marsden (Colorado Springs: Helmers & Howard, 1989), 145–55.

34. The quantity and quality of seminal studies is increasing rapidly. For starters, see the sources in notes 4 and 9, along with: Nathan O. Hatch, "Evangelicalism as a Democratic Movement," in *Evangelicalism and Modern America*, ed. Marsden; Donald G. Mathews, *Religion in the Old South* (Chicago: University of Chicago Press, 1977); Albert F. Raboteau, *Slave Religion: The "Invisible Institution" in the Antebellum South* (New York: Oxford University Press, 1978); Richard Lovelace, *Dynamics of Spiritual Life* (Downers Grove, Ill.: Inter-Varsity Press, 1979); Douglas Frank, *Less Than Conquerors: How Evangelicals Entered the Twentieth Century* (Grand Rapids: Eerdmans, 1986); Randall Balmer, *Mine Eyes Have Seen the Glory: A Journey into the Evangelical Subculture in America* (New York: Oxford University Press, 1989); Grant Wacker, "The Functions of Faith in Primitive Pentecostalism," *Harvard Theological Review* 77 (July/October 1984): 353–75; and Edith L. Blumhofer, *Restoring the Faith: The Assemblies of God, Pentecostalism, and American Culture* (Urbana: University of Illinois Press, 1991).

35. Lyman A. Kellstedt and Mark A. Noll, "Religion, Voting for President, and Party Identification, 1948–1984," in *Religion and American Politics from the Colonial Era to the 1980s*, ed. Noll (New York: Oxford University Press, 1990), 368.

36. On the shift of evangelicals to the Democratic party in 1896, see Paul Kleppner, *Continuity and Change in Electoral Politics, 1893–1928* (New York: Greenwood, 1987), 107–15.

37. Robert T. Handy, "Protestant Theological Tensions and Political Styles in the Progressive Era," in *Religion and American Politics*, ed. Noll, 283–88. In his own era, the religious-civil-social concerns of evangelist Billy Sunday were broadly

typical of Protestantism in general; see Lyle Dorsett, *Billy Sunday and the Redemption of Urban America* (Grand Rapids: Eerdmans, 1991).

38. Norris Magnuson, *Salvation in the Slums: Evangelical Social Work, 1865–1920* (Grand Rapids: Baker, 1990; orig. 1977).

39. See Richard Allen, *Religion and Social Reform in Canada, 1914–28* (Toronto: University of Toronto Press, 1971).

40. George M. Marsden, "Afterword: Religion, Politics, and the Search for an American Consensus," in *Religion and American Politics*, ed. Noll, 385.

41. *The Papers of Woodrow Wilson*, vol. 23: *1911–1912*, ed. Arthur S. Link (Princeton: Princeton University Press, 1977), 20.

42. Timothy L. Smith, *Revivalism and Social Reform: American Protestantism on the Eve of the Civil War*, expanded ed. (Baltimore: Johns Hopkins University Press, 1980); and idem, "Righteousness and Hope: Christian Holiness and the Millennial Vision in America, 1800–1900," *American Quarterly* 31 (Spring 1979): 21–45.

43. See Paul M. Waggoner, "The Historiography of the Scopes Trial: A Critical Re-evaluation," *Trinity Journal* 1984: 155–74.

44. George M. Marsden, *Fundamentalism and American Culture: The Shaping of Twentieth-Century Evangelicalism, 1870–1925* (New York: Oxford University Press, 1980); Joel A. Carpenter, *Revive Us Again: The Recovery of American Fundamentalism, 1930–1950* (Oxford University Press, forthcoming). Other useful studies include Ernest R. Sandeen, *The Roots of Fundamentalism: British and American Millenarianism, 1800–1930* (Chicago: University of Chicago Press, 1970); and Timothy P. Weber, *Living in the Shadow of the Second Coming: American Fundamentalism, 1875–1982*, rev. ed. (Chicago: University of Chicago Press, 1987).

45. Besides Carpenter, *Revive Us Again*, see also the works by proponents Lewis Sperry Chafer, *Dispensationalism* (Dallas: Dallas Seminary Press, 1951); and Charles Caldwell Ryrie, *Dispensationalism Today* (Chicago: Moody Press, 1968). For comment and critique, see C. Norman Kraus, *Dispensationalism in America* (Richmond: John Knox Press, 1958); and Clarence B. Bass, *Backgrounds to Dispensationalism: Its Historical Genesis and Ecclesiastical Implications* (Grand Rapids: Eerdmans, 1960).

46. See Marsden, *Fundamentalism and American Culture*, 55–62; and for background, George M. Marsden, "Everyone One's Own Interpreter? The Bible, Science, and Authority in Mid-Nineteenth Century America," in *The Bible in America: Essays in Cultural History*, ed. Nathan O. Hatch and Mark A. Noll (New York: Oxford Univesity Press, 1982); Theodore Dwight Bozeman, *Protestants in an Age of Science: The Baconian Ideal and Antebellum Religious Thought* (Chapel Hill: University of North Carolina Press, 1977); and Mark A. Noll, "Common Sense Traditions and American Evangelical Thought," *American Quarterly* 37 (Summer 1985): 216–38.

47. For example, Frank, *Less Than Conquerors*.

48. For example, Leo P. Ribuffo, *The Old Christian Right: The Protestant Far Right From the Great Depression to the Cold War* (Philadelphia: Temple University Press, 1983).

49. The examples in this paragraph are from Carpenter, *Revive Us Again*, where many more of a similar nature may be found.

50. The following two paragraphs rely upon the schema of Joel A. Carpenter,

"Contending for the Faith Once Delivered: Primitivist Impulses in American Fundamentalism," in *American Quest for the Primitive Church*, ed. Hughes, as well as my response to Carpenter, in ibid., 121–22.

51. John H. Leith, "Spirituality of the Church," in *Encyclopedia of Religion in the South*, ed. Samuel S. Hill (Macon, Ga.: Mercer University Press, 1984), 731.

52. Quoted in Samuel S. Hill, Jr., *The South and the North in American Religion* (Athens: University of Georgia Press, 1980), 128, which is in general an excellent meditation on its theme.

53. Ribuffo, *The Old Christian Right*.

54. David R. Elliott and Iris Miller, *Bible Bill: A Biography of William Aberhart* (Edmonton, Alberta: Reidmore, 1987); and Paul Boyer, *Mission on Taylor Street: The Founding and Early Years of the Dayton Brethren in Christ Mission* (Grantham, Pa.: Brethren in Christ Historical Society, 1987).

55. Joel Carpenter, *Revive Us Again*, does draw attention to a slim pamphlet by Judson E. Conant, "The Growing Menace of the 'Social Gospel' " (Chicago: Bible Institute Colportage, 1937), but this is no more than a rudimentary effort.

56. Nels F. S. Ferré, "Present Trends in Protestant Thought," *Religion in Life* 17 (1948): 336.

57. Donald Dayton in his contributions to Dayton and Johnston, eds., *The Variety of American Evangelicalism* and elsewhere has recently emphasized the anti-dispensational animus of these "new evangelicals."

58. See especially George M. Marsden, *Reforming Fundamentalism: Fuller Seminary and the New Evangelicalism* (Grand Rapids: Eerdmans, 1987); and for the role of more learned British evangelicals in pioneering a way, Mark A. Noll, *Between Faith and Criticism: Evangelicals, Scholarship and the Bible* (San Francisco: Harper & Row, 1986), 62–121.

59. Charles H. Malik, "International Order," in *Baker's Dictionary of Christian Ethics*, ed. Carl F. H. Henry (Grand Rapids: Baker, 1973), 332.

60. See the detailed study of the early *Christianity Today* by Dennis P. Hollinger, *Individualism and Social Ethics* (Lanham, Md.: University Press of America, 1983).

61. For this process of cross-pollination, see "Introduction," in Mark A. Noll and David F. Wells, eds., *Christian Faith and Practice in the Modern World: Theology From an Evangelical Point of View*, (Grand Rapids: Eerdmans, 1988), 1–19.

62. Of the many worthy studies, the following are among the most informative: Jerry Falwell (with Ed Dobson and Ed Hindson), *The Fundamentalist Phenomenon: The Resurgence of Conservative Christianity* (Garden City, N.Y.: Doubleday, 1981); Robert C. Liebman and Robert Wuthnow, eds., *The New Christian Right: Mobilization and Legitimation* (New York: Aldine, 1983); Richard John Neuhaus and Michael Cromartie, eds., *Piety and Politics: Evangelicals and Fundamentalists Confront the World* (Washington: Ethics and Public Policy Center, 1987); and Richard John Neuhaus, ed., *The Bible, Politics, and Democracy*, The Encounter Series, no. 5 (Grand Rapids: Eerdmans, 1987).

63. On the symmetry, see Hatch, in *The Search for Christian America*, ed. Hatch, Noll, and Marsden, 120–21.

64. For an illustration of his approach, written before he entered politics, see Paul B. Henry, *Politics for Evangelicals* (Valley Forge: Judson, 1974).

65. On the widespread intellectual influence of this thoughtful activist, see the glowing assessments in Lane Dennis, ed., *Francis A. Schaeffer: Portraits of the Man and His Work* (Westchester, Ill.: Crossway, 1986); the less favorable treatment in

Ronald Ruegsegger, ed., *Reflections on Francis Schaeffer* (Grand Rapids: Zondervan, 1986); as well as the comments in Wills, *Under God*, 320–32.

66. James Davison Hunter and Os Guinness, eds., *Articles of Faith, Articles of Peace: The Religious Liberty Clauses and the American Public Philosophy* (Washington: The Brookings Institution, 1990).

67. For especially helpful analysis extending beyond evangelical groups, see James W. Skillen, *The Scattered Voice: Christians at Odds in the Public Square* (Grand Rapids: Zondervan, 1990). A most useful earlier account is Robert Booth Fowler, *A New Engagement: Evangelical Political Thought, 1966–1976* (Grand Rapids: Eerdmans, 1982).

68. For example, Ronald Sider, *Rich Christians in an Age of Hunger* (Downers Grove, Ill.: InterVarsity Press, 1977); and *Christ and Violence* (Scottdale, Pa.: Herald Press, 1979).

69. For examples, Rousas Rushdoony, *The Institutes of Biblical Law* (Nutley, N.J.: Craig, 1973); Greg Bahnsen, *Theonomy and Christian Ethics*, 2d ed. (Phillipsburg, N.J.: Presbyterian and Reformed, 1984); and Gary North, *The Dominion Covenant* (Tyler, Tex.: Institute for Christian Economics, 1985). For analysis and commentary, the most helpful sources are William S. Barker and W. Robert Godfrey, eds., *Theonomy: A Reformed Critique* (Grand Rapids: Zondervan, 1990); and Richard John Neuhaus, "Why Wait for the Kingdom? The Theonomist Temptation," *First Things*, May 1990, 13–21.

70. For example, Rockne M. McCarthy, James W. Skillen, and William A. Harper, *Disestablishment a Second Time: Genuine Pluralism for American Schools* (Grand Rapids: Eerdmans, 1982), which draws on Dutch Calvinist insights.

71. As examples, Mark Amstutz, *Christian Ethics and United States Foreign Policy* (Grand Rapids: Zondervan, 1987); Doug Bandow, *Beyond Good Intentions: A Biblical View of Politics* (Westchester, Ill.: Crossway, 1988); Alberto R. Coll, *The Western Heritage and American Values: Law, Theology, and History* (Washington: University Press of America, 1982); and Dean Curry, ed., *Evangelicals and the Bishops' Pastoral Letter* (Grand Rapids: Eerdmans, 1984).

72. For example, Harold O. J. Brown, *The Reconstruction of the Republic* (New Rochelle, N.Y.: Arlington House, 1977).

73. Steve Bruce, *The Rise and Fall of the New Christian Right: Conservative Protestant Politics in America, 1978–1988* (New York: Oxford University Press, 1988); and the essays by George Marsden, Robert Wuthnow, and Robert Booth Fowler in Michael Cromartie, ed., *No Longer Exiles: The Religious New Right in American Politics* (Washington: Ethics and Public Policy Center, forthcoming).

74. Dwight Wilson, *Armageddon Now! The Premillenarian Response to Russia and Israel Since 1917* (Grand Rapids: Baker, 1977), 216.

75. This suggestion is from Leith, "Spirituality of the Church."

CHAPTER 4: "Protestants and Natural Law"
Carl E. Braaten

1. Abraham Kuyper, *Christianity and the Class Struggle* (Grand Rapids: Piet Hein, 1950), 14, note.

2. H. Richard Niebuhr, *Christ and Culture* (New York: Harper & Row, 1956).

3. Cf. Emil Brunner, *Justice and the Social Order* (New York: Harper & Row, 1945); and *The Divine Imperative* (Philadelphia: Westminster Press, 1947).

4. Karl Barth, *Church Dogmatics* (Edinburgh: T. & T. Clark, 1961), III, 4, pp. 11–12.

5. Barth, *Church Dogmatics*, II, 2, p. 523.

6. Jacques Ellul, *The Theological Foundations of Law* (London: SCM Press, 1960), 68.

7. Paul Lehmann, *Ethics in a Christian Context* (New York: Harper & Row, 1963), 148.

8. Stanley Hauerwas, "Natural Law, Tragedy and Theological Ethics," in Hauerwas and Richard Bondi, *Truthfulness and Tragedy* (South Bend, Ind.: University of Notre Dame Press, 1977), 58.

9. John T. McNeill, "Natural Law in the Teaching of the Reformers," *Journal of Religion* 26 (1946): 168.

10. Helmut Thielicke, *Theological Ethics* (Philadelphia: Fortress Press, 1966), 383–454.

11. Walter Künneth, *Politik Zwischen Damon und Golt: Eine Christliche Ethik des Politischen* (Berlin: Lutherisches Verlagshaus, 1954).

12. Cf. Theodor Herr, *Zur Frage nach dem Naturrecht im deutschen Protestantismus der Gegenwart* (Munchen: Verlag Ferdinand Schoningh, 1972); and Wilhelm Steinmuller, *Evangelische Rechtstheologie* (Koln: Bohlau Verlag, 1968), two volumes.

13. Cf. Michael Novak, "The Achievement of Jacques Maritain," *First Things* 8 (December 1990): 39–44; and Dennis P. McCann, "Natural Law, Public Theology and the Legacy of John Courtney Murray," *The Christian Century*, 5–12 September 1990, 801.

14. Cf. Dinesh D'Souza, "Illiberal Education," *The Atlantic*, March 1991, 51–79.

15. Evangelical Catholics in the Lutheran tradition can only applaud Pope John Paul II's encyclical *Redemptoris Missio*, which clearly sounds the clarion call for resumption of the Christian mission in all parts of the world and criticizes the kind of missiology that teaches that all religions are equally true and salvific.

16. Cf. James Luther Adams, "The Law of Nature: Some General Considerations," *Journal of Religion* 25 (1945): 88.

17. Ellul, *Theological Foundations*, 68.

18. Cf. C. H. Dodd, "Natural Law in the Bible," *Theology*, May/June 1946.

19. Karl Rahner, *Foundations of Christian Faith*, trans. William V. Dych (New York: Seabury Press, 1978).

Carl J. Peter

1. "Closing Messages of the Council," *The Documents of Vatican II*, ed. Walter M. Abbott, S.J. (New York: America Press, 1966), 731.

2. Ibid.

3. Ibid., 728.

4. Braaten in 1991 and Abraham Kuyper in 1891 (his comments are cited by Braaten with approval) are much more appreciative of Leo XIII's efforts than was H. Richard Niebuhr in 1951. Cf. *Christ and Culture* (New York: Harper, 1951), 138–39.

5. For Niebuhr on both, see *Christ and Culture*, 146–48.

6. *Summa Theologica*, I-II, q. 109, a. 2, c.

7. In *The Mystery of the Supernatural*, trans. R. Sheed (Montreal: Palm, 1967), 36–37, Henri de Lubac reflects with approval on this comment on Hans Urs von Balthasar and refers readers to the latter's *Theologie de l'histoire* (Paris: 1955), 167.

8. W. Kasper, *Jesus the Christ*, trans V. Green (New York: Paulist Press, 1976), 190–92.

9. *Gaudium et Spes* ("Pastoral Constitution on the Church in the Modern World"), sec. 13.

10. *Rerum Novarum*, sec. 21, in *The Papal Encyclicals 1878–1903*, ed. Claudia Carlen (Raleigh: McGrath, 1981), 246.

11. The question is prompted less by Braaten than by Niebuhr's universal judgment: "No synthesist answer so far given in Christian history has avoided the equation of a cultural view of God's law in creation with that law itself" (*Christ and Culture*, 145).

CHAPTER 5: "The Spirit of Freedom" Russell Hittinger

1. "The virtues arise in us neither by nature nor against nature, but we are able to acquire them, and reach our complete perfection through habit" (*Nicomachean Ethics* II.1 [1103a20]).

2. Gerard Verbeke, *Moral Education in Aristotle* (Washington: Catholic University of America Press, 1990), 47.

3. Religion, as James described it, is "the feelings, acts, and experiences of individual men in their solitude, so far as they apprehend themselves to stand in relation to whatever they may consider the divine. Since the relation may be either moral, physical, or ritual, it is evident that out of religion in the sense in which we take it, theologies, philosophies, and ecclesiastical organizations may secondarily grow" (William James, *Varieties of Religious Experience* [New York: Penguin Books, 1982], 31).

4. Ibid., 51.

5. Ibid., 95–96.

6. Ibid., 108.

7. Ibid., 111.

8. Martin A. Lee and Bruce Shlain, *Acid Dreams* (New York: Grove Press, 1985), 77.

9. John Wise, *The Churches Quarrel Espoused*, 1st ed. (1710), and *A Vindication of the Government of New England Churches*, 1st ed. (1717).

10. On the history of these new natural-law theories in the American context, see my essay "Liberalism and the American Natural Law Tradition," in *Wake Forest Law Review* 25, no. 3 (1990).

CHAPTER 6: "Abortion: Moralities in Conflict" Jean Bethke Elshtain

1. I draw generously on a previously published but, alas, little read piece, "Reflections on Abortion, Values, and the Family," in *Abortion: Understanding Differences*, ed. Sidney Callahan and Daniel Callahan (New York: Plenum, 1984).

2. Ironically, arguments against emotionalism in moral debate arise from precisely these views—views severing reason from passion and mind from body—that have provided the philosophical soil for sexist presumptions about women's ostensible incapacities for rational reflection and tendencies to be overrun by feeling.

3. Philip Abbott, *The Family on Trial* (University Park: Pennsylvania State University Press, 1981), 138.

4. Michael Tooley, "Abortion and Infanticide," in *The Rights and Wrongs of Abortion,* ed. Marshall Cohen, Thomas Nagel, and Thomas Scanlon (Princeton: Princeton University Press, 1974), 54–55.

5. Elizabeth Rapaport and Paul Sagal, "One Step Forward, Two Steps Backward: Abortion and Ethical Theory," in *Feminism and Philosophy,* ed. Marty Vetterling-Braggin, Frederick A. Elliston, and Jane English (Totowa, N.J.: Littlefield Adams, 1977), 410.

6. Jane English, "Abortion and the Concept of a Person," in Vetterling-Braggin et al., *Feminism and Philosophy,* 426.

7. Surely, it is fair for opponents of abortion to conjure up images of aborted fetuses even as it was fair for anti-war activists to react to pictures of napalmed Vietnamese children. Our emotions are complex, threaded through and through with thought, and should be engaged by moral debates lest we try to be, and perhaps succeed in becoming, monsters of abstract systematization.

8. One question for feminists and other social critics is whether they should challenge the atomistic construal of the social world or, instead, make their case in and through its reigning presumptions.

9. Charles Taylor, "Atomism," in *Power, Possessions, and Freedom: Essays in Honor of C. B. Macpherson,* ed. Alkis Kontos (Toronto: University of Toronto Press, 1979), 39–61.

10. Ibid., 48.

11. Ibid.

12. Rapaport and Sagal, "One Step Forward," 408.

13. C. B. Macpherson, *The Political Theory of Possessive Individualism* (Oxford: Oxford University Press, 1963), 3. I find Macpherson's readings of both Hobbes and Locke problematic; however, he has elaborated one striking feature of ultra-liberal argumentation.

14. Rapaport and Sagal, "One Step Forward," 414.

15. She is radical to the extent that we accept ultra-liberalism as radical.

16. Quoted in Daniel Callahan, *Abortion: Law, Choice, and Morality* (New York: Macmillan, 1970), 462.

17. English, "Abortion and the Concept of a Person," 417.

18. Cited in Lawrence Lader, *Abortion* (Indianapolis: Bobbs-Merrill, 1966), 156.

19. Ibid.

20. Callahan, *Abortion: Law, Choice, and Morality,* 457.

21. Quoted ibid., 540.

22. Lader, *Abortion,* 159. Another disquieting reference to light and darkness appears in Rosalind Pollack Petchesky, "Antiabortion, Antifeminism, and the Rise of the New Right," *Feminist Studies* 7, no. 2 (Summer 1981): 206–46. Petchesky gives a long recitation of good guys versus bad but fails to deal with the fact that

the "right-to-life" movement is, as the work of Kristin Luker demonstrates, grass-roots—not a conspiracy launched by the Catholic Church as Petchesky suggests.

Her piece, moreover, criticizes anti-abortion forces for being involved in politics, for working to pass or repeal laws. They "engage in political education and struggle, establish networks, support sympathetic candidates," and so on. Apparently meaning to condemn them, she states: "In other words, from the outset, the 'right-to-life' movement was set up to be a political action machine to influence national and local elections" (213–14). Would she attack the anti-nuclear movement or feminist organizations on similar grounds? Is politics an option only for those with whom we agree?

23. Abbott, *The Family on Trial*, 142.

24. Carol McMillen, *Women, Reason and Nature* (Princeton: Princeton University Press, 1982), 127.

25. Judith Blake, "Abortion and Public Opinion: The 1960–1970 Decade," *Science* 171 (12 February 1971): 544.

26. Rosalind Pollack Petchesky, "Reproductive Freedom: Beyond 'A Woman's Right to Choose,'" *Signs* 4, no. 4 (Summer 1980): 661–85, discounts the empirical evidence from Hilda Scott and Kristin Luker, who have shown how abortion policy encourages male disengagements.

27. Everett Carl Ladd, *The Ladd Report*, #8 (New York: Norton, 1990), 12–13.

28. Alasdair MacIntyre, *After Virtue* (South Bend, Ind.: Notre Dame University Press, 1981), 205.

29. John O'Neill, *Five Bodies: The Human Shape of Modern Society* (Ithaca, N.Y.: Cornell University Press, 1985), 83–84. O'Neill here relies on my work.

30. What I have in mind here is not the usual conservative lament but the emerging radical critique of welfarism and a politics of social control.

31. Peter Brown, *The Cult of the Saints: Its Rise and Function in Latin* (Chicago: University of Chicago Press, 1981), 30.

32. Ibid., 41–42.

33. As I write this, I feel uneasy. Precisely because our dominant surround is atomistic, self-sacrifice has become a dirty term in which we see a selfless self, a masochistic derangement.

34. Harry Boyce, *The Backyard Revolution* (Philadelphia: Temple University Press, 1980).

35. See Kristin Luker, *Abortion and the Politics of Motherhood* (Berkeley: University of California Press, 1984) for a discussion of the contrasting worldviews presented by pro- and anti-abortion activists.

36. Lisa Sowle Cahill, "Toward a Christian Theory of Human Rights," *Journal of Religious Ethics* 8 (Fall 1980): 284.

37. Ibid.

38. Pope John XXIII, "Ad Petri Cathedram," in *The Encyclicals and Other Messages of John XXIII* (Washington: TPS Press, 1964), 24–26.

39. U.S. Catholic bishops, "Economic Justice for All: Catholic Social Teaching and the U.S. Economy," *Origins* 16, no. 24 (27 November 1986): 415.

40. Ibid., 422–23.

41. David Hollenbach, "Liberalism, Communitarianism, and the Bishops' Pastoral Letter on the Economy," in *Annual of the Society of Christian Ethics*, ed. D. M. Yeager (Knoxville: University of Tennessee, 1987), 34.

42. Joseph A. Komonchak, "Subsidiarity in the Church: The State of the Question," *The Jurist* 48 (1988): 298–349, 301–2. I have recast Komonchak's principles in my own language.

43. Ibid., 326–27.

44. Stanley Hauerwas, "The Moral Value of the Family," in *A Community of Character* (South Bend, Ind.: University of Notre Dame Press, 1981), 165.

45. Ibid.

46. The "gender gap" shows that between the category "all women" and the category "all men"—after one has controlled for age, education, class, and so on— distinctions emerge primarily on matters of war and peace and social concern.

47. It is a world of such balance between rights and responsibilities that Mary Ann Glendon evokes in *Abortion and Divorce in Western Law* (Cambridge: Harvard University Press, 1987). Rights absolutism of the sort Glendon unpacks feeds into scientific fundamentalism of the sort I indict.

48. I take the lead staked out by Michel Foucault in a number of texts, including *Discipline and Punish* (New York: Vintage Books, 1979), in making these observations.

49. Petchesky, "Reproductive Freedom," 669, 683.

50. Such a historical faith is evident in Petchesky, ibid., when she presumes that only at some future point, when we have become both a socialist and feminist society according to her specifications, may we consider what exceptions might pertain to a woman's absolute right to control her body. (Petchesky says that this right is not absolute, but she also claims that we have no morality to tell us what the exceptions might be, thus making it absolute by default.) She also attributes the failures of contemporary socialist societies to approach anything like a new, egalitarian community to the fact that the "socialist transformation" is not yet complete.

51. Richard Cohen, "The Unequal Sexes," *Boston Globe*, 20 June 1982.

52. Harold M. Schmeck, "Twin Found Defective in Womb Reported De-stroyed in Operation," *New York Times,* 18 June 1981.

53. The first targets of Nazi racial policy were the retarded, who were sterilized, aborted, and gassed. The mentally ill were among the first to be sent to their deaths. The Hereditary Health Law, passed by the Reichstag, went into effect January 1, 1934. It authorized the sterilization of epileptic, insane, and "feeble-minded" persons. Eventually 70,000 "hereditarily defective" persons were shot or gassed.

54. Cited in George J. Annas, "Who's Afraid of the Human Genome?," *Hastings Center Report* 19, no. 4 (1989): 19.

55. Ibid., 20.

56. Erma Clarxy Craven, "Abortion, Poverty and Black Genocide," in *Abortion and Social Justice*, ed. Thomas W. Hilgren and Dennis J. Horan (New York: Sheed & Ward, 1972), 231, reported that, in 1969 at a White House Conference on Hunger, a doctor with the National Institutes of Health recommended (1) mandatory abortion for any unmarried girl within the first three months of her pregnancy and (2) mandatory sterilization of any woman or girl giving birth out of wedlock for a second time. Alan Guttmacher, president of Planned Parenthood, apparently gave this proposal "his strong support," but it was quashed under the leadership of Fannie Lou Hamer.

57. Ibid.

58. Abbott, *The Family on Trial*, 145.

Mary Ann Glendon

1. George Santayana, *Character and Opinion in the United States* (New York: Norton, 1967), 47.

2. Brigitte Berger and Peter L. Berger, *The War Over the Family* (Garden City, N.Y.: Doubleday Anchor, 1984), vii.

3. *Borough of Glassboro* v. *Vallorosi*, 117 N.J. 421, 568 A.2d 888 (1990).

4. The relatively advanced data-protection schemes of some European countries are resented by American businesses unaccustomed to being curbed in their collection, storage, and use of personal data. In 1991, American companies reacted with alarm at the news that the European Community was considering the adoption of a sweeping set of rules in the area. John Markoff, "Europe's Plans to Protect Privacy Worry Business," *New York Times*, 11 April 1991, sec. A, 1.

5. *Bowers* v. *Hardwick*, 478 U.S. 186, 199 (1986).

6. Maryland Code Ann. 20–103 and 20–208 et seq. (1991).

7. The lecture was still unpublished as of this writing, but similar views were expressed by Dworkin in a commentary on the Nancy Cruzan "right to die" case in "The Right to Death," *New York Review of Books*, 31 January 1991, 14, 17 n.6.

8. Richard Stith, commenting on Dworkin's views concerning the "right to die," has pointed out that Dworkin confuses sanctity of life with quality of life. "Letters," *New York Review of Books*, 28 March 1991, 73.

CHAPTER 7: "The Lay Vocation"
Christa R. Klein

1. Etienne Gilson, ed., *The Church Speaks to the Modern World: The Social Teachings of Leo XIII* (Garden City, N.Y.: Doubleday, 1954), 211–12.

2. Alasdair MacIntyre, *After Virtue: A Study in Moral Theory* (South Bend, Ind.: Notre Dame Press, 1981).

3. Mark A. Noll, *One Nation Under God?* (San Francisco: Harper & Row, 1988).

4. Ibid., 25–31.

5. For a potent account of the biblical origins of vocation, see Donald R. Heiges, *The Christian's Calling*, rev. ed. (Philadelphia: Fortress Press, 1984).

6. My own study of the Lutheran Church in America, a predecessor body of the Evangelical Lutheran Church in America, describes a denomination struggling with these temptations and sometimes expressing a coherent and illuminating theological ethic. Nevertheless, during the denomination's last years, the structuring of the conversation by interest groups has begun to undermine genuine argument over the tradition. See Klein with C. von Dehsen, *Politics and Policy: The Genesis and Theology of Social Statements in the Lutheran Church in America* (Minneapolis: Fortress Press, 1988).

7. *Leadership Is an Art* (East Lansing: Michigan State University Press, 1987).

8. For an effective summary of his theory, see Peter M. Senge, "The Leader's New Work: Building Learning Organizations," *Sloan Management Review*, Fall 1990.

9. Burton Weisbord, *The Nonprofit Economy* (Cambridge: Harvard University Press, 1988), 169 ff.; "The Nonprofit World: A Statistical Portrait," *Chronicle of Philanthropy* 2, no.6 (9 January 1990): 8. I am especially indebted to Peter Dobkin Hall of Yale University's Program on Non-Profit Organizations for conversations about these trends and their meaning.

Robert Destro

1. Editorial, "The Bishop and the Truce of Tolerance," *New York Times*, 26 November 1989: Church discipline "tear[s] at the truce of tolerance that permits America's pluralistic democracy to work"; and Editorial, "The Cardinal Gets Tougher," *New York Times*, 17 June 1990: if others—real Americans?—are not to be concerned, the Church should "stop leaning on Catholic public officials."

2. Max DePree, *Leadership Is an Art* (East Lansing: Michigan State University Press, 1987).

3. National Council of Catholic Bishops, "Brothers and Sisters to Us," 14 November 1979, *Pastoral Letters of the United States Catholic Bishops*, vol. 4, 342–55.

Chapter 8: "Christians and New World Disorders"
J. Bryan Hehir

1. Charles Krauthammer, "The Unipolar Moment," and William Pfaff, "Redefining World Power," *Foreign Affairs* 70, no. 1 (1991), 23–24, 35.

2. Seweryn Bialer, " 'New Thinking' and Soviet Foreign Policy," *Survival*, July/August 1988, 294.

3. Timothy Garton Ash, "Eastern Europe: The Year of Truth," *New York Review of Books*, 15 February 1990, 17–22.

4. Cf. K. Kaiser, "Germany's Unification," *Foreign Affairs* 70, no. 1 (1991): 179–205; Joseph Joffe, "One-and-a-half Cheers for German Unification," *Commentary* 89 (June 1990): 26–33.

5. Cf. Robert O. Keohane and Joseph S. Nye, Jr., "Power and Interdependence Revisited," *International Organization* 41 (1987): 725–53; Joseph S. Nye, Jr., "Neorealism and Neoliberalism," *World Politics* 40 (1988): 235–51; Samuel Huntington, "Transnational Organizations and World Politics," *World Politics* 25 (1973): 333–68.

6. Huntington, "Transnational Organizations," 333.

7. Krauthammer, "Unipolar Moment," 24.

8. Henry A. Kissinger, "Kissinger's World View," *Christian Science Monitor*, 6 January 1989; cited in Joseph S. Nye, Jr., *Bound to Lead: The Changing Nature of American Power* (New York: Basic Books, 1990), 235.

9. Robert Tucker, "1989 and All That," in *Sea-Changes: American Foreign Policy in a World Transformed*, ed. N. X. Rizopoulos (New York: Council on Foreign Relations Press, 1990), 204–37; Samuel Huntington, "America's Changing Stra-

tegic Interests," *Survival,* January/February 1991, 3–17; Nye, *Bound to Lead*; Pfaff, "Redefining World Power."

10. Stanley Hoffmann, "What Should We Do in the World?," *The Atlantic Monthly,* October 1989, 87–88.

11. Stanley Hoffmann, "A New World and Its Troubles," in Rizopoulos, *Sea-Changes,* 280–81.

12. Nye, *Bound to Lead,* 259–61.

13. For assessments of Niebuhr, cf. Richard W. Fox, *Reinhold Niebuhr: A Biography* (New York: Pantheon Books, 1985); Michael J. Smith, *Realist Thought from Weber to Kissinger* (Baton Rouge: Louisiana State University Press, 1986), 99–133.

14. Stanley Hoffmann's comment on Morgenthau has some applicability to Niebuhr also: "In short, Morgenthau's text provided both an explanation and a road map. . . . It was just what the elites of a disconcerted yet most powerful nation needed to hear" (*Janus and Minerva: Essays in the Theory and Practice of International Affairs* [Boulder, Col.: Westview Press, 1987], 76).

15. For assessments of Ramsey, see J. Johnson and D. Smith, eds., *Love and Society: Essays in the Ethics of Paul Ramsey* (Missoula, Mont.: Scholars Press, 1974).

16. John Langan, "Catholic Moral Rationalism and the Philosophical Basis of Moral Theology," *Theological Studies* 50 (1989): 25–43.

17. Cf. Paul Ramsey, *The Just War: Force and Political Responsibility* (New York: Scribner's, 1968); *The Patient as Person* (New Haven: Yale University Press, 1970).

18. For an assessment of Yoder, see Stanley Hauerwas, *Vision and Virtue: Essays in Christian Ethical Reflection* (Notre Dame, Ind: Fides Publishers, 1974), 197–221.

19. For a survey of this period of Catholic teaching, see Jean Yves Calvez and Jacques Perrin, *The Church and Social Justice: The Social Teaching of the Popes from Leo XIII to Pius XII* (Chicago: Regnery, 1961).

20. For a commentary on recent papal teaching, see Joseph Gremillion, *The Gospel of Peace and Justice* (New York: Orbis Books, 1976).

21. Cf. Keohane and Nye, "Power and Interdependence Revisited."

22. Recent interest in "regime theory," an extension of the interdependence analysis, does address incremental steps of limiting sovereignty and establishing rules and relationships among sovereign units; cf. Stephen Krasner, ed., *International Regimes* (Ithaca, N.Y.: Cornell University Press, 1983); Robert O. Keohane, *International Institutions and State Power* (Boulder, Col.: Westview Press, 1989), 101–31.

23. See John XXIII, *Pacem in Terris* (1963), for a representative statement of this position.

24. Hedley Bull, *The Anarchical Society: A Study of Order in World Politics* (New York: Columbia University Press, 1977), 24 ff.

25. John XXIII, *Pacem in Terris,* sec. 134–37.

26. John Courtney Murray, *We Hold These Truths: Catholic Reflections on the American Proposition* (New York: Sheed and Ward, 1960), 256–57.

27. John XXIII, *Pacem in Terris,* sec. 127. The text that attracted such notice read: "For this reason it is hardly possible to imagine that in the atomic era war could be used as an instrument of justice."

28. John Paul II, "Address in Drogheda, Ireland," *Origins* 9 (1979): 274; "Message to Youth on Nonviolence" (Lesotho), *Origins* 18 (1988): 253.

29. John Paul II, "World Day of Peace Message 1982," *Origins* 11 (1982): 477.

30. John Paul II, "Letter to President Bush," *Catholic News Service*, 16 January 1991.

31. John Paul II, "Pope: We Are Not Pacifists," *Arlington Catholic Herald*, 7 March 1991.

32. James Childress, *Moral Responsibility in Conflicts: Essays on Nonviolence, War, and Conscience* (Baton Rouge: Louisiana State University Press, 1982), 64–73.

33. John Paul II, "The U.N. Address," *Origins* 9 (1979): 258–66.

34. Paul VI, *Populorum Progressio* (1967), sec. 3.

35. John Paul II, *Sollicitudo Rei Socialis* (1987), sec. 9.

36. John Paul II, "Medellin: Ten Years After," *Origins* 8 (1979): 540; "Address at Puebla," *Origins* 8 (1979): 531–38.

37. Congregation for the Doctrine of the Faith, "Instruction on Certain Aspects of the 'Theology of Liberation,' " *Origins* 14 (1984): 193–204.

38. Congregation for the Doctrine of the Faith, "Instruction on Christian Freedom and Liberation," *Origins* 15 (1986): 715–28.

39. John Paul II, *Sollicitudo Rei Socialis*, sec. 20–24.

40. James Turner Johnson, "Just-War Theory: What's the Use?," *Worldview* 19 (July/August 1976): 41–47; George Weigel, *Tranquillitas Ordinis: The Present Failure and Future Promise of American Catholic Thought on War and Peace* (New York: Oxford University Press, 1987).

41. For commentary on the role of the moral arguments in the nuclear debate, cf. Robert Tucker, "The Nuclear Debate," *Foreign Affairs* 63 (1984): 1–32; Leon Wieseltier, *Nuclear War, Nuclear Peace* (New York: Holt, Rinehart, Winston, 1983); Joseph S. Nye, Jr., *Nuclear Ethics* (New York: The Free Press, 1986); William V. O'Brien and John Langan, eds., *The Nuclear Dilemma and the Just War Tradition* (Lexington, Mass.: Lexington Books, 1986); Weigel, *Tranquillitas Ordinis*; Michael Novak, *Moral Clarity in the Nuclear Age* (Nashville: Thomas Nelson, 1983); John Finnis, Joseph Boyle, and Germain Grisez, *Nuclear Deterrence, Morality and Realism* (New York: Oxford University Press, 1987).

42. John Ford, "The Morality of Obliteration Bombing," *Theological Studies* 5 (1944): 261–309.

43. Cf. Joseph S. Nye, Jr., "Nuclear Ethics," 104–31; William V. O'Brien, "Just War Doctrine in a Nuclear Context," *Theological Studies* 44 (1983): 191–220.

44. Cf. J. Bryan Hehir, "The United States and Human Rights," in *Eagle Without a Cause*, ed. K. Oye, R. Lieber, and D. Rothchild (New York: Publishers, Inc., 1991).

45. Krauthammer, "The Unipolar Moment," 33.

CHAPTER 9: "Culture First"
Michael Novak

1. Brochure for "A Conference to Mark the Centenary of Pope Leo XIII's Social Encyclical *Rerum Novarum*," Von Hügel Institute, St. Edmund's College, Cambridge, England.

2. What I find startling and disconcerting is that these massive historical trends [towards capitalism] have been largely unanticipated. The conventional wisdom with respect to socialism has been that it was, or would be, a success and that the future very likely

belonged to it. The same wisdom with respect to capitalism was that its future was clouded.

But what voice of the present generation has anticipated the demise of socialism and the "triumph of capitalism"? Not a single writer in the Marxian tradition! Are there any in the left-centrist group? None that I can think of, including myself. As for the center itself—the Samuelsons, Solows, Glazers, Lipsets, Bells, and so on—I believe that many expected capitalism to experience serious and mounting, if not fatal, problems and anticipated some form of socialism to be the organizing force for the twenty-first century.

That leaves the right. Here is the part that's hard to swallow. It has been the Friedmans, Hayeks, von Miseses, *e tutte quanti* who have maintained that capitalism would flourish and that socialism would develop incurable ailments. All three have regarded capitalism as the "natural" system of free men; all have maintained that left to its own devices capitalism would achieve material growth more successfully than any other system.

From this admittedly impressionistic and incomplete sampling I draw the following discomforting generalization: *The farther to the right one looks, the more prescient has been the historical foresight; the farther to the left, the less so.* [Emphasis his. Robert Heilbroner, "Was the Right Right All Along?" *Harper's* 282, no. 1688 (January 1991): 18–22. Reprinted from *Dissent*, Fall 1990.]

3. In his first use of the term, the pope says:

Socialists, exciting the envy of the poor toward the rich, contend that it is necessary to do away with private possession of goods and in its place to make the goods of individuals common to all, and that the men who preside over a municipality or who direct the entire State should act as administrators of these goods. They hold that, by such transfer of private goods from private individuals to the community, they can cure the present evil through dividing wealth and benefits equally among the citizens. [Pope Leo XIII, *Rerum Novarum* (Boston: Daughters of St. Paul), no. 7. All paragraph numbers in the text refer to this edition of *Rerum Novarum*, the authorized translation of the Holy See.]

4. The fact that God gave the whole human race the earth to use and enjoy cannot indeed in any manner serve as an objection against private possessions. For God is said to have given the earth to mankind in common, not because He intended indiscriminate ownership of it by all, but because He assigned no part to anyone in ownership, leaving the limits of private possessions to be fixed by the industry of men and the institutions of peoples. [14]

5. " 'Poisoning of the Soul': New Leaders of Russia and Central Europe Talk about the Evil Empire," comp. Kevin Acker, in *Policy Review*, no. 55 (Winter 1991): 60–65. Notes 5 through 14 refer to this compilation.

6. Tzvetan Todorov, Bulgarian author (*The New Republic*, 25 June 1990), ibid.

7. Tatyana Zaslavskaya, Soviet sociologist (*Voices of Glasnost*), ibid.

8. Gavrii Popov, mayor of Moscow (Cato Institute/Soviet Academy of Sciences, 10 September 1990), ibid.

9. Suyatoslav Fyodorov, Soviet laser scientist (*New York Times*, 11 March 1990), ibid.

10. Tadeusz Mazowiecki, prime minister of Poland, before the *Sejm* (Polish Parliament) (18 January 1990), ibid.

11. Oleg Kalugin, former KGB major-general and USSR people's deputy (*Moscow News*, 1 July 1990), ibid.

12. Timisoara Declaration, Romania (11 March 1990), ibid.

13. Václav Havel, president of Czechoslovakia (*Izvestia*, 23 February 1990), ibid.

14. Valtr Komarek, deputy prime minister of Czechoslovakia (*NRC Handelsblad* [Rotterdam], 6 February 1990), ibid.

15. Under a system based upon private ownership in the means of production, the scale of values is the outcome of the actions of every independent member of society. Everyone plays a twofold part in its establishment first as a consumer, secondly, as a producer. As consumer, he establishes the valuation of goods ready for consumption. As a producer, he guides the production-goods into those uses in which they yield the highest product. . . . And in this way, arises the exactly graded system of prices which enables everyone to frame his demand on economic lines.

Under Socialism, all this must necessarily be lacking. The economic administration may indeed know exactly what commodities are needed most urgently. But this is only half the problem. The other half, the valuation of the means of production, it cannot solve. It can ascertain the value of the totality of such instruments. That is obviously equal to the value of the satisfactions they afford. If it calculates the loss that would be incurred by withdrawing them, it can also ascertain the value of single instruments of production. But it cannot assimilate them to a common price denominator, as can be done under a system of economic freedom and money prices.

The problem of economic calculation is the fundamental problem of Socialism. That for decades people could write and talk about Socialism without touching this problem only shows how devastating were the effects of the Marxian prohibition on scientific scrutiny of the nature and working of a socialist economy.

To prove that economic calculation would be impossible in the socialist community is to prove also that Socialism is impracticable.

The discovery of this fact is clearly most inconvenient for the socialist parties. . . . Nothing has shaken the proof that under Socialism economic calculation is impossible. [Ludwig von Mises, *Socialism*, trans. J. Kahane from 2d ed. of 1932 (Indianapolis: Liberty Classics, 1981), 103–4, 116–17.]

16. In the nineteen-thirties, when I was studying economics, a few economists had already expressed doubts about the feasibility of centrally planned socialism. One of them was Ludwig von Mises, an Austrian of extremely conservative views, who had written of the "impossibility" of socialism, arguing that no Central Planning Board could ever gather the enormous amount of information needed to create a workable economic system. . . . Our skepticism [of Mises's views] was fortified when Oskar Lange, a brilliant young Polish economist, . . . wrote two dazzling articles showing that a Board would not need all the information that Mises said it couldn't collect. All that such a Board would have to do, Lange wrote, was watch the levels of inventories in its warehouses: if inventories rose, the obvious thing to do was to lower prices, so that goods would move out more rapidly; and if inventories were too rapidly depleted, to raise prices to discourage sales. Fifty years ago, it was felt that Lange had decisively won the argument for socialist planning. . . .

It turns out, of course, that Mises was right. The Soviet system has long been dogged by a method of pricing that produced grotesque misallocations of effort. The difficulties were not so visible in the early days of Soviet industrialization or in the post–Second World War reconstruction period. The dams and mills and entire new cities of the 1930s astonished the world, as did the Chinese Great Leap Forward of the 1950s, which performed similar miracles from a still lower base. But those undertakings, like the building of the Pyramids or the Great Wall, depended less on economic coordination than on the political capacity for marshalling vast labor forces. Inefficiency set in when projects had to be joined into a complex whole—a process that required knowing how much things should cost. Then, as Mises foresaw, setting prices became a hopeless problem because the economy never stood still long enough for anyone to decide anything correctly. [Robert Heilbroner, "After Communism," *The New Yorker*, 10 September 1990, 92.]

For a discussion of the famous debate between Lange and Mises (including the original articles), see Trygve J. B. Hoff, *Economic Calculation and the Socialist Society* (Indianapolis: Liberty Press, 1981 [1938]).

17. The main point of my argument is . . . that the conflict between, on one hand, advocates of the spontaneous extended human order created by a competitive market, and on the other hand, those who demand a deliberate arrangement of human interaction by central authority based on collective command over available resources is due to a factual error by the latter about how knowledge of these resources is and can be generated and utilized. As a question of fact, this conflict must be settled by scientific study. Such study shows that, by following the spontaneously generated moral traditions underlying the competitive market order (traditions which do not satisfy the canons or norms of rationality embraced by most socialists), we generate and garner greater knowledge and wealth than could ever be obtained or utilized in a centrally-directed economy whose adherents claim to proceed strictly in accordance with 'reason'. Thus, socialist aims and programs are factually impossible to achieve or execute; and they also happen into the bargain as it were, to be logically impossible. [F. A. Hayek, *The Fatal Conceit* (Chicago: University of Chicago Press, 1988), 7.]

18. From Zamyatin's novel *We*:

The state poet wrote a poem,
     Eternally enamored two times two
     Eternally united in the passionate four,
          Most ardent lovers in the world—
          Inseparable two times two. . . .
The state newspapers stated: You are perfect. You are machinelike. The road to one hundred percent happiness is free. . . . [Mihajlo Mihajlov, "Life = Freedom: The Symbolism of 2 x 2 = 4 in Dostoevsky, Zamyatin and Orwell," *Catholicism in Crisis* 3, no. 10 (October 1985): 20–24.]

19. Between 1798 and 1832 the new science of political economy was fully integrated into contemporary Christian social theory by a profoundly influential group of British economists. The ethical implications of a market economy had been rigorously analyzed from the standpoint of trinitarian orthodoxy, and a fairly robust theodicy constructed in order to account for the poverty and inequality in a world ruled by scarcity. "Christian political economy" passed into the mainstream of English-speaking culture and formed political attitudes down to the late 1970s.
     So far as the Church of Rome knew or cared, however, all this might have happened on another planet. After 1789 its attention, or at any rate that of the Curia, was engrossed by more pressing matters. When Leo XIII turned belatedly to economic matters in 1891 he issued an anti-socialist tract that steered well clear of any recognition of market forces in the social order. . . . The three most important elements of this explanation [are]: a misunderstanding of classical political economy, a misperception of the European economy in the nineteenth century, and philosophical commitment to a purely Scholastic understanding of liberty. [A. M. C. Waterman, "The Intellectual Context of *Rerum Novarum*" (first draft of unpublished paper, December 1990), 1, 7; to appear in *Review of Social Economy*.]

20. Václav Klaus, finance minister of Czechoslovakia (*Reason*, June 1990) in Acker, " 'Poisoning of the Soul,' " 64.

21. Anatoly Sobchak, mayor of Leningrad (Cato Institute/Soviet Academy of Sciences, 11 September 1990), ibid., 63.

22. Yuri Afanasyev, USSR people's deputy and rector of the Moscow Historical Archival Institute (*Dagens Nyheter* [Stockholm], 3 January 1990), ibid., 64.

23. St. Ambrose, for example:

In general, Ambrose apparently believes that almost all methods of acquiring wealth are unjust. That is certainly true of trade, which he regards with the abhorrence of a Roman aristocrat brought up in traditional values. Trade is based on lying and cunning, for the seller tries to make the merchandise appear more valuable than it is, and the buyer does the exact opposite. He goes so far as to declare that to use the sea for commerce is to twist its purpose, for the sea was given in order to produce fish and not in order to be sailed. . . . For Ambrose, travel to distant lands to procure what is not available locally is one more consequence of greed, of not being content with what is readily at hand.

The only source of wealth of which Ambrose occasionally approves is agriculture. As a true Roman aristocrat, he stands in the tradition of Columella and Cato. He can well understand and approve of Naboth's reluctance to give up his inheritance. Agriculture is also commendable in that it produces wealth without taking it away from another, which is more than can be said of other means of acquiring wealth. [Justo L. Gonzalez, *Faith and Wealth: A History of Early Christian Ideas on the Origin, Significance, and Use of Money* (New York: Harper & Row, 1990), 189. Gonzalez cites St. Ambrose, *De Officiis* 3.37, 57, 65–66, 71–72, in *Nicene and Post Nicene Fathers*, 2d series.]

24. . . . [T]he ideal of a liberal society could be fully achieved—that is, there could be universal compliance with the demands of contractual justice—and yet, according to the Scholastic view, widespread injustice and exploitation could still occur in the economic system. . . .

Reflection on the Scholastic procedure for distributive justice helps clarify the conception of exploitation implicit in the Pope's condemnation of the evils of capitalism. In the transition to a new mode of production, with the proletarization of the labor force, one whole class in society was deprived of that share of the community's property income proportionate to the *dignitas* of its members, with the result that capitalism, in the words of Leo XIII, "handed over the workers, each alone and defenseless, to the inhumanity of employers and the greed of competitors." . . .

According to the Scholastic division between the "parts" of justice, justice in distribution requires first and foremost that there be a community identified by a common desire to share in the exemplification of complementary personal excellences—a community characterized by what Aristotle, in *Ethics* IX, refers to as civic friendship. It is the communal perception of complementary excellences that provides the ground for judgment as to the relative *dignitas* of a society's members. Capitalism, so the great social encyclicals of Leo XIII and Pius XI indicate, has destroyed the sense of community and obliterated the moral vision required to establish distributive justice. Such destruction and obliteration . . . might very well originate in that *demotion of reason* whereby the technical means-end rationality characteristic of capitalism has displaced that *ontological* kind of reason mankind needs in order to perceive the good and the beautiful. When such demotion of reason occurs, perceptions of value cannot be articulated and distributive justice, therefore, can have no solid base. In a society afflicted by such a *malaise*, there is sure to be widespread alienation and a tendency, relying upon instrumental reasoning as the ground for social relationships, for members of society to use one another as instrumental means for the achievement of arbitrary egoistic ends. In such a society, it might very well happen, as Pius XI said of capitalism, that "dead matter comes forth from the factory ennobled while men are corrupted and degraded." . . .

[This is] exploitation derived from the demotion of reason, whereby a community is deprived of the vision required to perceive and appreciate instantiations of the good and the beautiful. [Stephen T. Worland, "Exploitative Capitalism: The Natural-Law Perspective," *Social Research* 48, no. 2 (Summer 1981): 294–95, 299, 304–5.]

25. Ambition must be made to counteract ambition. The interest of the man must be connected with the constitutional rights of the place. It may be a reflection on human nature that such devices should be necessary to control the abuses of government. But what is government itself but the greatest of all reflections on human nature? If men were angels, no government would be necessary. If angels were to govern men, neither external

nor internal controls on government would be necessary. In framing a government which is to be administered by men over men, the great difficulty lies in this: you must first enable the government to control the governed; and in the next place to oblige it to control itself. A dependence on the people is, no doubt, the primary control on the government; but experience has taught mankind the necessity of auxiliary precautions.

This policy of supplying, by opposite and rival interests, the defect of better motives, might be traced through the whole system of human affairs, private as well as public. We see it particularly displayed in all the subordinate distributions of power, where the constant aim is to divide and arrange the several offices in such a manner as that each may be a check on the other—that the private interest of every individual may be a sentinel over the public rights. These inventions of prudence cannot be less requisite in the distribution of the supreme powers of the State. [*The Federalist Papers*, no. 51, ed. Clinton Rossiter (New York: New American Library, 1961), 322.]

26. Heilbroner has lately noticed this:

Radical views are inherently more optimistic than conservative ones. Through radical glasses society always appears to fall far short of its potential, whereas through conservative ones it always expresses inescapable and insistent needs of abiding human nature. Conversely, the conservative view is always darker than the radical. It is more concerned with avoiding catastrophe than with achieving unrealized possibilities. It cannot be progress-oriented or teleological in the way that radical thought must be. [Heilbroner, "Was the Right Right All Along?," 20.]

Compare the words of Václav Klaus, finance minister of Czechoslovakia: "We wanted to create a new man, with only unselfish thoughts. I am afraid it is not possible" (Acker, " 'Poisoning of the Soul,' " 62).

27. Such "private life," of course, can be socially organized and publicly active; some forms of it (unions, associations, non-profit organizations) may be legally incorporated and thus, in a sense, "public." We should not confine the word "public" to the action of the state.

28. Long before Marx was on the scene, Madison stated the problem in *Federalist* no. 10:

The most common and durable source of factions has been the various and unequal distribution of property. Those who hold and those who are without property have ever formed distinct interests in society. Those who are creditors, and those who are debtors, fall under a like discrimination. A landed interest, a manufacturing interest, a mercantile interest, a moneyed interest, with many lesser interests, grow up of necessity in civilized nations, and divide them into different classes, actuated by different sentiments and views. The regulation of those various and interfering interests forms the principal task of modern legislation, and involves the spirit of party and faction in the necessary operations of the government. . . . The apportionment of taxes on the various descriptions of property is an act which seems to require the most exact impartiality; yet there is, perhaps, no legislative act in which greater opportunity and temptation are given to a predominant party to trample on the rules of justice. Every shilling with which they overburden the inferior number, is a shilling saved to their own pockets.

It is vain to say that enlightened statesmen will be able to adjust these clashing interests, and render them all subservient to the public good. Enlightened statesmen will not always be at the helm.

Madison suggests the solution in no. 51:

It is of great importance in a republic not only to guard the society against the oppression of its rulers, but to guard one part of the society against the injustice of the other part. Different interests necessarily exist in different classes of citizens. If a majority be united by a common interest, the rights of the minority will be insecure. [The method of providing] against this evil . . . will be exemplified in the federal republic of the United States. Whilst all authority in it will be derived from and dependent on society, the society itself will be broken into so many parts, interests and classes of citizens, that the rights of individuals, or of the minority, will be in little danger from interested combinations of the majority.

29. John Locke, *Two Treatises of Government, Second Treatise*, ed. Peter Laslett, rev. ed. (New York: New American Library, 1965), sec. 41, 339.

30. As a result of . . . steady and tireless efforts, there has arisen a new branch of jurisprudence unknown to earlier times, whose aim is the energetic defense of those sacred rights of the workingman which proceed from his dignity as a man and as a Christian. These laws concern the soul, the health, the strength, the housing, workshops, wages, dangerous employments, in a word, all that concerns the wage earners, with particular regard to women and children. Even though these regulations do not agree always and in every detail with the recommendations of Pope Leo, it is none the less certain that much which they contain is strongly suggestive of *Rerum Novarum*, to which in large measure must be attributed the improved condition of the workingmen. [Pius XI, *Quadragesimo Anno*, sec. 28, in *Seven Great Encyclicals*, ed. William J. Gibbons, S.J. (Glen Rock, N.J.: Paulist Press, 1963), 132.]

31. "How 'Poor' Are America's Poor?," *Heritage Foundation Backgrounder*, no. 791 (21 September 1990).

32. Boris Yeltsin, speech at Columbia University, cited in Acker, " 'Poisoning of the Soul,' " 64.

33. Michael Novak, *This Hemisphere of Liberty: A Philosophy of the Americas* (Washington: The AEI Press, 1990), 25-35.

34. The fundamental impulse that sets and keeps the capitalist engine in motion comes from new consumers' goods, the new methods of production or transportation, the new markets, the new forms of industrial organization that capitalist enterprise creates. . . . This process of Creative Destruction is the essential fact about capitalism. [Joseph Schumpeter, *Capitalism, Socialism and Democracy* (New York: Harper & Row, 1950), 83.]

35. See Friedrich A. Hayek, "The Use of Knowledge in Society," in *Individualism and the Economic Order* (Chicago: Henry Regnery, 1972).

36. Kirzner sees market capitalism:

not simply as a set of institutions governing exchanges . . . but as an ongoing process of creative discovery. What one witnesses in a market economy, at any point in time, are nothing but attempts by market participants to take advantage of newly discovered or created possibilities. . . . The process of creative discovery is never completed, nor is it ever arrested. [Israel Kirzner, *Discovery and the Market Process* (Chicago: University of Chicago Press, 185), ix–x.]

37. For example, *The American Heritage Dictionary* (1976) defines capitalism as "an economic system characterized by freedom of the market with increasing concentration of private and corporate ownership of production and distribution means, proportionate to increasing accumulation and reinvestment of profits." For others see the new Afterword in Michael Novak, *The Spirit of Democratic Capitalism*, 2d ed. (Lanham, Md.: Madison Books, 1991), 430.

38. George Gilder quoting Mikhail Gorbachev, "Freedom and the High Tech Revolution," *Imprimis* 19, no. 11 (November 1990): 1.

39. It is . . . a curious fact that a new country is most favorable—almost necessary—to the immancipation [*sic*] of thought, and consequent advancement of civilization and the arts. . . . I have mentioned the discovery of America as an event greatly favoring and facilitating useful discoveries and inventions.

Next came the Patent laws. These began in England in 1624; and, in this country, with the adoption of our constitution [*sic*]. Before then, any man might instantly use what another had invented; so that the inventor had no special advantage from his own invention. The patent system changed this; secured the inventor, for a limited time, the exclusive use of his invention; and thereby added the fuel of *interest* to the *fire* of genius, in the discovery and production of new and useful things. [Abraham Lincoln, *Abraham Lincoln: Speeches and Writings 1859–1865* (New York: Library of America, 1989), 10–11.]

See also Nathan Rosenberg and L. E. Birdzell, Jr., *How the West Grew Rich*:

Competition also became involved in innovation. The market rewards of innovation depended largely on the innovator's ability to charge a high price for a unique product or service until such time as it could be imitated or superseded by others. The rewards depended, in other words, on the innovator's margin of priority in time over imitators and successors. This was even true of patents, which go to the first inventor, and whose economic life is measured by the time it takes to find a better alternative. Given the multiplicity of Western enterprises, the possibility of forming new ones, and the possibility that old ones could shift to new activities, the process of gaining the rewards of innovative ideas takes on the characteristics of a race, informal but still competitive. The competitive nature of the process was intensified by the Western practice of leaving the losers to bear their own losses, which were often substantial. This use of a competitive spur to stimulate change was a marked departure from tradition, for societies and their rulers have almost always strongly resisted change unless it enhanced the ruler's own power and well-being. [New York: Basic Books, 1986, 23.]

40. *Det Fri Aktuelt* (Copenhagen), 2 December 1989; quoted in Acker, " 'Poisoning of the Soul,' " 64.

41. The Church's social doctrine *is not* a "third way" between *liberal capitalism* and *Marxist collectivism*, nor even a possible alternative to other solutions less radically opposed to one another: rather, it constitutes a *category of its own*. Nor is it an *ideology*, but rather the *accurate formulation* of the results of a careful reflection on the complex realities of human existence, in society and in the international order, in the light of faith and of the Church's tradition. Its main aim is to *interpret* these realities, determining their conformity with or divergence from the lines of the Gospel teaching on man and his vocation, a vocation which is at once earthly and transcendent; its aim is thus *to guide* Christian behavior. It therefore belongs to the field, not of *ideology*, but of *theology* and particularly of moral theology. [sec. 41]

Further, Pope John Paul II insists that the "right of economic initiative" is essential to economic development:

It is a right which is important not only for the individual but also for the common good. Experience shows us that the denial of this right, or its limitation in the name of an alleged "equality" of everyone in society, diminishes, or in practice absolutely destroys the spirit of initiative, that is to say, *the creative subjectivity of the citizen*. [*Sollicitudo Rei Socialis*, Vatican Translation, sec. 15.]

42. *Washington Post*, 30 November 1989, quoted in Acker, " 'Poisoning of the Soul,' " 63.

43. From a speech of 18 December 1989, quoted ibid.

44. Zhelyo Zhelev, cited ibid., 64.

45. St. Thomas Aquinas writes:

Our will can reach higher than can our intelligence when we are confronted by things that are above us. Whereas our notions about moral matters, which are below man, are enlightened by a cognitive habit—for prudence informs the other moral virtues—when it comes to the divine virtues about God, a will-virtue, namely charity, informs the mind-virtue, namely faith. [Disputations, "De Caritate" 3, *ad* 13, cited in *St. Thomas Aquinas: Philosophical Texts*, ed. and trans. Thomas Gilby (New York: Oxford University Press, 1960), 285.]

46. Mercy is supremely God's effectively rather than affectively. . . . The work of divine justice always presupposes the work of mercy and is founded thereon. Creatures have no rights except because of something pre-existing or pre-considered in them, and since we cannot go back and back, we must come to something founded on the sole generosity of the divine will, which is the ultimate end. . . . Mercy is the root in each and every divine work, and its virtue persists in everything that grows out of that, and even more vehemently flourishes there. . . . [T]he order of justice would be served by much less than in fact is granted by divine generosity, which far exceeds what is owing. [St. Thomas Aquinas, *Summa Theologica*, I.21.3–4; cited in Gilby, *St. Thomas Aquinas*, 116–17.]

47. The document goes on to say:

Whatever the forms of ownership may be, as adapted to the legitimate institutions of people according to diverse and changeable circumstances, attention must always be paid to the universal purpose for which created goods are meant. In using them, therefore, a man should regard his lawful possessions not merely as his own but also as a common property in the sense that they should accrue to the benefit of not only himself but of others. [*Gaudium et Spes*, sec. 69, in *The Gospel of Peace and Justice*, ed. Joseph Gremillion (Maryknoll: Orbis, 1976), 305.]

48. The person who works desires not only due renumeration for his work; he also wishes that within the production process provision be made for him to be able to know that in his work, even on something that is owned in common, he is working "for himself." This awareness is extinguished within him in a system of excessive bureaucratic centralization, which makes the worker feel that he is just a cog in a huge machine moved from above, that he is for more reasons than one a mere production instrument rather than a true subject of work with an initiative of his own. . . . In the mind of St. Thomas Aquinas, this is the principal reason in favor of private ownership of the means of production. . . . The personalist argument still holds good both on the level of principles and on the practical level. If it is to be rational and fruitful, any socialization of the means of production must be made to ensure that in this kind of system also the human person can preserve his awareness of working "for himself." [*Laborem Exercens*, sec. 15, in *Origins* 11, no. 15 (24 September 1981): 236.]

Compare Leo XIII in *Rerum Novarum*: "Private possessions are clearly in accord with nature" (sec. 15). "To own goods privately. . . is a right natural to man, and to exercise this right, especially in life in society, is not only lawful, but clearly necessary" (sec. 36). Pope Leo then quotes St. Thomas Aquinas: "It is lawful for man to own his own things. It is even necessary for human life" (*Summa Theologica*, II-II.66.2).

49. Genesis 3:19.

50. Whether we consider natural *Reason*, which tells us, that Men, being once born, have a right to their Preservation and consequently to Meat and Drink, and such other things, as Nature affords for their subsistence: or *Revelation*, which gives us an account of those Grants God made of the World to *Adam*, and to *Noah*, and his Sons, 'tis very clear, that God, as King *David* says, *Psal.* CXV.xvi. *has given the Earth to the Children of Men*, given it to Mankind in common. [Locke, *Two Treatises of Government, Second Treatise*, sec. 25, 327.]

For an analysis of chapter 5 of Locke's *Second Treatise*, see Robert A. Goldwin, "A Reading of Locke's Chapter 'Of Property,' " in *Why Blacks, Women, and Jews Are Not Mentioned in the Constitution, and Other Unorthodox Views* (Washington: The AEI Press, 1990), 99–109.

51. . . . [H]e who appropriates land to himself by his labour, does not lessen but increase the common stock of mankind. For the provisions serving to the support of humane life, produced by one acre of inclosed and cultivated land, are (to speak much within compasse) ten times more, than those, which are yielded by an acre of land, of an equal richnesse, lyeing wast in common. . . . I have here rated the improved land very low in making its product but as ten to one, when it is much nearer an hundred to one. [Locke, *Two Treatises*, 336.]

52. Whenever, in any country, the proprietor, generally speaking, ceases to be the improver, political economy has nothing to say in defense of private property, as there established. . . . When the "sacredness of property" is talked of, it should always be remembered that any such sacredness does not belong in the same degree to landed property. No man made the land. It is the original inheritance of the whole species. Its appropriation is wholly a question of general expediency. When private property in land is not expedient, it is unjust. . . . Even in the case of cultivated land, a man whom, though only one among millions, the law permits to hold thousands of acres as his single share, is not entitled to think that all this is given to him to use and abuse, and deal with as if it concerned nobody but himself. . . . The rents of profits which he can obtain for it are at his sole disposal; but with regard to the land, in everything which he does with it, and in everything which he abstains from doing, he is morally bound, and should whenever the case admits, be legally compelled to make his interest and pleasure consistent with the public good. [Mill, *Principles of Political Economy*, ed. William Ashley (New York: Augustus M. Kelley, 1969), 231, 233–35.]

53. See Roger Heckel, S.J., *Self-Reliance*:

Self-reliance does not project the idea of "falling back upon oneself" or of isolation, but rather of a genuine return to the living subject and his/her dynamism. The connotation, therefore, is of an eminently positive nature. The full meaning of the concept appears less in the *noun* (self-reliance) and more in the *adjective* (self-restraint) coupled to the word *development* with which it finds its full meaning. . . . [Self-reliance] is of the same order as *freedom*. It is through voluntary and reasoned action that a people becomes aware of its own law of development and implements it as a vital capacity or power. Self-reliance would therefore be an internal vital principle which manifests its presence under the guise of a power. It is the ever-increasing capacity of a people to assume its past, decide upon its future, and, on a level of equality, contribute to the shaping of humankind and the universe of which it is part. [Vatican City: Pontifical Commission Justice and Peace, 1978, 4–5.]

54. According to a 1989 report by the Morgan Guarantee Trust Company, at the end of 1987 Latin American foreign investment was as follows: Brazil, $31 billion; Mexico, $84 billion; Venezuela, $58 billion; Argentina, $46 billion. According to Mark Falcoff, these amounts would cover the following percentages of foreign debt for each country if invested at home: Brazil, 30–40%; Mexico, 60%; and for Argentina and Venezuela, 100%.

55. Foreign aid does not in fact go to the pitiable figures we see on aid posters, in aid advertisements, and in other aid propaganda in the media. It goes to the governments, that is to the rulers, and the policies of the rulers who receive aid are sometimes directly responsible for conditions such as those depicted. But even in less extreme instances, it is still the case that aid goes to the rulers; and their policies, including the pattern of public spending, are determined by their own personal and political interests, among which the

position of the poorest has a very low priority. [P. T. Bauer, *Reality and Rhetoric: Studies in the Economics of Development* (Cambridge: Harvard University Press, 1984), 50.]

56. Of one of his intellectual predecessors, Rorty approvingly notes, "Wittgenstein . . . cheerfully tosses out half-a-dozen incompatible metaphilosophical views in the course of the *Investigations*" (*Consequences of Pragmatism* [Minneapolis: University of Minnesota Press, 1982], 23). Rorty draws an explicitly historicist deduction from this: "We Deweyan historicists . . . think that 'first principles' are abbreviations of, rather than justifications for a set of beliefs about the desirability of certain concrete alternatives over others; the source of those beliefs is not 'reason' or 'nature', but rather the prevalence of certain institutions or modes of life in the past" (Richard Rorty, "That Old-Time Philosophy," *The New Republic*, 4 April 1988, 30). See also: "No specific doctrine is much of a danger, but the idea that democracy depends on adhesion to some such doctrine is" (Richard Rorty, "Taking Philosophy Seriously," *The New Republic*, 11 April 1988, 33).

57. Schlesinger writes:

> The American mind is by nature and tradition skeptical, irreverent, pluralistic and relativistic. . . . Our relative values are not matters of whim and happenstance. History has given them to us. They are anchored in our national experience, in our great national documents, in our national heroes, in our folkways, traditions, standards. Some of these values seem to us so self-evident that even relativists think they have, or ought to have, universal application: the right to life, liberty and the pursuit of happiness, for example; the duty to treat persons as ends in themselves; the prohibition of slavery, torture, genocide. People with different history will have different values. But we believe that our own are better for us. They work for us; and, for that reason, we live and die by them. [Arthur Schlesinger, Jr., "The Opening of the American Mind," *New York Times Book Review*, 23 July 1989, 26.]

See my reply, "Relativism or Absolutes: Which Is the American Way?" in *National Catholic Register*, 29 October 1989.

58. Murray wrote:

> The Catholic community faces the task of making itself intellectually aware of the conditions of its own co-existence within the American pluralistic scene. We have behind us a lengthy historical tradition of acceptance of the special situation of the Church in America, in all its differences from the situations in which the Church elsewhere finds herself. But it is a question here of pursuing the subject, not in the horizontal dimension of history but in the vertical dimension of theory.
>
> The argument readily falls into two parts. The first part is an analysis of the American Proposition with regard to political unity. The effort is to make a statement . . . of the essential contents of the American consensus, whereby we are made "*e pluribus unum*," one society subsisting amid multiple pluralisms. Simply to make this statement is to show why American Catholics participate with ready conviction in the American consensus. The second part of the argument . . . is an analysis of the American Proposition with regard to religious pluralism, especially as the proposition is embodied in our fundamental law. Again, simply to make this analysis is to lay bare the reasons why American Catholics accept on principle the unique American solution to the age-old problem. [John Courtney Murray, S.J., *We Hold These Truths* (New York: Sheed & Ward, 1960), 27–28.]

And Maritain writes:

> Not only does the democratic state of mind stem from the inspiration of the Gospel, but it cannot exist without it. To keep faith in the forward march of humanity despite all the temptations to despair of man that are furnished by history, and particularly contemporary history; to have faith in the dignity of the person and of common humanity, in human

rights and in justice—that is, in essentially spiritual values; to have, not in formulas but in reality, the sense of and respect for the dignity of the people, which is a spiritual dignity and is revealed to whoever knows how to love it; to sustain and revive the sense of equality without sinking into egalitarianism; to respect authority, knowing that its wielders are only men, like those they rule, and derive their trust from the consent or the will of the people whose vicars or representatives they are; to believe in the sanctity of law and in the efficacious virtue—efficacious at long range—of political justice in face of the scandalous triumphs of falsehood and violence; to have faith in liberty and in fraternity, an heroical inspiration and an heroical belief are needed which fortify and vivify reason, and which none other than Jesus of Nazareth brought forth in the world. [Jacques Maritain, *Christianity and Democracy* (New York: Scribner's, 1950), 59–60.]

59. Freedom of religion and of thought and of speech were achieved by denying both to the state and to the established church a sovereign monopoly in the field of religion, philosophy, morals, science, learning, opinion and conscience. The liberal constitutions, with their bills of rights, fixed the boundaries past which the sovereign—the King, the Parliament, the Congress, the voters—were forbidden to go.

Yet the men of the seventeenth and eighteenth centuries who established these great salutary rules would certainly have denied that a community could do without a general public philosophy. They were themselves the adherents of a public philosophy—of the doctrine of natural law, which held that there was law "above the ruler and the sovereign people . . . above the whole community of morals." [Walter Lippmann, *The Public Philosophy* (New York: New American Library, 1956), 76–78.]

60. David Hollenbach, S.J., writes:

The thesis proposed here is that Catholic teaching on human rights today presupposes a reconstruction of the classical liberal understanding of what these rights are. The pivot on which this reconstruction turns is the traditional natural law conviction that the human person is an essentially social being. Catholic thought and action in the human rights sphere, in other words, are rooted in a communitarian alternative to classical liberal human rights theory. At the same time, by adopting certain key ideas about constitutional democracy originally developed by classical liberalism, recent Catholic thought has brought about a notable new development of the longer tradition of the church while simultaneously offering an alternative to the standard liberal theory of democratic government. ["A Communitarian Reconstruction of Human Rights: Contributions from Catholic Tradition," unpublished paper prepared for a project on "Liberalism, Catholicism, and American Public Philosophy," at the Woodstock Theological Center, Georgetown University.]

Cf. Ernest Fortin:

For centuries, the cornerstone of Catholic moral theology was not the natural or human *rights* doctrine but something quite different, called the natural *law*. Rights, to the extent that they were mentioned at least by implication, were contingent on the fulfillment of prior duties. . . . Simply stated, what the church taught and tried to inculcate was an ethic of virtue as distinct from an ethic of rights. . . .

The bishops may have confused some of their readers by using language that looks in two different directions at once: that of rights or freedoms on the one hand, and of virtue, character formation, and the common good on the other. They would certainly be ill-advised to give up their vigorous defense of rights, especially since the pseudomorphic collapse of Neo-Thomism in the wake of Vatican II has left them without any alternative on which to fall back; but they have yet to tell us, or tell us more clearly, how the two ends are supposed to meet. ["The Trouble with Catholic Social Thought," *Boston College Magazine*, Summer 1988, 38, 42.]

61. Even so, Jacques Maritain reminds us that we need not be completely despairing. Every age sees itself as falling off in morals (*"O tempora! O mores!"*). Yet in a chapter called "The Old Tag of American Materialism," Maritain says:

The American people are the least materialist among the modern peoples which have attained the industrial stage. . . .

Americans like to give. . . . Not only the great foundations, but the ordinary course of activity of American institutions and the innumerable American private groups show us that the ancient Greek and Roman idea of the *civis praeclarus*, the dedicated citizen who spends his money in the service of the common good, plays an essential part in American consciousness. And let me observe that more often than not the gifts in question are made for the sake of education and knowledge. Frequently people who were unable to have a college education make large gifts to universities.

There is no materialism, I think, in the astonishing countless initiatives of fraternal help which are the daily bread of the American people, or in the profound feeling of obligation toward others which exists in them, especially toward any people abroad who are in distress. . . .

There is no materialism in the fact that the American charities, drawing money from every purse, and notably to assist people abroad, run every year into such enormous sums that charity ranks among the largest American industries, the second or third in size, according to statisticians. . . . Let us not forget what an immense amount of personal attention to one's neighbor and what personal effort is unceasingly put forth in all the groups which exist in this country, and which spring up every day, to meet some particular human misfortune or some particular social maladjustment. . . .

There is a perpetual self-examination and self-criticism going on everywhere and in every sphere of American life; a phenomenon incomprehensible without a quest for truth of which a materialist cast of mind is incapable. [Jacques Maritain, *Reflections on America* (New York: Scribner's, 1958), 29–30, 34–36, 38.]

62. See Hernando de Soto, *The Other Path* (New York: Harper & Row, 1989), 12–13. In Peru, "48 percent of the economically active population and 61.2 percent of work hours are devoted to informal activities which contribute 38.9 percent of the gross domestic product recorded in the national accounts" (12). "Informals have managed to gain control of 93 percent of the urban transport fleet" (13).

63. Heilbroner goes on to write:

The Soviet Union, China and Eastern Europe have given us the clearest possible proof that capitalism organizes the material affairs of humankind more satisfactorily than socialism: that however inequitably or irresponsibly the marketplace may deliver the goods, it does so better than the queues of a planned economy. . . . Indeed, it is difficult to observe the changes taking place in the world today and not conclude that the nose of the capitalist camel has been pushed so far under the socialist tent that the great question now seems how rapid will be the transformation of socialism into capitalism, and not the other way around as things looked only a half century ago. [Robert Heilbroner, "Reflections: The Triumph of Capitalism," *The New Yorker*, 23 January 1989, 98.]

64. As I have said elsewhere:

The market, then, is a social device for achieving the common good. Alone, the market cannot attain the *whole* common good. It is a device chiefly of the economic order, which is, in turn, only a part of political economy. Many constituent parts of the common good can only be supplied outside of markets. More than markets can accomplish cannot be asked of them. On the other hand, matched with institutions of invention and innovation, no economic institution has ever succeeded better in raising up so many of the poor. None has generated a higher standard of living, brought about a more regular and swifter circulation of elites, or inspired more extensive creativity.

Its founders intended a market order based upon invention and patents to excel in its achievement of the common good. That was the experiment. In promoting the general welfare, measured empirically against what has been achieved by other systems, the market system based upon creative invention has no peer. In that respect, the common good has been a basic underlying criterion for measuring both its successes and its failures. The new concept of the common good does not require intentions, but it does require achievements. It does not require the perfect, but only the greater, good. Its essence is to establish an order promoting the free cooperation of all, for the benefit of all, among those who are not saints. . . .

If we had to prove that markets are perfect instruments of the common good, we could not. But we do not have to do so. All that is required is to show that markets, however imperfect, are better social instruments for their limited purposes than any other known alternatives, traditionalist or socialist; and that their deficiencies may be made up through supplementary agencies of the polity and culture. [Michael Novak, *Free Persons and the Common Good* (Lanham, Md.: Madison Books, 1989), 108–9.]

65. See Michael Novak et al., *The New Consensus on Family and Welfare* (Milwaukee: Marquette University, 1987).

66. "The 1984 survey by the Bureau of Labor Statistics, based on complete income figures submitted by several thousand nationally representative households, shows that the poorest 20 percent of households had average reported income before taxes of $3,200 and annual expenditures of $10,800" (U.S. Department of Labor, Bureau of Labor Statistics, "1984 Consumer Expenditure Survey").

67. David Popenoe has recently written:

The Swedish marriage rate is now the lowest in the industrialized world, and the average age at first marriage is probably the highest. The rate of nonmarital cohabitation, or consensual unions, outranks that of all other advanced nations; such unions, rather than being a mere prelude to marriage (as is more often the case in the United States now), have become a parallel institution alongside legal marriage. About 25 percent of all couples in Sweden today are living in consensual unions (up from 1 percent in 1960), compared with about 5 percent in the United States. The growth of nonmarital cohabitation among childbearing couples has given Sweden one of the highest percentages of children born out of wedlock in the industrial world—over 50 percent of all children, compared with about 22 percent in the United States. . . .

There is one thing about growing up in Sweden today that should give pause even to those sympathetic to the welfare state. There is a strong likelihood that the family has grown weaker there than anywhere else in the world. What has happened to the family in Sweden over the past few decades lends strong support to the proposition that as the welfare state advances, the family declines. If unchecked, this decline could eventually undermine the very welfare that the state seeks to promote.

The modern welfare state was founded with the goal of helping families to function better as decentralized welfare agencies. It sought to strengthen families, not to weaken them. Over time, however, welfare states have increasingly tended not so much to assist families as to replace them; people's dependence on the state has grown while their reliance on families has weakened. In a classic illustration of the law of unintended consequences, the family under the welfare state is gradually losing both the ability and the will to care for itself. ["Family Decline in the Swedish Welfare State," *The Public Interest*, no. 102 (Winter 1991): 65–66.]

68. "Today a significant population of able, nonelderly adults stay on welfare for more than two years (and sometimes for more than one intermittent spell). Rather than supporting the elderly and the young [who cannot enter the labor force], they themselves are long-term dependents" (Novak et al., *New Consensus*, 58–59). This is based on data presented by Mary Jo Bane and David Ellwood in a paper prepared for the assistant secretary for planning and evaluation, Department of Health and Human Services. They say, "Fewer than half the women who go

onto AFDC are off within two years. Of those who remain into the third year, 60 percent will be on at least six years" (*New Consensus*, 68).

69. "The dependency of the 5 million or so who are in that situation [both poor and concentrated in cities in which 20 percent of the population is also poor], is of a depth not exhausted by the catch-all phrase 'below the poverty line' " (Novak et al., *New Consensus*, 25–26). This is based on data provided by Richard P. Nathan in "The Underclass: Will It Always Be With Us?" (presented at the New School for Social Research, 14 November 1986). On the underclass in Britain, Charles Murray explains:

> "Underclass" is an ugly word, with its whiff of Marx and the lumpenproletariat. Perhaps because it is ugly, "underclass" as used in Britain tends to be sanitised, a sort of synonym for people who are not just poor, but especially poor. So let us get it straight from the outset: the "underclass" does not refer to degree of poverty, but to type of poverty.
>
> It is not a new concept. I grew up knowing what the underclass was; we just didn't call it that in those days. In the small Iowa town where I lived, I was taught by my middle-class parents that there were two kinds of poor people. One class of poor people was never even called "poor." I came to understand that they simply lived with low incomes, as my own parents had done when they were young. Then there was another set of poor people, just a handful of them. These poor people didn't lack just money. They were defined by their behaviour. Their homes were littered and unkept. The men in the family were unable to hold a job for more than a few weeks at a time. Drunkenness was common. The children grew up ill-schooled and ill-behaved and contributed a disproportionate share of the local juvenile delinquents. [Charles Murray, *The Emerging British Underclass* (London: The IEA Health and Welfare Unit, 1990), 1].

70. See Charles Murray with Deborah Laren, "According to Age: Longitudinal Profiles of AFDC Recipients and the Poor by Age Group" (presented at the Working Seminar on the Family and American Welfare Policy, Washington, D.C., 23 September 1986). Murray cites a Michigan study that shows that of all men ages 20 to 64 who had completed high school—with no more education—less than 1 per cent are poor.

71. Lawrence Mead, "The Work Problem in Workfare" (presented at the Working Seminar on the Family and American Welfare Policy). "For example, the poverty rate for black families with no workers, is 69 percent; with one worker, 35 percent; with two workers, 8 percent. Clearly, work is an effective path out of poverty, and the number of workers per family matters a great deal" (Novak et al. *New Consensus*, 59).

72. Guy Sorman, *Barefoot Capitalism: A Solution for India* (New Delhi: Vikas Publishing [distributed by Advent Books, New York], 1989).

Index of Names

Medellín conference, 237–38
Medicaid, 266
Memorial and Remonstrance (Madison), 305
Mencken, H. L., 299
Mennonites, 62, 71, 83–84, 86
Methodist Episcopal Church, South, 81
Methodists, 61–62, 80
Middle East, 43, 78, 225, 239
Midrash, 160
Mill, John Stuart, 140, 273
Mises, Ludwig von, 257, 260
Missouri Synod Lutherans, 62
Monetary Reform (Keynes), 289
Montesquieu, 154
Moody Bible Institute, 77–78
Moody, D. L., 66
Moral Criticism of Law (Richards), 28
Moral Education in Aristotle (Verbeke), 154
Moral Majority, 84
Moral Man and Immoral Society (Niebuhr), 290
Morgenthau, Hans J., 223, 230
Moscow, 225
Mouw, Richard, 86
Münzer, Thomas, 44
Murray, John Courtney, 3, 15, 19, 30, 112, 158, 234, 278
Muslims, 39, 215
Mussolini, 78

National Association of Evangelicals, 82
National Conference of Catholic Bishops, 43
National Council of Churches, 12, 24
National Recovery Administration, 78
National Socialism, 195
Nation, The, 305
NATO, 225
Nazis, 112
Nebraska, 59
New Christian Left, 85

New Christian Right, 61, 84
New Deal, 40
New Haven, 5
Newman, John Henry, 11, 24
New Testament, 35, 37, 69, 146, 291
New World Order, 31, 52
New York, 170, 246
New York Times, 5, 6, 185, 215, 220
Nicaragua, 280
Niebuhr, H. Richard, 40, 42, 106, 122–23, 159, 299
Niebuhr, Reinhold, 40, 46, 75, 95, 229–30, 290
Nietzscheans, 303–4
Nietzsche, Friedrich, 48, 145–46, 150, 298, 301
Noahide laws, 7
Noll, Mark, 200–201, 206
North America, 275
Nye, Joseph, 228–29

Ockenga, Harold John, 82
Octogesima Adveniens, 2, 237
Office of Technology Assessment, U.S. Congress, 186
Old Testament, 146
"On Consulting the Faithful" (Newman), 24
O'Neill, John, 174
Orwell, George, 258
Ottaviani, Alfredo, 11
Oxford Movement, 206
Oxford University, 195

Pacem in Terris, 2, 6, 16, 19–20, 57, 232–33, 236
Pacific Rim, 25
Paine, Thomas, 94
Pannenberg, Wolfhart, 113
Papal States, 36–37
Paris, 225
Pascal, Blaise, 298
Paul, Saint, 99, 125, 133, 147, 160–61, 271, 291